LETTERS OF
BEDE JARRETT

1916

DOMINICAN SOURCES IN ENGLISH   VOLUME 5

LETTERS OF
BEDE JARRETT

Letters and other papers
from the English Dominican Archives

selected by Bede Bailey OP

edited by
Simon Tugwell OP & Dom Aidan Bellenger

Downside Abbey & Blackfriars Publications
1989

Downside Abbey
Stratton on the Fosse
Bath, England, BA3 4RH

Blackfriars
64 St Giles
Oxford, England, OX1 3LY

© 1989 Downside Abbey and Blackfriars Publications.
All rights reserved. No part of this book may be reproduced, stored in a retrieval system or transmitted in any form or by any means without the permission of the publisher.

British Library Cataloguing in Publication Data:
Jarrett, Bede, *1881-1934*
   Letters of Bede Jarrett.
   1. Religious orders. Dominicans—Biographies
   I. Title II. Bailey, Bede III. Bellenger, Dominic Aidan
     IV. Tugwell, Simon V. Downside Abbey VI. Series
   271'.2'024

ISBN 0 9502759 6 4 (Downside Abbey)
ISBN 0 9511202 4 7 (Blackfriars)

Cum permissu superiorum tam OSB quam OP

Printed and bound by Hobbs the Printers of Southampton

DOMINICAN SOURCES: NEW EDITIONS IN ENGLISH aims to provide reliable English texts of significant Dominican sources, especially those which are not already available in a dependable form in English. It is intended that the series should in time include texts of spiritual and historical interest from all periods of Dominican history and from all branches of the Dominican family.

VOLUMES PUBLISHED
1 Jordan of Saxony, *On the Beginnings of the Order of Preachers*. (ISBN 0 9511202 9 4)
2 Henri Lacordaire, *Essay on the Re-establishment in France of the Order of Preachers*.
(ISBN 0 9511202 1 2)
3 St Catherine de' Ricci, *Selected Letters*. (ISBN 0 9511202 2 0)
4 Juan de Torquemada, *A Disputation on the Authority of Pope and Council*.
(ISBN 0 9511202 3 9)
5 Bede Jarrett, *Letters*. (ISBN 0 9511202 4 7)

VOLUMES IN PREPARATION
Humbert of Romans, *Opus Tripartitum* (trans. Augustine Thompson OP, with an introd. by Alexander Murray).
Girolamo Savonarola, *Spiritual Writings* (selected and introduced by Alvaro Huerga OP)
Juan de la Cruz, *On Vocal Prayer* trans. T. O'Reily.
St Albert and St Thomas, *Sermons* ed. Louis Bataillon OP, trans. M. Justin Lane OP.

DOWNSIDE ABBEY publishes *The Downside Review* as a focus of learning and scholarship in theology, metaphysics, history and spirituality in the hope that it may stimulate a catholic and far-reaching view of religion. A small number of books are also published especially in the field of post-Reformation Catholic church history in England.

VOLUMES PUBLISHED
Aidan Bellenger, *English and Welsh Priests 1558-1800* (ISBN 0 9502759 2 1)
Aidan Bellenger, *The French Exiled Clergy in the British Isles after 1789*
(ISBN 0 9502759 3 X)
Essays in honour of Godfrey Anstruther; *Opening the Scrolls* (ISBN 0 9502759 5 6)

VOLUMES IN PREPARATION
Geoffrey Scott, *The English Benedictine Congregation and the English Mission 1685-1794*
Charles Fitzgerald-Lombard, *English and Welsh Priests 1801-1914*

CONTENTS

	page
Letter from the Master of the Order	v
Introduction by Simon Tugwell OP	vii
Text and Notes	1
Biographical Notes	206
Index of Names	277

Fr. Bede Jarrett has been one of the outstanding figures in the Order of Preachers in the 20th century. His 'Life of St. Dominic' has often been spoken of as a self portrait, so clearly did his life pattern that of Dominic. He combined in an extraordinary way the gifts of administration with those of a preacher, writer and counsellor.

His brothers remember him as a man of great understanding, unperturbable and joyous in adversity, gentle and friendly. His courageous leadership of the English Province over a period of sixteen years did much to revive it with new foundations at Oxford and Edinburgh and the establishment of the Order in Southern Africa. His patient understanding of others and their needs endeared him to all.

Others remember the gifted preacher, the writer and counsellor who spent long hours in the confessional. He once humorously declared that he became a preacher as he was unable to sing. He had a gift for words and a genius for sensing the need of his audience. This deeply spiritual man had a word for everyone. Like Dominic he had a special appeal for young people. This is clearly seen in the letter with which he introduces the 'Space of Life Between'.

His memory is still green. This volume will sharpen that memory.

fr. Damian Byrne, O.P.
Master of the Order.

INTRODUCTION

When Father Bede Jarrett died in the early afternoon of 17 March 1934, he was undoubtedly one of the best known Dominicans in England and one of the best known English Dominicans in the world. He died in hospital in London, a simple friar, assigned to St Dominic's Priory, London, but he had been in a position of authority almost continuously between 17 June 1914, when he was elected prior of London, and 27 February 1934, when he resigned as prior of Oxford. He had been prior provincial of the English province for sixteen years, during which, under his leadership, the shape of the province and the orientation of its work had changed considerably. The province he joined in 1898 was still essentially the product of the bleak centuries during which the Dominicans, like other religious in Britain, functioned primarily as missionaries, trying to rebuild the Catholic faith in a country which had lost it. The province in which he died in 1934 was in many ways the product of his own provincialate.

Immediately after his death, his successor as provincial, Father Bernard Delany, wrote a spontaneous obituary of him in the Provincial's Diary, which can serve as an admirable introduction to this admirable man:

> Father Bede Jarrett was a very great man, a religious of rare virtue and (with sober deliberation weighing my words) I can say that he is the most perfect Dominican I have ever met. He was full of charity, humble and patient. As a superior he carried almost to excess the virtue of putting himself in the subject's place. He was always just; most courageous and his courage was of the very rare (and perhaps unnoticed) kind which accepts responsibility cheerfully and without fuss and murmuring. He was a living example of religious observance, remarkable for his silence, never absent from choir when in the house: an apostle, preaching in the pulpit and by means of his writings. The marvel is how he managed to get through all the work he did, yet there was never any sense of agitation or 'rush' about him—always serene and always the same calm presence—ready to listen to you as if he had all day to spare for your troubles or questions. He wore his virtues naturally without affectation or self-consciousness—nothing grotesque, freakish or odd about his saintliness. On fire yet not fanatical. He sparkled with fun and humour, he was witty yet never at the expense of charity. He had a rare supernatural commonsense. He trod the dangerous path of authority without ever seeming even to be affected by its dangers. He was utterly without ambition. His natural gifts,

his personal charm, eloquence, brilliance, marked him out for high honours in the church and he was always talked of for every bishopric that fell vacant. He only escaped being elected Master General by a few votes. He had an enormous power of dealing with detail and minutiae: he never forgot anything however small—or anybody—except F.Bede. He had a great natural capacity for friendship and this supernaturalized became a great force for winning souls to Christ. How many renunciations were implied in this natural gift given back to the highest Love, God only knows. His was a nature responsive and affectionate, yet he accepted nearly all his life the loneliness of office and no one could have been more just and more opposed to anything having the semblance of favouritism. His scholarly instinct was suppressed in the interests of the common good and the administrative work of a religious superior. We thank God for the gift He gave us in F.Bede and ask God to make us worthy of that gift by following where he always led. R.I.P.

*

When Bede Jarrett became a Dominican in 1898, the English province was still enjoying a revival that would have seemed impossible fifty years earlier, even if, in retrospect, we can see that this revival was just about to 'peak'.

In 1846, when Newman was wondering what to do with himself, now that he had become a Catholic, the Dominicans appeared to him to be pretty well finished. 'If indeed we could be Dominicans *teaching*,' he wrote on 6 July, 'it were well. Meanwhile I am doubting whether the Dominicans have preserved their traditions—whether it is not a great idea extinct.' When he wrote that letter, the Dominicans in England were certainly not flourishing. In the previous month they had bravely decided that the improved position of Catholics in England warranted their resumption of the religious habit, which they had not worn in England since the time of Queen Mary; but it was far from certain that there would for much longer be any Dominicans in England to wear it. Of the eight members of the province one was a sick old man of 90, who died later in the year, and one was living in retirement in Antwerp; another had left the Order in 1842 and, though he returned to the Catholic church in 1847, he never returned to the Order. There were a few postulants in the school run by the brethren at Hinckley, in Leicestershire, yielding a small trickle of vocations, but the results were on the whole not encouraging. Two novices had been clothed in 1841, but one had died during his noviciate; the other had just been ordained, in April 1846. One novice had been clothed in 1844 and was now doing his studies. A young man of 23 was waiting to join the Order, and he received the habit in October 1846 (but he left the Order in 1863). Of the three who entered in 1847 not one stayed long enough to be professed.

The old province, originally established in 1221 when the first English Dominican house was founded, in Oxford, had been entirely swept away by the Reformation, as had its daughter province of Scotland, erected in 1481. The Irish Dominicans had seized the opportunity to become a separate province in 1536 and, in spite of appalling difficulties throughout the penal period, they had managed to maintain some kind of continuous existence and, in the course of the nineteenth century, they underwent a remarkable revival; but their story is largely independent of that of their English and Scottish brethren.

Dominican work in Scotland had been carried on intermittently, thanks to a handful of individual friars, some of them Irish, but it had petered out altogether soon after the middle of the eighteenth century, and the Scottish province as such had not been able to retain any institutional existence. To this day dreams of its restoration still await their fulfilment.

The English had, for a time, fared somewhat better, at least since the middle of the seventeenth century. The erection of a formal priory of the province at Bornhem, Flanders, in 1657, followed by the establishment of a monastery for English Dominican nuns near Brussels in 1660 and the opening of a college in Louvain in 1697, gave the province a proper institutional structure, underpinning its missionary work in England and providing for the religious and intellectual formation of its recruits. But the achievements of a century and more were brutally wiped out by the French occupation of Belgium in 1794. The English friars and nuns, together with a few Belgian refugees, were forced to transfer their centre of operations to England, where they had no institutional structures to accommodate or support them.

The nuns found a home at Hartpury Court in Gloucestershire in 1794, moving to a newly built monastery at Atherstone, Warwickshire, in 1839. In 1858 they had to leave Atherstone for financial reasons, but after a brief sojourn at Hurst Green, near the Jesuit college of Stonyhurst, they found a permanent home at Carisbrooke, on the Isle of Wight, in 1866. There they remained until 1989.

The brethren were less fortunate. Their work in England, like that of most Catholic clergy, had depended primarily on Catholic gentry, whose chapels provided a base for their missionary labours, but could naturally not take the place of the properly constituted priories which were the normal context for Dominican work and the essential context for the training of new recruits. A first attempt to open a school (1794) and then a noviciate (1806) at Carshalton proved too ambitious and achieved little except an enormous debt; it was abandoned in 1810.

The hopes of the province were then focused on Hinckley. The Dominicans had first gone to that neighbourhood in 1734, when they were asked to supply a chaplain to the Turville family at Aston Flamville. They had moved into the town itself in 1765, and in 1814 their house was formally designated a priory and noviciate. But, to maintain even the semblance of a convincing priory, the province had progressively to close down its other mission stations until, by 1835, only Hinckley and Leicester were left.

It was indeed surprising that the province had even continued to exist. After the loss of Bornhem two fathers had gone to America in 1804 to launch a new province there, and in 1805 two more fathers had followed them, against the wishes of the English provincial. The American venture prospered and the province of St Joseph, rather impetuously brought into official existence in 1805, looked so much more promising than its English progenitor that for years there was talk of abandoning the English province entirely in favour of St Joseph's. In 1822 the chief decision which the English Provincial Chapter had to make was whether to resist a proposed forcible absorption of the remains of the province into the new American province. If they had lost their nerve at that point, the province would have ceased to exist.

At the beginning of 1850 (the year which was shortly to see the restoration of the Catholic hierarchy in England) the Provincial Chapter, meeting at Hinckley, could not even muster enough voters to elect a new provincial. There were eight members of the province, but only four were eligible to vote, of whom one was too sick to attend. The Master General appointed a new provincial and named two extra diffinitors to carry out the remaining business of the chapter, including, rather pointlessly, the father who was too sick to attend, so in fact only one extra diffinitor was effectively produced. With this minimal reinforcement, the chapter reconvened on 28 August and deliberated, disconsolately and inconclusively, where on earth the province could send novices to be trained. Viterbo? Perugia? France? No solution seemed to be in sight, when suddenly a 'fairy godmother' appeared, in the unlikely guise of the squire of Woodchester Park, Gloucestershire, one William Leigh, the great-uncle, as it happens, of Bede Jarrett.

Leigh had become a Catholic in 1844, a year before Newman. In 1845 he bought Woodchester Park and determined to create there, if he could, a model Catholic estate. In the same year, through the agency of a former president of Oscott, Henry Weedall (1788—1859), he made a donation to the Dominican nuns at Atherstone.

After consulting Bishop Wiseman (1802-1865), soon to become the first archbishop of Westminster, Leigh invited the Passionists to take charge of his projected new mission, and in 1846 Dominic Barberi (who had received Newman into the church the previous year) took up residence, with one laybrother, in a rented house near Woodchester, which he opened as a public Mass Centre on 25 March. In the same year work began on the building of a church at Woodchester itself, and on 10 October 1849 it was consecrated. By then Barberi had moved to London, but he was actually on his way to visit Leigh when he died in August 1849.

The Passionists were not able to commit themselves to Leigh's project to the full extent that he wanted, so in 1850 he decided to offer the church to the Dominicans, together with land for a priory and financial support for a certain number of friars. He arrived at Hinckley on 30 August, just after the Provincial Chapter had completed its business. At first, not surprisingly, the brethren were reluctant to take on a responsibility that it was manifestly beyond their present resources to honour, but Leigh persisted and finally the newly appointed provincial wrote to the Master General asking for permission to accept Woodchester and for support in creating there a proper priory and noviciate.

By the end of 1850 the Dominicans had taken charge of the church at Woodchester, and in 1851 the foundation stone of the priory was laid. In 1853 the building was far enough advanced for the brethren to move in, and in 1854 a formal priory was erected. But already in 1851 novices were being received. In the course of the year, on four separate occasions, eight novices received the habit, one of them from the hands of Master General Jandel, who was visitating the province. Jandel was so impressed by Woodchester that in 1852, expecting soon to be relieved of his office, he announced his intention of moving there himself. In fact he continued to be Master General, but he saw to it that men from other provinces, notably the Irish, were sent to boost the new foundation, so that, at last, the province had once more got a viable place to receive and to train vocations. From its paltry eight members in 1850 it grew to 100 by the end of the century and to just over 200 on the eve of the second World War.

The increase in its numbers meant that the province could resume its traditional missionary work in England, so once again we find the brethren undertaking new mission stations, such as Littlehampton, and developing stations they had served before, such as Nuneaton. Sometimes they worked with the newly burgeoning congregations of Dominican sisters, so that, for instance, they took on responsibility for the missions at Stone and at Stoke on Trent for a time, where the sisters had made foundations. But increasingly they directed their attention to rebuilding the proper institutional structures of Dominican life. The mission launched in London in 1861 developed into a formal priory in 1868, and that begun in Newcastle upon Tyne in 1860 became a priory in 1882. The mission in Leicester also became a priory in 1882. And their work continued to expand. In 1895 they tried to make a foundation in Liverpool, but the bishop would not allow it, and in 1898 they opened a mission at Pendleton, Manchester, which became a priory in 1901.

As the balance of the province shifted towards more classic Dominican structures, with most of the brethren assigned to fairly substantial priories, the pattern of its work changed accordingly. Although many of the brethren were engaged in parochial work, a significant number of them were officially designated 'missioners', which meant that they were available for preaching work anywhere in the country, whatever their house of assignation. Typically they were asked to give parish missions, courses of special sermons, convent retreats and that sort of thing. The more successful of them spent most of their time on the move, from one preaching job to the next. The whole operation was governed directly by the provincial, who allocated preachers to the places that asked for them.

Since the foundation of Bornhem, education had been an important concern of the province, but dwindling numbers had made it impossible for it to maintain a serious school or even to educate its own recruits. In 1825 there was a grandiose plan for a 'Catholic Academy' at Hinckley for the education of twelve 'young gentlemen', but it dwindled to being no more than a postulant school and as such it was closed in 1854, when the postulants were moved to Woodchester. It was re-opened in 1858, but lasted only until 1886. Another attempt was made in 1885, and this time the school proved more durable, though only as a postulant school.

Thanks to the support of other provinces, the noviciate at Woodchester was able to provide at least a basic priestly training for the Order's recruits, though it was still necessary to send them to Louvain or elsewhere if they were to pursue more rigorous theological studies, leading to the lectorate (the Dominican teaching qualification). In 1867 the new priory in London was designated a study house, and for a few years the studies were divided between there and Woodchester, but this scheme was abandoned in 1872 and all the studies were re-united at Woodchester. Some attempt was made to maintain continuity among the teaching staff at Woodchester, but the lectors were very few—sometimes only one, and rarely more than two; it was only in 1891 that a steady total of three was reached.

And the lectors nearly always had to play an active and demanding part in the extensive parochial and missionary work of the priory in addition to their academic responsibilities.

In 1894, thanks to an extremely generous benefaction, a new house was opened at Hawkesyard in Staffordshire and the bulk of the studies was moved there, leaving only the first year of studies at Woodchester. The teaching staff at Woodchester was again reduced to two, and there were two lectors at Hawkesyard. The main advantage of Hawkesyard was that, as a house, it had no pastoral or parochial responsibilities, so the lectors, however much incidental extra work they might take on, were not burdened with too many other institutional commitments. But, at least at first, the professorial team was rather less stable than it had been at Woodchester. And it continued to be far too small to allow the lectors to develop any real professional interest or competence in some particular subject.

In 1898 the tide was beginning to turn. On 30 June of that year Hugh Pope took his lectorate in Louvain and he, both as professor of scripture and, for many years, as Regent of Studies, was destined to play a vital role in the development of more serious studies in the province, and he was a true specialist. For twenty-seven years of his life he was a professor (in Rome for four years, but otherwise in Dominican study houses in England), whereas the previous 'stalwart' of Dominican studies in England, Placid Conway (1854–1913), spent only twelve years as a teacher, and for three of these he was also, to all intents and purposes, a parish priest as well. The year before Bede Jarrett joined the Order, he was taken off teaching altogether and sent to work in the parish in Newcastle, and in the following years there was little sign that the province was interested in or capable of building up a stable body of professional teachers.

In 1898 the postulant school was moved from Hinckley to Hawkesyard, which reinforced the role of Hawkesyard as the academic centre of the province, though the school, like the study house, suffered from the lack of a stable teaching staff. Also in 1898 the Provincial Chapter called for the establishment of a Grammar School in London, which was duly opened in 1899, under the rectorship of Benedict Tickell, but Tickell was removed the following year, and the school was closed in 1903.

The English Dominicans were certainly not lacking in intellectual seriousness, but the traditional working of the province called for versatility in its men rather than sustained commitment to the intellectual life, and their training did little to facilitate easy contacts with educated circles outside the Catholic church. They were given a solid foundation in Thomistic philosophy and theology, but they put it to work chiefly in the practical context of their endeavours to revivify Catholicism in England (and, occasionally, Scotland). Moral theology and sensible piety were more important to them than adventurous speculation. And, above all, they saw their task as consisting in apologetics: the Catholic church, emerging from the dark days of persecution, was finding a new confidence to proclaim its message in the ringing tones of absolute conviction. The English Dominicans seem to have been remarkably unaffected by the agonising questioning associated with 'Modernism'. They knew what they believed and rejoiced in it. Those who could not do this (and there were some) generally left the Order, if not the church. And if the province did produce an occasional scholar and full-time intellectual, like Peter Paul Mackey, whose conversation so impressed Bede Jarrett when he visited London in 1906, he was most evidently an exception.

The role of the province in the expansion of the Order at large was somewhat more hesitant than it was on the home front. The English brethren gladly received recruits from California to be trained at Woodchester and London in the 1860s and 1870s, but they were less enthusiastic, as a province, about committing their own men to work overseas. In 1863 Louis Gonin, a Frenchman who had become prior of Woodchester, was appointed archbishop of Trinidad and, when he sailed in 1864, he took an English Dominican, Thomas Greenough, with him. Greenough remained there for over thirty years, but in 1895 he was recalled by the provincial, John Procter, and it was only on the insistence of the pope that two other English Dominicans were sent to the West Indies in his place, though since then there have always been English Dominicans working in the Caribbean.

In 1887 and again in 1893 individual friars were sent to Australia, but this was due to their state of health rather than to any desire to expand the horizons of the province. No doubt their work in the antipodes was one of the factors which prompted John Procter in 1894 to write to the Master General to propose the setting up of an Australian province; but his note in the Provincial's Diary is revealing: 'We are invited, but are not numerous enough to undertake it' (26 June 1894).

By the end of the century, the first wave of Dominican revival in England had nearly achieved all that it was capable of. Numbers continued to rise until 1904, but then they levelled off at about 121 until after the first World War. The province increased its commitment in the West Indies in 1901, in response to an appeal from the archibishop of Trinidad, an Irish Dominican, Vincent Flood, who wanted English fathers to take charge of the island of Grenada, subject to a general vicariate based in Trinidad. The English agreed to accept the invitation only on condition that Grenada was made independent of Trinidad, with the result that Trinidad became a vicariate of the Irish province and Grenada a vicariate of the English province, headed, not surprisingly, by Greenough, and staffed by considerably more men than had ever before been supplied from England to work in those parts. But otherwise it continued to be a matter of individual initiative, rather than of provincial policy, for English Dominicans to work overseas. In 1900 Benedict Tickell, after his failure as rector of the ill-fated Grammar School in London, got permission from the Master General to go and work in New Zealand, where, in the outcome, he remained until his death in 1905. In 1907 he was followed by Gilbert Tigar, after some correspondence with the bishop of Auckland, and he worked there until 1914. In 1904 Maurice Watson, who had already worked in China as a priest before he became a Dominican, volunteered for the foreign missions and was sent back to China, where he remained until 1915. The outbreak of the first World War naturally prompted some of the brethren to want to serve as chaplains to the forces (C.F.s), but, after an initial offer of five men in December 1914, the provincial, Humbert Everest, did his best to prevent others going to join them. When Cardinal Bourne asked urgently for four more men, Everest replied that he was unable to oblige, and altogether only three more men slipped through his net during the rest of his provincialate.

The home mission settled down to a period of consolidation rather than expansion. An attempt to make a foundation in Glasgow was foiled by the archbishop's veto early in 1905 and after that, until Bede Jarrett became provincial, nothing new was attempted. The opening of a small house in Byker in 1907 was hardly a new venture, as it was no more than the separating off of a new parish from the parish the Dominicans were already running in Newcastle, and in 1911 they tried to hand it over to the diocese, which was probably what they had in mind all along.

The most important developments were in the field of studies. In 1906 the study house at Hawkesyard was erected into a formal studium. As in the early days at Woodchester, the English province was not able to sustain a proper studium on its own, but it was rather less lucky this time in the help it received from elsewhere. Jean-Dominique Folghera arrived from France in 1905, and he became the first Regent of Studies, but he was lost to the province in 1914. Dominic Prümmer (1866–1931) was sent to Hawkesyard in 1906, but he seems not to have approved of what he found there. In 1908 he went to Fribourg, calling in at Florence on his way, where he vehemently urged a stray French Dominican he found there not to think of going to the English province!

Steps were soon taken to secure properly trained and qualified

English lectors. Hugh Pope was sent to Rome in 1908 and 1909 to get the licentiate and then the doctorate in scripture, and in 1909 Ethelbert Rigby was sent to Rome to study for a doctorate in canon law. In 1912 Luke Walker was sent to the École Biblique in Jerusalem, and it was unfortunate that the outbreak of war prevented him from completing his course. If, in the outcome, it was only very gradually that the province managed to build up a reasonably stable and competent body of professors, so that most of the task still remained to be done during the provincialate of Bede Jarrett, at least it was clear in which direction the province was trying to move.

It was also beginning to think in more positive terms about contacts with the non-Catholic intellectual world around it. In 1900 and 1901 Raphael Moss gave two series of conferences to the students in Oxford, and it looks as if it was then that some people began to think about a possible Dominican foundation there, though it was left to Bede Jarrett to realise this dream. Most strikingly of all, Bede Jarrett himself was sent to Oxford as a student in 1904, the first Dominican to attend the university there as a student since the Reformation. But that brings us at last to the story of Bede Jarrett, under whose leadership the second great wave of development and revival occurred in the province.

*

This is not the place to attempt a full-dress biography of Bede Jarrett, but an outline of his life, particularly the early period, which is less well represented in the documents that follow, will perhaps be useful.

Born on 22 August 1881 at Blackheath, he was baptised Cyril Beaufort on 30 August. His father Henry Sullivan Jarrett, was an officer in the Indian Army and a man of considerable culture. His mother, Agnes Delacour, née Beaufort, was the granddaughter of the famous hydrographer, Sir Francis Beaufort (1774–1857). They had six sons, of whom Cyril was the fifth. One of his brothers died at school, the others all followed in their father's steps and joined the army. By 1919 they were all dead, except the youngest, who outlived Cyril (Bede) by a mere two years and died in 1936.

Cyril's aunt (his father's sister) had married William Leigh's son (also called William), who inherited Woodchester Park in 1873. So it is not surprising that, shortly after Cyril's birth, the Jarretts took a house near Woodchester at Amberley. When, in 1883, they returned to India, the children were entrusted to their grandmother, Mrs Thomas Jarrett, who was already bringing up the Leigh children at Woodchester Park after the death of Mrs William Leigh. So from 1883 until he went to school at Hodder Park, Stonyhurst, in 1891,

Cyril was actually living at Woodchester, where the family had retained a strong link with the Dominicans, whom indeed they rather tended to think of as their family chaplains, which led inevitably to a protracted and rather bitter row, which Bede Jarrett had to resolve diplomatically when he became provincial. In 1884 we know that the Jarrett children were taken to 'the Monastery' (as the Dominican priory was called) on St Dominic's day, and we can be sure that this was not the only visit.

It was the belief of his family, and they were probably right, that it was in these years at Woodchester that Cyril first conceived his desire to become a Dominican.

First, however, it was to the Jesuits that he went, to receive his schooling. In 1891 he went to Stonyhurst, where he was a student first at Hodder Park, then, from 1892-1898, at the college proper. All his older brothers were already at Stonyhurst, and his younger brother was soon to join him there. Among the Jesuits who taught him was Alban Goodier, later archbishop of Bombay, to whom he confided his intention of becoming a priest. His first years at school were not marked by any special success, though he worked hard, but in his last years he excelled. He was a good runner and played football quite creditably. He was a notable debater. In his last year he won the Poetry Gold Medal and the prize for English Verse, nearly winning the History prize as well. He was also a competent classicist, an interest he developed later as a Dominican student at Hawkesyard, where he used to read Latin and Greek literature with his friend, Aelred Whitacre.

In 1896 Col. Jarrett retired from active service and returned to England, where he settled at East Grinstead, in the house that was to remain the family home until Mrs Jarrett's death in 1930. It was in the same year that Cyril intimated to his father his desire to become a Dominican.

In 1898, in spite of some pressure to keep him on at school, both his family and the English Dominican provincial, John Procter, decided to let Cyril join the noviciate at Woodchester without further delay. So on 12 September he returned to the place he had known so well as a child, and two days later he began the retreat which was required before clothing. From his notebook we know that he chose for his reading, first of all, a book by a veteran missioner of the province, Reginald Buckler, who had just finished being novice master at Woodchester, *A few First Principles of Religious Life* (London 1896), in which he would have met the sane and practical Thomism which was traditional in the province at this period. Cyril soon finished reading Buckler and, after a few other short works, he then turned his mind to Bernard Chocarne's *Inner Life of P. Lacordaire*, often reprinted since its first publication in English in 1867. Here he would have learned of a rather different vision of Dominican life, shaped by the rather different circumstances of the French mission. For Lacordaire the intellectual apostolate of the Order was paramount, not the running or creating of parishes, which had been the typical work of the English brethren.

At 9 a.m. on 24 September Cyril received the Dominican habit from the prior of Woodchester, Ambrose Smith, and was given the religious name of Bede. The prior had previously, for fifteen years, taught at Woodchester until, in 1887, he was made an STM (Master of Sacred Theology), which paradoxically seems to have been the cue for him to be moved out of the study house to devote himself to parochial work elsewhere, though it is true that, throughout his time as a lector he had also undertaken heavy pastoral responsibilities, walking as far as Cirencester at weekends for four years. In 1897 he had returned to Woodchester as prior, and he also did a certain amount of teaching, though, for some reason, he did not offer any lectures in the year in which Bede Jarrett was a student there.

The novice master was Antoninus Williams, who epitomised more than most the rebuilding of the province in the previous decades. It was he who had got the church in Newcastle built and later supervised the completion of the church in London, both of them impressive monuments to the new spirit of confidence and expansiveness in the Church in England and in the Dominican order. In 1894 he was appointed the first superior of Hawkesyard, becoming its first prior in 1895. On 11 September 1898, when he finished as prior there, he was immediately appointed novice master at Woodchester.

On 24 September 1899 Bede pronounced his simple vows, promising obedience to his superiors until death (temporary profession had not yet been introduced). Two days later he embarked on his first year of Dominican studies. His teacher of philosophy was Leo Moore, who initiated him into the textbook which would see him through all his philosophical studies, the *Summa Philosophica* by the Dominican Cardinal, Tommaso Zigliara, founder of the Leonine Commission (of which the English Dominican, Peter Paul Mackey, was at this time a distinguished member). He also received a course on scripture from Laurence Shapcote, who in addition taught him Sacred Eloquence and Hebrew. It was evidently not considered necessary at that time to teach Dominican students Latin or Greek, which they could be presumed to have learned at school, or at the Dominican postulant school, if necessary, before entering the noviciate.

Bede's first academic year ended with examinations on 20–21 July 1900, at which the provincial presided.

Apart from his studies, Bede had the chance to observe, if only from a distance, something of the machinery of Dominican government at work, as on 7-9 May 1900 the provincial Inter-Chapter met at Woodchester (a formal gathering of the priors of the province in between Provincial Chapters). He would also have learned at first hand something of the mobility of the brethren. As soon as the Inter-Chapter was over, Ambrose Smith's term of office as prior came to an end, and Vincent McNabb was elected to succeed him on 10 May, arriving almost at once to take up his new office. On 16 May Bede's novice master (at this time even after profession students were still called 'novices' and remained subject to the novice master) was elected prior of Newcastle, and the following day Gabriel Whitacre, whom he had known as prior of London, was appointed novice master in his place. Also on 17 May Laurence Shapcote, who had been teaching him at Woodchester, was appointed to take charge of the studies at Hawkesyard.

Bede himself arrived at Hawkesyard on 21 September 1900, three days after the beginning of term, after spending a week's holiday in London. The prior at the time was Henry Bartlett, who had spent most of his priestly life as assistant novice master or novice master, and who had first moved to Hawkesyard in that capacity in 1895. In 1896 he had been sent to London, but in 1898 he had returned to Hawkesyard as prior. In September 1901 he was succeeded by Raphael Moss, who had first met Bede in 1884, when, as he later recalled the episode, young Cyril was 'so small that I never spoke to him'.

The lector primarius was, as we have seen, Laurence Shapcote, but in March 1901, after the death of Antoninus Williams, he was elected prior of Newcastle, and his place was taken by Humbert Everest until September, when Raphael Moss took over his job in addition to being prior.

The novice master (or, as we would now say, student master) was Humbert Everest, who had been sent to teach at Hawkesyard when it was first opened in 1894, fresh from winning his lectorate in Louvain. He had been appointed novice master in May 1900. He was later Bede's predecessor as provincial and, throughout most of Bede's own provincialate and for ten years afterwards, he was a very successful provincial bursar.

For two years Bede continued to study philosophy, first under Shapcote, then under Alban King. For four years he studied scripture under Hugh Pope, who was, as has been said already, the harbinger of a new spirit of scholarship in the province. In his second year he also did a course with Pope on what would later be called 'fundamental theology'. Pope also taught him Hebrew for a year, and later gave him and Hilary O'Neill extra Hebrew tuition on their own. In the second year he started three-year courses on moral theology and canon law, both taught by Humbert Everest. In his last two years he did dogmatic theology with Raphael Moss. Both morals and dogma were taught from the text of St Thomas. Throughout his four years at Hawkesyard Bede was always top of the class, either on his own or sharing first place with Hilary O'Neill.

In many ways life in the studentate was not unlike life in a public school, and there was frequent contact in fact with the boys at Hawkesyard School, even after Laurence Shapcote, the new provincial, imposed some restrictions in October 1902. The boys and the students played football and cricket together and often combined forces in liturgical (or more secular) performances. In their relatively closed world quite small events, such as the occasional parental visit, acquired a significance they would not have had elsewhere. In 1902 Col. Jarrett came for Holy Week, and a concert was laid on in his honour, at which Bede's great friend, Aelred Whitacre, played the violin. And great excitement was caused in August of that year, when two of Bede's schoolfriends came to visit him in a motor car, supposedly the first car ever to 'come up our ancient drive', as Bede remarked in the students' chronicle (he was chronicler for much of his time at Hawkesyard). When they were given some free time, the students used to bicycle the most extrordinary distances, though they had to seek their entertainment in such harmless pursuits at train-spotting at Stafford railway station (another of Bede's friends, Jerome Rigby, was a keen train-spotter).

The religious discipline of the cloister and the personal poverty of the friars were not all that different from the discipline of a public school and the chronic impecuniosity of the schoolboy, and relief from both was occasionally available in a way that would have been familiar to the students from their schooldays. At Hawkesyard the resident benefactress of the young was the lady who had given the estate to the Order, Miss Helen Gulson, who lived in a cottage in the grounds and called herself the 'mother general' of the students. She was always willing to put up small sums of money behind the novice master's back to enhance the funds of the cricket club, and from time to time she invited the students to a much better tea than they could normally look forward to.

There is no reason to doubt the genuineness of the students' religious concerns, but faith does not exempt anyone from the foibles of fallen humanity nor does religious life shut them out: the believer's advantage is that he has a context of christian wisdom in which to understand the muddles of life, and the cloister provides an extra incentive to face up to them with increasing self-discipline. At Hawkesyard, as at any public school, emotions could easily run wild, with passionate friendships springing up and as quickly turning to the most bitter disappointments and feelings of being alone and unloved. Some of Bede Jarrett's letters from this period show how vulnerable he was to such emotional storms. It is only with hindsight that we can see that he was even then laying the foundations for some friendships that would last until his death, including notably that with Aelred Whitacre.

The task that was most obviously and immediately on the agenda was to seek guidance from the past and to try to establish some sort of orderliness amid the riot of emotions—not, of course, to smother the emotions themselves, but to try to get them working properly and coherently, instead of flapping around knocking each other out. It is the old ascetic ideal of a sanity so effective that it renders mere self-control superfluous. Bede plunged himself into such classics as Cicero's book on friendship and the writings of St Aelred, and the fruits of his researches, both theoretical and practical, are evident in many of the documents which follow. In this perennial tradition he found validated his own high ideals of friendship and could begin to see how they had to be cultivated by an absolute insistence on not allowing feelings of jealousy and mistrust to take root, and how attachments must always be kept sane by a deep inner detachment. He could learn the difference between genuine affection for another and a selfish exploitation of other people in the interests of self-gratification. As his letters attest, he had not always found it easy to love without falling into doubts and fears, but the evidence of his mature friendships makes it clear that he did learn the necessary self-discipline and did become capable of an intensity of affection that still left him and his friends free to be themselves and to go their own ways. His letters on friendship, not least those to young men wrestling with the problems he had had to face himself, are full of a kindly wisdom which he had learned the hard way.

In the chapter on friendship in *The Space of Life Between*, first published in 1930, Bede Jarrett sums up his message to young men with refreshing candour, and it is the message he had had to start looking for when he was himself a young man, torn hither and thither by his as yet untamed affections:

> What difference is there between love and friendship? It is hard to determine, perhaps, with any absolute exactness. To Shelley, the word friendship had a meaning of greater unselfishness than love. Friendship was less passionate than love, and implied that a man gave more of himself and received less in return. Perhaps more usually a man's friends are thought of as of his own sex. If this be so then in spite of Shelley's distinction, the friendships of boyhood, school friendships, can be passionate enough and

hard to distinguish from what Shelley has called love. ... The friendships that a man makes with his friends of school-days or of later life may be as passionate as any others. In the artificial surroundings of school and its necessary isolation from home interests, the spontaneous affection of a boy finds no outlet other than the other boys; if he be of affectionate nature, he will turn passionately to his friends. ... This may be perilous: let us admit, however, that it is certainly inevitable. ...

The friendships that we have with others of our own sex may be as valuable to us as those we speak of usually as our loves. They can possess us as wholly, can give us as high a measure of unselfishness, can form as great a joy. But friendship, no less than love, has its rubrics, conditions, and limitations. It must be entered into deliberately and with eyes wide open to the consequence. A friend, like a lover, is for all time: 'That is not love which alters when it alteration finds and bends with the removers to remove.' I must choose warily, for I choose for always. Again, with friendship as with love, with loss of reverence comes friendship's own ruin, for respect is the basis of the enduring qualities of love; so that passion beyond control, a blundering, vulgar thing, which destroys the freshness and fragrance of affection, destroys friendship as completely as it does love. Friendship is a great gift, if we remember that it is carried in an earthen vessel, delicate, 'a seldom pleasure', and is only to be kept from evil by the thought of Our Lord present as a third in it. Thereby it becomes full of unselfishness and sacrifice. It may become evil, it is not necessarily an evil, it may be a great good.

Bede's doctrine, with its echoes of Cicero and St Aelred, insists on the real problem that besets any kind of love, whether it would naturally be designated 'love' or 'friendship': to be truly love, it must be unselfish and sacrificial. It must be faithful enough to respect the freedom of the other to change, even when this results in the loss of some comfort one had grown used to. In this way the passing of whatever extravagances of ardour there may have been at the beginning leaves behind, not another bitterness to soothe away and in time forget, but another friendship that can endure. There is a long christian tradition of the 'order of charity', in which an ideal is clearly depicted of a way of loving which allows for multiple loves which do not exclude each other. In the case of Bede, it is clear that he was capable of a fidelity in friendship which was not, for him or for his friends, thrown into jeopardy by new attachments. The testimony of those who were his friends proves this entirely. After Bede's death, Aelred Whitacre wrote a most moving account of their friendship, in which he says, 'His deep rooted affection for me never failed throughout life, although we always lived apart. As Provincial it was his duty to rebuke me sometimes when I truly deserved it and he did not fail to administer the rebuke. But I would know by a word or touch of hand that his extraordinary affection for me was the same as it had always been.' Another friend, Leonard Parker, who was a schoolboy when Bede first knew him, referred to his friendship with him as 'the most wonderful friendship I could ever experience.' It is clear that Bede's love for his friends was neither threatened by nor threatening to the development of other loves—Bede was overjoyed at the marriage of such young friends as Leonard Parker and George Bellord; their new family commitments enriched the friendship that had been there before.

The temptations to which friendship is prone are essentially emotional ones—doubt and mistrust and possessiveness. Contrary to what might be supposed, these are far more deadly, if they are not firmly checked, than sexual temptations. Bede himself seems to have been gifted with a deep and unworried chastity, but, as his comments on Eleonora Duse and Sybil Hart-Davis reveal, he was unusually tolerant of sexual misdemeanours in those whose loves he believed to be genuinely unselfish. In their regard he more than once cited our Lord's words about the woman who was a sinner: 'Much is forgiven her *because* she loved much.' Of course chastity is a freedom and a strength, part of the delicacy of love even in marriage; but love is the greater commandment and it covers a multitude of sins.

To return to our story, the community at Hawkesyard, when Bede arrived there in 1900, contained some interesting men. Aloysius Crosse was headmaster of the school; soon he was to cause considerable consternation (and amusement) in the province by his habit of constantly leaving and then rejoining the Order. His assistant was Peter Reader, who was to become one of the leading botanists in the county. Maurice Watson, who had been a missionary in China, was assigned there, though he was one of the province's band of itinerant preachers. Another such itinerant was Bertrand Wilberforce, one of the great 'characters' of the province. He was away so much that the student chronicler remarked on one occasion, 'Although he is nominally assigned here, it is the first time we have seen him for several months.' On 20 April 1902 Bede reports in the chronicle, 'Sermon by F. Bertrand on the day's epistle. It was one of St Peter's, which he described as the first of the Great Papal Encyclicals. It was a stirring Tory sermon on loyalty to the king, thanking God for our religious liberty in England.' The students were, of course, aware that such liberty was not guaranteed elsewhere. On 2 December 1902 Bede noted in the chronicle, 'Heard today French Dominicans expelled from "la belle patrie".'

It is hard to imagine Bede not being a Dominican, but, as the time for his solemn vows approached, he seriously contemplated leaving the Order, to escape 'once and for all' (fond hope!) from the perplexities and anxieties he was experiencing in the Order. Although simple vows were made for life, it was not difficult to obtain a dispensation from them, so it was solemn profession that was the real, irrevocable commitment, made three years after simple vows. Bede, like the rest of us, knew how to be tempted by the apparently simple, drastic solution of running away from situations which appeared to be preventing him from living at his best; it was perhaps in 1902, with the help of Aelred Whitacre, that he first really learned to see such temptations for the foolish nonsense that they are. In some of the documents that follow, we can see how well he learned that lesson and how firmly he could pass it on to others.

On 20 September 1902 he received minor orders, and on 24 September he made his solemn profession in the hands of the prior, Raphael Moss. On 9 November he was ordained subdeacon. He was made a deacon on 19 September 1903.

In 1904 a decision was made, which was unprecedented in the modern history of the province: instead of carrying on with his theological studies, Bede was to go to the university of Oxford to study modern history. It is likely that this decision was at least profoundly influenced by Raphael Moss, who was both prior and lector primarius, and who had been much impressed, it seems, by his own visits to Oxford in 1900 and 1901, which appear to be one of the shadowy roots of the idea which soon began to emerge into people's consciousness, both inside and outside the Order, that it was time the Dominicans returned to the city and the university in which they had had their first English house.

At this time, of course, there was no Dominican presence in Oxford, so Bede was to be accommodated by the Benedictines of Ampleforth, who had a Private Hall (Hunter-Blair's) in the university. It was accordingly to Ampleforth that Bede was sent in September, to prepare for responsions (the qualifying examination). Then, on 26 September, he went to Oxford to take the exam (which he passed). He returned to Hawkesyard on 1 October. In his absence Humbert Everest had been elected prior of Hawkesyard and Charles Halpin had replaced him as novice master.

On 15 October Bede took up residence in Oxford and was matriculated on 18 October. Without delay, he put his new-found independence to good use by making his own arrangements for his ordination. He heard from his cousin, Blanche Leigh, that his friend, Bishop Burton of Clifton, would be staying at Woodchester Park before

Christmas (at which time, conveniently, the bishop of Birmingham would be safely out of the way in Rome), so he asked if he and his contemporaries could be ordained at Woodchester, which was granted. In fact two of his contemporaries, Anthony Lowe and Norbert Wylie, were already at Woodchester under a new scheme introduced in 1903, whereby the first year of philosophy was transferred to Hawkesyard and some of the less bright theologicial students were sent to finish their studies at Woodchester.

On 7 December Bede went to Hawkesyard for his pre-ordination retreat. Then, on 15 December, he went to London to visit his brother Hubert, who was being sent to India (he had joined the Indian Army, like his father). On 18 December he was ordained priest at Woodchester. After that, it seems that he spent some days at home at East Grinstead, then returned to London. There, on 5 January 1905, he was rather brusquely informed that he was not to go back to Hawkesyard. Instead he was to spend his vacations in London. It looks as if the new novice master at Hawkesyard was not keen to have his young men exposed to the corrupting influence of an Oxford undergraduate. But for Bede the resulting situation was, especially at first, rather painful. He felt that he belonged nowhere. In term time he was in Oxford, which he loved, but he missed having Dominican companions around him. During the vacation he had to go to London, but he was not assigned there, so it was not strictly his home, and he found the brethren there largely uncongenial.

In Oxford he worked hard and successfully, passing his examinations without difficulty. On 11 and 13 March 1905 he took his first public examination, which at the time consisted of scripture and Latin and Greek; then he was able to concentrate on his historical studies, until he began his finals on 6 June 1907. The results, published on 7 August, reveal him to be among the select list of nine people who won first class honours in the History school. On 10 October he took his degree (becoming an MA four years later without any further examination, in accordance with the Oxford system).

Although he felt obliged always to wear clerical dress in Oxford, he did not live the life of a clerical recluse or a swot. He was not averse to spending an afternoon with a friend at a cricket match or going to tea parties. And his keen sense of fun was readily provoked by the eccentricities and pomposities of some of the dons. In a letter to Jerome Rigby written in October 1904 he quotes with delight one old chap whom he had heard remarking, quite seriously, 'I am labouring under an apprehension which is fast approaching to a certainty that the humidity from the greensward is penetrating into my galoshes.'

He also interested himself in local Dominican history, with the help and encouragement of one of the outstanding local historians, the Dominican tertiary, Baroness Frances de Paravicini. He also offered to edit some of Raymund Palmer's papers for publication, if the Oxford Historical Society would be willing to print them. And he had the satisfaction of publishing a pamphlet on the life of Cardinal Howard.

If he was happy in Oxford, he nevertheless felt acutely unhappy to be strung between Oxford and London, as he was. The intellectual atmosphere of Oxford, combined with his historical studies, sharpened his sense of what Dominicans in England ought to be, and this made him all the more unhappy with the Dominican life he actually found in London, where traditional Dominican values were, he felt, not sufficiently honoured, and where his own obligations as a student were not respected, so that he had to do much of his work on the top of buses and trams, as he went about the priestly business which his superiors imposed on him. Once again he had to discipline his instinctive reactions, of rebellion and distaste, learning the hard way how to entrust himself effectively to the mysterious ways of providence. It is not surprising that it is at this period that he begins to cite as his favourite doctrine the Thomist theory of 'physical premotion', which insists in the most radical possible way on the absolute and all-pervasive effectiveness of God's omnipotence in every single thing that happens in this world.

After graduating in Oxford, Bede went to Louvain to finish his theological studies, arriving there on 25 October 1907. In less than a year he completed his lectorate, which he was awarded on 6 July 1908. The Regent of Studies there at the time was Antoninus Dummermuth, who had made his name as a staunch defender of Bede's favourite doctrine of 'physical premotion', Among the other professors was the future Master General, Martin Gillet, who was lecturing on moral theology.

It might have been expected that, armed with his Oxford BA and his Louvain lectorate, Bede would have been sent to teach at Hawkesyard, but in fact he was assigned to London on 3 August 1908, to work in the parish.

To begin with he found the work unappealing, but, as always, he threw himself into it with his usual generosity. And he found aspects of it which did engage his interest. One such was the scout troop, founded in 1909, allegedly the first Catholic troop in the world. In May 1910 its chaplain was sent to Grenada and Bede took it over. For all practical purposes he was scoutmaster as well as chaplain, leading his boys enthusiastically in all kinds of activities, from swimming to cooking, from Morse Code to first aid. He solicited funds for them wherever he could, so that they could go on expeditions and have a thoroughly good camp every year. Even after he relinquished official responsibility for them when he became provincial in 1916, he kept in touch with them for years. This kind of work with young people attracted him and he was evidently very good at it. His talent for friendship, disciplined so that it would not be burdensome or oppressive, enabled him to enter easily into their world in such a way as to let them regard him both as a leader and as a friend.

An interest of a more sombre kind was his concern to know about and understand the social conditions of the people he was meant to serve. He had studied social theory at Louvain; now he studied it on the ground, being appalled at some of the things he discovered. Although, at least in public, he aimed to maintain a position of political neutrality, he took pains to learn what the Socialists were saying, and some of them became his lifelong friends, like Joseph Clayton, whom he received into the Catholic church in 1910, and Miss Calthrop, whom he also received into the church and who became a Dominican tertiary and a great ally of his.

He did not abandon his intellectual pursuits. Two of his more scholarly books were published in this period: *Medieval Socialism* (1913) and *S. Antonino and Medieval Economics* (1914). He also became a member of the Catholic Records Society, being elected to the committee in 1909 to replace John Procter. He had also, since 1904, been one of the people responsible for seeing what manuscripts the various English Dominican houses possessed and cataloguing them, and in 1908 he officially became provincial archivist. In 1909 he was appointed librarian of London.

There can be no doubt of the brethren's confidence in the young priest. In February 1911 he was made a 'depositarius provinciae', one of the two fathers responsible, with the provincial, for keeping an eye on the province's finances. In 1912 the Provincial Chapter wanted him to become novice master at Woodchester, but the Master General refused to give him the dispensation his youth required. On 16 June 1914 he was elected prior of London. In 1916 he should have been one of the representatives of the province at the General Chapter at Fribourg, only neither he nor the provincial was able to get a passport, because of wartime conditions.

With his accumulating responsibilities and increasing calls for his services as a preacher, he became extremely busy, and he seems not to have found it easy at first to cope with all the demands made on him. The impression of serene leisureliness for which he was later famous was not acquired in a day. But he was never too busy to cultivate his friendships, some of which provided him with a much-needed escape and with an intellectual companionship which he valued. The Bellords, for instance, allowed him to relax in a friendly family atmosphere, and Lady Margaret Domvile gave him books to read, which he almost invariably enjoyed.

One wonders when he found time to read anything at all, but he plainly did discover the secret of remaining at leisure in spite of everything. After his death extraordinary testimonies were sent in to his readiness to drop everything at a moment's notice, however busy he was, to respond to what most people in his position would have regarded as utterly trivial demands. Even as provincial he could respond to the call of a harassed mather, who did not know how to handle her boy's bad temper. Bede Jarrett went down the road at once and told him stories until he calmed down. He was quite willing to spend hours visiting some little girl in hospital, whom he had never seen before. And he never lost his ability to take a full part in any childish romp that came his way, sometimes to the consternation of his more serious-minded brethren.

On 5 September 1916, at the Provincial Chapter at Woodchester, which he attended as prior of London, Bede Jarrett was elected provincial in the first scrutiny, with twelve votes out of seventeen. At the time he was barely 35 years old, which made him easily the youngest provincial in the Order. At the end of the 1916 General Chapter the average age of the provincials was 51, the youngest being 43, and only three of them being under 45. He was the youngest English provincial to be elected since 1870, when the province was scarcely half the size it had attained in 1916.

It never occurred to Bede to refuse any job he was given, but, being entirely without vanity, he reacted to his new eminence with typically boyish humour. 'Do pray for me,' he wrote to Miss Calthrop, 'I feel such a fool!' In response to a letter of good wishes from Leonard Parker and his family, he composed a mock encyclical, 'given at Wheeler in the first week of our Provincialate.' 'The wishes of such excellent people,' he wrote, 'took almost entirely away the nasty taste of the office. It was almost worth being made Provincial to have so nice a letter... It shall be put in the coffin with Us when We go.'

As provincial, he was required by the Constitutions to visitate his whole province annually, or at least to send a visitator, and to pay special attention to the houses of formation (Woodchester, Hawkesyard and, after 1929, Oxford). It was customary for the provincial to attend studium examinations, which ensured regular visits to Hawkesyard, and Bede often attended meetings of the lectors too. He was not expected normally to perform clothings or professions, but Bede was very regular in his visits to Woodchester as well as Hawkesyard. He also visitated each house of the province in person every year, usually in the latter half of the year. Sometimes these visits must have been rather a scramble; in 1929 he got round the whole province, except Woodchester and Hawkesyard, between 1 October and 2 November. He also visited the province's overseas missions several times. In addition he had to attend General Chapters in 1924 (Rome), 1926 (Spain) and 1929 (Rome).

Under his provincialate the province resumed its expansion, both in its numbers (from 124 in 1916 the province rose to 183 members in 1932) and in its territory. By the end of his last term of office, the province had acquired a large new mission abroad (South Africa), was on the verge of starting a new mission in Persia, and had a new monastery of nuns (Headington), a new school (Laxton) and two major new houses of friars (Oxford and Edinburgh).

Like St Dominic, Bede Jarrett believed in dispersing rather than in hoarding his manpower. His predecessor, Humbert Everest, had been reluctant to spare men even to become chaplains to the forces; Bede Jarrett not only allowed their number to be increased considerably, he drew the moral that, since the province was evidently quite capable of functioning without them, it had people to play with to launch new initiatives. And from the outset his vision stretched far beyond the traditional horizons of the province.

Already at the chapter which elected him there was talk of starting a mission in India and, since no invitation had come from India, it seems likely that this was Bede's own inititative. In 1917 an invitation was received from South Africa, and Bede was keen to accept it and easily let himself be persuaded by Laurence Shapcote to do so without even waiting for the army chaplains to return from the war. He responded eagerly to a suggestion put to him by Cyprian Rice, when Rice was but a novice, that there was work to be done in Persia, and he did all that he could to secure a space there for the English Dominicans to work. He also interested himself in the Order's plans to revive the old province of Lithuania. In 1930 a booklet was published in Russian in Lithuania, explaining what the Order of Preachers was, and in the following year a serious attempt was made to gather brethren to go there. Casimir Chases, an English Dominican of Lithuanian extraction, was sent for by the Master General in 1933, but even before this, in 1932, Bede was urging that George Taylor (who had been born in Russia) should be sent to study in Rome (presumably at the newly founded Russicum) in view of the possibility of his working in Russia. The lectors were also thinking of sending him to Rome, but they wanted him to do canon law there! In the outcome he got no nearer to Russia than the Centre d'Études Istina in Lille (from which he was re-assigned to the English province in 1935).

On the home front, Bede had no wish to undermine the traditional work of the province, but he had very clear views of how he wished it to be developed and diversified. The band of missioners continued to function as it always had, and he was a stalwart defender of Dominican parochial work; but he wanted the province to have a higher profile in the intellectual and cultural life of the country. He believed deeply that wherever the Dominicans worked, they should tackle their territory from within its educational centres. Not only were they the traditional recruiting ground of the Order, they would also be the places where Dominicans were formed to be able to talk to (and, if necessary, dispute with) their countrymen within a common culture and on the basis of genuine mutual respect. Bede Jarrett accordingly wanted as many of his brethren as possible to have some kind of university experience. And all the projects which most interested him had an educational aspect.

Few of Bede's projects originated with him. But it was his enthusiasm, his hard work, and above all his willingness to pounce on opportunities, without worrying where the money was to come from, that turned them into realities. Both of the two innovations which he considered to be the most important works of the province—the return to Oxford and the lectures to non-Catholics—had been talked of before he became provincial, but nothing concrete had been done about them. Already in 1911 Baroness de Paravicini altered her will, leaving £1000 to go, if possible, towards a Dominican house in Oxford, instead of £500 to go to London, and even before that it is clear that the idea of a return to Oxford was being mooted. But it was Bede who attracted and motivated benefactors to give the money, it was he who took the plunge and bought a property (which, on his own account, he could not at the time afford to pay for).

Similarly the idea of laying on public lectures aimed at non-Catholics had been proposed by Felix Couturier, who even had a benefactress lined up to pay for them, but it was Bede's hard work, first as prior of London, then as provincial, that got the first series of lectures off the ground in 1916. It was also he who got others to work for the idea, not least Lady Cadogan, who was a sort of 'Catholic first lady' in London. Later on, it was Bede who persuaded London University and the Catholic Evidence Guild to take the lectures under their wings.

Another medium which Bede got the province to exploit was the press. In 1911 the provincial council had turned down the idea of starting a magazine, on the grounds that it would cost too much. But lack of funds never discouraged Bede Jarrett. On 7 May 1919 he informed the council that he had been offered *The Catholic Review* for 30 guineas and that he proposed to buy it out of his own, provinicial's, funds. The next year it was relaunched as *Blackfriars*, with Bernard

Delany as its first editor.

The idea of starting something in Scotland had long been around, and various attempts had been made, including one scheme, which seems to have originated with that very determined tertiary, Miss Baker (whose godmother was the wife of the Jarretts' landlord at East Grinstead), to get some of the French Dominicans who had been expelled from their priories in France to come and settle in Scotland. But what finally did secure a Dominican house in Scotland was Bede Jarrett's success in persuading people that the Dominicans were the right Order to appeal to, where a university venture was in question, so that the archbishop of Edinburgh invited the province to go there, when he thought there was a chance of setting up a chair of scholastic philosophy in the university. After that, all that was needed was Bede Jarrett's willingness to cast prudence to the winds and buy a house he could not pay for and endow it with an impressive overdraft.

At home and abroad it is interesting to see how Bede's vision of the province matured. He was a pioneer of what is now called 'inculturation'. The Dominicans in England must be genuinely English, at home in and acceptable to English culture. Similarly the Order's work in Scotland must attract Scottish vocations so that the Scottish province could be revived. In South Africa he wanted to move to the intellectual heart of Afrikaanerdom, Stellenbosch, in the hope that eventually the brethren could penetrate the university there, for all its Calvinism and Dutchness, and begin to attract young South Africans to join the Order. In the West Indies he dreamed of a West Indian province (an idea which his Irish counterpart, Finbar Ryan, confessed had never even crossed his mind); the first step would be to open a house for West Indian young men, where they could study and, in due course, in some cases, join the Order.

The trouble with an expansive vision like this of what the province could and should be doing was that it was also rather an expensive vision, and the finances of the province were in a most parlous condition. Some of the documents which follow show that Bede Jarrett, as provincial, was well aware of this and concerned that the economics of the situation should be understood by the brethren. He was no idle dreamer, rising above the crude realities of pounds, shillings and pence. Even if he had wanted to, he could not have afforded to give up his gruelling schedule of talks and sermons, up and down the kingdom and in the fabled Eldorado of North America. He simply needed the money. A great deal of the financing of the province depended on his personal earnings. If he wanted to send someone overseas, he probably had to earn the fare himself. It is not surprising that he came to think of most of the money involved in the affairs of the province as 'his' money; most of it had been acquired by his labours or by his ability to attract generous and wealthy benefactors. Not that he abandoned his strict ideal of personal poverty; it was simply that he was far more likely to end up paying the bills than the provincial bursar was. All the expenses of the building of Oxford, for instance, were met out of his pocket, and the bills were addressed to him personally. It is amusing to notice, in a letter written soon after he became prior of Oxford (no. 239), that he automatically wrote 'you ought not to give me that cheque' and had to correct it to 'give us'.

However much he needed the money, he never lost the limpidity of his spiritual vision. He was, above all, a preacher, whether he was giving talks or delivering sermons or conferences, and his preaching was evidently remarkably effective. In an unselfconscious way he radiated to others the solid faith and down-to-earth charity that were his.

He gave himself tirelessly to the task, indeed the multiple tasks, that were laid upon him, and he expected that everyone else would similarly give of their best. It was always a shock to him to discover that people were not doing this, and it seems that he sometimes showed this, to the discomfort of the offenders. In this way he could appear to be a hard man, and this impression was reinforced by his conviction that, as superior, he ought not to have friends amongst his subjects, lest he give even a hint of having favourites. People who had been happy in his friendship before they joined the Order sometimes found this difficult to take, particularly as he seems not always to have explained the reason for his seeming coolness towards them. In fact he was phenomenally willing to give his time to any of his subjects, from the most junior novice to the most senior fathers, for as long as they wanted, and his affection for his Dominican friends was in no way dimmed. His intention was not to withhold himself from anyone, but to deny himself the comfort of seeking out the company of his friends within the Order, in case he appeared to be giving them preference over the rest.

He manifestly continued to enjoy the confidence of his province. In 1920 and in 1924 and again in 1928 he was re-elected provincial with an easy majority in the first scrutiny, and he shouldered the task afresh each time, in spite of his increasing weariness. Particularly during his last term he was worn out and his health was beginning to suffer; but he did not complain.

Only in 1932 was he relieved of his burden, when Bernard Delany, who had been the first prior of Oxford, was elected provincial. But Bede was not to be allowed to rest even then. The chapter appointed him to replace Delany as editor of *Blackfriars* and, as soon as Delany's election as provincial was confirmed by the Master General, the

Oxford community unanimously elected Bede to succeed him as prior, on 17 September 1932. He was allowed a brief holiday, paid for by friends, but on 19 October he arrived in Oxford to take up once more the burden of office. In addition, he was asked to give a course on preaching to the Dominican students there. He also became house chronicler.

As prior, he felt it was his duty not to absent himself without serious reason from his priory, but in the first part of 1933 he paid a final visit to the United States, where he had many invitations to preach and give talks. This absence was justified because of the financial benefit it would bring to the house. Otherwise he generally declined invitations. However he did accept a weekend invitation from the Little Oratory in London. On 17 February 1934 he arrived at the Oratory and prepared his first conference, with his usual scrappy little notes. After the conference he went to the confessional, and there he was found, some time later, manifestly unwell. Two days later he was taken to St John and St Elizabeth's Hospital, run by the Mercy nuns, among them an old friend of his, whom he had professed as a nun, Sr Elizabeth Stourton. On 21 February he received the last sacraments. On 24 February he resigned his priorship.

On 17 March the provincial went to see him in hospital and was overjoyed to find him much better. He died later in the day.

*

Part of the story and a great deal of the character of Bede Jarrett will emerge from a reading of the documents presented in this volume. They reveal a man with a lively sense of fun and a deep seriousness about the mission of the Order of Preachers to make known effectively and attractively to each generation the Word of God, in which our hope of salvation resides. He instinctively rediscovered the medieval notion of the *gratia praedicationis*: the effect of grace is to make the Word spoken by the preacher a 'graceful', alluring word, which will win favour with those who hear it. Bede Jarrett, because he was humble and unselfconscious, was not afraid of his own personal charm. He let it be put to work as an instrument of the gospel. His own affectionate nature, refined by self-discipline, became for many who encountered it a kind of sacramental of the very love of God. It is not hard to believe that Bede Jarrett was, as Delany affirmed, the most perfect Dominican his contemporaries had ever met.

*

The documents edited here all come from the archives of the English Dominican province, save one (no. 196), which comes from the house archives of Blackfriars, Oxford. Many of them are letters whose recipients kindly offrered them to the province after Bede's death. In some cases, a copy was made and the original returned; in some cases it was a copy that was sent in in the first place. In many cases the original is now in the possession of the province. A few letters were copied by people who came across them during their travels. The Provincial's Diary, from which some of the items come, is an official record, kept by the provincial, of his movements and his official acts. The records of the provincial council were also normally kept by the provincial.

The selection of documents to be published was originally made by the archivist of the English Dominican province, Fr Bede Bailey OP. The documents were then edited by Fr Simon Tugwell OP, who made a few minor changes in the selection. Bede Jarrett's spelling was notoriously erratic and it has normally been regularised without comment. Similarly abbreviations have normally been filled out without comment. Any other changes made in the text are pointed out in the notes. We have printed most of the documents in their entirety, but omissions have occasionally been made, and these are indicated by a row of dots (...). To avoid confusion, where there was a row of dots in the manuscript, these have been printed as dashes (---).

We have done our best to avoid anything that could cause upset to people still alive. If we have inadvertently printed something which is distressing to anyone, we hope that our apologies will be accepted. We have tried to secure the consent of all the people most closely concerned in the documents printed here, either as recipients or because they feature in them, or as the immediate relatives or descendants of the people mentioned. Where we have been unable to track down anyone whose consent we could ask, and fear that there might be some risk of giving offence, we have suppressed personal names. Since some of the people who have graciously given their consent to our publication prefer to remain anonymous, we do not list any of them here.

In the notes, compiled by Fr Simon Tugwell OP and Dom Aidan Bellenger, we have tried to supply sufficient historical context for an understanding and appreciation of the documents themselves, and to comment on any salient points of interest or on points which might cause perplexity. Where the editors themselves are perplexed, we have said so, and we invite any readers who can do so to relieve our perplexity. On one point we must admit that we conceded defeat almost immediately: we have largely failed to identify the literary quotations and allusions which feature in some of the letters.

In addition to the notes attached to individual documents, we have supplied a fairly copious annotated catalogue of names, giving a biographical outline of most of the people mentioned in the documents themselves or in the notes. This catalogue was started by Fr Bede Bailey, but most of it was compiled by the other two editors. The over-all editing of the book was the responsibility of Fr Simon Tugwell.

In the preparation of this edition we have become indebted to so many people for various kinds of help that we run the risk of being branded as major public nuisances if we name them all. Nevertheless their kindness cannot go unmentioned. First of all, we must thank the nephew and nieces of Bede Jarrett for their encouragement and for the family information they have so generously supplied: Lt. Col. C. J. B. Jarrett, Mrs Allpress, Mrs Thesiger and Mrs Wykeham-George. Then we must thank the staff of the Bodleian Library, the library of the Jesuit Generalate in Rome, the Fawcett Library and the National Railway Museum. Archivists galore have come to our rescue, some of them responding with heroic forbearance to one question after another: Sr M. Martin Barry OP (San Rafael), Fr André Duval OP (Paris), Dame Eanswythe Edwards OSB (Stanbrook), Fr Hugh Fenning OP (Irish Dominican province), Mr Ian Gardner (English Dominican Laity), Sr Borghild Gundersen SHCJ (Mayfield), Fr T. G. Holt SJ (Farm Street), Mrs Clare Hopkins (Trinity College, Oxford), Sr M. Hugh OP (Stone), Sr M. Albert Hughes OP (Carisbrooke), Sr M. Aquinas Major (Mercy Convent, St John's Wood), Fr Bernard Montagnes OP (formerly Rome), Anne Neavy (Gonville and Caius College, Cambridge), Sr Mary Ormerod (Assumption Convent, Kensington), Miss Elizabeth Poyser (Westminster Diocesan Archives), Mrs M. E. Rattue (St Anne's College, Oxford), Sr Sheila OP (Bushey), Fr F. J. Turner SJ (Stonyhurst) and Mrs June Wells (Christ Church, Oxford). Then we have had parish priests and religious superiors turning over their records on our behalf: Sr Aelred (Abbess of the Poor Clares, Arundel), Fr Pawl Cremona OP (Malta), Fr Adrian Dowling OP (Newcastle), Revd G. J. Duckett (Clacton), Revd K. F. Gaskin (Torquay), Canon Francis Grady (Oxford), Fr Anthony Nye SJ (Farm Street), Fr Bernard O'Donovan (Prior of Parkminster), Fr Richard Price (Provost of the London Oratory), Mgr Nicholas Rothon (Blackheath), Dom Alberic Stacpoole (St Benet's, Oxford) and, not least, the parish secretary of Woodchester, who spent much time and trouble looking for information that turned out not to be there. Other people who have, in various capacities and in various ways, helped us with information and advice are: Mr Charles Bellord, Fr George Bowring SSJ, Fr Peter Duncker OP, Fr T. J. Ertle OP, Dom Charles Fitzgerald-Lombard, Fr Jonathan Fleetwood OP, Mrs Ian Haigh, Sir Rupert Hart-Davis, Dom Philip Jebb, Sr Marguerite-Andrée

Kuhn-Regnier, Mr Philip Moss, Dom Gregory Murray, Br Robert Nisbet, Fr Bob Ombres OP, Mr Simon Parker, Fr Timothy Radcliffe OP, Miss Rosemary Rendel, Fr José Vicente Rodrigo OP, Sr M. John Ronayne OP, Major General J. Scott Elliot, Frère Pascal Vennin OP, Miss Julia Walworth. To all of these and to all who have helped this volume on its way, we tender our cordial thanks.

Simon Tugwell, OP
10 October 1989

1. *Col. H. S. Jarrett to the English Dominican provincial.*[1] *From East Grinstead. 30 September 1896. Autograph.*

One of my boys, who is now 15 years of age—(16 next August) and at Stonyhurst College, tells me that he desires to be a priest and his inclination is to the Dominican order. He seems very decided about this last and the parish priest here to whom I sent him, believes that he has a vocation. I am in doubt what to do regarding him. His education is, of course incomplete, and he is not of age yet I presume,[2] to be put into a seminary. I write to ask your advice as to whether it is advisable that he should continue his studies for the present at Stonyhurst or what course I should best pursue in his regard. He thinks himself capable of bearing the rule of perpetual abstinence.[3] I think the inclination to the Dominicans is due to Woodchester Park where he was brought up as a little boy.[4] However he has long talked of the priesthood, and during these holidays he has been advised to come to some determination regarding his future career. He is decided about the church and the order, and we are of course, glad to learn his excellent choice and will do all we can to forward it.

I should be grateful to you, if you would give me the benefit of your advice.

1. John Procter.
2. In fact the Dominican constitutions in force at the time (the 1872 edition, Const. 214) permitted clerical aspirants to receive the habit any time on or after their fifteenth birthday, but sixteen was a more normal age for young men to enter the noviciate.
3. Originally the Dominicans abstained from meat in all their houses (Primitive Constitutions I 8, edited in A. H. Thomas, *De Oudste Constituties van de Dominicanen*, Louvain 1965, p. 319), but by this time there was fairly generous provision for dispensations allowing meat to be eaten, though only outside the refectory (Const. 157). In 1898 the Provincial Chapter petitioned the Master General to dispense the whole province from perpetual abstinence, so that the brethren in all the houses in the province would be allowed to eat meat, even in the refectory, four times a week; Master General Frühwirth granted the desired dispensation, excepting only the noviciate house at Woodchester, though even there he insisted that the rule of abstinence must be applied with moderation (R. Palmer, ed., *Acta Capitulorum Provincialium Provinciae Angliae Ord. Praed. 1730-1916*, London 1918, pp. 198, 201).
4. When BJ was two years old, his parents went back to India and he was sent to join his cousins, the Leighs, at Woodchester Park, to be looked after by his and their grandmother, Mrs Thomas Jarrett. He lived there for eight years. His cousin, Blanche Leigh, was also convinced that it was during these early years of his life that his Dominican vocation was born (letter to Bernard Delany, 6 June 1934).

2. *Col. H. S. Jarrett to the English Dominican provincial. From East Grinstead. 3 October 1896. Autograph.*

I am much obliged for your letter and the book which I shall read and, as you kindly permit, send it on to my son.

I shall particularly point out to him the necessity of a sound study of Latin together with the general course of education which is obligatory at Stonyhurst. I think he is diligent and his conduct has always been exemplary. His reports are always good in this regard. He is not a clever boy but willing, studious and very docile, which are stepping stones to better things.

Next year I hope you will be able to see him and pronounce on his vocation and capacity.

3. *Col. H. S. Jarrett to the English Dominican provincial. From East Grinstead. 25 July 1897. Autograph.*

I saw my son during the Whitsuntide holidays at Stonyhurst. He seemed as much disposed as ever to enter the church and the Dominican order. I spoke to Father Walmesley, the Rector, about the boy's wish and my own approval. He expressed himself pleased at the boy's intention and seemed to think he had all the makings of a vocation. His conduct and character and work are always well reported, and he has this last year made great improvement in his studies; but he is still very young—16 next month—and (he thought) scarcely advanced enough to begin a noviciate. I am inclined to think that the boy had better complete the course at Stonyhurst. He is now in Syntax and has Poetry and Rhetoric before him.[1] He would enter Poetry in September next, and Rhetoric the following year. That would bring him to eighteen years of age.

The idea of entering the noviciate at Woodchester would, I am sure, be tempting to him, but whether it would be advisable I am in doubt, and would be glad to know your opinion. He will be here for his summer holidays on August the 3rd. Perhaps some day, you might like to see him in London—or if you cared to come here on a visit, we should be very glad to see you.

1. The Jesuit system of education was regulated by the *Ratio atque Institutio Studiorum Societatis Iesu*, published in 1599. Stonyhurst followed the format for the faculty of letters legislated for in the *Ratio*. There were six classes or 'schools': Rhetoric, Poetry or Humanities, Syntax or Upper Grammar, Grammar or Middle Grammar, Rudiments (or Great Figures) and Figures (or Little Figures). Rhetoric corresponds to the sixth form, Poetry to the fifth, Syntax and Grammar, roughly, to the fourth and third forms. Stonyhurst and other Jesuit schools retain some of this nomenclature.

4. *John Procter OP to Ambrose Smith OP.*[1] *From Eastbourne. 26 August 1898. Autograph.*

You will see from enclosed that Col. Jarrett has decided for his son to enter the noviciate *this* year—I am very glad.

Please communicate with him
    South Lodge
    Imberhorne
    East Grinstead[2]
as to date of retreat[3], and arrange all particulars about Bishops Testimonials etc.[4]

... Fr Antoninus will be with you before the retreat to enter upon office of Novice Master.[5]

1. Prior of Woodchester.
2. BJ's family home.
3. The ten-day retreat postulants were required to make before receiving the habit (Const. 107).
4. By decree of Pius IX no one could be admitted to the order without testimonial letters both from the bishop of his original diocese and from the bishop of any diocese where he had been living for more than a year since his fifteenth birthday (Const. 216).
5. Antoninus Williams was appointed novice master at the Provincial Chapter in June 1898, which had also re-elected John Procter provincial. The provincial sent him his assignation to Woodchester and his letter of appointment on 11 September, the date on which his term of office as prior of Hawkesyard expired.

5. *Col. H. S. Jarrett to the English Dominican provincial. From East Grinstead. 27 August 1898. Autograph.*

I am obliged by your letter and await the instructions from the Prior of Woodchester about the boy's despatch and the date of it. I sincerely hope and pray he may be confirmed in his vocation and that it is a real call of which it has all the appearance. I suppose he must take with him the clothes he usually requires for Stonyhurst, contained in one portmanteau. Fr Gabriel, the Prior,[1] mentioned a nephew of his as joining the noviciate at this time[2] and perhaps the two might go down together. Is he to take any money with him? I mean any pocket money if usually given to novices.

Regarding the pension[3]—its amount—when required and to whom payable, I presume the Prior at Woodchester will inform me, if it is his province to do so—otherwise will you kindly instruct me?[4]

1. Gabriel Whitacre, at this time prior of London.
2. Charles Whitacre, who received the Dominican habit at Woodchester at the same time as BJ and took the name Dunstan. He made simple profession a year later, with BJ, and went to Hawkesyard for the second year of studies in 1900, but left the order and was dispensed from his vows in December 1900. His brother, Bernard, joined the order in 1899 and took the name Aelred: he had met BJ briefly in London just before BJ went to Woodchester, and when they

3

met again at Woodchester in 1899 he became one of BJ's closest friends and remained so till BJ's death.

3. The noviciate could be a serious financial burden on the province, and it was hoped that, at least in some cases, the novices' living costs during the noviciate would be covered by their families, i.e. their 'outfit' (the clothes they needed as religious) and their 'pension' (the cost of feeding and housing them etc.).

4. Procter annotated this letter, before sending it on to the prior of Woodchester: 'I have said (a) give him £10 for outfit, (b) pension £40 a year to be paid to Prior of Woodchester, (c) no pocket money needed, (d) will be met at Stroud if the Prior knows time of train.'

6. *Joseph Browne SJ[1] to the prior of Woodchester. From Stonyhurst. 18 September 1898. Autograph.*

I have sent a testimonial to Mgr Hill[2] regarding Cyril Jarrett. He is a most excellent youth, and I trust will be an honour to his Order as well as a credit to his alma mater.

1. The new Rector of Stonyhurst.
2. William Hill (1849-1929), secretary to the bishop of Salford. Stonyhurst being in the diocese of Salford, a testimonial letter from its bishop was required (cf. note 4 on letter 4).

7. *BJ to Jerome Rigby OP. At Hawkesyard. 23 May [1904]. Autograph.*

Wishing Br. Jerome a Happy Feast Day on B. Jerome Savonarola's Anniversary.

I have had such bad 'pip' lately; I hope it has not made me rude to you; I tried to come up and tell you after Matins, but when I got there, I was too shy. I wanted to go up the Park last night.

. . . Please don't laugh! This is a sonnet I once wrote on him—

> O hark to that grand fugue which forward flies
>   Adown the aisle, confused it seems to sound
>   Each several part by each succeeding drown'd
> Each several part in swift succession vies
> To 'whelm the theme incept, which seeming dies.
>   Yet all harmonious and undying crown'd
>   For then in soaring melody around,
> The thrilling theme alone is heard to rise.
>
> The music ceased. Me thought that in a dream
> Upon mine ear a voice angelic fell,
> 'Thus, thus the Frate's life to men did seem
> Confused sounds of heaven and earth to tell
> But diadem'd by death the single theme
> Of "All for God" burst forth in louder swell.'

8. *BJ to Jerome Rigby OP. At Hawkesyard. 14 August 1904.*[1] *Autograph.*

As I am in a hurry, could you please accept this note? I would have come, but I don't know when you will return; you were not in your cell when I last called. . . .

3°. Tomorrow is the anniversary of the OPs first going to Oxford Aug. 15. 1221. Please remember me in your Holy Communion (I *always* remember you in mine). If I go to Oxford, you will be sure to follow, if you keep up your classics and keep interest in them.

4°. The Abbot of Ampleforth comes here on Tuesday.[2]

5°. Philip[3] and I (wind permitting) cycle to Stafford tomorrow afternoon, couldn't you go there for the day? Heaps of engines on a Monday[4] (with Austin[5] of course).

6°. I picked some unripe grapes for you this afternoon. They're not at all bad. The plums are nearly ripe at the end of the garden. . . . (I put in the n°s. It looks intellectual doesn't it?)

1. This note, written on a used envelope, is undated, but internal evidence places the date beyond doubt; in 1904 15 August fell on a Monday.
2. The Abbot of Ampleforth at this time was Oswald Smith. No doubt he was coming to discuss the sending of BJ to Oxford to become a student at the Ampleforth Hall there (Hunter Blair's Hall). On 22 August BJ went to Ampleforth for a fortnight to prepare for his Oxford entrance examinations.
3. Philip Darley.
4. Jerome Rigby was an enthusiastic train-spotter.
5. Austin Barker.

9. *BJ to Jerome Rigby OP. At Hawkesyard. October 1904.*[1] *Autograph.*

I just want to thank you for all in your kindness in putting up with me during these last months. You have put up with me as no other has done, and borne with me when I must have been really a dreadful nuisance.[2] I cannot repay you as I would like to do, nor can I say my thanks. I belong to that select class of Johnnies who can only speak when they should not and never when they should. However I can feel deeply.

I'm afraid this is getting dreadfully sentimental, and you are the last person in the world I should dare to be sentimental to. There is too much of the F. Humbert[3] about you as I have always said. Still put up with this as you have put up with the rest.

I meant what I put into that sonnet[4] that you came at a time when F. Raphael[5] had left me for Austin[6], when Philip[7] never came near me, when everybody seemed to find me heavy and a bore. That I can never forget, and I shall repay you in every little way I can. All that I have ever done for you has been intended to do this. These last days have been dreadfully full of pip. Oxford is grand and full of interest and loveable, but it is not home; and much as I like the OSBs they are not OPs, and there is ever a gulf between. Perhaps if I was fond of railways etc I should never feel the home-sickness, but being what I am I do feel it.

This letter is probably rather flat and rambling but I wanted to thank you somehow or other and to tell you that I love you very much (don't laugh or be vexed) and shall do even beyond death. Friendship to be so, must be eternal.

1. The letter is undated, but evidently must have been written after BJ returned to Hawkesyard on 1 October 1904 after passing his entrance examinations in Oxford. He left for Oxford again on 15 October.
2. Rigby had been the constant recipient of BJ's emotional outpourings, even though he was himself temperamentally disinclined for such displays of feeling.
3. Humbert Everest, until very recently student master at Hawkesyard; on 24 September he had become the prior there.
4. On 1 July BJ had written a sonnet to Jerome Rigby, beginning, 'Amid the loneliest year of all my days.' He appended a note in pencil, 'I wrote this in intense pip. Please make away with it when you have done and *don't laugh*!!!' (In spite of BJ's plea, Rigby kept all or almost all of BJ's communications to him, and BJ, in a letter written slightly later in the year, explicitly refrains from *demanding* that they should be destroyed.)
5. Raphael Moss, until very recently prior of Hawkesyard.
6. Austin Barker.
7. Philip Darley.

10. *BJ to Jerome Rigby OP. From Oxford. March 1905.*[1] *Autograph.*

It is hard having to go to London and never to be back at Hawkesyard again[2] at least not for some time. You can imagine how I felt when the Prior[3] told me in his offhand way. It is part of the religious life one has vowed, so it must be all for the best, though that at times is somewhat difficult *to see*. However don't you get upset with F. Charles.[4] I know you feel it more than most but it is what one has to accept within the cloister. It's training and one knows it is best (though hardest) to obey, but after all Deut. 20 is the true view—we mustn't make the hearts of our brethren to fear.[5] Go on in your own way, obeying and trusting; I shall make a memento of you in my daily Mass, and that will speed across time and space. I did hope to be able to help you as best I could, but your Helper now will slumber not nor sleep for he watcheth over Israel.[6] Pray for me occasionally—for half the year I do not see an OP, for the other half I am among OP who are uncongenial.

1. The date is conjectural, but internal evidence suggests that the letter was written towards the end of Hilary term 1905.
2. After his first term in Oxford, BJ returned to Hawkesyard on 7 December 1904. On 15 December he went to London to visit one of his brothers, who was leaving for India. After his ordination, at Woodchester, on 18 December, it seems that he went back to London, without

revisiting Hawkesyard; there, on 5 January 1905, he was informed that henceforth he was to spend his vacations in London and not return to Hawkesyard.
3. Laurence Peach.
4. Charles Halpin, who had taken up the role of student master at Hawkesyard on 30 September 1904, after the election of Humbert Everest as prior. It was probably Halpin who was responsible for BJ's 'banishment' from Hawkesyard, no doubt fearing the 'corrupting' influence of an undergraduate from a secular university on the young of the province. He was a most unsuccessful and unpopular student master and resigned in August 1905 'in view of the recent unpleasantness aroused in the noviciate' (i.e., in later terminology, the studentate), as he explained to the students.
5. Deuteronomy 20:8.
6. Psalm 120:4 (Vulgate).

11. *BJ to Austin Barker OP. From St Dominic's, London. 30 March 1905. Autograph.*

. . . I have just come back from a day at Oxford to close my written exams by an oral one.¹ I have managed to get through, and my tutor told me (spare my blushes, gentle maid) that I had done 'a splendid paper' . . .

The more one sees of Oxford, the more one longs for us to be able to get back there. One can see the effect it has had on the OSBs. It has given them a tone and a feeling of work that should be part of the everyday habit of an OP. In places like this London everyone has so much work to do that you have to have a good firm will to be able to settle down and get through good sound work. I mean those who have their districts. It seems to be quite a byword amongst people outside that Dominicans are passable Parish Priests, good pious men; but no scholars. That if a priest needs a good preacher, the last place to which he should apply would be the Order of Preachers; and all this makes one very sad. I always say that Oxford would cure all this and give us the spirit of work. It is so absurd to say we're not ready for it; we shall never be ready for it ourselves; we need to go there to be made ready. I can only hope that you will be able to go for I am sure you would do good work and would be able to serve well for us hereafter. You will excuse this gush of mine; and I would not write like this to another, but you understand me well enough I should think to see what I mean. Nor need you show this to any who is likely to be scandalised thereby. But the OP work is simply waiting for us to do it. We have a glorious future before us if we care to make use of it; and jump at it and do our best. . . .

1. On 11 and 13 March BJ had taken the examinations in scripture and in Latin and Greek, that all undergraduates had to take, regardless of their subject.

12. *BJ to Jerome Rigby OP. From St Dominic's, London. 22 April 1905. Autograph.*

. . . Buck up with your studies;[1] you will find little time afterwards for such luxuries, you'll be swamped with parochiality till one's OP ness is squeezed out of one. I have watched this operation in another. One can never tell what will happen to oneself. . . .

I watched the boat race from the top of some railings clinging with my right hand to a lamp post, and saw Oxford leading by 3 lengths, i.e. 189 ft. My Card. Howard has been accepted by C.T.S. but when it appears I don't know.[2] Tell no man.

1. Judging from his grades in the annual examinations, Rigby was perhaps not doing as well as he could have done in his studies. In 1904 he secured 19 out of 25 (while BJ got 21, Austin Barker 20 and Ethelbert Rigby 22), putting him only in the top eight out of a total of eighteen students. In July 1905 he sank to 10 out of 15 (Austin Barker got 14 out of 20 and Ethelbert Rigby 19 out of 20), so that this time there were nine students with higher marks and eight with lower. In 1906 he got 14 out of 20, which put him near the bottom of his class (though no one got more than 15). In 1907 he and Austin Barker got 16 out of 24, with only one student getting a lower mark in their class (Ethelbert Rigby, in his class, got 21). In 1908 a different system was adopted, percentage marks being given separately for a written examination and for an oral; Jerome Rigby got 76 percent in his written examination and 70 in his oral, putting him near the top of his class (Austin Barker got an average of 76.5% and, in the class ahead of them, Ethelbert Rigby got an average of 83.5%). In the same year Jerome Rigby was accepted as a 'formal student' (a candidate for the lectorate). In 1909 he got one of the highest marks of all the students, and far and away the highest in his class (an average of 85%). In 1910 he successfully passed the examination for the lectorate.
2. This was BJ's first published work. He wrote his pamphlet on Cardinal Howard in 1903; it was published by the Catholic Truth Society in October 1905.

13. *BJ to Jerome Rigby OP. From Oxford. 16 May 1905. Autograph.*

I want to write to B. Philip for his feast day[1] so I will put this in with it. But I have so little time that I can only write lengthily in bits. Hence I am beginning this in the Bodleian (on the paper they provide for notes) waiting for the small boy to bring me my books.
. . . I have had pressing invitations from a friend of mine from St Edmund's Hall (popularly known as Teddy Hall) to play cricket with them. I rather fancy they must be hard up for a man. At any rate I hardly fancied that my reputation for brilliant leg hits had spread so far as this. However I explained as well as I could that I did not think it right for a priest to indulge in whites before a lot of people. And really one can't play in blacks. I think that, Prot. as he was, he understood. For he quite agreed with me. So here I am with a clean conscience; and the glory of my cricketing powers all unsullied . . .

Talking of cricket, an old school friend of mine, Philip Walton,[2] has offered to take me to the Australians v. Oxford today. I suppose I ought to take the opportunity, though I can only be there for some

3 hours at the most. I hardly like to get him to pay a bob for that. Those beastly Australians want a 'gate' so everyone has to pay—(Here comes the youth; so ta ta for the present.)

(Continued at All Souls, waiting for my lecturer on 'the Military History in England till 1485'[3]). One 'fresher', i.e. a chap who came up last October with me, the Hon. C. N. Bruce,[4] has got into the XI and last night made 46 not out against the Australians.

(Later still) Went to the match. Rather fun, but we were hopelessly beaten. More's the pity.[5] The Gentlemen of England come down this week against the Varsity. I hope C. B. Fry comes as well.[6]

You will be interested I'm sure to hear that on Wednesday I am going to a lecture by Flinders Petrie (whose name no doubt will be familiar to your scriptural ear) on 'the Egyptians on Mt Sinai'.[7] On the 7th of June Sayce is to lecture on 'Canaan in the century before the Exodus'.[8] They ought both to be interesting. I'm sorry some of you bright Hebrew scholars can't come to listen to these words of wisdom. But we hope the time will come when all these things will be accomplished.

You would think it weird if you came to one of my lectures. A gent of the name of Fletcher[9] lectures on the Tudors at Magdalen College. He sits there; and on his lap all the while is a big cat which he strokes the whole time. I thought he must be cracked, but I am told he has always done so since he started lecturing—and his hair is grey now. . . .

1. Philip Darley. 26 May was the feast day of St Philip Neri.
2. Philip Walton (1882-1915) went to Stonyhurst in 1892; he was at University College, Oxford, 1901-1904, when he obtained a 4th in History. He became a barrister and, in 1912, went to work in Singapore. He died there, by a tragic accident, during the mutiny in February 1915.
3. These lectures were given at mid-day by Charles (later Sir Charles) William Chadwick Oman (1860-1946), at this time Deputy Chichele Professor of Modern History. From what BJ says, he was evidently lecturing on Tuesdays, in spite of the lecture list for the term, which assigns his lectures to Thursdays and Saturdays (though at the end of the previous term he had announced he would lecture on Tuesdays and Thursdays).
4. Clarence Napier Bruce (1885-1957), who became the 3rd Baron Aberdare in 1929. At New College, Oxford, 1904-1908, when he obtained a 3rd in History. He had played cricket for Winchester before coming up to Oxford, and was a very successful cricketer at Oxford. *The Oxford Magazine* 23 (1904-1905) commented on 24 May 1905 (p. 342), 'Undoubtedly the best batting performance was the innings of C. N. Bruce.' After serving in the first World War he became a distinguished cricketer, playing for Middlesex 1919-29. It was evidently at the end of the first day of play in the match against the Australians, Monday 15 May, that he was 46 not out; on Tuesday he was bowled out, having scored 69.
5. The match against the Australians was played 15-17 May. By the end of play on Tuesday 16th the Australians had had two innings, in which they scored 241 and 266, and the University had had one innings, in which they scored 167 all out. The University did no better on Wednesday.
6. The match against the Gentlemen of England was played 22-24 May, and C. B. Fry was not in the team. The University won. Charles Burgess Fry (1872-1956) had a long career in cricket. He was captain of cricket at Repton and at Oxford (in 1894 he made a century against Cambridge), perhaps affecting what might otherwise have been a more glorious academic

record (in 1893 he got a 1st in Classical Moderations, but in 1895 he only managed a 4th in Literae Humaniores). Later on he played for Sussex and then for Hampshire, and sometimes for England. Even as late as 1921 he was invited to play for England, though he was unable to do so.
7. Flinders Petrie (1853-1942) was professor of Egyptology at London University 1892-1933; he was knighted in 1923. On 24 May he was due to address the Oxford Architectural and Historical Society on the topic indicated by BJ; there is an account of his lecture in *The Oxford Magazine* 23 (1904-1905) pp. 357-358.
8. Archibald Henry Sayce (1845-1933) was professor of Assyriology at Oxford 1891-1915. He was to give a public lecture on the topic indicated by BJ on 7 June.
9. Charles Robert Leslie Fletcher (1857-1934) got a 1st in History at Oxford in 1880 and became a fellow of All Souls in 1881; fellow and tutor at Magdalen College 1889-1906. He was a man of fiercely Protestant and Tory views.

14. *BJ to Jerome Rigby OP. From St Dominic's, London. 28 June [1905]. Autograph.*

. . . Now I must stop, having to range through Aristotle's Politics, Hobbes' Leviathan and Rousseau's Contrat Social in the next 2 or 3 days, not to mention some 12 volumes of the Chronicles of Matthew Paris—this is exclusive of 40 other books which, so says my tutor,[1] I have to get through in this Vacation (called the Long Vacation, or by 'Varsity people (ahem!) simply 'the Long'). But it lasts till October. . . .

1. Ernest Barker.

15. *BJ to Jerome Rigby OP. From St Dominic's, London. 21 August 1905. Autograph.*

. . . There are times when I feel the strain is more than bearable. I know I oughtn't to do so, but I worry over what I can't help regarding as lack of observance here. Probably I'm wrong and all that; but feelings worry nerves and nerves worry brain, and the whole thing at times makes me quite ill. It seems absurd for a young priest, hardly a few months ordained, to set himself up against the rest, but I dread all thought of what our S. Dominic would say; and dreading it my head whirls round.
. . . I have got through all my books for my tutor except some 8 vols of the Rolls Series—the Chronicles of Matthew Paris in Latin. They are such bulky things to take about, for I do no small portion of my work on the top of trams and buses. . . .

16. *BJ to Austin Barker OP. From St Dominic's, London. 1 September 1906. Autograph.*

Mea maxima culpa! But I did really intend to write to you for S. Austin's day,¹ only this is the first free day I have had. Yesterday, the hottest day of the year so far in London (92 in the shade, though of course 2 in the shade is squeezing point), I had to give French class for 3 hours, and this besides all my Oxford work. So please accept my most humble apologies for this very late affair.

I do hope you are sticking to your Scripture if I may thus launch into an homilia Venerabilis Bedae presbyteri.² F. Peter Paul³ is here, or rather he has just left. I don't think that I have ever met so scholarly a man. He is well-read in all the modern histories and gives one a criticism of each, just and true as far as my poor wits could judge. From which I supposed that beyond his 5 hours a day at S. Thomas, he devoted his time to History. Not a bit of it. No sooner had a question come up on biology than off he went again, showing that he had read and inwardly digested a good deal of modern science. But in Scripture he was just as down to date. He laid special emphasis on this last which he said was so necessary for Catholics to take up and that seriously. We must as far as we can take up all these modern questions. And, if I may be pardoned for adopting this high and mighty tone, I do hope you will go in for Scripture. Perhaps you can keep this to yourself, but if I get a chance of saying anything to the Provincial⁴ (though as you know what he is like, you can understand that I may get no such chance) I shall ask him to send you and B. Luke⁵ to Oxford, you for Scripture and him for Classics. I feel that it is absurd looking at Oxford as a sort of nursery for the College Masters,⁶ every OP ought to be given the opportunity of making himself proficient in some branch, so far as L.S.D. will permit. He ought not to be driven to it, for such is not our spirit, is it? But he ought to have the opportunity and the encouragement. After that he may be trusted to do his own work for God. The OSBs say that with them where the Professor has precedence of the monk, the monastery becomes lax. But with us, I fancy, the reverse has been true, though of course I do from my heart abhor the Lectors or at least all their works and pomps. Yet on the other hand we have been a learned Order, and nowadays we live on the reputation of our spiritual ancestors instead of trying to revive the old traditions for ourselves. Have you read Watson's poems, they are in your library, a green and gold book that once was given to me. In his 'Apologia' there are lines which we OPs must greatly feel:-

'E'en such pride was mine
As is next neighbour to humility,

> For he that claims high lineage yet may feel
> How thinned in the transmission is become
> The ancient blood he boasts; how slight he stands
> In the great shade of his majestic sires.'[7] . . .

P.S. I go to Woodchester for retreat.

1. 28 August.
2. 'Homily of the Venerable Bede, presbyter'—a phrase used often enough in the Breviary to introduce readings from the Venerable Bede at Matins.
3. Peter Paul Mackey OP, of the Leonine Commission, charged with the editing of the works of St Thomas Aquinas.
4. Laurence Shapcote. He had been provincial since 1902, having been re-elected on 8 May 1906.
5. Luke Walker. BJ soon changed his mind about the usefulness of biblical studies in Oxford and began to think that Jerusalem would be better. In the outcome, both Walker and Barker were sent to Jerusalem.
6. The schoolmasters at Hawkesyard, that is.
7. Sir William Watson (1858-1935), *The Father of the Forest*, London 1895, pp. 67-68.

17. BJ to Jerome Rigby OP. From St Dominic's, London. 29 September 1906. Autograph.

. . . I have just come back from Brighton. It was very nice there, as I stayed with some cousins of mine who have a sweet little boy (aetat. 7, but very precocious).[1] I attended every conference.[2] There were many there whom I knew and not a few from Oxford. The Bishop of Christchurch (New Zealand)[3] at the reception asked me where I came from and when I told him, he said I was too young and too good-looking to be there by myself.[4] Of course he must be a distinguished and far seeing prelate, and I shall watch his career with interest. Of all the papers, F. Benson's[5] was the most amusing. Do read it in the 'Tabby'[6] or elsewhere. It is clever and true, though many seem to think he ought to have been more serious, as the theory has more in it than may appear.[7] But I fancy that humour of a refined kind, as is his, is quite a good solvent. F. Hugh's retreat[8] was very good. 'Be ye English, as your Heavenly Father is English' was the refrain. Sorry to scandalise you.

1. Almost certainly Francis Beaufort Palmer (1845-1917) and his wife, whose son Julian Arthur was born in 1899 (died 1973). F. B. Palmer was a cousin of BJ's mother.
2. BJ and Vincent McNabb had been attending the Catholic Conference, organised by the Catholic Truth Society, held in Brighton 23-26 September.
3. John Grimes (1842-1915), an Englishman who had been appointed first bishop of Christchurch, New Zealand, in 1887. As he told the conference, the pope at the time 'had laid upon him the duty of building a cathedral. He had set to work and had had the consolation of opening a building which the Governor had described as the finest in New Zealand' (*The Tablet* 108 (1906) p. 489).
4. A modern echo of the story widely circulated in the early years of the Order, reported in the *Vitae Fratrum* (cf. S. Tugwell, *Early Dominicans*, New York 1982, p. 137).

5. Robert Hugh Benson gave a talk on 'Christian Science' in the morning of 25 September.
6. Benson's talk was printed in *The Tablet* 108 (1906) pp. 515, 495-498.
7. Benson concluded his talk with some recommendations: 'First, I am sure we must keep our tempers; and secondly, our sense of humour. If it is true that Protestantism rises in any degree from the absence of this latter virtue, I am certain that Christian Science, its latest development, rises almost entirely from it . . . Let us therefore bring to bear this genial solvent of laughter and see whether Christian Science is as impervious to it as to so many other facts of the world in which we live. But supremely let us remember that the sacramental system is the one and only positive scheme which can be advanced with any hope of success. It is from the loss of this that this new heresy has had its rise . . .'. Benson's own exposé of Christian Science is very funny and quite devastating.
8. BJ had been attending the retreat preached at Woodchester by Hugh Pope.

18. BJ to Jerome Rigby OP. From St Dominic's, London. 8 December 1906. Autograph.

. . . Well I hope you feel very settled now after the Solemn Profession.[1] I fear that we are to reap a fair crop of scandals[2], but please don't let that worry you. These odd things are bound to happen. The only cause as far as I can see is that people don't take a sufficiently manly view of life. They expect that everyone will sympathise etc., instead of expecting and almost wishing for the hard things of life. I trust that none of us are such fools as to come to the cloister for the pleasure of the thing. Consequently comes the temptation to skimp work and to be underhand with superiors, instead of taking things on principle and letting one's own pet ambitions go to the wall. To me personally S. Thomas' efficient premotion[3] is the ideal guide to help one along. The whole scheme of one's life is already laid out before God. It is all His will, though of course it is all equally our own free choice—a mystery if you will but not a contradiction.[4] It is no use grumbling, rather is it harmful; besides being childish and feminine. Of course one is always tempted to give way and be depressed. But we have to be men and strong ones in mind, to be healthy in spirit.

Excuse this hortatory tone, but I am so upset at present that I can take little interest in anything else. . . .

1. He made his solemn profession on 23 September 1906.
2. BJ is referring to Hilary O'Neill leaving the Order. As he wrote on the same day to Austin Barker, 'Hilary O'Neill has gone off with a girl and written to his prior to say he can't come back and live as a priest.' O'Neill had been clothed at Woodchester half way through BJ's noviciate, and they had gone to Hawkesyard together in 1900. His time at Hawkesyard was characterised by ill health, resulting in his being ordained early, in December 1903. From BJ's comments, it appears that he at least suspected that O'Neill had been skiving.
3. The controversial Thomist teaching, developed especially by 16th-century theologians like Domingo Bañez OP (1528-1604), that God is the *first* cause of all that happens in creation, in as much as he imparts causal efficacy to all created secondary causes and determines their particular effects in each particular case (hence *pre*motion), and that he is the *efficient* cause of all causality within creation, including that exercised by human free will. One of the most vigorous defenders of this doctrine was the Regent of Studies at Louvain, Antoninus Dummer-

muth OP (1841-1918), who published two books on it in 1895 and 1896, defending the 'orthodox' Thomist interpretation of St Thomas against the Jesuit V. J. Frins (1840-1912). Although BJ had not yet himself studied at Louvain, his teachers had. Dummermuth was Regent there from 1885-1915, and among his students was Humbert Everest, who had taught the course involving the topic of physical premotion in 1901-1902, when BJ was a student at Hawkesyard.

4. For a modern exposition of the Thomist doctrine, cf. Herbert McCabe OP, *God Matters*, London 1987, pp. 10-24.

19. *Oswald Hunter-Blair to the finalists at Hunter-Blair's Hall, Oxford.*[1] *6 June 1907. Autograph.*

To You Three.[2]

Every kindest wish I send you:
May the best of luck attend you,
Saints and Angels all befriend you,
Hem you round about, defend you
From the foes who fain would rend you!

Prospere procedite, et regnate. Egomet pro felici eventu S. Sacrificium hodie oblaturus sum.[3]

1. The ancestor of the present St Benet's Hall, Oxford. Under a statute passed in 1882 any Oxford MA above the age of 28 could apply for a licence to open a Private Hall, which would be known by his own name. Both the Jesuits and the Benedictines made use of this provision to open Halls in the university, the Jesuits in 1896 with Clarke's Hall, the Benedictines in 1899 with Hunter-Blair's Hall. In 1918 a new statute allowed for the creation of Permanent Private Halls (with correspondingly permanent names), and the Jesuit Hall became Campion Hall and that of the Benedictines St Benet's Hall.
2. The copy of this poem in the Dominican provincial archives is annotated in BJ's hand, 'Verse written by Fr Hunter-Blair OSB to three of us taking the final schools, Oxford June 6th 1907', but it is not entirely clear that BJ was meant to be included, as there were three Benedictine finalists in 1907: Justin McCann, who got a first in Greats; Aelred Dawson (1881-1914), who got a second in Theology; and Dominic Willson (1879-1943), who got a third in Chemistry.
3. 'Go forth prosperously and reign (Psalm 44:5, Vulgate). I will offer the Holy Sacrifice today for a happy outcome.'

20. *BJ to Austin Barker OP. From Louvain. c. June 1908.*[1] *Autograph.*

When F. Paulinus[2] told me the good news,[3] I could hardly believe my ears and had to read through slowly Zigliara's proof of the perse-validity of the testimony of the 5 senses,[4] before I could satisfactorily commit an act of certitude sine formidine errandi.[5] For the next half hour I could do no work but chortle out broken choruses of some chic French songs, interspersed with the Soldiers' Chorus from Faust and with bits of 'To all you ladies etc.' Now however having more or less recovered my stable equilibrium I venture to write and congratulate you and the Province and everybody all round. It is a splendid opening, for you who have such interest in things scriptural. You go out into the scene of labours, and will work under the guidance of perhaps our greatest biblical scholar since the days of Santes Pagnini and Sixtus of Siena; for Père Lagrange is a great theologian as well and can know when to lead and when to follow the Church. But it is not of Père Lagrange that I want to write. I have no intention of giving advice for that is not my strong point and I have none to give even if I wanted to. But remember that it is on you that the Province will depend in a few years' time for all her scriptural tradition, that scripture is the study above all others that appeals to the religious side of the English character, and that it is in the realm of scripture that many of the Modernist problems will be fought out, that is, both in the theological and in the practical side of biblical studies. These are facts, and the advice relating to them or the conclusions to be drawn from them are questions personal to yourself, which I have not the impudence to interpret. Only I can say that my prayers will be with you that all you may do may be worthy of our master, of our order, and of yourself. One thing I should like to say is that F. Jerome[6] wrote to me that much of his first class work was wasted in Jerusalem because some of the lectures were given in French. I should fancy that getting B. Jerome[7] to talk French rapidly with a clothes-peg saddled on his proboscis might produce the nasal effect which it is difficult at first to decipher.

I am glad too B. Ethelbert[8] is coming here, for three reasons. (1) To take off the bad effect on the prestige of the English Province which will be produced by any failure. (2) That I shall not feel so criminally like Jacob, the supplanter.[9] (3) Because he will benefit by Louvain and well deserves it, having served like Jacob for Rachel for 7 years.[10]

Here everyone is glad you are going to Jerusalem. It means the opening out of the Province; it means that the curious modernistic ravings have not frightened the Provincial;[11] it means that Père Lagrange will see that he has not lost but gained confidence in this day of trial; it means also, says the Regent,[12] though happily this is of no meaning in England at present, that the scriptural professors are to be men who are up to date.

I suppose F. Hugh[13] is very pleased over it all. By the way in January soon after the beginning of the year a post card from Australia with his superscription, and dated September, reached me here. It had evidently also been voyaging for its health's sake. I will try and thank him for it some day.

And now I will leave you to revert to your Hebrew grammer. You must be beginning to pack up your mosquito curtains and Keatings Powder,[14] to press your nasal eruption into the Jewish arch of triumph, and to talk Hieroglyphics and Cuneiform.

Hoping to see you before you leave England.

1. The moves mentioned in this letter (Austin Barker to Jerusalem, Ethelbert Rigby to Louvain) were announced by the provincial in a letter sent to Hawkesyard on 3 June 1908. Probably the news reached Louvain fairly quickly, so BJ's letter can be dated to the middle or end of June.
2. Paulinus Sweeney, who was also studying at Louvain.
3. That Austin Barker was to go to the École Biblique in Jerusalem to study for his lectorate.
4. T. M. Zigliara OP, *Summa Philosophica*, was the textbook of philosophy used both at Woodchester and at Hawkesyard when BJ was a student. At Woodchester in 1899-1900 he had been taken through Zigliara's epistemology by Leo Moore, and had had to do a paper on his refutation of 'absolute scepticism'. In the edition published in Lyons and Paris in 1884, the proof referred to here is in volume I, pp. 210-211.
5. 'Without fear of error'—part of the classic scholastic definition of certainty (cf. Zigliara, op. cit. I p. 188).
6. Jerome Brookes, who had been sent to Jerusalem in 1902, where he died in the following year.
7. Jerome Rigby.
8. Ethelbert Rigby.
9. Ethelbert Rigby had been accepted as a 'collegial' or 'formal student' (i.e. a candidate for the lectorate) in 1907, a year before Austin Barker, so might well have expected to go to Louvain immediately, had not BJ himself been sent there in that year. Jacob supplanted his brother Esau as his father's heir (Gen. 27:36).
10. Gen. 29:20. Rigby had not literally served for 7 years; he started his studies in 1902.
11. John Procter.
12. Antoninus Dummermuth (cf. above, no. 18, note 3).
13. Hugh Pope. He had been ill early in 1907, and it was decided that he needed a proper chance to recuperate, so he was sent off on what was almost a world cruise, paying his way by serving as chaplain. In June he sailed for Australia from Naples, and there he remained for most of the summer. He then went to Cairo and Jerusalem, returning home via Rome, reaching Hawkesyard in December.
14. A precaution against fleas.

21. *BJ to Jerome Rigby OP. From East Grinstead. 22 August 1908. Autograph.*

The whole tribe of Jarrett, i.e. both parents and two brothers, are off for a ball tonight and have left me alone here. Consequently here goes for an epistle of natal congratulations[1]. . . . I hope this year will go quickly by till it brings you that which is the great centre of your life, to which all the past leads up and from which all the rest will have its being.[2] You have always the memento[3] and I have nothing else to give you.

I have just been two weeks here in absolute peace. Tennis has been the most violent exercise I have taken, and motoring the most pleasurable. You remember the Blounts' house[4], the chapel of which I showed you and the park of which we crossed? It is their motor (or one of them, for they have four) which has hurtled me over hill and dale. This I find pleasant. One need never talk, and the company is excellent. One can see the perfect Sussex scenery, the most gentle and peaceful in the world, as far as I know it. The whole effect is soothing, and this is the holiday I like. They wanted me to go to the Franco.[5] But I struck at that. It is no holiday for me to dash round those sort of places. By the way my eldest brother was there, i.e. at the Franco, the other day when the explosion took place.⁶ He was some 30 yards off but uninjured by the flames. The excitement was immense.

Would you do something for me? A Belgian collegiate OP is very keen on the study of comparative religions. He read an article in the H.R.⁷ (not *the* article,⁸ but one of the unimportant ones) on 'Buddhism and Christianity' (?) by B. Bruno (?).⁹ I fancy I am right so far. Well he would like to work with him, by correspondence if it could be managed. Is the aforesaid B.B. keen? Is he very learned? The Belgian is. (Besides being my best friend over there). Is it any use B.B.'s writing? The Father is Bernard Kübben. Use your own judgment and do nothing if you think it best.

Also F. Ceslas Rutten OP wishes for a young English Father to take up his sociology work. Does that attract you or is there anyone else you know keen on it? . . . The other day I went up to lunch with Miss Baker.¹⁰ She had been up to Haverstock Hill the very Saturday he left to see F. Austin¹¹ to give him the address of Père Le Vigoureux (the Père Etienne of the book¹²) who lives in Paris and is just leaving for Jerusalem. It was very nice of her but of course too late. Have you heard as to how he fared in Paris and how his voyage suited him? Miss B. is very keen on Oxford and thinks she has captured a lady (with £80,000 per annum) who might be fascinated into an endowment. I have to go to tea some time to fascinate! Do lend me your face for a while. Personally I fear that the good lady is lost to us as Lady Edmund Talbot is trying to squeeze her for the poor of London, and, much as I hope for an Oxford house, I cannot honestly give it preference (even if I had the power) to the Catholic poor. Moreover I cannot bring myself to 'work' people for some scheme. It's hardly a priestly office, is it? She (i.e. Miss B.) is leaving her own money in that way I believe; though she has not explicitly told me so. Personally I do not fancy we have enough in the Province for that at present and it would seem to be wiser to found single burses, say at Oxford, Jerusalem, Fribourg, etc. That with London and Pendleton¹³ ought to afford sufficient for the Province for some time to come. This is at least what I put before her and I think she agreed with me. . . .

1. 24 August was Rigby's birthday.
2. I.e. his ordination to the priesthood (he was ordained on 6 March 1909).
3. The 'memento' for the living in the canon of the Mass.
4. The Blounts were the owners of Imberhorne Manor, and South Lodge, where the Jarretts lived, was part of their estate. They were a staunchly Catholic family. Until his death in 1905 the patriarch of this branch of the family was Sir Edward Charles Blount (1809-1905), who was an important banker and pioneer of the railways in France; his wife was Gertrude Frances Jerningham, granddaughter of the 6th Baronet. The manor was inherited by Sir Edward's son,

Henry Edmund (1844-1911), then by Henry Edmund's son, Edward Aston Charles Marie (1874-1953), who was 'like another brother' to the Jarrett children (letter of Sr Elizabeth Stourton to Bernard Delany, 15 August 1934).
5. The long-running Franco-British Exhibition at Shepherd's Bush, London.
6. On 14 August an airship, which had already been displayed in America and was due to make its first ascent in England at the Exhibition, exploded at about 11.30 a.m., killing the aeronaut's secretary and wounding five workmen. BJ's eldest brother was 'Charlie' (Charles Henry Brownlow Jarrett), born in 1874; he was killed in the war in 1915.
7. *The Hawkesyard Review*.
8. The first issue of the new series, begun in 1908, contained an article by Jerome Rigby on 'St Thomas and the Immaculate Conception' (pp. 29-44).
9. There was an article in the same issue by Bruno Walkley on 'Buddhism and Christianity' (pp. 56-67). Walkley had gone to Hawkesyard School in September 1904, so must have been almost, if not entirely, unknown to BJ.
10. Elizabeth Anstice Baker.
11. Austin Barker, who was on his way to Jerusalem, via Paris.
12. Miss Baker's book, *A Modern Pilgrim's Progress*, London 1906.
13. The province was greatly burdened with the debt incurred in the building of the new priory at Pendleton, opened on 20 January 1901; and the parish in London urgently needed a larger building for its parish school, currently (and quite inadequately) accommodated in Blackfriars Hall.

22. BJ to Jerome Rigby OP. From St Dominic's, London. 25 December [1908].[1] Autograph.

I had made up my mind not to write to you. But your 8 pages has made me scrawl something. Like M.S.A.[2] I have been en route for the Dead Sea, there to spend my Xmas. As a matter of fact I am not ill, only at Parish work for which I feel myself quite unfitted. Of course every one says that it will do me a lot of good etc., and that I shall be pleased to look back on it. Really I should be quite pleased even already to look back on it; only unfortunately my only chance is to look forward at present. This has given me the Almighty Pip, so I came to the conclusion that it would be wiser and more charitable to leave you alone. However you have pulled the chain and all the water has come down. It is entirely your own fault.

As for my best behaviour, I was quite as sick of it as you were. But I felt that I must somehow try the oyster dodge and shut up. The result seems to have been unfortunate, more so for myself. However as Lady Macbeth remarked as she tried to loosen the knot of her boot before retiring to bed, 'What's done cannot be undone'. Ergal,[3] my good behaviour has vanished as quickly as it came. . . .

The Prince[4] and his companion spoke French. We did Abbey, Cathedral, Westminster Hall, National Gallery, Tower, British Museum by tube, electric underground, motor bus, horse bus, cab, hansom, taxi—that is all between 10 a.m. and 4.55. Quite a record. We counted spoons after he had gone. I think he was genuine.
P.S. What an idiot! A merry Xmas and a bright New Year! It shows how my mind is wandering!!

1. The two possible dates for this letter (when Austin Barker was in Jerusalem and Jerome Rigby was working for his lectorate) are 1908 and 1909. The latter seems excluded by the beginning of this letter, which is hardly compatible with BJ having written a four-page letter on 22 December, as he did in 1909.
2. Most Sweet Austin (Austin Barker).
3. BJ is presumably thinking of 'argal', a comic corruption of 'ergo' found, for instance, in Shakespeare, indicating, as often as not, the triumphant conclusion of a dubious bit of reasoning.
4. The Prince has not been identified.

23. *The Editor of Votes for Women*[1] *to BJ. From London. 15 July 1909. Original typescript.*

Your little article is very interesting, and we hope to be able to publish it in a future number of 'Votes for Women'.[2] It shall certainly be anonymous as you wish it.

1. *Votes for Women* was a suffragette journal, launched in October 1907 by the Women's Social and Political Union, founded in 1903 by Mrs Emmeline Pankhurst (1858-1928) and her militant daughter, Christabel (later Dame Christabel) (1880-1958). It was edited by Frederick William Pethick Lawrence (1871-1961) and his wife, Emmeline (1867-1954), who joined the WSPU in 1906. She was a social worker in the grand tradition of Victorian philanthropy. He later became a Labour M.P. (1923-31 and 1935-45), and was Secretary of State for India and Burma 1945-47; in 1945 he was created the 1st Baron Pethick Lawrence. In 1912 the Pankhursts' decision to increase their militancy led to a split between them and the Pethick Lawrences.
2. BJ's article seems not to have been published or to have been heard of again. We are grateful for the help of Michael Doyle OP and the Fawcett Library in our fruitless quest for it.

24. *BJ to Jerome Rigby OP. From St Dominic's, London. 20 July 1909. Autograph.*

. . . Lagrange and Cie[1] were here of late and were most pleasant and nice. A day at the British Museum among Assyrian monuments I found most interesting. Père Dhorme (whom naturally the lay-brothers called the 'Door-mat') read off cuneiform inscriptions as I would English and the sound of that quaint tongue was very soft and smooth-running like the wheels of the LNWR 'Owl'.[2] They spoke very kindly of 'Miss Barker'[3] who has won golden opinions out there and is liked by all.

Your mother says that you can give them no help about holidays, so I don't know whether to expect you or not. Anyway I have had so much stuck on me to do of late that I shall see but little of you even if you do come. There are times when I feel as though my head would burst, with numberless little things to think of and do, and I spend nights half-waking and half-dreaming how I am to fit in all the little duties of the morrow. But of course in my saner moments (for I have reverted to the morning cold bath as a restraint of some kind) I call myself a fool and try and take things calmly. Or perhaps like the Scottish preacher, I 'look the matter squarely in the face and—pass on.' But there is so much that says, 'Oh you were not made for this, you are stupid at that, run away and study history and let the rest go.' Then I get a letter from an old Oxford professor[4] who has been at Harrogate with the Provincial[5] and who writes to tell me that he is so pleased to hear that I have time and leisure to pursue my historical studies. Then my mind revolts. Then I see others allowed to miss this, that, and the other, so as to amuse themselves—or being let off parish work altogether. Again I feel revoltful. Then come guests or any other thing you like and it or they are dumped on me, and I feel inclined to go from the Province or the Order or from life. Then God sends a thought of physical premotion, the all-powerful, all-pervading will—and I have peace and am ready to bear with it all. So am I tossed to and fro from hour to hour a sinner or a saint. Fortunately I have no one here to say a word to, so that I am driven to spiritual things for help. It is only just this once that I allow myself to burden even you.

1. The 'compagnie' consisted of P. Vincent and P. Dhorme. Lagrange and Vincent spent fifteen days at St Dominic's, London, returning to Paris on 16 July. Dhorme was with them for eight days. On 17 July Lagrange wrote to Master General Cormier that they had been 'very charitably received'; they visited Oxford and Cambridge, he says, 'but particularly the British Museum'. See letter 143 in the forthcoming edition of Lagrange's correspondence with Cormier: Bernard Montagnes OP, *Exégèse et Obéissance, La Correspondance Cormier-Lagrange 1904–1916*, Paris 1990. We are grateful to Fr Montagnes for drawing our attention to this letter and for supplying a text of it.
2. LNWR had a locomotive named 'Owl', built at Crewe in 1860; however it had been retired in 1903. We are grateful to the librarian of the National Railway Museum, York, for this information. Presumably it was a train that Rigby had 'spotted' on one of his train-spotting expeditions to Stafford.
3. I.e. Austin Barker, at this time studying in Jerusalem.
4. Probably Sir Ernest Barker, who had been BJ's tutor at Oxford. In his autobiographical *Age and Youth*, Oxford 1953, p. 54, he recalls BJ with affection and says that he 'was the inspiration of a little book I once wrote (now long forgotten) on "The Dominican Order and Convocation"' (Oxford 1913).
5. John Procter, who had been elected provincial again in 1907, after Shapcote's resignation.

25. *BJ to Austin Barker OP. From Mercy Convent, Westbury on Trym. 30 December 1910. Autograph.*

I got your p.c.[1] forwarded to me here where I am retreating to a parcel of nuns. It was a pleasant ray of light amid the dark clouds of my work. But it also reminded me of my neglect in not writing to you before. So here goes.

The news of the Province, such as it is, will no doubt already have reached you, the MacNamara trial etc.[2] F. Ceslaus[3] is very ill, dying I should say, from enlarged liver pressing on enlarged heart. When I left London his mind was wandering and he kept asking for

F. Gabriel[4] and demanding who sent him out of London. Of course he is in London still.

Then poor F. Wilfrid[5] has collapsed. His mind has quite gone. At first it was merely a harmless lapse; now I understand that he is getting violent and either has been or is to be removed from the 'home' that he is in to an asylum.[6] It is a sad case; but one to be expected from so diligent a scholastic. How can one ever write treatises in English on Universals or venture on translating the *Summa*[7] and hope to retain that healthy balance of nonsense which is necessary for living? S. Thomas could and Cajetan could;[8] but, I fancy, only such genius as they.

F. Vincent[9] did a splendid exam in Rome I'm told. He told me that F. Hugh[10] examined him in inspiration. He tried to fence and not commit himself over the *secundum apparentias*,[11] but F. Hugh drove him further and further into a corner; at last he was forced to blurt out the whole Lagrangean theory and trembled in his shoes for the result. The bowed head of the Master General[12] looked up gleaming for a second; the masters in theology shook their plumage as though there had been a momentary breeze, but no one objected and he returned from the sacred city unburnt. Some people have all the luck; but he is one of the few who get it and deserve to get it.

I have been giving the Oxford Conferences; but am now being prodded by the Provincial to write them—an intolerable nuisance as they are set down only in scrappy and unintelligible notes[13] and not worth much even at that. These are the occasions when one chafes at obedience.

Please tell Père Lagrange that Evans has not yet brought out a proper catalogue of his Cretan remains.[14] Should one come out, I'll send it to him.

1. Post card.
2. Richard MacNamara OP, currently assigned to Hawkesyard, had left the priory without permission and taken up residence in his mother's house in Leicester in April 1910. She then sued him for the cost of his board and lodging. He accepted her claim, but maintained that the Dominican Province was responsible for settling it. The case was heard on 19 December at Leicester County Court, and was written up in *The Tablet* on 24 December. The court did not accept the Province's liability and found against the defendant.
3. Ceslaus Fletcher.
4. Gabriel Whitacre. He and Fletcher had been boys together at the Dominican school at Hinckley, and had joined the Order within a year of each other, so that they were together for most of their studies.
5. Wilfrid Lescher.
6. It had been decided by the provincial on 22 December that he must be moved to an asylum.
7. In 1893 Lescher wrote and had privately printed a pamphlet on Universals. In 1907 he pioneered the translation of the *Summa Theologiae*, and the Inter-Chapter in April 1910 put him in charge of it, though in July Laurence Shapcote had been appointed editor of the translation.
8. Neither St Thomas nor Cajetan actually wrote any treatise specifically on universals, but Thomas discusses universals intermittently in many of his works, and Cajetan's treatment of them in his commentary on *De Ente et Essentia* is cited as an important source, for instance, in

J. Gredt, *Elementa Philosophiae Aristotelico-Thomisticae*, vol. I, ed. 2, Freiburg im Br. 1909, p.105.
9. Vincent McNabb had been taking the examination for the STM at the Angelicum, Rome. Until the 1969 Constitutions came into force, the STM was acquired in several stages: first the lectorate, then a period of teaching, then the examination 'ad gradus', which is what McNabb took in 1910. If the candidate passed this examination, he became a 'Bachelor' or 'Praesentatus'. After some more years of teaching, he could become a Master of Sacred Theology, if his Provincial Chapter recommended him and if the Master General or a General Chapter approved. McNabb received his STM in 1916. The system derives from late medieval university practice, which is still reflected in the system at Oxford and Cambridge, whereby someone who has passed the examinations for the BA can become an MA after a few years without taking any further examination. There was a further requirement in the Order that each province could only have a limited number of STMs. NcNabb was proposed in 1916 to replace John Procter, who had died in 1911.
10. Hugh Pope, currently teaching at the Angelicum.
11. 'Inspiration' had become a hotly debated topic, as a result of the application of modern critical methods to biblical study and the consequent 'discovery' of a number of 'factual errors' in the supposedly inerrant bible. In 1893 Leo XIII attempted to defuse the problem of apparent scientific errors in the bible by pointing out that, in many cases, the biblical writers were not offering any 'scientific' comments on the nature of the world, but were simply 'following appearances' (*Acta Sanctae Sedis* 26 (1893-94) pp. 286-287); taking up a hint from the same encyclical (which he later admitted he may have misunderstood) Lagrange applied the same principle, that the biblical writers were speaking 'secundum apparentias', to apparent historical errors in the bible. His views were expressed in *La Méthode Historique*, published in 1903 and subsequently re-issued in 1904 and 1907, and they aroused considerable controversy and were attacked particularly by A. J. Delattre SJ (1841-1928). An edict of the Biblical Commission in 1905 effectively disallowed the theory of 'historical appearances' except in such narrowly defined circumstances that it would have almost no application (*Acta Sanctae Sedis* 38 (1905-1906) pp. 124-125), and the Modernist crisis, which was coming to a head in these years, tended to cast suspicion on the whole historical method. The Master General of the Dominicans, Hyacinthe Cormier, published a sort of answer to Lagrange in his very successful *Lettre à un Étudiant en Écriture Sainte* (Fribourg 1905; Italian translation 1906; French reprint 1907; Spanish translation 1907). He also forbade Lagrange to publish his response to Delattre in 1905, nor would he permit a reprinting of *La Méthode* in 1909. An edict of 30 June 1909 from the Biblical Commission insisted on a literal historical reading of Genesis 1-3 (*Acta Apostolicae Sedis* 1 (1909) pp. 567-568). No wonder the situation was rather fraught during McNabb's examination in Rome. He had himself earlier contributed to the debate with his book, *Where Believers may Doubt* (London 1903). Not long afterwards, on a suspicion of Modernism, Lagrange was banished from Jerusalem (1912) and Hugh Pope from Rome (1913). In 1915 McNabb himself got into trouble with Cormier because of a letter he published in *The Tablet* on 30 October on inspiration, and, in spite of a spirited defence by Humbert Everest, the provincial, he was forced to publish a second letter making clear his loyalty to the edicts of the Biblical Commission. Lagrange himself later conceded that his doctrine of 'historical appearances' was misleading. Cf. R. de Vaux's introduction to the re-issue of *La Méthode Historique*, Paris 1966.
12. Hyacinthe Cormier.
13. Quantities of BJ's lecture notes survive, usually consisting only of a few headings jotted down on a piece of paper. For an example, cf. below no. 254.
14. Sir Arthur Evans (1851-1941), the archaeologist who did most to uncover the remains of ancient Crete, published his big work, *The Palace of Minos*, London 1921-1936, though he had already published his *Scripta Minoa* in Oxford in 1909. Lagrange had published *La Crète Ancienne*, Paris 1908.

26. BJ to Austin Barker OP. From St Dominic's, London. January 1911.[1] *Autograph.*

As I was the first to tell you of the Hilary scandal, may I be the first to tell you that all is put straight now![2] For he says that I may say everything. I got him to write to F. Hugh[3] and work through the Provincial etc and not through the Archbishop as he had first attempted. After a couple of months he sent up his petition formally and left everything to the decision of the Holy See. They sent back a sealed envelope which he was to forward to a 'discrete confessor'; I was the one selected so that I knew before anyone else the terms of the dispensation. He is freed from everything *salva castitate*, his office being commuted into 5 mysteries of the Rosary per diem, and he can live with the good damsel as brother with sister. It is a very generous act on Rome's part, and poor Hilary is evidently surprised at their leniency. He has petitioned the Provincial to be made a Tertiary. That chapter then is ended.

I was so glad to hear that your lectorate was so successfully accomplished and you must be right glad to have passed that milestone. I suppose that after your 2 years, you'll return via Rome, snapping up Licentiates and other such grandiose marks of learning, up and down Europe. But you'll be wanted sadly here, when come you do. The studies at Hawkesyard must be desperately uninteresting for the most part when the Lectors have each some half-dozen subjects to profess[4] and have little time, opportunity, or encouragement to dig deeply in any one of them. It is easy enough, when one has had the chance to specialise in a subject, to take it up and carry it on without any encouragement at all; but what is difficult is to go on working away at the outer fringe of the weaving, while every possible inducement is being held out to take up other work as well and so spoil any attempt at a real whole-hearted endeavour to acquire some knowledge.

The Province remains as it was, *sedit aeternum sedebit* perhaps.[5] F. Ceslaus has gone after a month of illness, and the last week unconscious.[6] Aloysius[7] comes backwards and forwards as of old, one week in religious life, one week out of it. Then you have no doubt heard of the MacNamara incident; he is applying for secularisation and hopes to get taken by a colonial Bishop.[8] It will be a good way out of the trouble, if he can be got away to outdoor work etc. There was a danger at one time of the Protestant Alliance.

1. Judging from BJ's 'news', the letter was probably written on or after 18 January.
2. Hilary O'Neill (cf. above, no. 18). In November 1910 he had expressed a desire to regularise his position in the church, as John Procter notes on 11 November in the Provincial's Diary.
3. Hugh Pope.
4. When Barker returned to Hawkesyard in 1911, the lectors there were: Folghera, Shapcote, Whitacre, Moore and Everest. In the four year cycle 1909–1913 Folghera taught Eschatology, De Deo Uno, Trinity, Creation, Church History, the Incarnation, Logic and Sacraments. Shapcote taught Morals and Grace. Whitacre taught Ontology, Psychology and New Testament. Moore (who joined the team in 1910) taught Logic and Ecclesiology. Everest (who left the studium in 1911) taught Apologetics, including Ecclesiology.
5. 'It has sat down, it will sit for ever.'
6. Ceslaus Fletcher died on 8 January and was buried on 11 January.

7. Aloysius Crosse had by now a long history of being unsettled. Indeed, his Dominican life got off to a shaky start: after he had been accepted to enter the noviciate in 1882 he changed his mind and wrote to say he was not coming after all. Then he changed his mind again and got the Jesuits to intercede on his behalf, pleading that he should nevertheless be allowed to go to Woodchester. As a result he entered the noviciate late, in November. In the Order he had been a successful and apparently happy schoolmaster at Hinckley and then at Hawkesyard until 1902, when he was taken off school work. Since then he had never settled down. There had been talk of his becoming a secular priest in 1907, and in January 1908 he was given leave of absence to look for a bishop. In June he announced he was not going to leave and was assigned to Stroud, but he walked out the following March. In May 1908 he was assigned to Pendleton, but only a few weeks later he wrote to the Provincial that he had 'finally' decided that he could not face community life and was going to live outside the Order. A week after that he wrote and apologised and said he did not want to leave the Order, so his assignation to Pendleton was renewed, and he went there in the middle of June. By the middle of July he had left again. In August he wanted to return, and, on the Master General's instructions, he was assigned to Woodchester. He left again on 6 October. Early in February 1910 he wanted to come back, and the Master General gave permission for him to go to Hawkesyard, and he was assigned there on 21 June, but the very next day the Provincial wrote to the Master General that he was getting restless again, and he left on 25 June. In November he was back again, but he only stayed for little over a fortnight. Early in January 1911 he wrote to the Master General asking to be taken back yet again, and on 18 January he went to see the Provincial about this. This is probably the point at BJ wrote to Austin Barker. The same pattern continued until in 1913 the Provincial Council persuaded the Sacred Congregation for Religious to give Crosse (against his own wishes) leave to live outside the Order. He became chaplain to the Assumption nuns at Boxmoor, and the Province thereafter stolidly refused to allow him back.

8. Richard MacNamara (cf. above, no. 25). On 9-10 January the provincial had held a meeting at Hawkesyard with the official committee responsible for judging the case of 'incorrigible' brethren deemed worthy of expulsion; MacNamara had failed to present himself to them, and the whole matter had been passed on to Rome. But on 14 January the Master General had written to say that MacNamara had applied for secularisation and was hoping to find a colonial bishop to take him. In the outcome it was not until 1913 that he was accepted by such a bishop (the Archbishop of Vancouver).

27. *BJ to Lady Arundell. From St Dominic's, London. 11 June 1915. Autograph.*

I hardly like writing to beg from you as you are sure to have very many appeals at this time, and you have been so good too to dear Father Cuthbert,[1]—for whom I hope something more permanent may be arranged by the coming winter.

But as soon as the war is over we shall have to build schools here for 800 children, and it is estimated that the cost of them will lie between £12,000 and £13,000, an almost impossible sum in these drear days.[2] It is simply the hugeness of this figure that forces me to apply to every possible quarter in order to secure what I can, for our parish capacities are wholly incapable of such an effort.

Our actual schools are condemned with their playground as wholly inadequate and we shall have to surrender our own garden so as to save the expense of buying a site. We are already overcrowded and have had to refuse nearly 100 Catholic children—all the more painful as on either side of us the parishes have given up their schools.

Please excuse my troubling you in this way after all your kindness to us, especially as I had hoped one day to intercede with you about a house at Oxford. But the children are the more immediate need.

Building expenses in London are said to work out at £13 or £14 per head per child, so that £13 or £14 means the education of one Catholic child for ever.

1. Cuthbert Wolseley, who was a 'cousin' of Lady Arundell's. He did important pioneering work in Grenada 1896-1906 and worked there again 1907-1913; unfortunately he was incapable of managing his finances and incurred considerable debts, and his attempts to raise money to pay them off generally landed him in worse trouble. Lady Arundell had several times intervened to help him. In 1913 she gave him £300 towards the repayment of his debts, but the problem was still there in June 1915. For reasons of health he had been allowed to winter in Ibiza, from where he returned to London on 21 May 1915. It seems that no provision was actually made for him to escape the winter of 1915-16.

2. The parish school, housed in Blackfriars Hall, built in 1867, urgently needed more space, especially as there had been an influx of Belgian refugees into the parish. Earlier in the year there had been a lot of correspondence with the authorities about the problem, and permission had been obtained to use the Priory Hall for extra accommodation. In spite of the need, it was not until 1931-32 that a new school was built, and even then it was a huge financial adventure.

28. *Provincial's Diary. 5 September 1916.*

F. Bede Jarrett was elected Provincial.[1]

1. He was elected at the first scrutiny, with 12 votes out of 17.

29. *Provincial's Diary. 12 September 1916.*

Wrote to Archbishop of Simla[1] *re* Indian mission after the war to be started by 5 of our C.F.s.[2]

1. Anselm Kenealy. The Provincial Chapter had instructed the provincial to investigate the best way of starting a mission in India, and evidently BJ wasted no time. No invitation had been received from India, and it looks as if the initiative may have come from BJ himself; it certainly came from within the province. Master General Theissling, in his letter of 12 November approving the Acts of the Chapter, demanded more details about the Indian project before anything was done about it. On 22 November he wrote again saying the project must be dropped.

2. Chaplains to the Forces. At this time the province was supplying one naval chaplain and seven army chaplains, but it was already foreseen that more of the brethren would be offering their services to the army (cf. below, no. 33b). Three more were commissioned in October, and one in January 1917.

30. *Provincial's Diary. 26 September 1916.*

Interviewed Norbert over my Scotch scheme.[1] He seemed unwilling at first, then more willing.

1. BJ was hoping to start a small house in Scotland (cf. below, no. 35), and no doubt was thinking of Norbert Wylie, a Scotsman, as one of the priests who might be sent there. He was currently assigned to London.

31. *Provincial's Diary. 4 October 1916.*

At Hawkesyard interviewed Lectors. They asked me to get Folghera back;[1] else Paulinus as Pro-Regent.[2] And no Bacc. nor Master of Students.[3] Urged Luke[4] and Austin[5] to prepare for licentiate and doctorate in S.Scripture; Paulinus[6] for Fribourg degree; Chrysostom[7] and Walter[8] for Brum[9] degrees. Ditto students.[10] They agreed to get Syllabus and send me a report. Asked Prior[11] to act as Pro-Regent for the time and to arrange for monthly outside lectures.

1. Folghera was still officially Regent, though he had been in France since 1914. He was unable to leave France, because he could not obtain a passport, owing to a confusion over his nationality. The Italian authorities thought he was French, and the French thought he was Italian.
2. Paulinus Sweeney, currently 'novice master' (in modern terms 'student master'). Since he was not an STM he could not be appointed Regent, but he was officially made pro-Regent later in the month.
3. The three officials of a studium were: Regent of Studies, Bachelor (Baccalaureus), and Master of Studies (or Students). The first was meant to be an STM, and the other two were meant to be at least Bachelors (i.e. they had to have passed the examination necessary to become an STM). The last Bachelor at Hawkesyard was Humbert Everest, who had become prior of London in November 1911. The last Master of Studies was Laurence Shapcote (who had indeed only been pro-Master), but in July 1914 he had become prior of Leicester. In the outcome, the studium carried on without Bachelor and Master of Studies until 1928, when the Master General pointed out its lack of necessary officials. BJ explained, as he notes in the Provincial's Diary, that he had found no such officials when he became provincial 'and presumed all was well'. A pro-Bachelor and pro-Master of Studies were duly appointed.
4. Luke Walker.
5. Austin Barker.
6. Paulinus Sweeney.
7. Chrysostom Egan.
8. Walter Gumbley. None of BJ's academic plans indicated here was realised.
9. A popular nickname for Birmingham.
10. I.e. 'interviewed students', though 'they' in the next sentence must refer to the lectors again.
11. Vincent McNabb, who had already been acting as pro-Regent since Folghera's departure, it is not clear on whose authority.

32. *Provincial's Diary. 5 October 1916.*

Wrote to Folghera.

33a. *Provincial's Diary. 10 October 1916.*[1]

Vicar Apostolic of Johannesburg wrote offering a South Africa mission, Boksburg (near his city) to us, suggesting a contract.[2] Forwarded with comments to Frs Pope, Shapcote, Everest.[3]

33b. *BJ to Hugh Pope OP. From St Dominic's, London. 10 October 1916. Autograph.*

Will you please read and consider the following letters which I received yesterday. My own inclination runs thus:—
(1) Impossible while war is on. Every available priest should go as C.F.
(2) No mention made of who is to pay passage out.
(3) Else I should say 'Yes' and send 2 C.F.s after the war. There'll be twelve of them, of whom, say 5 can go to India, 2 to S. Africa, the rest will be needed here.

Personally I think the wider variety of life offered the easier will it be to content all and to secure subjects. Then we could have novices precisely for our 3 foreign missions. After noting, please forward to Prior of Leicester[4] to be sent on here with this letter.

1. The date is given in the Diary as 11 October, but it is more likely that the date of the letter sent to Hugh Pope is correct.
2. Bishop Charles Cox OMI had written on 15 August, offering Boksburg, with Boksburg North and Vogelfontein thrown in, mentioning the plans of the Dominican sisters to build a 'fine Convent and Boarding School' there. In a postscript he warns, 'I cannot promise that the Fathers will give missions, as the Redemptorists are here for the purpose and there is not enough for them to do. Possibly there might occasionally be a Convent retreat, but even in that work the Redemptorists have the first claim.' He sent this letter to the Sacred Congregation for the Propagation of the Faith in Rome and to his OMI superiors there. His letter, together with the response of Propaganda, was forwarded to the English provincial, with a covering letter from the OMIs, on 3 October.
3. These were for the moment the only members of the Provincial Council. The councillors, known as 'fathers of the province' (*patres provinciae*), were all ex-provincials and STMs in the province; if these did not suffice to yield a council of at least six members, others could be appointed, for life, by the Master General (1913 General Chapter, para. 145). Although the provincial was rarely obliged to consult them, he was expected to do so whenever serious decisions had to be made (ibid. para. 138). In 1915 four extra councillors had been appointed by Master General Cormier; but their position had been questioned and they had all resigned on 5 September, and they were not re-confirmed by Master General Theissling until 12 November. Pope was an STM, Shapcote and Everest were ex-provincials, so there was no doubt about their entitlement to be councillors.
4. Laurence Shapcote. Humbert Everest was evidently staying at Leicester at this time.

34. *Provincial's Diary. 8 October 1916.*

All in favour of S. Africa, wrote to Bishop in sense of criticisms.[1]

1. Apart from BJ's own question about who would pay for someone to go to South Africa, the only councillor who expressed any doubts was Everest, who wrote: '(1) The exclusion of our Fathers from our characteristic work of missions and retreats (see Bishop's PS) I should not agree to. (2) The acceptance of novices specifically for this or that mission is a new departure of sufficient importance (to my mind) to merit discussion at a meeting of the Provincial Council.' BJ seems to have dropped his suggestion of ear-marked novices, but he raised the other points with Bishop Cox. Laurence Shapcote, as well as formally responding, 'I agree with all my heart', sent BJ two more letters in which he expressed his own great desire to go to South Africa himself (he had been born there), and asked whether the invitation held good until after the war. 'If not, I think the council should be consulted on the point of *immediate acceptance*. India is certainly not to be despised—but we are not yet even invited.'

35. *BJ to Mrs Tayleur. From The Cenacle, Grayshott. 2 November 1916. Autograph.*

Thank you for your very kind letter. How wonderfully God works to have brought you to Himself in that seemingly chance way. But then we are always learning, aren't we, that there's no such thing as chance at all.

Now this is in confidence to you and *please* to no one else because it really isn't quite settled. But I am hoping to open a Dominican house in Scotland next year—not of course in a big way, for that would be much too expensive. But what I thought of doing was to take quite a small house, a private house, where 2 Fathers could live and say Mass in a little Chapel of their own and go out to preach. Of course that would depend partly on the amount of preaching they could get: whether it would be enough to keep them alive. But in order to have enough work they must be right in the centre of some large town where there were plenty of Catholics and churches: or at least in a centre whence many towns could be easily approached. I would try to get a benefactor to pay their first year's rent and then trust to Providence for the rest of it.

Now if this were to succeed, then Kirkconnel[1] would make a charming noviciate house: quiet for the spiritual training and the studies. However that would not be for many years (ten at least, possibly 30)[2] in which case the Irish OPs would have got it.[3] You see if my private house worked, benefactors would offer Priories, I suppose, and once one had 3 Priories the old Scotch Province OP could be re-born.[4]

But the Irish being there would complicate things, though of course one would gladly welcome any help. —Still, you won't say anything to anyone else except God, will you? And I'll try to see about letting Kirkconnel.

1. A house, about five miles from Dumfries, the property of the Duchess of Norfolk (Baroness Herries), whose lease belonged to Mrs Tayleur. After being converted to Catholicism by an Irish Dominican mission in Dumfries, Mrs Tayleur became a Dominican tertiary in Ireland in 1913 and was keen that the Dominicans should take over her house, with a view to restarting the Scottish Dominican province. In 1927 BJ agreed to take over the lease, and it was formally conveyed to him in 1928, but no permanent Dominican community was ever established there and Mrs Tayleur continued to live there until 1938, when she was no longer able to keep it up. Between 1924 and 1938 it was the regular holiday home for the Dominican students, and Mrs Tayleur moved out to make way for them. She was evidently an extremely kind and generous hostess, whose hospitality was much appreciated. In 1938, since she wanted to give up the house, the province proposed to return ownership of the lease to her, but her lawyers were not in favour. In 1940 she entrusted the lease to her nephew, and in 1941 the Provincial Council decided that the best course was to sell the house and give her the proceeds.
2. BJ originally wrote 'ten at least', then corrected it to 'ten at least, probably 20', before finally settling for 'ten at least, possibly 30'.
3. Mrs Tayleur had originally offered her house to the Irish Dominicans, but they refused it, saying that it would be more appropriate for the English province to have it.

4. By custom, at least three formally constituted priories were required for the establishment or re-establishment of a province (cf. 1913 General Chapter pp. 151, 158, 164), but the principle does not seem to have been enshrined in Dominican law until the 1932 Constitutions, Const. 280-II.

36. *Provincial's Diary. 15 November 1916.*

Lectures on *Summa* began:- only 20 present.[1]

1. The idea of laying on public lectures, aimed particularly at non-Catholics, had been floated in 1915 by Felix Couturier, and it was accepted by the Provincial Council on 1 June 1915, which also noted that Miss Evelyn Coats, who was a friend of the province, had promised to make a donation so that an endowment fund could be set up to finance such lectures. However Couturier had become a military chaplain and had not been able to do anything more to realise his project. It was taken up enthusiastically by BJ, even before he became provincial, and he worked especially with Lady Cadogan to get some lectures organised for 1916. After months of searching for a suitable and available venue, the series was launched at Caxton Hall with a lecture by Vincent McNabb. The lectures became an annual event, in spite of the small numbers attending the first session, and they were later taken under the wing of the London University Extension Lectures (see below, no. 73), and the *Summa* lectures were joined by other series, first on the bible, and later on Catholic philosophy. BJ is on record as having said to the Master General that he thought these lectures for non-Catholics were one of the two most important works pioneered by the English Dominicans (the other being the foundation of the priory at Oxford).

We have been unable to discover much about Miss Coats. She later gave the money to build a Carmelite monastery.

37. *Provincial's Diary. 21 November 1916.*

Letter from General *re* S. Africa.[1] Which I answered . . .
(i) If we don't others will.
(ii) Growing in importance and Catholics.
(iii) Healthy.[2]
(iv) Nuns OSD.[3]

1. Master General Theissling wrote on 17 November, expressing his concern about the province's lack of personnel to undertake any new missions; he had noticed that the existing mission in Grenada was suffering from a lack of manpower.
2. Bishop Cox had urged that Boksburg was in a situation that would be good for people's health, and this had evidently impressed BJ, who wanted the province to have somewhere where it could send brethen whose health was giving concern. In a letter to Shapcote on 3 July 1917, replying to one in which Shapcote had unguardedly given the impression that he had not been too well since his arrival in Boksburg, BJ says, 'You know I am beginning to lose faith in S. Africa. We thought of it as a sanatorium . . . instead you seem lately to be in trouble.'
3. 'The Dominican Nuns from Newcastle (Natal) are arranging to build a large Church, a convent of 60 nuns, and a boarding school. They have bought a large piece of ground there' (Letter of BJ to the Master General, AGOP XIII 65101). It is ironic that on 24 November Sr M. Rose Niland OP wrote from Newcastle, Natal, to the Master General, pleading for Dominican fathers to be sent to them, but adding, 'I do not think English or Irish Fathers would do as they never care for native work' (ibid.).

38. *Provincial's Diary. 4 December 1916.*

Letter from M.G.¹ . . . authorising S. Africa and India *if* Grenada not thereby weakened.

1. The Master General. In fact his letter of 28 November only approves South Africa: 'I should prefer to see you start to develop the work in S. Africa before that in East India.' In an earlier letter he had already called for the abandonment of the Indian project (cf. above, no. 29 note 1).

39. *Provincial's Diary. 20 December 1916.*

Two letters from Bishop of Johannesburg offering to pay £40 passage for 2 fathers etc. Held on S. Africa meeting of Priors assembled for Seventh Centenary¹ (minus McNabb) and read correspondence.² Unanimously agreed to send out one father,
(a) To take Bishop's £40,
(b) To accept for first year £50 as per letters,
(c) To add £30 from Province.

1. On 21 December there was a celebration at St Dominic's, London, of the 7th centenary of the founding of the Order; among those present was ex-King Manoel II of Portugal (1889–1932).
2. The problem of financing the new mission had been addressed by the bishop, but he had hardly yielded any ground on the question whether Dominicans would be allowed to do their typical work of mission-preaching and retreats: 'I don't see how the Redemptorists can object to your Fathers helping at the Convent retreats, particularly at the Dominican Convent retreats;' that much he concedes, but otherwise he insists that he has to be fair to the Redemptorists, and so, 'I must ask you *not* to put missions and retreats in a prominent way in your programme.'

40. *Bishop Joseph Robert Cowgill to BJ. From Bishop's House, Leeds. 12 January 1917. Autograph.*

Please excuse delay in acknowledging your letter, but I could not send an answer till I had an opportunity of consulting my Chapter. I have at last been able to do so. They fully appreciate your kind offer to come into the diocese and are much alive to the good you would do, but at present they see many difficulties, and as there is no immediate need for the kind of work you specially mention they think it better to put off the consideration of your request. I am afraid my answer will be a serious disappointment to you, but I must be guided by my Chapter, and moreover I must say that for the present at least I am in agreement with them. At the same time I thank you for your offer.

Annotated in BJ's hand: What's to be done? I asked for a preaching house!¹

1. The Dominicans had had a mission in Leeds 1802–33, but lack of personnel forced them to abandon it. Their pioneering work there had however laid the foundation for many parishes, including the Catholic cathedral in Leeds. In the autumn of 1916 BJ had sounded out the prior of Pendleton, Alban King, on the possibility of developing non-parochial work in Yorkshire. In a letter to him on 13 October 1916 he says, 'Personally I am keen on houses not parochial but preaching, I mean without parishes attached. Now would there be any chance of getting enough work, say, for 2 fathers in Leeds?' Evidently King had already raised the matter informally with Bishop Cowgill of Leeds.

41a. *Provincial's Diary. 15 January 1917.*

Appointed F. Shapcote to the S. African mission, he therefore resigned his Priorship of Leicester, which I accepted and notified to his community. Forwarded this letter to all the houses:

41b. *BJ to the English Dominican province. From St Dominic's, London. 15 January 1917. Autograph.*

I am to announce to you that in the name of the English Province I have taken over a mission in S Africa, and I have appointed the Very Rev F. Laurence Shapcote, S.T.L. Ex-Provincial, to take charge of it.

The Vicar Apostolic of Johannesburg, Bishop Cox OMI, invited us there in a letter dated Aug 15: 1916, which reached me through the Procurator General of the OMI and which had received the authorisation of the Cong. of Propaganda. I consulted the *Patres Provinciae* who encouraged me to continue negotiations. The Bishop replied on Nov 10th with the definite offer of Boksburg, Boksburg North and Vogelfontein, which form 3 townships about a dozen miles from Johannesburg. We shall start with one priest, but more will follow in a year's time. The actual conditions etc were submitted to a meeting of the Priors of the Province on Dec 21st and by them approved. The Master General has authorised the venture. Please pray that the work may prosper and that the blessing of God, our Lady and S. Dominic may be on it.

42. *Provincial's Diary. 18 February 1917.*

Interviewed Mgr Morris, V.G. of Edinburgh,[1] concerning a house in Edinburgh. My plan was for 2 Fathers to live there privately for preaching. His statements were:
(1) Private house would not appear seemly to secular priests who certainly would never invite (OSBs had asked for same and been refused).
(2) No objection to a Priory, properly constituted.

(3) Suggested a Parish. (To my question as to whether that meant taking over an existing parish or establishing a new one, he answered that no new one was wanted)

1. Patrick Morris (1848-1929) had been Vicar General of St Andrews and Edinburgh since 1905.

43. *Provincial's Diary. 19 February 1917.*

Interviewed Archbishop of Edinburgh.[1]
(1) Ditto to above 3 points.[2]
(2) Suggested S. Cuthbert's, Gorgie, where debt of £9000—or rather didn't suggest but mentioned as all he could offer though he knew we could not accept.
(3) St Andrews for students at varsity of no use to us until after we were established in Scotland.
(4) Aberdeen a better university.
(5) Dundee a better city (25000 Catholics).
(6) Better to visit Scotland and spy out land.

He was very friendly and hoped for our ultimate appearance in Scotland. Would have no objection to our having a parish in Edinburgh, if it could be arranged. This remark repeated by me to Mr Raffalovich drew from latter a proposition which I must keep secret. It gives hope for a sure foundation of OPs in Scotland. In case I die, the secret has been communicated to Frs Bracey and O'Gorman[3] under vow.

1. James A. Smith.
2. See above, no. 42.
3. Respectively prior of London and socius of provincial.

44. *Provincial's Diary. 25 June 1917.*

Went to see Oblates *re* Clacton.[1] Saw F. St Lawrence the Superior[2] and Canon Wyndham.[3] Chief points mentioned were:—
(1) They only leave because of anomaly of their position as Priests of Westminster in another diocese.
(2) The whole thing, house and Church, etc cost £13,000; of which £5000 was gift. They don't want to make money but only be recouped, hence offer for £7000 i.e. what they spent.
(3) Conditions of benefaction are:—
    £60 a year to Mrs St John[4]
    Rosary every day.
(4) Chaplaincy at Mercy Convent £60 a year; less from OSF nuns.[5]

(5) Part of Presbytery can be and has been leased.
(6) Income not known at present; promised to find out.
(7) Away from tripper end for in residential but not shopping centre.
(8) Willing to come to terms over payments i.e. times etc.
(9) Can be worked by one able bodied + one less A.B. person.

1. The Oblates of St Charles Borromeo were a society of priests living the common life, without vows; they were founded in 1857 by Manning. In 1971, with only nine priests and one house left, the society was suppressed by the Holy See. Their mission at Clacton-on-Sea was started in 1894; the first priest who was actually sent to live there was Alfred Swaby, who built a new church there in 1903 and, except for about four years in other houses, he remained at Clacton until he joined the Dominicans in 1918. The parish was in the diocese of Westminster when it was founded, but on 22 March 1917 the new diocese of Brentwood was formed, including Clacton. The Dominicans' interest was chiefly in obtaining a site by the sea-side, which could be of value as a health resort for ailing brethren; Lady Arundell offered her enthusiastic support.
2. William St Lawrence (1874-1961), the superior of the Oblates, who lived at their mother house in Bayswater.
3. Francis Merrick Wyndham (1838-1919), Oblate of St Charles and a canon of Westminster Cathedral. He was a writer and an authority on St Joan of Arc.
4. In 1895 Mrs St John and a friend of hers bought a house in Clacton and land for a church, where they could establish the devotion to Our Lady of Light, with a particular statue of Our Lady that they possessed. The devotion goes back to the eighteenth century, when St Louis Mary Grignon de Montfort (a Dominican tertiary) discovered some villagers in Brittany gathered round a statue of Our Lady which attracted his attention; he named it 'Our Lady of Light'. The devotion caught the attention of Sir Henry Trelawny, who later became a Catholic priest and introduced it into Cornwall, renaming his estate 'Sclerder' (the word used in Cornish for 'Light'). The devotion was revived by Mrs St John and another lady late in the nineteenth century, and they had a special statue carved for it, and in May 1883 an association they had formed received approval from the Holy See. In 1894 they left Cornwall, and Cardinal Vaughan recommended thay they should go to Clacton. Having set up house there, with a chapel, they found it difficult to secure the services of a priest, so they approached the Oblates of St Charles, who in due course established a parish there, under the patronage of Our Lady of Light.
4. These were the two convents in the parish, whose chaplaincy would bring in a little income. The Franciscan sisters ran a school in the parish, and the Mercy sisters ran a home for crippled girls.

45. *Provincial's Diary. 25 July 1917.*

Answer of Council[1] on the whole unfavourable to expense of Clacton. Bishop Ward simultaneously desires us to pay him something extra as to Diocese. This seems to make it out of question.

Miss Coats sent in £5000 to our Bank for missions to Non-Catholics:[2] £3000 Exchequer Bonds and £2000 War Loan.

1. The Provincial Council.
2. Cf. above, no. 36. On 25 June of this year Miss Coats had written to BJ, 'I am handing over to you securities for the sum of £5000 (of which £4000 must be invested as a capital fund) to be used for the spread and development of the faith in England and Scotland, by affording means either for the giving of lectures explanatory of Catholic doctrine or for the higher education at Oxford or elsewhere of students for the priesthood or for any other purpose absolutely that shall commend itself to you or to your successors as securing the same end.'

46. *Provincial's Diary. 7 September 1917.*

Bishop Ward wrote to say that the Senior Priests of diocese refused to allow us Clacton and offered Dovercourt. Refused provisionally or rather asked instead for Frinton.

47. *BJ to Lady Margaret Domvile. From St Dominic's, London. 3 October 1917. Autograph.*

I am going to call this afternoon so as to let you go out of London at once and I am shifting till tomorrow the work that ought to have been done today.

As a matter of fact I am seeing very few people at present as I have just now an immense amount of work to get through and cannot conceive how it can be got done. So it means blocking hard all day and every day. Then it gets cut into by sermons and the consequent travelling, and people plague one all day long till I feel inclined to retire with my books into the heart of France and be bothered only by guns. I feel every day indeed more and more desirous of throwing up my whole job and just going off as a C.F. That would be one way out of all the entangled threads in which for the moment I happen to be caught; but even without them it is positively painful to find oneself fit and well, and doing nothing, while all about are either wounded or khakied folk.

I celebrated S. Michael's day with the Consolation Book and its perfect poem; and I have finished *Campion*.[1] The latter is really admirable as a fearless biography which is also at once alive and learned. The man stands out clear and distinct and life-ful; and although such defects as he had are apparent, the general air of charm is too attractive to be affected by them.

I don't like your Hospital fad one bit. Those agitated and betubed aliens are another symptom of distress. I shall probably preach in U.S.A. during Lent. None of these things are connected but only 'topics' of conversation.

1. We have not identified either of the books mentioned.

48. *Provincial's Diary. 14 November 1917.*

Bishop Ward writes that he's heard definitely that Clacton is retained by Oblates, hence his offer of Frinton and Walton is withdrawn. Answered. . . .

Wrote to Bishop Cox for territory in S. Africa.

49. *BJ to Lady Margaret Domvile. From St Dominic's, London. 23 November 1917. Autograph.*

... No, Guy's memoir of George Wyndham I haven't seen, but I have had the loan of 2 volumes of his correspondence (perhaps that is what you mean)[1] which fascinated me hugely. His wonderful devotion to his mother is quite touching so that to the end his letters are as boyish as ever. There is in it, do you remember, a rather wonderful description of his mother which will become a classic in our language.[2] It is so exquisite and delicate an analysis and synthesis of her womanliness—a delicious miniature. Then of course a perfect little poem by 'Perfoo'[3] ending on the strange note of the music of the hills as the 'Horn of distress'—another of those inspirations of childhood which suddenly lay bare hidden thoughts and feelings. Of course his devotion to *Romance* explains and gave its basis to the charm of his character; it all fits in to make him the darling of the gods. One notices at the end that his intimates are nearly all Catholics, Romantics like Belloc, G.K.C.[4] and Gatty, and Schoolmen like W. Ward. It seems to make his sudden death more sudden and less understandable.

Didn't you like Lord Hugh Cecil's speech with its vehement protest against the advanced doctrine of state supremacy?[5] G.K.C.'s *History*,[6] Wyndham's *Letters*, and Lord Hugh's *speech* are all of a piece, fragments of a larger faith that once was Christendom. Why should it be left to 3 Protestants to voice the immemorial[7] teaching of the Church? I believe our Bishops are to issue a manifesto in the New Year, composed by Plater SJ.[8] Perhaps I shall be glad then to seek U.S.A.! I shall be a new S. Francis and preach to, not fishes, but submarines.

1. Guy Wyndham (1865-1941), George Wyndham's younger brother, edited the *Letters of George Wyndham*, 2 volumes, Edinburgh 1915. There is an introductory memoir in this edition; he had not written any other memoir of his brother.
2. *Letters*, ed. cit. I pp. 333-336.
3. 'Perfoo' was the nickname of George Wyndham's son, Percy Lyulph (1887-1914). The poem, written when Perfoo was seven, is in *Letters* I pp. 322-323.
4. G. K. Chesterton, not yet actually a Catholic, though perhaps already fairly obviously on his way towards Catholicism. He was received into the Catholic church in 1922.
5. *The Times* for 22 November 1917, p. 10, reports a powerful speech made in parliament by Lord Hugh Cecil, member for Oxford University, in support of the rights of conscientious objectors, appealing to 'a higher law than the law of the State'. 'We will not listen to the doctrine that the State's interest is to be supreme.'
6. G. K. Chesterton, *A Short History of England*, London 1917.
7. BJ actually wrote 'immemorable', but presumably this is what he meant.
8. Cardinal Bourne's pastoral letter on 'Catholics and Social Reform' (printed in *The Tablet* 131 (1918) pp. 222-226).

50. *BJ to Lady Margaret Domvile. From Our Lady of Lourdes Church, New York. 17 April 1918. Autograph.*

Just before I leave for B.W.I.[1] I send[2] a line of wishes for Ireland.[3] At present there's a regular tangle which I, not being Irish, cannot think can be well undone. But I believe so firmly in the British star that I know some way out will be found. No less firmly do I believe that even this last loss of Messines,[4] which seems the worst of all, cannot mean the end of things as people here prophesy. I am content to wait and hope and pray, and God help us all!

I have really liked this wonderful people and have enjoyed all my stay here though it has meant a good deal of vocal effort. Lectures not a few have been added to sermons; and I have 2 days' retreat to Ladies tomorrow and Friday in the Cenacle convent—which reminds me of Grayshott and our friendly though infrequent talks.

I have bought (but not paid for! I'm a real Catholic priest) land at Oxford for an OP house and all after the war. I want still £6,000, where am I to find it? I am trying S. Joseph. Do ask your friends in Heaven to help him to find it!

1. The British West Indies.
2. BJ actually wrote 'sent', but presumably he means 'send'.
3. Lady Margaret was Irish, and the Irish Question was much in the news these days. In 1917 the British government had opted for an Irish Convention as the best way towards a solution, thereby at least theoretically leaving it to the Irish to decide on what form of Home Rule (if any) would be acceptable. On 5 April 1918 the Convention at last adopted a scheme for limited Home Rule, but there was a strong dissenting minority; the Nationalists were far from united, and Sinn Fein had refused to take part in the Convention at all. And the Unionists remained deeply suspicious of any form of Home Rule. The British government did not ease the situation by connecting Home Rule with the proposal to extend conscription to Ireland—a move considered necessary in view of a serious deterioration in the Allies' position in the war with Germany. The English newspapers during these days were full of reports of the debates in parliament on the Military Service Bill (which in fact received the Royal Assent on 18 April) and the extension of conscription to Ireland and the pledges being given by David Lloyd George (1863-1945) to do all he could to ensure the passing of a Home Rule Bill. In the outcome, conscription was so unpopular in Ireland that it achieved an unprecedented unity of purposes between all the different Nationalist groups. 'It provided the final legitimization of Sinn Fein as a 'national' political party, and the culmination of the wartime government's record of disastrous Irish decisions' (R. F. Foster, *Modern Ireland 1600-1972*, London 1988, p. 490). Cf. S. Hartley, *The Irish Question as a Problem in British Foreign Policy 1914-1918*, Basingstoke 1987.
4. Possession of the Messines ridge, a ridge some 150 feet high, running to the south of the Ypres salient on the western front of the war, had given the Germans a certain strategic advantage. In June 1917 the British army, under Douglas Haig (1861-1928), had captured the ridge in what was (and is) considered an impressive victory. But in April 1918 the British had had to retreat under strong pressure from the Germans, prompting Haig, on 12 April, to issue his famous exhortation, 'With our backs to the wall and believing in the justice of our cause, each one of us must fight to the end.' On 17 April *The Times* reported that 'the town of Bailleul fell into the hands of the enemy on Monday night, and the greater part of the Messines ridge has also been lost.' The first leader comments, 'Of the two local reverses recorded this morning that of the withdrawal from the centre of the Messines ridge is certainly the more serious . . . The Messines ridge was a prime factor in our defensive battle in this area' (p. 7).

51. *BJ to Lady Margaret Domvile. From the Hospital of St John & St Elizabeth, London. 1 January 1919. Autograph.*

My first letter of the New Year goes to you to wish you in 1919 every good and pleasant thing! May God hold you away from all the flames of trouble and keep you sheltered always in His Blessed Peace!

Your Ghost story is most interesting. I should have died of fright nor do I believe I should have been clear enough in my mind to have invoked[1] the Holy Name. I wonder you were not paralysed with fear. But for Heaven's sake, don't please let the horrid woman have her way, for we don't want you to go yet. So please invoke the Holy Name again and get rid of the old Lady, despite her perfect features and her clinging and graceful garments. That sort's the worst, I believe.

I am here rounding off this morning a retreat! So I shan't get the poems till I return to the Priory today. You are so nice to send me such jolly and distinctive presents. No one ever gives me what you give in that way. Yours are always *chosen*.

You ask my plans? Well, at present I am absorbed chiefly in the Oxford Priory. We have bought 3 houses and hope in a couple of years' time to build a Priory, partly by adapting the present 16th century houses (with Queen Anne fronts) and partly by building a wing and a chapel. The idea is to convert the young man there by pandering to his love for the picturesque—a Priory to the Holy Ghost, the white forms, the chanted office, lectures, sermons etc. One of the houses turns out to have been the last home of Walter Pater. We are going to have a little *Pater Museum* and have that as an excuse to find the undergrad in; then when he's least attentive baptise him. We shall have to have very weak tea always served so weak as to be valid matter for Baptism.

Well, now I must get ready to wind up the Nuns.

1. BJ wrote 'to have invoke', falling between 'to invoke' and 'to have invoked'.

52. *BJ to Leonard Parker. From East Grinstead. 10 January 1919. Transcript.*

May I send you a letter in answer to all 3 of yours which I found awaiting me when I returned on the 6th?

I should just like to say 2 or 3 things because I have been so touched by your saying that as prefect you find there's less fun in school life, more responsibility, and less friendliness.

I should say first that you will find that every step upwards in life tends to isolation and loneliness in the sense that general comradeship ceases; that's so always.

But it means that you have to choose between the mere amusements of life and the real work of life. Everyone who strives really to live can't help getting isolated.

However there is this compensation that you have in return to keep hold of the 2 or 3 friends who are real friends. The rest are pals etc; but the real friends of life are very few. They should be and must be. The rest will drop from you at every promotion, a few not worth having will come to you now for what they can get, the 2 or 3 will alone be your support. It was because of this that I did so want you to have Terence[1] as a friend for this last year, else you are likely to become bitter or at least cynically aloof.

Then hold on to your friends, and trust them sufficiently to know you never bore them. Once you find yourself tempted to keep away lest you should be a nuisance to them remember it is a temptation against friendship and unfair to them. Don't give way to your blessed self-consciousness, but be frank and free and open, be yourself. Say the first thing that comes into your head; and it will be easier for you to talk if you begin by getting him to talk about himself.

1. Terence Geoghegan.

53. *BJ to Lady Margaret Domvile. From St Dominic's, London, 11 February 1919. Autograph.*

I was thinking of you last night and when your letter came this morning I wondered whether it was she of the white coif who had made you come into my mind. But no, it wasn't that *she* but another, your late cook, who has come into service with some delightful friends of mine, who's sight carried me off to the lift and ever open door of Sussex Mansions.[1]

First for Walter Pater. I dare say that unbeknown he did a good deal to develop a view of life that was largely to prove at first unhealthy, but re-read the ending of his Greek Studies and you will be struck by his exceeding *appreciation* of Christianity and Catholicism; he says of the Greeks thay they 'almost merited revelation'[2] which is a perfect way of placing the true values of both ways of Faith. Moreover towards the end the Catholicism that was hereditary in his family[3] began to peep out more and more to those who watched and loved him, and all the evil side of his teaching got burnt up in that noble forbearance to Jowett and his crew of suspicious, unrelenting and misunderstanding satellites.[4] The chapel at Balliol has done more to overwhelm religion than all the pagan sympathies of Marius and his prototype.[5] It may not be wise perhaps as you say to push W.P. too much, but I am convinced that it is his Catholic tendencies more than his pagan ones which put most of his Oxford enemies agin him. But it is rather[6] pretty to think of the 'comely Dominican habit' as he calls it in the last chapter of that unfinished *Gaston de Latour*[7] coming as a white symbol of forgiveness, like the snow that witnessed and testified to the forgiveness of Charles I.[8]

In those lectures[9] I am not reconstructing politically, for in public I have no politics. I only urge people to think unselfishly and tolerantly though of course I feel sympathy with the new and affection for the old. As a priest I advocate no measures, for so many are allowable and good, but only hope that supernatural motives will weigh with all. Above all I should like to urge courage *and* hope.

Let Pico della Mirandola[10] be the symbol of all the future, his brilliant intelligence, his personal beauty, his deep devotion, his Dominican death-shroud. About him is the fragrance of youth, so eager, so foolishly wise, so sure it has found its 900 theses to explain all life's problems, so humbly patient of authority, so reverent to the painstaking fragments of past wisdom, so buoyantly hopeful of the added wisdom which the future is to bring,[11] yet dying prematurely as all youth dies, as indeed all die who are young in heart and sympathy, tender to the oncoming generations. You are so, tender to the new verse and the new ideas, even all the more so since you feel they are wrong though not in their temper but in their judgements.

1. Lady Margaret lived at 16 Sussex Mansions, London.
2. Walter Pater, *Greek Studies*, London 1895, pp. 314-315.
3. Pater's partly Catholic background is discussed in A. C. Benson, *Walter Pater*, London 1906, p. 2, and in Thomas Wright, *The Life of Walter Pater*, London 1907, vol. I pp. 2-6. Pater himself was brought up as an Anglican.
4. This picture of 'noble forbearance' in face of Jowett's active hostility comes from Benson, op. cit. pp. 54-58, and Wright, op. cit. vol. I pp. 255-259. It is challenged by Geoffrey Faber, *Jowett*, London 1957, pp. 379-384, and little of it survives in Michael Levey, *The Case of Walter Pater*, London 1978, pp. 143-144, though it seems clear that Jowett disapproved strongly of Pater's *Studies in the History of the Renaissance*, London 1873.
5. Walter Pater, *Marius the Epicurean*, London 1885. In many ways Marius is a literary persona for Pater himself.
6. BJ actually wrote 'But it rather . . . '.
7. Walter Pater, *Gaston de Latour*, London 1896, p. 193.
8. Charles I was buried at Windsor on 8 February 1649. 'As the coffin was brought to the chapel snow began to fall, and gave to the pall, as the little company loved to remember, "the colour of innocency" ' (S. R. Gardiner, *History of the Great Civil War*, reprinted London 1987, vol. IV p. 324). A bit of the page has been cut out of BJ's letter here.
9. On 11 February BJ started a series of six weekly lectures at the Catholic Women's League in London on 'The Church and Reconstruction'.
10. Giovanni Pico della Mirandola (1463-1494) was an Italian scholar and humanist, who proposed to defend 900 theses in 1486, drawn from an immense range of sources; however, on learning that Innocent VIII considered some of them heretical, he abandoned the project. He was a friend of Savonarola's and received the Dominican habit from him on his deathbed. Pater included an essay on him in his *Studies in the History of the Renaissance*. There is an edition of the 900 theses by Bohdan Kieszkowski, *Giovanni Pico della Mirandola, Conclusiones sive Theses DCCCC*, Geneva 1973.
11. BJ actually wrote 'to be bring'.

54. *BJ to Lady Margaret Domvile. From The Cenacle, Grayshott. 11 April 1919. Autograph.*

I was sorry to have to let *G.W.*[1] disappear unread though dipped into! However I know a young man who has the volume (a railway clerk to whom *Recognita*[2] made such appeal that he saved up his Bradburys[3] to buy these essays) and shall borrow it later and read it with care. It really does interest me very much. —One of the retreatants (horrid word! of pure Jesuit coinage) came to me with her difficulty—viz. the subject for an historical novel, as she's a novelist and so far the retreat had yielded no clue or sign from God (I had not realised before that one entered retreats for *copy*).[4] However, I whipped out *G.W.*, read to her the account of Eleanor of Aquitaine, and gave her the date of 1147.[5] So you see neither of us have lived in vain. We have suggested a masterpiece and shall have helped to erect a monument to literature.

1. Evidently George Wyndham's *Essays in Romantic Literature*, edited posthumously by Charles Whibley, London 1919.
2. C. T. Gatty, *Recognita*, Naas 1914 (a memoir of George Wyndham).
3. Pound notes. When paper money was introduced in 1914, John Swanwick Bradbury (1872-1950), first Baron Bradbury, was joint permanent secretary at the Treasury, and his signature was reproduced on each note over the promise to pay.
4. The lady novelist has not been identified.
5. Wyndham, *Essays* pp. 18-21, 30-31. He assigns a crucial role in the development of Romance in European literature to the marriage of Eleanor of Aquitaine and Henry of Anjou (King Henry II) in 1152: 'It is when they married, and where they married, that most of the Springs of Romance commingle in the literature of Europe. Nor were the results of that commingling accidental. They were produced by design: and the designers were largely the poets of Henry's and Eleanor's cosmopolitan court' (p. 31). 1147 is the year in which Eleanor went on the Second Crusade with her first husband, Louis VII of France.

55. *Provincial's Diary. 9 May 1919.*

Went to Oxford for day with P.C.[1] to view site of Priory and compare with proposed plans, which hopelessly 'out' by measurements and size.

1. The Provincial Council. Vincent McNabb, Humbert Everest and Lewis Thomson were present. The date of the expedition is not entirely certain. In the minutes of the Provincial Council, BJ records that there was a meeting in London on 7 May, at which it was decided to go to Oxford 'the next day'; in the Provincial's Diary he originally dated the meeting in London 7 May and the trip to Oxford 8 May, but he then corrected both dates, making them read 8 May and 9 May respectively.

56. *Provincial's Diary. 13 May 1919.*

Wrote to F. Leo[1] *re* Leicester's loans to buy site for new Church, which has to be done without reference to the Congregation—pledged

by Prior McNabb.² Advised loans at Bank. The site is now complete and consists of 3 different sales:
Corpus Christi house to Province   £3280
12 New Walk & 36 Wellingon St   £1200 at 5%
14 New Walk   £2150
They have banked £1500 with Province.

1. Leo Moore, at this time subprior of Leicester (he was shortly afterwards elected prior of Pendleton).
2. Vincent McNabb was prior of Leicester 1908-1914. In 1911 he proposed building a new church there, and he promised that the Dominicans would provide the site, leaving it to the congregation to raise the money for the actual church.

57. BJ to Leonard Parker. From Dominican Convent, West Grinstead.¹ 26 August 1919. Transcript.

I don't want to bother you and as the newspapers say, 'This correspondence may now cease', for it is horrible to expect people to write during holidays, but I should like most awfully to say: 'Do tell him'. There is nothing really so blessed in life as a friendship and by not telling him and talking to him you are missing the one thing which makes school-life worth the having. You never afterwards have such opportunities for making friends or for seeing so much of them. I am sure if you don't you will regret it always. Of course you are by nature exceedingly sensitive and afraid of being a bore and you don't like to force yourself on him; but probably he's feeling the same as you. I think we can nearly always feel instinctively when people are fond of us. May I then say 'Do tell him what you feel and have it all out; and don't funk it.' You have to wait for your opportunity of course, and then, with heart thumping away like a Ford Motor, just blaze away. I am sure you will be most awfully glad ever after.²

Will you distribute these notes for me? There are no envelopes in the village and this is all I could buy.

1. The Dominican convent of West Grinstead was founded in 1876 by Mother Vincent Ferrier (Victoire-Thérèse Chupin) (1813-1896), who had sought refuge in England from the Franco-Prussian war. She was the foundress of the Congregation of Notre-Dame de Grâce, whose motherhouse was at Châtillon from 1880 until very recently. The sisters were invited to West Grinstead by the parish priest, Mgr John Francis Denis, a Breton priest brought to the English mission by the first bishop of Southwark, Thomas Grant. After working for a few years in Alderney and, very briefly, in Rotherhithe, Mgr Denis was appointed to West Grinstead, where he remained until his death, in 1873. He wanted sisters to run a school for boys as well as girls, and previous attempts with the Daughters of the Cross and the Servites had not proved successful. Mother Vincent herself only remained a few months and then returned to France. Under pressure from the parish priest and Bishop Danell of Southwark the new convent soon became independent, and its first novices were professed there in 1880. After being subjected to an almost incessant succession of harassments, caused by their isolated situation and their entire dependence on the parish priest and the diocese, the sisters decided in 1915-16, on the advice of Raphael Moss OP, to seek contact with other Dominican sisters, beginning with

Mother Rose Niland, who had in 1915 established a community at Launceston, Cornwall. But Bishop Amigo objected to the idea of the sisters of West Grinstead joining a Congregation whose motherhouse was in South Africa. He similarly vetoed a suggestion that they might be reunited with Châtillon. An approach to the sisters of Portobello Road, London (another offshoot from Châtillon), was rebuffed by the sisters' Chapter there. So West Grinstead struggled on on its own. In 1925 a fresh blow was struck when Bishop Amigo countermanded a permission already granted to receive postulants to the habit, and the sisters sought the help of BJ, who had long been a friend of theirs and who generally visited them when he was staying at his family home nearby at East Grinstead. He discussed the situation with Bishop Amigo in September 1926, and learned that the bishop was in favour of West Grinstead amalgamating with some other Dominican sisters (he favoured Harrow). He then went to West Grinstead and formally asked each sister what she thought ought to be done. A majority was in favour of amalgamation with Mother Rose's Congregation, which was in the process of establishing its new motherhouse at Bushey. BJ undertook the necessary negotiations with Mother Rose and with the bishop, and in 1927 the amalgamation formally occurred. Further harassment from the parish priest eventually made Mother Rose decide to abandon West Grinstead and in 1932 the community moved to Ponsbourne Park, Hertford. The convent there was closed in 1972.

2. On 16 November Parker wrote to BJ, 'I've done it! I screwed up my courage and told Terence. We talked it over coming back from the match on Saturday.' Terence is, of course, Terence Geoghegan.

58. *Provincial's Diary. 16 October 1919.*

Saw Theodore and Vincent[1] over Oxford plans. Promised to secure exact measurements. Forwarded these on Oct 19.

1. Theodore Bull and Vincent McNabb.

59. *BJ to Leonard Parker. From St Dominic's, London. 7 November 1919. Transcript.*

Just to say: *of course you must settle as to whether the affair is now impossible.* But don't ever again hold off in such matters, please, despite your natural diffidence, for life goes so quickly that we have to seize every gift of God as it comes, else (as you have found) it floats past us down the river of time. We get such few second chances in life.

Responsibility is, people say, the salt of life, but there are times when it is chiefly pepper and mustard. However it has its own satisfactions as well and these are to be found in the character it creates in us.

With every best prayer for your success in your prefectship and your friendships.

60. *BJ to Leonard Parker. From St Dominic's, London. 25 June 1920. Transcript.*

I have hardly had a letter in my life that left me happier than yours did—to know that you had had such a perfectly delightful time, the perfect setting and your own greatest friend as a gem in the midst of all that loveliness. You have no idea how much such happiness of his and yours makes me happy, and I walked all these hours on air, high and wonderful air that made the whole world full of lightness. Yet you strike one note that jars terribly, damnable, simply damnable, and I am jolly well going to pitch into you for the last time—at the risk of breaking any friendship you have ever had for me. Yet for Terence's[1] sake and yours know that what I write, I write because I love both of you very much indeed. Well, you have no business at all to say that you wondered 'whether by that time he'll have forgotten all about me'. Now really that is not diffidence at all, though it is caused by diffidence, just because you think you have so little to recommend you to him. Now whether that last is true or not (of course it isn't true, for you have all the things that hold and attract people), you have no business whatever to suppose that he will ever forget you. He's a friend and he's worthy of your friendship and he's called himself a friend. Do friends, real friends, who are fit to hold the title, forget? Would you care if he doubted for one instant your loyalty and your remembrance and thought that the pleasures and jollities of Oxford would make you forget him? Now, my dearest old pal, do forgive me, but really diffidence may reach a point when it begins to distrust and once you distrust your friend, the friendship is gone. You *must* just trust him as he trusts you and as you wish him to trust you. You can say that the cases are not parallel, that you have everything to receive and he nothing to gain from you, but really be as humble as you can in the matter of love but only there is a point where such a diffidence is reached as will make it no longer love. I know perfectly well that you do love him and believe him when he says he loves you; so, for pity's sake, check all those temptations and just humbly accept his friendship as finely as he accepts and trusts yours.

I dare to say this because as a boy I made my days miserable by always doubting, knowing how little I had to give, how endlessly I was receiving; but now I see how wickedly really I was unknowingly blaspheming human love. Trust always, despite all appearance, else you will never have the right to have a friend. Forgive me and pray for me.

1. Terence Geoghegan.

61 *BJ to Leonard Parker. From St Dominic's, London. 6 July 1920. Transcript.*

You are such a good friend that I am going to venture one more letter of scolding and then have done. Don't you think that sentimentalism may sometimes be your fault? And sentimentalism is at times unconscious selfishness. There, I shall never say anything more against you till I die and I have never even thought of saying that much to anyone else but you. But from one or two things you and Terence[1] said laughingly in my cell at Downside, and from one or two remarks in your letter, I have come to the conclusion that sometimes you get very hurt and show your feelings very openly and perhaps scare Terence and then you think no one understands you. It has happened to me in my boyhood—now as I look back—that I used to be morbidly sentimental, nursing my sadnesses and like Rachel 'refusing to be comforted'.[2] Now as I look back I see I gave my friends the very devil of a time. One of them who was killed in the war told me so just before he went out to France the last time, and made me realise what a beast I had really been, determined to be hurt, keeping silence, putting their affection to a big strain and simply intent on my rotten little self and my jealousies and expressing them openly and generally making an ass of myself—which is of no consequence—and particularly, in that, showing myself thoroughly selfish—which is of very great consequence. Instead of trying to think of my friends and their points of view and trying to give them a good time, I worried over my sorrows and enlarged them. Knowing this of myself, I am wondering whether you have any of my sins. Why should I think so? Well, because you read (as I loved doing) endless poetry.

You see I am horribly motherly in all this, grandmotherly, so this is a letter you musn't keep. It will keep me in a bad light in your memory; but I do so want you to keep friends with Beloved Terence and at times I wonder whether you will. Oh, I know I am a brute to say it; but I do wonder whether you will. All I can say (and it must sound horribly priggish) is Be unselfish and keep him happy and seldom let him see your sadness, indeed, so long as he's with you, you should have none. Never inflict sadness on him, trust him as you wish to be trusted, and his love and friendship will endure.

1. Terence Geoghegan.
2. Jeremiah 31:15, Matthew 2:18.

62. *BJ to a Dominican prior.*[1] *From Scarcroft Lodge, Thorner, Leeds. 3 August 1920. Autograph.*

I must apologise for not coming on Sunday after all and for not letting you know of my inability to come either. As a matter of fact I was summoned here earlier on account of some family business[2] and I could not get a telegram off to you from Liverpool from the station. There were none being sent at that hour.

I have written to the Abbot of Ampleforth and told him to let you know definite details. I am most grateful to you for taking the retreat for me.

Perhaps on the eve of S. Dominic's day[3] I may be allowed to say as briefly as I can what I consider to be amiss with us as a whole in this Province.

(i) I think we suffer from a lack of the sense of responsibility. Religious life is left almost entirely to the individual. It cannot now-a-days be overseen. It has become largely a matter of trust. Yet it appears to me that for some of us there is too much of the schoolboy sense of dodging a master e.g. in district work, in punctual attendance at the confessional, in breaking silence, in spiritual reading, in coming in late. Also under the same heading, the vow of poverty seems at times imperilled by spending money on outings and pleasures, not for ourselves so much as for others.

(ii) On the part of the Priors, I would suggest the strict observance of the fortnightly Chapter,[4] careful instructions on the vows and higher principles of religious life, and insistance on (a) the discipline of punctuality, (b) silence, (c) devout saying of divine office, the due pauses customary in the Province, brisk yet dignified,[5] not with any sense of 'getting it over' but realising that it was *intended to break up the day.*

On the vexed dispute over observance[6] I have nothing to say except that to me it is not a matter of doing more but of doing better. The Province has a fine record of work, a record of mutual charity, both of which are admirable. The lack is chiefly in discipline, in Dominican discipline, wherein we are put on our honour to obey.

1. We have not been able to identify the prior to whom this letter was sent.
2. Scarcroft Lodge was the home of Lady Mary Louisa Savile (1864–1945), sister of the 6th Earl of Mexborough. The nature of the 'family business' that took BJ there is not known.
3. Until the reform of the calendar after the second Vatican Council, St Dominic's feast day was 4 August. The rest of this letter is clearly a circular, presumably sent to all the priors and superiors of the province; it is a good example of how BJ wove such circulars (which he wrote out by hand) into letters which would still be personal to each recipient.
4. The Constitutions in force at the time (the 1872 edition) required Chapter at least once a fortnight (Const. 823). Chapter provided an Official occasion for the prior to address the assembled members of his community.
5. From the beginning the Dominican Constitutions specified that the Divine Office should be sung or recited briskly and without delays (Dist I 4 in the earliest known Constitutions, edited

in A.H.Thomas, *De Oudste Constituties van de Dominicanen*, Louvain 1965, p. 316). This was maintained in the Constitutions until the 1969 revision (in the 1872 text, see Const. 59).

6. Since the revival of the Order in the nineteenth century, under the influence of Lacordaire and Jandel, there had been a heated dispute about the extent to which primitive observances, such as midnight Matins, could or should be restored. In England, Woodchester was established as a house of full observance, and some members of the province wanted to revive a more rigorous observance in other houses and, as part of this campaign, they questioned the propriety of Dominican parishes (cf. below, nos. 198 and 220). A strong supporter of Jandel's view of Dominican religious life was Raymund Devas, who published *The Dominican Revival in the Nineteenth Century*, London 1913, as a sort of manifesto, followed by a selection of documents associated with Jandel, *Ex Umbris*, Hawkesyard 1920.

63. BJ to Lady Margaret Domvile. From Thornton College.[1] 10 August 1920. Autograph.

Yes you have judged rightly. Here I am, a gigantic house, acreage of garden immense, endless greenhouses, a fishing stream and 23 ladies! One part of the house dates from the 12th century and there used to be ghosts—only unfortunately they only undertook to haunt the drive until Catholics got back the property, and when the Nuns bought the place 3 years ago they apparently downed chains and other noisy instruments and quit this world for the other they had certainly after all these years deserved. Anyway we are no longer haunted alas! except by retreatants, as you say an odious word. But I discovered a worse one than that. Of course it served me right, but I had been browsing on S.J. piety and came on the word 'exercitant'. Isn't that worse?

Your note on the Ward lectures[2] fascinated me. But don't bother to send the volume along. I shall get hold of it later after I get back from Bruges.[3] Your words however about Mrs Studd[4] worried me. What can I do? Tell me and I'll do it. She's such a Catholic mind that it musn't go astray! I wish I knew an artistic defence of the faith. Do you think she'd write an apologia for Catholicism based on painting and literature and music?

As for yourself, your description of your irresolution, your power of making mistakes when you do decide, and their being over-ruled by Providence so as to avert their evil consequences, reminds me curiously and flippantly of the Coalition Cabinet.[5] However that's by the way. I fancy that the Holy Spirit, devotion to the Holy Spirit, is the best remedy; and the remembrance that so long as we take pains to form our judgements we can let the rest rip as far as God is concerned. All He asks is that we should try to secure the grounds of judgement, try to be impartial in our choice of alternatives, and then leave it to Him to mop up the mess afterwards. Isn't it one of your own principles to leave room for God? Well that is what you've got to do.

What you say about *Blackfriars* interests me. You know I've tried hard to get someone to defend the present economic system and can get hold of no one. A man has written something for September, but I'm told it isn't attractive.[6] We have tried to secure someone and so far failed. . . . .

The Lambeth Conference article has excited much comment, unfavourable from most Catholics,[7] but favourable from Lord Halifax and others. Mrs Lane Fox, his daughter, told me that it had brightened her father up immeasurably and he's urging a Conference between the High Church and the Dominicans. I'm hoping we shall fix something up[8]—but we'll get condemned by Rome and burnt. Margarine will be cheap!

How about Mgr Mannix?[9] Yet he once received King Edward to Maynooth, hung with the king's racing colours![10] Why don't they send him to Ireland to be converted again to that earlier mood?

1. Thornton had been acquired in 1917 by the Sisters of Jesus and Mary, who opened a college for girls there.
2. *Last Lectures by Wilfrid Ward*, edited by Mrs Wilfrid Ward, London 1918.
3. BJ was in Bruges 14-30 August; he gave a retreat to the English Canonesses there.
4. See below, no. 69.
5. In December 1916 Lloyd George came to power as head of the coalition war cabinet, and in the General Election in 1918 the coalition was returned to power with a huge parliamentary majority. Although Lloyd George was not averse to disagreeing sharply with some of his colleagues, his cabinet was an 'exceptionally united one' (K. O. Morgan, *Consensus and Disunity: The Lloyd George Coalition Government 1918-1922*, Oxford 1979, p. 176). However, one item much in the news at this time might lie behind BJ's flippant comment, and that is the government's attitude to the war between Russia and Poland. Winston Churchill (1874-1965), in the cabinet, maintained an extremely 'hawkish' stance against the Bolshevik régime in Russia and it was widely believed, especially in Socialist circles, that he was forcing Lloyd George, against his better judgment, to commit Britain to intervening militarily in support of Poland. The behaviour of the government had indeed been somewhat contradictory, with the provision of military supplies going hand in hand with blunt refusals of military help. Lloyd George's own insistence that he had no intention of going to war with Russia lost much of its credibility because of his retention of Churchill in the cabinet (on 3 July 1920 *The Daily Herald* called for Churchill to be impeached for treason because of his warlike intentions towards Russia). Matters were largely taken out of the government's hands as a result of the formation of a Council of Action on 5 August 1920 by the TUC and the Labour Party, pledged to mobilise all the forces of organised labour to prevent any military involvement of Britain in support of the Poles. On the day BJ's letter was written, there was an editorial in *The Daily Herald* denouncing, yet again, the government's warmongering: 'They are planning war against Socialist Russia because they like wars and because Russia is Socialist.' Cf. L. J. Macfarlane, 'Hands off Russia: British Labour and the Russo-Polish War, 1920', *Past and Present* 38 (Dec. 1967) pp. 126-152.
6. The article was evidently never published.
7. 'The Lambeth Conference', by Vincent McNabb, in *Blackfriars* 1 (1920) pp. 221-230, was delated to the Holy Office, which simply referred the matter back to the Master General, and nothing came of it except the appointment of censors for the review. Cf. B. Delany, 'The Beginnings of "Blackfriars" ', *Blackfriars* 34 (1953) pp. 316-318.
8. Nothing came of this suggestion at the time, but later on conversations were held between the Dominicans and the Anglican Society of the Sacred Mission, Kelham; more recently, there have been regular conversations between the Dominicans and the Community of the Resurrection, Mirfield.

9. Daniel Mannix (1864–1963), the Irish-born archbishop of Melbourne (1917–1963), was on his way to Rome for his *ad limina* visit. He had been addressing large crowds in the United States in support of Irish independence. On 31 July there were noisy anti-British scenes as he boarded his liner in New York to cross the Atlantic, saying that he 'cared not a whit' for the British government's declaration that he would not be allowed to go to Ireland (*The Times*, 2 August 1920, p. 8). the whole affair featured prominently in the newspapers every day thereafter. On 9 August *The Times* noted that the government's decision had caused widespread excitement and that it was 'generally condemned as a blunder' (p. 11). On 10 August (the day BJ's letter was written) it was reported that, on the evening of the 8th, Mannix had been taken off his liner and put aboard a destroyer, and had been landed at Penzance on the 9th (*The Times*, p. 11). For a comment on the whole episode, cf. Leslie Shane, 'Archbishop Mannix', *Blackfriars* 1 (1920) pp. 322–326.

10. Mannix was Vice-President of Maynooth when King Edward VII visited there on 24 July 1903.

64. *BJ to the Members of the English Dominican province. 9 February 1921. Printed.*

I feel that since this opening year of 1921 begins the 700th anniversary of the death of S. Dominic, I ought to send you a few words of greeting. I am diffident of appealing to the Province for a deeper attention to the Dominican vocation vouchsafed us all, since I am always sensibly conscious of my own grave failures in this affair of the soul, yet on the other hand, I suppose as Provincial, I ought to say something to you.

Moreover it seems to me, that since we are ourselves being pushed on, invited, welcomed, to take over new works, clearly Dominican in temper and character, it looks as though this full cycle of 700 years finds the world at large suffering from the same defects as were peculiar to the age of S. Dominic. The work he sought to achieve is still to be done, in the same spirit and by the same endurance. Of this there can be no doubt. By pen and, above all, by the spoken word, the need is even greater for the truths of faith to be proclaimed strongly, clearly, without fear yet without offence, not intruding into quarrels, but at least laying down those noble principles of the Gospel which S. Thomas has arranged for us shortly and orderly in his *Summa Theologica*.

The work then certainly is there, as it was in Languedoc, and the whole world over in 1221.

And the workers? Are they equipped for their task? We are the workers. Now we are naturally conscious of the great gulf between ourselves and our fathers. But between ourselves and those thirteen friars, under Gilbert de Fraxineto or Gilbert Ash, who entered this kingdom on August 6. 1221?[1] Certainly there are differences, obvious and natural. We are less austere, more comfortable, less used than they to the harder and more inclement side of life. Above all, I dare say, we are less heroic, but I do not think that we are less well trained in study. Probably however the gap that separated them in knowledge and learning from the people about them was much greater than separates us from the ordinary folk of these islands. But you will notice this about them, that they tried by their immediate settlement at Oxford to improve themselves and to benefit the leaders of English thought and life. They had ideals, they had daring, but they were practical and were whole-heartedly devoted to their calling, attempting by all means to their hand to become good followers of S. Dominic. Grossetête, from his knowledge of some of them said jokingly, that all a friar needed was to study well, to pray well, and to eat well.[2] Perhaps we may easily take these as hints or brief suggestions as to our work. Somehow we may be too apt to excuse ourselves as though our failure was due to our conditions of life or surroundings, to suppose we would become better Dominicans elsewhere. The fault is in ourselves, not in our circumstances.

Our religious life should above all centre upon (i) the punctual discipline of community life, (ii) the law of silence, (iii) the devout attention to the Divine office. We should add to this the obligation of study, not merely in the abstract sense, but in careful attention to our works and our hobbies.

Have we a parish? Do we study the working of parishes, read books on it, try to take the matter seriously and scientifically, or merely drift? A district perhaps we have? Is it as properly worked as it should be? A Dominican cannot say that parish work is incompatible with his vocation, but bad parish work, negligent, slipshod parish work will always be incompatible with it. Has he a guild, a boys' club, Scouts? Then as a Dominican, he must do it well (i.e. as well as it can be done), learning by the experiments of others, reading; not content with the pleasure it gives him, not restless under its drudgery and necessary failures, but driving onwards to a more perfectly developed work. Preaching and professing are necessarily requiring much attention, much preparation of material, of arrangement, learning the tricks of the trade. Am I a professor? Then have I ever studied pedagogy, the art of teaching, and have I not rather trusted to chance, to the sense of duty on the part of the students, to anything and everything, rather than my obligation not only to learn but to teach. The Boys' School at Hawkesyard is, equally with the other business of the Province, a matter of very high concern. Other schools must be studied and learnt from. Even the Procurator has to do his business in the best way possible, realising that this too is an art in our day, requiring much training. So too a Dominican laybrother must not be content merely to do his work, but to try to find out how others, outside the cloister, work at his particular job, and to copy their newer methods and more satisfactory ways. Above all with our highest gift, the contemplative life. That too is a science, an art, nay the very art of arts without which my Dominican vocation will not ride evenly, but overleaning in the direction of my work. Contemplation needs careful and professed study, particularly of Dominican authorities. Am I trying to do this as conscientiously as I can? Not only our works of obligation but our hobbies must be done in the same fashion, writing, composing, painting, printing, embroidery; every energy devoted not only to Dominican work, but to work in a Dominican way.

Who is sufficient for these things? The daily Mass and Communion, are (say the Constitutions) the source whence we draw the strength necessary for our day.[3] Is any more needing to be said? In those silent moments alone with God, we can measure ourselves against all our terrifying obligations and be filled with courage.

Of mutual charity, of patience, forbearance and tolerance, in this province, there is happily no need to speak. We have a unity that is not the least of God's blessings to us. That, and our sense of humanity, our friendship and our love of laughter, and that humility among the brethren which to watch has been to me the most touching and edifying part of my Provincialate, these under the high patronage of S. Dominic, and his 'Holy Queen' will give us the quiet temper needed.

May God in the memory of our past glories and through the endurance of all these generations dead, give us to feel the responsibility of our vocation, and enable us to meet as fitly as we can the immense opportunities that now beckon to us!

Asking the help of your prayers, I beg to sign myself
yours affectionately in S. Dominic.

1. BJ argues for this date in one of his contributions to *The English Dominican Province 1221-1921*, London 1921, p. 2.
2. BJ was probably thinking of the remark Grosseteste is quoted as having made to some Dominican in Thomas Eccleston, *De Adventu Fratrum Minorum in Angliam*, ed. A. J. Little, Paris 1909, p. 115, 'There are three things necessary for material well-being: food, sleep and fun'. He certainly cites this remark, as constituting 'Grosseteste's description of Dominican qualifications', in his review of Coulton, *Blackfriars* 4 (1923-24) p. 1369, though the reference he gives there (to Grosseteste's letters) is entirely false.
3. In a retreat BJ gave to the Dominican sisters at Portobello Road in August 1914, he is reported to have quoted the 'Constitutions' as saying, of the conventual Mass, 'There they draw the springs of water, which are to make fruitful the day's labour'. But there does not seem to be anything in the Constitutions remotely resembling this. BJ was perhaps thinking of a comment made by Humbert of Romans in his commentary on the Constitutions (ed. J. J. Berthier, *Opera de Vita Regulari*, vol. II, Rome 1889, p. 80) about daily Mass providing 'nourishment for our souls and bread to support our daily failing life'.

65. *BJ to the Priors and Superiors of the Province. From St Dominic's, London. 9 February 1921. Typescript.*

I should like to give you for my sake as much as for your own, and for the sake of all the Province generally, some idea of the state of our finances. To do this in a clear way, I am making use of figures supplied me by the Procurator of the Province, F. Humbert Everest, from the accounts of last year, i.e. the financial year ending March 1920.[1]

I. As to Income:—

A. First of all, there are receipts from the Burse monies connected either with the Noviciate or the School.[2] These are simply of the nature of 'Transfers', i.e. the whole of the sum so received is paid out for its specified object; the entries balance each other on either side.

With these, too, go also the taxes payable by Grenada and the several houses of the Province; and the collections made annually in May in each House in England for the upkeep of the Noviciate.

All these sums, of course, are earmarked, and cannot be touched by us except for the purpose for which they are intended.

The whole amount thus coming to us for the year 1919-1920 was £659.19.2 (Noviciate £557.16.0; School, £102.3.2).

* * *

B. Secondly, of the same nature (Transfer) is the Interest on Miss Coats' Benefaction of £5000, the Income from which is to be spent on Catholic Evidence Lectures, or works of that kind.[3]

This again is to be considered merely as a Transfer. It comes in and goes out again, applied to its specific object.

* * *

C. Thirdly, we have in process of time acquired certain properties and Investments, the Income from which reaches us in the form of Dividends, Interest or Rentals.

Over these of course we have full control.

They amounted last year to £635.3.3, viz.

Dividends	254.14.7
Interest on Loans	69. 2.5
Rentals, after deducting Rates, Taxes, Tithes, Insurance	311. 6.3

* * *

D. Fourthly, there are certain incidental sums which come in from one source or another, and are not Income from Properties or

Investments, nor settled revenues. In the last financial year these amounted to £124.15.11.

* * *

It will be seen, therefore, that apart from mere Transfers (sums collected for transmission to Rome, Power Honoraria[4] to be distributed etc.) and earmarked Receipts equivalent to Transfers, we had at our disposal last year the sums:—

$$\begin{array}{r} 254.14.\ 7 \\ 69.\ 2.\ 5 \\ 311.\ 6.\ 3 \\ \underline{124.15.11} \\ \underline{£759.19.\ 2} \end{array}$$

So far, as to Income. Now, as to Expenditure.

II. As to Expenditure:—

E. Now, on the other hand, as against this, we have certain definite charges which must always be met. Of these I give the figures for the year ending March 1920.

Annuities (Pickering £80,[5] Delhaise £6,[6] Wortley £30,[7] Hinckley £30,[8] Woodchester Fathers £100)[9]   246.0.0

Interest (Carisbrooke £569,[10] Hinckley Loan £16,[11] Mrs Cogan £10,[12] Int. on (then) uninvested items of Burse Capital and Buckler Deposit £45)[13]   640.0.0

On these, the chief things to note are:—

(i) that owing to the increased charges, whereas last year we had to pay £80 for Br. Sylvester Pickering at Belmont Park, this year the figure will be nearer £95.

(ii) The large sum of Interest to Carisbrooke is due to the Loan (now reduced to £15,225) which we have from the Nuns, over half of which the Province has had to contract to meet expenses at Pendleton.[14] On 31 March 1920 Pendleton's Capital amount of Loan from the Province was nearly £10,000 (viz. £9822) and the amount the Province had paid in Interest for Pendleton was more than another £5000 (£5371.4.3).

Pendleton pays off £150 a year by means of its outdoor collections, but at present is doing nothing more.[15]

(iii) The Cogan Loan is a sum of £200 lent to F. Peach at 5%.

(iv) The 'uninvested Burse money and Buckler Deposit' means that we had to spend money that was given us to Capitalise. Instead of funding it, we borrowed it (crediting it, of course, with Interest). By the present date, all this Burse Capital and Interest due to it has been invested.

F. Lastly, there were certain incidental expenses—£243.4.6—of which the chief items were: £150 travelling expenses of two Missioners to Grenada;[16] and £45.7/- for outfits for two Fathers.[17]

* * *

G. Moreover, owing to demands made on us by Woodchester and the Apostolic School at Hawkesyard, we had to pay, *in excess of our receipts for Burses* as recounted above, £289.8.2.

* * *

Thus, over and above the Transfers named under paragraphs A and B—

We received—		We paid out—	
Dividends	254.14. 7	Annuities	246. 0.0
Rentals	311. 6. 3	Interest	640. 0.0
Incidentals	124.15.11	Incidentals	243. 4.6
Interest	69. 2. 5	Extra, Nov. and Boys	289. 8.2
	£759.19. 2		£1418.12.8

* * *

H. It will be seen, therefore, that our Income was deficient to the amount of £658.13.6.

Naturally, we had to meet this deficit by borrowing. The result of this is that we have a larger interest payment to face this year.

* * *

J. Perhaps, for the sake of clearness, I may make the following points:—
(i) Hawkesyard (though the Province paid Pensions for the *Simple* Novices while they were there) has throughout, from the time Miss Gulson's Endowment[18] was received, supported the Professed Novices and Student Priests without any help from the Province. Happily, the Endowment payment was maintained without reduction even during the war. But in the present increasing numbers of the Noviciate, Hawkesyard cannot go on indefinitely without assistance.

As the Province has no further funds to draw upon, and we dare not add to the large sum already borrowed, unless fresh help reaches us, we shall inevitably be compelled to limit the Noviciate.
(ii) When any extra expenditure falls upon a House (e.g. Woodchester has to find 4½ guineas a week for F. Francis Wade)[19] the Province is unable to help.
(iii) F. Reginald Ginns at Jerusalem costs £120 a year. I have to pay that myself. I had to pay £150 to send F. Gilbert Tigar and F. Gabriel Bezzina to S. Africa. I had to pay for F. Aidan Elrington to go to

the United States. The province could do nothing.[20]

(iv) BLACKFRIARS has had to be supported simply on what I was able to save. The Province could do nothing.

K. We are in this hopeless state largely through the huge sums in Capital Expenditure and in unpaid interest that have resulted from Pendleton.

Without any reflection on any member of the Province, living or dead, we are likely to remain thus insolvent, until Pendleton is established financially, and able to repay to the Province something of what it has cost us.

When, therefore, projects are put before me, or before the Chapter, or Provincial Council, it is well the Brethren should realise that much as we may wish to do for the Province, our works are necessarily restrained by conditions not of our choosing. The apparent nearness of successive Provincial Procurators, the repeated 'dunning' appeals that not unnaturally irritate, these things may perhaps now be better understood.

* * *

Let this point, at least, emerge:

The set charges on our Income (Annuities and Interest i.e. £246 and £640) are in excess of our Income (i.e. Dividends £254.14.7; Rentals £311.6.3; and Interest receivable £69.2.5).

Our fixed payments—£886—exceed our fixed receipts £635.3.3 by £250 odd; and to meet 'incidental' payments there is nothing.

I know that you will realise the necessarily confidential nature of this report, and will not divulge it beyond the limits of the Province. But I am sure that you ought to have at least this general knowledge of how we stand.

You will see that had it not been for the kindness and trustfulness of the Sisters at Carisbrooke, the Province would have had to borrow elsewhere at a higher interest; and this must financially have[21] threatened its very existence.

1. The accounts of 1919-1920 evidently proved quite a shock to Humbert Everest (who had just become provincial bursar), once he worked out what they really implied. He wrote to BJ in March 1920, 'I had not realised it myself. The details are like dust in one's eyes. But it seems to me to be a fact that our general income does not meet even the interest we have to pay on loans. In other words, we are borrowing in order to pay interest on previous borrowings'. In a letter of 2 December 1921 he writes to BJ, 'Your letter of Oct. 1 1920 betrays the shock it had been to you to find that the other Province Funds amounted only to £648 and that they had to meet a constant annual payment of at least £921.' BJ therefore drafted his letter to all the superiors in the province and sent it to Everest, who made some slight changes and corrections.
2. The province had various burses, endowed by benefactors such as Lady Arundell, for the training of students either in the Studium or in the school at Hawkesyard.
3. See above, no. 45.

4. On 28 November 1916 John Power (otherwise unknown to us) made a formal arrangement with BJ and the provincial bursar (Laurence Peach) to leave a substantial sum of money to the province in his will, and to make annual contributions until his death, for three masses to be said daily for his intentions. These intentions, with the stipends attached, were one of the ways in which the province gave financial support to some of the brethren, e.g. those studying at Louvain.

5. Since 1913 Silvester Pickering, who had had a complete mental breakdown as a student at Hawkesyard, had been hospitalised, at the expense of the province, at Belmont Park, Waterford, Ireland, a home run by the Brothers of Charity 'for the treatment and cure of mentally afflicted gentlemen', as their advertisement in the Catholic Directory put it.

6. In 1916 the Revd Hubert Joseph Delhaise (1857–1926) gave the province £120 in return for a life annuity of £6. He was a Belgian priest, who had worked for nearly 30 years in the diocese of Newport and Menevia (later the archdiocese of Cardiff). Owing to chronic ill health, much of his time was spent as chaplain to various convents of sisters, and he died in a nursing home in Bristol.

7. In 1885 Miss Eleanor Wortley of Leicester gave the province £600 in return for an annuity of £30. She died in 1925.

8. Carrington Francis Turville of Aston Flamville left the province £5000 in his will, on condition that £30 a year was sent to the local mission, which by this time meant Hinckley.

9. When William Leigh gave the church at Woodchester to the province in 1850, he also gave a lump sum of £2500 instead of the £100 per annum he had previously offered, on condition that the province accepted responsibility for paying an annuity of £100 to the priests staffing the church.

10. The province had been borrowing from Carisbrooke since 1862; they repaid £1100 in 1911, but otherwise the debt continued to grow until, by 1920, it stood at £16,225. In 1920 £1000 was repaid, but in the same year a further £2100 was borrowed.

11. In the period 1918–1920 the province borrowed £400 from Hinckley at 4%. The debt was paid off in 1930.

12. In 1912 Mrs Sillery Cogan (about whom we could discover nothing) offered the province a loan of £200 at 5%.

13. Charles Alban Buckler (1824–1905) was the architect of St Dominic's church, London. In his will, made in 1905, he left the residue of his estate in trust for his three Dominican brothers. The sum received was £1141, which was administered by the provincial bursar. When the last of the three brothers (Reginald) died in 1927, the money was handed over to the London priory.

14. The province had incurred enormous debts to pay for the building of the priory in Pendleton, opened in 1901. A loan of £5000 was negotiated with the bank; Raffalovich had promised to give this sum, if the province could first borrow it, and he undertook to pay the interest on the loan until he could repay the capital. In fact, though, he paid the interest only until 1904 and in 1903–1904 he paid off £1400 of the capital. He later announced that he would leave £9000 in his will to cancel Pendleton's debt, but he did not die until 1934 and he actually left his money to Canon Gray and it came to the province shortly afterwards on the death of Canon Gray, but then it was earmarked for the Order's work in Edinburgh.

15. By the time of BJ's letter, judging from Everest's letters to BJ from this period, Pendleton was not even bothering about the regular collections, so that Everest thought they would fall short of the £150 target.

16. Lambert Cuypers and Osmund Barker were sent to Grenada in 1920. Cuypers died there very shortly afterwards, and Barker returned to England in 1922.

17. One outfit was for Cuypers, going to Grenada, the other for Anthony Lowe, who returned from Grenada towards the end of 1919 and was assigned to Pendleton.

18. Miss Gulson left most of her estate to the province when she died, asking that the bulk of it should be devoted to the maintenance of Hawkesyard and its inmates. In 1922 this fund was formally turned into a Trust.

19. In a nursing home in Bristol.

20. BJ earned money for such purposes by giving retreats and lectures.

21. The typescript actually has 'must have financially have'.

66. *BJ to Lady Margaret Domvile. From St Dominic's, London. 9 February 1921. Autograph.*

I was welcomed from Scotland last night by your charming present, the portly and valuable volumes which I shall greedily devour.

Unfortunately I am just off by train to Downside as my dearest boy friend has just died suddenly of pneumonia.[1] I have prepared him for all his sacraments save the last and go to put him to his rest. Pray for me.

1. Terence Geoghegan died at Downside on 7 February 1921.

67. *BJ to Mother Dominic Geoghegan. From Downside. 9 February 1921. Transcript.*[1]

I came down here with them this afternoon and just send a line to say that Terence's death has done more than anything else to bring about that long wished for peace and union. Really there is something wonderful in it all, his death after happy school years, before the disappointments of life had touched him, so radiant, so modest, so unselfish. And to be buried within sounds of prayer and praise, a perpetual memory, were he in need of it, crying for the prayers of monks and boys. But the two are wonderful, offering up everything in the flame of sacrifice.

1. Mother Dominic, of the Holy Child sisters at Mayfield, was the aunt of Terence Geoghegan. The priest who transcribed this letter notes: 'Mother Dominic tells me that he (BJ) and Terence G. were very close friends. Terence G. had a remarkable influence among his seniors and contemporaries in the School. Boys, who were too shy to bring their difficulties to the monks, used to come to Terence and ask his advice. Terence would submit the difficulties and problems to Fr Bede who would send his solution by return of post. This particular aspect of their apostolic activities only came to light after Terence's death.' It appears from the letter that BJ was taken to Downside by Terence's parents.

68. *BJ to Leonard Parker. From St Dominic's, London. 11 February 1921. Transcript.*

Just to enclose the last I had from him, because you will see by the last page he has a reference to you, and to the pleasure your letter gave him. There is always that mood of yours, radiant, happy, your true self, that so appealed to him and made him love you, though he loved you in all your moods. At Christmas some dream you told him of, him as a priest saving you, rather worried him at the time. But, my dear, he will always be a priest for you. Always you can consider him standing by God's side, and always with you in his mind and memory, your cares and troubles, failures, successes, you always. He will be giving to God your prayers and taking to you God's graces. It will be a comfort to you all life long, to have so unforgetful an advocate: it will rob death of half its terrors to know he will be waiting for you. Death has ended all chance of misunderstandings, of jealousies. Always he's your best friend.

69. *BJ to Lady Margaret Domvile. From St Dominic's, London. 5 March 1921. Autograph.*

Really I had no intention of saying Dividends were necessarily wrong. The 2 points Mr Clayton made were to my mind perfectly just.[1] (i) They are money-lending and (ii) they arise from the service of others i.e. the interest is the result of the labour and skill of the business or trade in which they are employed. But these 2 points don't make dividends wrong; they only make them dangerous and to be carefully examined in each case. They are money-lending: and the fact that I get interest at all is because there are clever managers, directors, skilled and unskilled labour, with whose wits my bit of money-lending works big things.

The Cheyne Walk visit was very interesting, 4 till 6.15!.[2] First I had a talk with her for an hour or so (she is, to my mind, staunchly Catholic), then Bernard Holland[3] came in, and eventually Col. Studd who sat next to me and whom I much liked. Of course Ireland was the topic.[4] I think we (i.e. he and I) agreed thoroughly as to the[5] terrible harm the B. and T.[6] were doing to the name of England (you'll see a hair-raising article in *Blackfriars*[7] put in deliberately to make people realise how the name of England to us who love her is being dragged hatefully through mud), and as to the abomination of the Murder Gang!

I should say all their instincts were Catholic, their temper Catholic and their refinement Catholic, both of them, a charming couple in a delightful house! There!

1. BJ was due to lecture that evening at Caxton Hall on 'The Morality of Dividends' in the series, 'Modern thought and ancient morals'. He had presumably been discussing with Lady Margaret the article by Joseph Clayton, 'The meaning of dividends', *Blackfriars* 1 (1920) pp. 231–238.
2. 97 Cheyne Walk, Chelsea, the home of Col. Herbert William Studd and his wife, Mary. BJ had gone to visit them at the instigation of Lady Margaret (cf. above, no. 63). Col. (later Brig. Gen.) Studd (1870–1947) joined the Coldstream Guards in 1891 and served with distinction in South Africa (1899–1902) and in the first World War.
3. Bernard Holland (1856–1926) was a prominent civil servant, who had become a Catholic in 1915. He later edited the *Selected Letters of Friedrich von Hügel*, London 1927. He lived close to the Studds, at 4 More's Garden, Cheyne Walk.
4. Mrs Studd was Irish, descended from the de Veres of Curragh Chase, Co. Limerick, who had since the middle of the previous century been much involved with the plight of the Irish. She had been received into the Catholic church in 1916.

5. BJ wrote 'as the the terrible', and then crossed out the second 'the', but he no doubt intended to write 'as to the'.
6. Black and Tans. In 1920, as the Irish 'troubles' increased, the British government recruited reinforcements for the Royal Irish Constabulary, dressed, not in the traditional bottle-green uniforms of the R.I.C., but in makeshift costumes which included a wide use of khaki. The force, which was to reach 7000 in strength and to receive an unenviable reputation for brutality, was first seen in County Tipperary, where it received its nickname after a pack of hounds there called the Black and Tans. See Robert Kee, *Ireland, A History*, London 1980, pp. 182-185.
7. 'Ireland today under England', by an English officer's son, *Blackfriars* 1 (1920-21) pp. 699-712.

70. BJ to Miss Savielle. From St Dominic's, London. 19 March 1921. Autograph.

'Nobody's asked me, Sir—she said'—so I am silent during these next days and not sorry for it.[1] One needs to listen as well as talk. May Easter bring you its joys and gladnesses! These come to those who strive quietly and in few words to find God in the heart of their being.

1. Cf. the end of the nursery rhyme, 'Where are you going to, my pretty maid' (Iona and Peter Opie, *The Oxford Dictionary of Nursery Rhymes*, Oxford 1951, no. 317), '"Nobody asked you, Sir," she said'. Miss Savielle had evidently asked BJ where he was preaching during Holy Week and Easter (20 March was Palm Sunday).

71. BJ to Leonard Parker. From Ampleforth. 25 March 1921. Transcript.

Just to wish you all good things for Easter, especially that peace at heart and contentment which Frum[1] always wished you to have. I suppose you will have seen the letters by now: but were they in chronological order? I haven't had the heart to read them again, as I haven't even yet read Charlie's[2] to me. I am such a fool now-a-days that I cannot read those things without being perfectly miserable. If therefore there was anything you were not meant to see, I know you will perfectly understand. He was so affectionate, so natural and so sane that nothing he ever wrote could possibly have done you harm to see. More and more I find I miss him: and you must discover his loss even more than I do, who saw him so little, really, all these last years, whereas you have had him with you almost to the last. However now we both have him and there are times when his smile, his laugh, his lazy-looking walk surge up to my memory and seem as real and vivid as though this life still coloured them. One after another, three of the people whom I loved most have gone, but I don't think for a moment that I have lost them. They are all the more mine in a way[3] than are my living friends. Somehow one is sometimes fearful of them, whether they will be as bored as they naturally should, whether life's distance and interests may not separate them from me: but of these 3 I am sure. I pray to them to help me and once or twice when Frum has got me things I wanted there has been a certain prankishness in the way the things came to me that I almost fancied I could hear his laughter, with his dear head on one side, half-profile, as he used to put it when he had 'pulled one's leg'.

I think of you all at Downside and wonder what it all has meant, how it has been seen through tears. 'The memory of happy memories' is certainly not all sorrow, yet it has a pathos as well as a pleasure of its own. Give them my love. I feel I dare not write to them at present.

And I am wondering whether you would write an article for *Blackfriars*. I have tried to think over an article on Schools and Books on them by Boys: but I feel I don't know enough. Will you try? I make you a present of the title, which is all I have so far achieved. It is to be called *Waughs and Rumours of Waughs,* to show how *Sinister Street* has opened the floodgates of an unpleasant and unclean water which threatens to be prolonged.[4] S.S. was happy as a description: the L. of Youth[5] is unhappy as a reform.

1. Terence Geoghegan.
2. Charles Bellord, who died in 1918.
3. BJ actually wrote 'in the way'.
4. Parker refused the invitation to write this article, so finally BJ wrote it himself; it was published in *Blackfriars* 2 (1921-22) pp. 716-723.
5. Compton Mackenzie, *Sinister Street*, vol. I, London 1913; Alec Waugh, *The Loom of Youth*, London 1917.

72. *BJ to Leonard Parker. From St Dominic's, London. 7 April 1921. Transcript.*

You must forgive a note written while I am waiting for someone to call who is already over-due, in order to acknowledge two of your letters, April 1 and April 5.

I was indeed most glad to find that you had stayed at No. 64[1] and that all went well. It is just like them to have put you into dear Frum's[2] room and to have given you, who depend so much upon environment, the proper surroundings whereby to reconstruct Frum's life and thereby better to understand him. I am always sure of that, that the nearer one can get physically to anyone's way of life the nearer one is to understanding them themselves; and the result is that your 4 days at No. 64 will have suddenly made you realise better than ever before or at least with a swift completeness all that he was.

I am sorry the article doesn't tempt you.[3] I had hoped that it would. However we must go elsewhere for it.

I think that your interpretation of *Yours ever* in Frum's last letter is indeed a perfectly just one for in some unconscious way (the quacks would use the word 'subconscious') friendship is most instinctive of the future. I feel pretty sure that the nearness of death always makes itself felt or nearly always, a brooding, an instinct, a vague surmise, and though one may no doubt hold down the thought and keep it from becoming effective and promise oneself instead years of life, none the less the matter remains in a vague feeling. Anyway I am sure that he with that perfect sincerity of character which was part of his charm would never have written what he did not mean and *yours ever* was no doubt truly the note of his mind. It is the greatest of helps to remember that, for one must often do things that make one wonder whether the friends who now see us so clearly won't be shattered in their friendship, seeing so plainly what we're like really; the answer must be to re-encourage oneself that love is eternal, 'for better, for worse', whatever betide. Not that one can do anything knowing that the lover across the other side of death won't mind: that would not be love at all. But we can I fancy always be sure that they will have pity, have sympathy and wholly understand and forgive. After all they are the friends of God, like Him and through the very effect of their love for Him made even more like Him, and so wholly able to go on loving to the end. *Yours ever* was a true statement and will be always. And that is exactly what he meant it to be, an inspiration, a stimulus, a re-heartening. After that it were blasphemy against love, human and divine, ever to despair, to lose hope of yourself. We can do nothing of ourselves, but all things in Him that strengtheneth us;[4] and that you will be ever strengthened is now guaranteed you by Frum's unfailing presence before God.

1. 64 Parliament Hill, Hampstead, the Geoghegans' family home.
2. Terence Geoghegan.
3. See above, no. 71.
4. Philippians 4:13.

73. *Provincial's Diary. 6 May 1921.*

Went to London University to interview Extension Lectures Registrar, Mr John Lea, to secure (if possible) recognition of Caxton Hall lectures.[1] Found Committee or Board had received application most favourably. Apparently my name was known to them and my work (which? what?) and they would accept my personal guarantee. But several conditions:—
- (i) To be open to public.
- (ii) Admission to full course tickets.
- (iii) Syllabus, bibliography, and questions and lecturers' names all submitted.
- (iv) Questions after lectures to be allowed.

(v) Examination at end of year.
(vi) Fee of £23.5.0 paid to 'Varsity for advert. expenses.
(vii) On the *Summa*.

1. Cf. above, no. 36. Henceforth the lectures were given under the auspices of the University Extension Lectures at the Catholic Evidence Guild Hut, Westminster Cathedral. Once again, Vincent McNabb was the first lecturer. In 1929 a new series was launched, also by McNabb, on the New Testament. The circumstances are recounted by McNabb in a memorandum he wrote on 4 May 1936 on the back of a poster advertising the first series (now forming part of the house chronicle of St Dominic's, London): a French lady, who kept a little girls' school, asked McNabb one day where she could find Catholic lectures on the bible in London, and he had to admit that he did not know of any, and, in response to her evident astonishment, he promised to try and do something about it. 'After a few months she came again, and asked, "Has anything been done? You told me to come and worry you. So I have come." I said apologetically and with contrition, "No! I have done nothing." I cannot remember more than the atmospheric condition of her disappointment. I think she used a little of the liberty of the sons (and daughters) of God to wonder why only those outside the Church were setting store by the scriptural riches of the Church. Then she went away and not without a look of disappointment. Now it happened that the Provincial, Fr Bede Jarrett, was at home and in his cell. I went at once to him. On my way upstairs it occurred to me that perhaps we could arrange for the Bible what we had arranged for the Summa—a series of Extension Lectures approved by the University of London. On entering his cell, I knelt and said, amongst much else, "Dieu le veut. A woman from the crowd has asked for lectures on the bible." Then I told him all. In his own quiet way he listened, hardly saying a word. But I knew his love of God and of God's word and of God's people so well that his silence was nowise threatening. That afternoon he was at the University of London offices, interviewing the University Extension registrar, Mr Lea. In a few weeks' time the lectures were approved.'

74. *Provincial's Diary. 25 June 1921.*

Wrote to Archbishop McIntyre for leave to open Hawkesyard School to boys other than postulants giving as reasons (α) Bishop of Salford's declaration that shortage of Catholic Secondary Schools.[1] (β) Our School been in existence 400 years.[2] (γ) Deluged with applications. (δ) Willing to exclude Birmingham diocesans.

First Mass said by Oxford Dominican on Dominican ground.[3] I sacrificed this enviable privilege by going to Hawkesyard for S.T.L. exams.[4] What it is to be Provincial and yet to have to miss so much of its emotional privileges!

1. The bishop of Salford was Louis Charles Casartelli. We have not been able to identify the declaration BJ is referring to. We are grateful to the diocesan archivist of Salford for the information that there is no trace of it in the Casartelli papers preserved in the diocesan archives.
2. As it stands, this cannot be true. What BJ actually wrote in his letter is not clear, since there is no trace of the letter in the Birmingham diocesan archives (we are grateful to the archivist for this information). The English Dominicans opened their school at Bornhem, Belgium, in the 1660s. When they were driven out of Bornhem by the French, they opened a school in England at Carshalton in 1794, which they kept going until 1810. The revival of the province in England took a major step forward with the opening of the priory at Hinckley in 1825, followed immediately by the opening of a school there (coinciding with the final closure of the school at Bornhem). This school lasted until 1854. In each case the school was intended to cater for the educational needs of English Catholics, not just to provide for postulants

intending to enter the Order. In 1858 a postulant school was opened at Hinckley, which lasted until 1866, and was then restarted in 1885 and moved to Hawkesyard in 1898. Since Archbishop McIntyre refused permission for the school to be enlarged there to include pupils other than postulants, the school was moved to Laxton in 1924. It was finally closed in 1967.
3. The Mass was said by Bernard Delany.
4. On 24 June Wilfrid Ardagh and Adrian English were examined for the Lectorate at Hawkesyard (both of them successfully).

75. *BJ to Leonard Parker. From the Priory of Our Lady of Good Counsel, Haywards Heath. 25 July 1921. Transcript.*

... Now on the 15th I shall hope to have you as a fellow acolyte with Van Zeller to keep Card. Bourne in order.[1] ... You and the Zeller (unless I can discover someone of your own height. Do you know anyone who would suit you better and who would be available?) shall shove the performing prelate through his paces. In that exam you certainly must not fail.[2]

... Here I am giving a retreat and have some pleasure out of the priest who has a love for modern poetry. He has a book called *Oxford Poetry 1910-1913* which contains a great deal of real twaddle, perfectly dreadful stuff, that the war probably has killed. But there are some things by Douglas Cole of Magdalen and Balliol which are quite excellent (do you know anything of him? He seems to have published poems in 1910, so that he'll have left long ago. Is he the *Guild Socialist* fellow who used to write in the *Herald*?).[3]

Again Godfrey Elton of Balliol has done amongst other pieces a good attempt called *NEWS*. I shall copy it out for you, in case you have not fallen across it, for it is a real picture and a painfully accurate memory. But really though Ronnie Knox and Eric Shepherd have given some value to the volume,[4] the rest really is dreadful, full of passion and women and mud and the dreadful nonsense anyone can compose when wrestling with a sick headache and the intermittent attentions of Cascara.[5]

You really are a delicious person to talk as you do of your great age and the happy effect of Zeller as his presence will ensure you the laughter of a child.[6] I do hope you will never grow up and change all that, for though it does worry some people to hear you I just love it; but then I suppose I would love it whatever you did.

1. On 15 August the foundation stone was to be laid of the church at Blackfriars, Oxford. In the outcome, it was Leonard Parker and George Bellord who served as Card. Bourne's acolytes.
2. Parker had just failed his preliminary examinations in Law in Trinity term. He seems not to have been much interested in his exams. On 16 March 1922 BJ wrote to him, 'You are a ridiculous person! Why take an exam when you don't expect to pass?' Sure enough, in Hilary 1922 he failed his Scripture exam. In his first years at Oxford he was much more concerned about raising money to fund a scholarship for Downside.
3. G. D. H. Cole, who read classics at Balliol (1908-12) and then won a prize fellowship at Magdalen in 1912, was one of the editors of this first volume of *Oxford Poetry* published by

Blackwell in Oxford in 1913. He left Oxford in 1919, but returned as fellow of University College in 1925. He was a regular contributor to the *Daily Herald*, which was relaunched as a Socialist daily paper in 1919, and he was the leading exponent of Guild Socialism, which was at its most influential in about 1920, in which year he published his book, *Guild Socialism Restated*. In the 1920s and 1930s he also wrote, with his wife, 'thirty solid but dull detective stories' (*Oxford Today* 1 (1989) no.2 p. 23).

4. Knox contributed four poems, including 'Absolute and Abitofhell' (pp. 195-205). Elton's 'News' is on p. 77. R. A. E. Shepherd, an up-and-coming Catholic poet, contributed five poems (pp. 135-142).

5. Cascara Sagrada, at the time a favoured remedy for constipation.

6. BJ and Parker had been planning a holiday together in France; BJ had written to ask whether it would be all right for Van Zeller to come too. Van Zeller was about three years younger than Parker.

76. *Provincial's Diary. 15 August 1921.*

FOUNDATION STONE AT OXFORD. Assembled in Randolph Hotel at 11.30: and left in procession at 11.55. Card. Bourne and Card. Gasquet preceding. For ceremony, full account in local papers. Principal items were the sermon by Card. Gasquet, singing by *Schola Cantus* (under F. Jerome,[1] including Frs Vincent,[2] Eustace,[3] Bertrand[4]), and speech at luncheon by Card. Bourne. In Foundation Stone, besides inscription, were medal of Donald Carden,[5] coins, medals, Blackfriars, Rosary, Times.[6]

1. Jerome Rigby.
2. Vincent McNabb.
3. Eustace O'Gorman.
4. Bertrand Pike.
5. Donald Carden (born 1898) was at Hawkesyard School January-July 1915. We have not been able to discover anything else about him, but he is perhaps to be identified with the Donald Carden who died in the war in 1918.
6. It seems likely that it was the August number of *Blackfriars* and *The Rosary* and that day's *Times* that were put in with the foundation stone. Walter Gumbley published a piece on 'The Blackfriars at Oxford' in the first (*Blackfriars* 2 (1921-22) pp. 306-315), and the other two both contained announcements of the forthcoming laying of the foundation stone (*The Rosary*, revised series 1 no. 8 (1921) p. 98; *The Times*, 15 August 1921, p. 11).

77. *BJ to Leonard Parker. From the Augustinian Priory, Ealing. 3 September 1921. Transcript.*

What can I say to such a letter as yours![1] It is just perfectly yourself to say such touching things in such a way as to make one feel as though one was rather a nice person. I am indeed glad you didn't *say* anything of this, else I should have broken down altogether at the station; for there are tears in human things[2] and despite all one's faith and confidence in friendship, all one's declared belief that distance and separation do not really exist where friendship is concerned, and all the other very fine things one proclaims in order to show the essential greatness of friendship as above death or parting, somehow poor old human nature can't possibly always live up to the wonderful things it believes and teaches, so that though I feel that to part should not be a sorrow, for it is a parting only of material things, yet actually it is a sorrow indeed. It was horrid after those jolly days and those lengthy and often nonsensical and even rude nightly discussions to have to drift apart again.

Well at least I feel I know you better and am closer to you than before. That is something of a gain.

But, my dear, realise that friendship makes people equal. Hence though (as I said) my asking of you to be candid is all over, finished with, really it did not mean that you were to pick holes. Heaven knows that I wasn't picking holes in you. Only I was so fond of you, oh yes and so blooming talkative, that I had to say to you and in the presence of someone else who was also fond of both of us, whatever came into my head. All I asked was for you to do the same. But you are such a dear idealist that your friends are without fault and you have nothing to say. All's well however and I quite understand. I'm not hurt at all, and I shan't bother you again with that matter.

But I will ask you to believe one thing, namely that I cannot possibly have done more for you than you have done for me. You will believe that, won't you? Not because you think it true or untrue, but just because I say it. My older friends have all gone over to the other side: and as a Superior one cannot possibly have any friendships within one's own Order. It would make life intolerable for everybody else; hence one is forced to go outside. Charlie Bellord and Terence[3] were very kind to me: and I still go to both of them in my troubles. But you are the only one I have left here, and I am selfish enough to cling to you very much. You have been of enormous help to me just by being yourself, for friends are of assistance never because of what they do but because of what they are, i.e. friends. Jelly[4] is a dear, but I like to hold on to you as my friend.

However I don't want to come under your ban as a sentimentalist—which I really am for I revel in sentiment and even sentimentality—so I stop saying anything more. But I do want you to realise that you have given me as much as I have ever given you since you have given me yourself. For my holiday was so bound up with you that I felt I should be refreshed after a fortnight of your company wheresoever in the world we should be; of course in that romantic setting of the chateau, with its scenery, its historic roots, its dungeons, and even the curious psychological background of the party at the Chateau, all served to make the holiday even more delightful than I had guessed. It was worth not being able to sleep to have you and your talk and in the strength of it I shall be able to forge ahead in my work.

Therefore my dear I do from my heart say *Thank you*.

It is rather amusing here for I am waited on at my meals by a venerable lay sister who comes from Nantes and who is so delighted to wait on a fellow-Breton (as she calls me) that we talk nothing else but French. At least she does, I listen in French. We discuss coifs, velvet streamers, and the sermons of the Dominican Fathers who have preached the Lent in Nantes. . . .

I trust the smokelessness and winelessness do not trouble you too much and above all that your mother's better.

1. Thanking BJ for the holiday they had been taking in Brittany and Normandy (cf. above, no. 75). Hubert van Zeller refers to this holiday, spent 'under the inspiration of Father Bede', in *Willingly to School*, London 1952, pp. 118-119, 149.
2. Cf. Vergil, *Aeneid* I 462.
3. Terence Geoghegan.
4. The nickname of all the van Zellers (in this case Claud, later Dom Hubert).

78. *BJ to George Bowring. From St Augustine's Priory, Ealing. 7 September 1921. Transcript.*

. . . Well, I shall pray for you every day at Woodchester.[1] You must be quite yourself and you will then certainly do well. Don't worry about yourself or fuss or add potty little devotions. Keep to the big things of religious life, the office etc and remember that at first you will have so much material memory work as to spoil your devotion in the Office, Mass, and Communion; but once it has become a habit the rest will return. You will find your Novice Master[2] kind and with a knowledge older than he seems.

1. Bowring was shortly to join the noviciate at Woodchester.
2. Eustace O'Gorman, chosen by the Provincial council at the end of May 1921; he accordingly resigned as prior of Hawkesyard and was formally appointed novice master on 8 September.

79. *Provincial's Diary. 6 October 1921.*

Went to Oxford taking Jerningham vestments,[1] with F. Fabian Dix. Saw the foundations of Chapel and entrance and all the front of No. 62[2] (that was) finished, and watched the workmen setting the first upright stone above ground, namely the left pier of corner of main entrance.

1. A set of Italian Baroque vestments (a chasuble and two dalmatics) from Costessy Hall, Norfolk, the home of the Jerninghams. BJ bought them at a reduced rate (£1000) from the 11th Bart, Sir Henry William Stafford Jerningham (1867-1935), in July 1920. In April 1918 an expert assured Sir Henry that they were 'a most wonderful set and the finest I have ever seen'.
2. 62 St Giles. The Dominicans had acquired nos. 62, 63 and 64 St Giles, Oxford.

80. *Provincial's Diary. 17 February 1922.*

Went to Kirkconnel Lea.[1]

Difficulties	*Advantages*
Lights	Stable as Chapel
Finance	Duchess of Norfolk landlord
9.45 buses	Shooting rights over grouse[2]
Distance 12.45 to	View, gardens
6.45 Dumfries	Well-built
Need to leave one priest at home always	Summer resort, growing
	Novices, wild and free
	L.N.W.R. Glasgow, Edinburgh
	Bishop may agree more readily to country place
	Lady Herries[3] left £500 to build Chapel

1. Cf. above, no. 35.
2. BJ actually wrote 'greese', perhaps a supposed plural of 'grouse'!
3. Lady Angela Mary Charlotte Herries (died 1 March 1919), mother of the Duchess of Norfolk, had added a codicil to her will in 1916, leaving her daughter £500 'towards the chapel she proposes to build . . . in memory of her father'.

81. *BJ to Sr M Suso Hurdle-Williams OP. From St Dominic's, London. 24 February 1922. Autograph.*

Thank you for your letter.
(1) By all means get your mother to visit you while you are at Oxford.[1] It certainly seems at least a chance of something being done, and it will show that you are doing everything in your power to ease things. One never regrets in life any attempt to make peace: one always reproaches oneself afterwards for opportunities (however remote) that one has missed for securing it.
(2) I am sure that financially you need not worry at all. You may have hardships: you must have 'em or should at the foundation of a new house. That is the way of God: and hardships will unify your community and make it a single body in a way nothing else can. Hardships produce gaiety and peace, two essential qualities of the Dominican spirit. Moreover there is an especial blessing that God always gives to new beginnings, a *fervor noviticus*,[2] a sacredness that brooded over the early history of the order, is found in the story of Fra Giovanni Dominici in Fiesole, retold in the group round Lacordaire.[3] Even the beginnings of rivers have been held holy by christian people. On you will come all this, trouble and blessing both, a double portion of the spirit and blessing of God.

1. Sr M. Suso (shortly to become the first prioress of the new Dominican monastery at Headington, Oxford) and Mother Veronica Ashworth, prioress of Carisbrooke, visited Oxford to examine the house it was proposed to buy for the nuns, 19-22 April 1922. Sr M. Suso hoped to take the opportunity to meet her mother, who disapproved of her being a Catholic, let alone a nun.
2. 'Enthusiasm associated with new beginnings'. BJ was probably thinking of the phrase *fervor novitius* found in the Rule of St Benedict (1.3). *Noviticus* is a made-up word.
3. BJ is referring to the foundation in 1406 of the reformed Dominican convent of Fiesole and to the group associated with Lacordaire in the revival of the French province in 1839-41. Of the former BJ wrote in 1914, 'In 1408, the Convent, dedicated in honour of S. Dominic, was finished at Fiesole, so back again the novices came to their first home. There is a fragrance that always attaches to the spring-time of things, when life begins afresh, radiant, and full of hope and promise. The early days, the first records, the primitive sources of things, the tumultuous origin of dynasties are the periods round which gather legends and myths. Even the places where rise the great and famous rivers have been consecrated by pious tradition and deemed sacred by the custom of the race. So too has God dealt with His own people . . . And so was it with the Convent of Fiesole' (*S. Antonino and Mediaeval Economics*, London 1914, pp. 25-26). BJ's account of the members of the community there, which was in line with current beliefs, has been significantly undermined by more recent scholarship: St Antonino was among them, but it is now not generally accepted that Fra Angelico was his fellow-novice, nor is there any reason to believe that Bl. Lorenzo of Ripafratta was their novice-master (cf. S. Orlandi, *B. Lorenzo da Ripafratta*, Florence 1956, p. 23).

82. *BJ to Mrs Mortimer.*[1] *From St Dominic's, London. 17 March 1922. Transcript.*

Well I like that! Badgering me to remember D.[2] in my daily Mass! What next, I wonder! As though I didn't do it already indeed and have for years. But pray for his vocation? Ah well, I am not so sure that I'll do that. Really I find it so very difficult to press such points on God. You see, one never quite knows whether he should be or not; and if not, then heaven forbid he should ever come in at all. It is so often that disasters have attended the pressure of vocations, not that you are the person to do that; but I say this only to prevent disappointment to you if he finds another way home to God. After all, what you really want is that God's will be done. It is being done and must be if we all leave it to Him and take no care except diligently to watch and see which way he is led and help that on. It is not your desires nor my hopes, but D.'s own soul that we have to watch and try to sympathise with, enter into its odd little views and gifts, nor make any effort to insinuate our own into him. He's such a dear little person, so very shy and so afraid of betraying himself that one has to have the tact of an archangel not to rub him all in a way against his own wishes. However drawn to the OP vocation, he'd be terrified of anyone's guessing it and be equally terrified of revealing it: this makes his task harder to him and ours harder too.

With every best wish and remember me at the tomb of S. Peter.

1. A parishioner of St Dominic's, London, about whom we have been able to discover almost nothing except what is contained in these letters.
2. Her 14-year-old son.

83. *Provincial's Diary. 12 June 1922.*

Wrote to Bishop of Galloway[1] about Mrs Tayleur's offer for Kirkconnel Lea,[2] having heard from the General his approval on June 10.

1. James McCarthy.
2. Cf. above, no. 80. Mrs Tayleur had made a definite offer to give the property to the English Dominicans, and the Interchapter (8–11 May) had provisionally accepted her offer.

84. *BJ to Mrs Mortimer. From Ireland. 9 September 1922. Transcript.*

Thank you for your kind letter with its jolly news of my beloved D. Of course you never have had any reason to worry over D.; he always has had a larger slice than either of us of the grace of God, so that he has much more reason to worry over our salvation than we have to worry over his. The great thing is to go on being very careful not to interfere. It is so terribly tempting just to jostle him into the path we think good for him and to put things in his way, but really all one can do is to leave him in God's hands. You know he has a very sensitive little soul, which makes him endeavour to hide his feelings by talking big. It is never what he says that you need ever pay attention to, only what he does. His words are the attempt of a thin-skinned and sometimes tortured bloke to put one off the scent. He's always been like that to my knowledge, though I don't see very much of him, not because of his fault or mine but just the odd jobs of life that part us.

So just thank a kindly Heaven for giving you such a boy whose prayers will probably save your soul and perhaps that of
                Yours sincerely,
                F.B.J.

85. *BJ to Mrs Mortimer. From St Dominic's, London. 11 September 1922. Transcript.*

Thank you for letting me see this letter which I return. May I suggest that you never pay very much attention to what he says when he talks about having no principles? He really bristles with un-science[1] and whatever he may do that is wrong ever it won't be done with[2] feeling in himself much turmoil and protest. He is by nature exceptionally sensitive to evil and opposed to it: but he loves to shock people with his language. It is his words which will always be the worst part of him.

1. Almost certainly this should be corrected to 'conscience'.
2. Presumably BJ meant 'without'.

86. *BJ to Leonard Parker. From St Dominic's, London. 23 September 1922. Transcript.*

Yes, Oxford in September, in the quiet, the scarlet creeper, and the mist, is the Oxford of dreams and visions: 'She needs not June for beauty's heightening.'[1] And yet, you know the real charm of the *place* is not the quiet but the contrast (at least remembered) between the venerable grey walls and the unvenerable pink humanity that floats noisily between the walls. Mere venerable appearance would have an air of stragery[2] and death: but against such a background make parade of youth, futile, rowdy, and busy, and you have the complete thing at its best. And it is precisely *that* you remember, and its remembrance sets off the place to perfection. Were it always as you see it now, you would feel its need of noise and laughter and perhaps mild drunkenness, something to keep vivid and alive the otherwise dead stones. In one of those endless memoranda that Prince Albert lavished on Edward VII as Prince of Wales there came a sentence quoted by Lytton Strachey I think in words like these: 'The only use of Oxford is that it is a place of study, a refuge from the world and its claims.'[3] Shows what he knew about it, doesn't it? And then to Lacordaire it was the 'resort of the beautiful for all who appreciate it.'[4] Now that is the real *use* of Oxford. It affects whoever is wishful to be affected but none others. It doesn't shout its message through some megaphone at the passer-by, but throws off radiant messages, distilled from walls that are and lives that now are not, which you must yourself be tuned up to in order to receive. Still to my way of thinking, in retrospect rather than in reality, it is the decay of the buildings and the youth of the inhabitants that please jointly and each sets the other off.

Ah but then I am a bloated optimist whereas you are, well, you are you: for you as for John Keats, happiness is a fleeting dream
> And joy whose hand is ever to his lips
> Bidding adieu.[5]

Now to me it is the noise, the tumult, the cries, the bare legs, mud, sweat, the whole apparatus of youth, its colour, smell, ideas, that charm because these radiate out life, intense, eager, alert. I only can bear life, for even decay has its beauty gathered out of the hints, and glimpses it affords of 'immortal longings'.[6] Thus to me Shakespeare is more wonderful than the delicate group of Keats, Shelley, and Mat Arnold, for these give you a fretted outline, fragile, mournful, incomplete, and threatening collapse and ruin; they give you death and bid you notice its grey and fading colours. Whereas Shakespeare peers through the grey and fading colours to the real life behind it. Falstaff is life with an incredible fat belly; but then Ariel is alive too and Rosalind, and Othello and Cordelia promise life, and the tragedy of Richard II makes one still 'even through the hollow eyes of death see life peering.'[7]

This is sane, human, real, and Catholic. The other is Paganism with the hump.

Well what think you of the new Abbot, Leander Ipse?[8] I am told that the Abbot of Belmont[9] led at one time by 10 votes but that L.R. caught him up and went beyond. The school will be little interfered with, I'm told:[10] but monks and boys will fare less sumptuously and the austerity which you know I missed will be restored, and the picture will be perfect. So cheer up. Downside will prevail.

1. Matthew Arnold, 'Thyrsis' line 20.
2. This is what BJ wrote, and it is difficult to think of any other word he might have meant, though there is no such word as 'stragery'. It presumably means 'destruction' (from Latin *strages*), unless BJ was thinking of the Italian *stregheria*, 'witchcraft'.
3. Lytton Strachey mentions Prince Albert's long memoranda to the Prince of Wales in *Queen Victoria*, chapter VI (pp. 179-180 in the 1924 London edition), but, at least here, he does not cite his comment on Oxford, which, in any case, does not come in these memoranda but in a letter of 27 October 1859 to the Prince's Governor, Col. Robert Bruce. The text is printed in Viscount Esher, *The Influence of King Edward*, London 1915, p. 28. Col. Bruce (1813-1862) was one of the sons of the 7th Earl of Elgin, and was appointed Governor to the Prince of Wales in 1858.
4. BJ is referring to the ecstatic letter Lacordaire wrote to Mme Swetchine from Oxford on 16 March 1852, contrasting the French universities with Oxford, where 'the university is a whole world', where the doors of the colleges are wide open 'and the stranger goes in as to a refuge belonging to anyone who loves the fragrance of learning and the beautiful.' In the edition of the letters to Mme Swetchine published Paris 1886, see p.489. The editors are grateful to Fr André Duval OP for identifying this reference.
5. 'Ode on Melancholy' lines 22-23.
6. Shakespeare, *Anthony and Cleopatra*, Act V scene 2.
7. Shakespeare, *Richard II*, Act II scene 1.
8. Leander Ramsay.
9. Aelred Kindersley.
10. Leander Ramsay, as headmaster of Downside (1902-1918), had modernised the school, which was remodelled along the lines of an English public school. He saw the running of an efficient school as the community's principal task, a work ideal for a resident Benedictine community.

87. *Provincial's Diary. 9 October 1922.*

Heard from Bishop of Galloway that Canons have refused to let us into diocese (to Kirkconnel Lea) near Dumfries. (1) No use to diocese in so remote a spot. (2) No scope for OP work, I acknowledged without comment.

88. *Provincial's Diary. 8 November 1922.*

F. Vincent McNabb began course on *Summa* at Cambridge in Henry Martyn Hall to an audience of 57.¹

1. McNabb's success in attracting large audiences to lectures on St Thomas was something which impressed the province, and was used as an argument in favour of lecturing in English in the studium in Oxford. At a lectors meeting at Hawkesyard on 10 January 1925, presided over by BJ, 'the question of teaching in English at Oxford was again briefly discussed. The success of Fr Vincent McNabb's English lectures on the *Summa* at the Catholic Evidence Hut, Westminster, where there is an average attendance of 200 per week, shews that English lectures will at least secure an audience.'

89. *Provincial's Diary. 9 November 1922.*

Feast of All Saints OP. Said the first Mass in the new Chapel of OP nuns at Headington, after blessing the Chapel, using the form *Pro Receptione Conventus* in Processional.¹ In afternoon at 2.30, Archbishop of Birmingham² preached in Chapel; we then processed all through the Priory, Frs Aidan,³ Bernard,⁴ J.B.⁵ and myself, also OSB including F. Justin McCann,⁶ Frs Steuart and Burdett SJ⁷, and many others, quantity of women local and otherwise. Then Archbishop and I locked the large gate into garden, after he had read the heavy curse out of Pontificale.⁸ Enclosure of Nuns. Benediction was given by Archbishop of Birmingham, and Mrs Davies confirmed:⁹ and so home. I went to Blackwell to see about Aristotle for text book of philosophy at Hawkesyard¹⁰ and ordered 24 copies each of Tauchnitz ed.¹¹ of Metaphysics, Ethics, and De Anima; also translations of Ethics by Williams,¹² of Metaphysics by Rose¹³ —to be forwarded to F. Austin Barker at Hawkesyard.

1. *Processionarium iuxta ritum S.O.P.*, Rome 1913, pp. 135-138.
2. John McIntyre.
3. Aidan Elrington, superior of the Oxford community.
4. Bernard Delany, a member of the Oxford community.
5. John Baptist Reeves, the third member of the Oxford community.
6. The Master of St Benet's Hall.
7. The superior and another priest from St Aloysius' church, Oxford.
8. In the rite for the blessing and consecration of virgins, contained in the *Pontificale Romanum*, the bishop pronounces an extremely comprehensive curse on anyone who tries to interfere with them or their goods.
9. The mother of Sr Mary Magdalen and a great benefactress of the community. She had been baptised on 12 October.
10. BJ wanted philosophy to be taught directly from the original text of Aristotle instead of from such modern manuals as that by Zigliara, which had been used in the Studium. His suggestion caused considerable debate and some perplexity among the lectors at Hawkesyard, but it was discussed very fully with an eye to its possible implementation in the academic year 1923-24. One of its most enthusiastic supporters was Daniel Callus, recently arrived from Malta. A major reason given for adopting Aristotle was that 'Aristotle is the Oxford text-book' (minutes of the lectors meeting on 20 July 1923). In the outcome the new system was introduced

in October 1923, with Austin Barker being largely responsible, as the main teacher of philosophy at Hawkesyard. On 21 December 1923 Hugh Pope wrote to BJ, 'The Aristotle has more than justified itself and Austin deserves high commendation.' However the lectors' enthusiasm did not last. In their planning for the first academic year after BJ's death, the lectors at Oxford unanimously decided (on 11 July 1935) that teaching psychology and metaphysics on the basis of Aristotle had not worked and that a 'modern manual' would be better.
11. A series of cheap editions of classical texts.
12. R. Williams' translation was published in London 1869, 2nd ed. 1876.
13. W. D. Ross's translation was published in 1908 in the Oxford translation of the complete works of Aristotle.

90. *BJ to Mrs Bellord. From St Dominic's, London. 17 January 1923. Autograph.*

Really it will be a sad day for me when you all go.[1] So long as you have been within rush, it has meant that any time there was a chance to see you; but now even Knightsbridge sounds acres away. I am glad to go off to U.S.A. till the dreadful deed is thoroughly done; else in the fashion of the Japanese I might commit suicide on your steps while the furniture was being carted away as a protest. . . .

But I really don't feel at all like joking now over such a thing; it seems horribly sad.

However partings says Shakespeare are 'such sweet sorrow'.[2] No doubt Ann Hathaway may have been of such a kind as made her William think so; and in a way to have a letter like yours does make one understand something of the kindliness, almost of the fragrance, that there may be in them, to temper the sorrow that is there.

But really one finds that death (which makes folk further than Knightsbridge) does not really make people very far off, if we care to remember and perhaps if they care to let us know that they remember, so that one does understand that between friends there never can be ever any partings at all, never need be.

However far then you and yours wander, as far as I am concerned, they can never wander at all. They are always here with me.

In the old days when I had things I thought to be troubles, it was always to Bedford Lodge that I went, not to mention them but to have them banished at a nursery tea by the laughter, the affection, even the furious engagements that might ensue. Your house still has the same healing balm for me, and I suppose horrible though Knightsbridge sounds to me now it will one day have the same effect.

I must try to come in e'er I sail.

I missed speeches and tea and all Thursday,[3] feeling very overpowered by the collection of people and escaped in Lady Morris' car.

1. The Bellords had moved house twice since BJ was first sent to London in 1905, but they had remained in Hampstead, within easy reach of St Dominic's. Now they were moving to Ennismore Gardens, S.W.7.
2. Shakespeare, *Romeo and Juliet*, Act II scene 1.
3. We have not been able to discover what function BJ missed with the help of Lady Morris' motor car.

91. *BJ to Mrs Campbell.[1] From St Dominic's, London. 17 January 1923. Transcript.*

... Your prayers were most useful. I had the luck to have by me quotations which made my fellow disputant's arguments a little off the spot,[2] and that luck was the answer to other people's prayers. He, my fellow-wrestler, was not very unpleasant, and once when he tried to be, I don't think the audience approved. But I don't think these things do any good.

... Mother Connelly[3] was fascinating as the study of a soul driven by others into strange paths, a life exceptional in what it included and apparently completely at the mercy of others. That's rather a comfort. So much of what we do is forced on us by the action of others, and here one sees how circumstances can be exalted into the very machinery of God, the shepherding of God, His driving us like startled and clucking hens into an open door which in our agitation we miss and only brush and bang our wings against the wire netting, rousing dust, feathers all out at right angles, with the door, mind you, open in front all the time.

Again many thanks for your prayers.

1. Amy Elizabeth Catherine Campbell (née Marchant) was the wife of William Edward Campbell (1875-1957), whom she had married in 1907; he was a master at Downside 1905-32 and 1941-45.
2. On 16 January BJ had engaged in a public debate with the Revd Walter Limbrick (1867-1936), secretary of the Protestant Reformation Society (founded in 1827 to 'proclaim the Gospel of the Lord Jesus to nominal Protestants and Roman Catholics'), on 'The Open Bible', at The Dome, Brighton. Originally the invitation had been made to Hugh Pope, after an address he had given on the beach at Brighton, in which he maintained that the 'open bible' ('open' in the sense that it was open to any individual to interpret it in any way he saw fit) was the greatest curse that had befallen England. It is not known quite when Pope delivered this address, but as early as 1920 BJ was encouraging him to 'get to Brighton if you can and get a flip up there on the esplanade' (letter of 16 February 1920). Since 1921 Pope had been persistently unwell and he had gone away to recuperate, so the invitation was passed on to BJ. The whole debate was published later in the year as a booklet, *The Open Bible: Is it a Blessing or a Curse?*, London 1923. BJ's 'quotations' can be found particularly on pp. 35-36.
3. *The Life of Cornelia Connelly 1809-1879, Foundress of the Society of the Holy Child Jesus*, by a Member of the Society, London 1922.

92. *BJ to Aidan Elrington OP. From Chicago. 8 April 1923. Autograph.*

Thanks for your letter and its good wishes.

There are various points[1] I have thought of as result of seeing seminaries and convents here: I jot them down at haphazard.

(1) The book-cases for the cells can be under the writing table, running the width of the table in 2 shelves on either side. That saves room.

(2) Incinerator in each floor so that paper and rubbish can slip down into furnace.

(3) Blackboards on 2 walls, behind rostrum and along wall opposite windows—to be of slate and not composition.

(4) No benches but chairs with reading desk attached on right hand side—for classrooms.

(5) Electric lighting to be by white globes, enclosing bulb.

(6) Ventilator in cells not to be transom, by piercing wall about door, but top panel of door folds back into cell on ordinary hinge—with chain to arrest it half way to moderate its opening if not desired to open full.

(7) Water laid on to each room.

Can you keep your eyes on these if any of them crop up before my return?

Have not much money, alas!, only about £150. . . .

1. BJ involved himself in all the minutest details of the construction of the Oxford priory. Elrington was appointed superior in Oxford to be BJ's 'man on the spot'.

93. *BJ to Claud (later Dom Hubert) van Zeller. From St Dominic's, London. 22 July 1923. Autograph.*

Yes all your letters have come home to me at last and all of them display a depressed and worn out Jelly,[1] ready to join the sad procession of decayed horses on their way to Antwerp to become the food of the democracies of the world.[2] Even the Reynolds'[3] visit illumining as with patches of sunshine the clouded sky of your life read almost like a tale of misery. The Butler and the Valet seemed but grim figures in a fantastic nightmare, the Butler a sinister representative of unjellified respectability and the Valet undoubtedly the original of the phrase 'valet of tears'. For the rest all is gloom. Just a flash in the pan on the Anselmian[4] return, no doubt a snobbish gleam when the P.W.[5] arrived, perhaps the plastered hair and the prefecture[6] (wasn't Pontius Pilate a Roman prefect?) filled for a while with vanity the vanquished and aged spirit, probably the good aunt passing a glow of her copper hair to gild (this sounds like a discovery of the mediaeval adventure of transmuting metals) the horizon, else gloom, gloom, gloom.

Oh I forgot; there is the pleasure of examinations, of sleeping out in the open, of poetry. Do you know you are at last becoming infected by Downside pessimism? It has taken years to develop, but, my good Jelly, it has come. I behold you already advancing along the path in the centre of which, a long way ahead and nearing the entrance, is our friend Leonard.[7] Him I have not seen save for ½ hour in Mrs Bellord's room. He did invite me out to lunch; but forgot all about it as he was engaged in taking a girl to Lords to watch the Varsity match. Since he asked me to lunch I have never heard another word from him; it was Mrs Bellord who told me he was out with the girl. He has now made up his mind to go to Salt Lake City as others[8] he will never be able to choose only one and settle to her. He has a Catholic heart I think.

I am waiting to hear of you next off in the same direction. At present you are in the pessimistic mood:

> 'Let not young souls be smothered out before
> They do quaint deeds and fully flaunt their pride.
> It is the world's one crime its babes grow dull,
> Its poor are ox-eyed, limp, and leaden-eyed.
> Not that they starve but starve so dreamlessly,
> Not that they sow that they seldom reap,
> Not that they serve but have no gods to serve,
> Not that they die but that they die like sheep.'

There now, that's your style isn't it? 'Not that they die but that they die like sheep.' Of course for myself I have left pessimism behind: I used to dabble in it when I was a boy and could then afford to dabble in it. But now I think if persevered in too long it hardens and cramps and narrows:

> 'Who loves the rain,
> And loves his home,
> And looks on life with quiet eyes,
> Him will I follow through the storm
> And at his hearth-fire keep me warm;
> Nor hell nor heaven shall that soul surprise
> Who loves the rain
> And loves his home
> And looks on life with quiet eyes.'

There, that's my style!

But I think it is good to write verse for all that. One is sometimes the victim of one's rhymes and has to say what one doesn't mean because the word is necessary to finish the piece. However you are much bolder and sacrifice rhyme to reason. I don't see why you shouldn't. Only, beloved, don't rhyme *Law* and *'tor*, for it suggests that you pronounce the first word *'lor'*. The *R* is the trickiest of letters when you are rhyming.

However ignore all these nasty remarks of mine when we meet as I trust we shall in the summer time when you come to town for your brief interlude betwixt hearty school and heartier holidays with the Aged Parents.

A bloke on board my ship from B.W.I. told me that your Papa was not going to be cashiered under the new Egyptian Govt.[9] but will linger on in state and have charge of the coast guards for many dynasties yet. I trust this is true.

1. Van Zeller's nickname.
2. Belgium had been notorious for its trade in worn-out horses; in 1919 the secretary of the National Equine Defence League wrote to the King of Belgium, asking him to 'prohibit the traffic in old and decrepit horses between England and Belgium' (*The Times*, 13 May 1919, p. 17). On 25 June 1923 questions had been raised in parliament about the export of old horses, though without any specific reference to Belgium.
3. William Reynolds was a boy at the school at this time, and he was a great friend of the van Zellers. His father was Sir James Philip Reynolds Bt. (1865-1932). It is his family that is being referred to here.
4. Dom Anselm Rutherford, since April stationed at St Osburg's, Coventry. He must have paid a brief visit to Downside.
5. The Prince of Wales visited Downside on 18 July 1923.
6. Van Zeller was made a school prefect in 1923; together with the other prefects, he was presented to the Prince of Wales during his visit to the school.
7. Leonard Parker.
8. Perhaps BJ meant 'otherwise'. Salt Lake City was the Mormon capital—an ideal place, as BJ jokingly suggests, for a young man unable to choose between his girl friends, since the Mormons allowed polygamy.
9. Van Zeller's father, Francis van Zeller (1874-1935), was an official of the Egyptian government, in command of the Egyptian coast guard. He finished his career as Governor of the Red Sea Province.

94. *Provincial's Diary. 6 September 1923.*

Spent day at Leicester, inspecting Stoneygate site,[1] discussing with community the 2 plans, interviewing Mrs Price, who wishes to leave £30,000 for the purpose of a new Priory on site of Holy Cross,[2] and talking to F. George Naylor whose mother is there dying. He tells me that he has 2 unmarried sisters and an unmarried brother, the brother is consumptive, one sister looks after him and the mother, the one is at work; it looks as though he could have to become a Chaplain somewhere to support them.

1. The Leicester community was considering the possibility of moving to a new site on the corner of London Road and Victoria Road, adjacent to Victoria Park.
2. Mrs Eliza Dundas Price, in a will made on 12 March 1924, left her estate to her daughter, with the specification that after the daughter's death it was to pass to the Dominicans in Leicester. Mrs Price died in 1934.

95. *Provincial's Diary. 8 September 1923.*

Prior of Leicester[1] writes that Council of the House at Leicester has reversed its decision of March and now plumps for old[2] site:-
March voting was: Council unanimous for new site
                     Chapter only one adverse vote.
Sept 7 voting was: Only one vote in Council in favour of new site.

1. Stephen Fitzgerald.
2. BJ accidentally wrote 'new', but it must be 'old' that is meant.

96. *Notes of a sermon preached at Headington, 9 September 1923.*

God's Will means *everything* to us. It is the only reason for our being at all. When we try to think of God's reason for creating us, or in fact, of anything, we come upon one of the profoundest mysteries. What on earth could God want with us? He was content, infinitely content in his own divine life. Three in One, he had no need of anyone or anything. The only possible reason for us is that we should carry out his will.

When we study the Gospels and see the supreme Character therein spoken of, we find that our blessed Lord practically never let slip an opportunity of showing that he is on earth only to accomplish his Father's will. His first words recorded, 'Did you not know that I must be about my Father's business?'[1] He is astonished that our Lady shouldn't know. 'Didn't you know', he says. I am surprised. Didn't you *know* that is why I have come? And again, 'I am come to do the will of Him who sent me.'[2] And his last words almost, 'It is consummated.'[3] What? The work the Father had given him to do.

It is the same with our blessed Lady, 'Fiat mihi',[4] the expression of her whole life.

But Our Lord does not only see in this life the will of God as such. He is the expression of the Father's tenderness and care of the least thing he has made. He is extraordinarily sensitive to the beauty of the world he sees about him, and it is his Father's world; extraordinarily sensitive to the seemingly cruel and sad things that happen. It is not only to comfort his apostles that he says, 'Not even a sparrow falls to the ground without my heavenly Father willing it.'[5] Mark this well; he does not only say 'God's will', but 'the will of my Father'. This little creature of song lying dead, probably killed by some or other of God's creatures—a trivial thing, perhaps, and yet in its way a tragedy—still, it is by the will of the Father that it has happened, and our blessed Lord seems to find sweetness in the very name of 'Father', and the thought of his Providence brooding over all creation.

For us too, if we would keep a sane view of things in the face of all that is incomprehensible, even sad, and there is so much that is cruel in nature—we must always remember that nothing happens but by the will of the Father and his tender providence rules all.

Then with regard to the work we may be called upon to do, and each one of us has some special work to do for God. God made his plans for us before we came into the world at all—for the work is of primary importance, it comes first in God's thought, and we follow as instruments. When an architect is commissioned to build a house, he has to know first its destined use, its locality, and the weather conditions etc. Every detail must be taken into consideration. Only then can he collect his materials and begin to work. The foundations are very slowly made, with pain and trouble and much work if the building is to endure. Anyone seeing the monks of Buckfast building their church[6] will realise how work done for God should be done— each brick carefully shaped, lovingly put in its prepared place—all done quietly, without haste. Not only is it a labour of love, but each moment is a prayer—'laborare est orare'[7]—for the building is to last as long as the ancient churches endured—the more trouble and work, the greater the endurance. So it is with our souls.

God is the architect. He has made our souls a certain size and shape, to fit certain holes, so to speak. It is not for us to say that we are incapable, or unfitted for the work given to us. That is not only to criticize ourselves, which wouldn't matter at all, but it is to criticize God. If meant, it is a blasphemy. He has placed us in a certain position, and if he wants us to do a certain work, we *shall* do it. If he doesn't, we shan't. In any case, it is not for us to judge, but to obey his will. The doing of his will is not only the reason for all our Lord's life, but of our life, of *all* life. In its accomplishment lies the fulness of life. 'Now this is eternal life—that we may know thee.'[8] The will of God is made known to us through the interplay of our own interior impulses and desires, and our exterior circumstances. Why, for instance, are we here? Why have we come into this Order? Well, we felt an impulse, a something we couldn't resist—it seemed to answer to something in us. And have we found just what we desired and hoped for? Well, no, not exactly. It is not quite what we thought. Some things are different—some better, some worse. Nothing is ever quite what we anticipated. There is the interplay of circumstances on our desires. It makes known to us what is God's will for us; and so we give up in our desires what does not fit in with God's plan for us, content to do as he wishes.

I dare say we have all seen an old woman driving a hen. She stands, with her dress held out, trying to get the hen into the open door of the hen-house. But, for some reason or other, the hen doesn't seem to see the open door and she gets terribly excited, all her feathers get ruffled and she makes any amount of dust and fuss, clacking away, with the old lady behind trying to show her in. She hops up and down and beats herself against the netting, and it never seems to occur to her to go through the wide-open door. Then, suddenly, she realises and sees the door. All her feathers go down and she walks in quite quietly, without another sound. Well, God is rather like the old woman. He drives us. He blocks our way. We try one path, and then we come to a stop—it is a cul-de-sac. God is blocking us, and we have either to go back, or to the right or left, and find another path . We go down that, and again God blocks it, and so on , until at last God gets us into *our way*. It may seem unnecessary, all this going backwards and forwards, but it isn't. It is God's way of showing his will for us.

In the same way God allows our faults and temptations. But surely God cannot want me to have such a weakness, temptation? Oh yes. He does. He made each of us with our individual character and its difficulties. If we look back we can see how through all our lives it has been the same thing—so we can't help it, can we? For some reason, God has given these things to us to enable us to carry out his will. We must remember that circumstances are always favourable to God's plan, always, always. To our own, no, very fortunately for us. God does not always give us our desires, at any rate not now. He may later on—in ten years, or a hundred. But what seems to us so unfortunate is the best possible thing in God's plan, and so we must never look back. 'No man setting his hand to the plough and looking back is worthy of the kingdom of heaven.'[9]

Never look forward to the future with anxiety. 'Be not solicitous. Consider the lilies'.[10] The present is the will of God. Therefore no over-compunction for past faults, no worrying over the future, no anxious peerings into the darkness. 'Watchman, what of the night?'[11] We can safely leave all that in God's hands. They are the hands not only of a clever, but of a wise architect, and all power is in them. In our Lord's last hour, when he seemed utterly forsaken, and gave that cry, 'My God, my God, why hast thou forsaken me?',[12] even then he yet realised that it was by his Father's will that he suffered, and presently, when dying, again cried out, 'Father, into thy hands I commend my spirit.'[13]

Whatever happens to us through God's will is always the best possible thing for us. God is not only good, very good, supremely good, but the only good. Therefore his will is and must be always the best for us.

It often seems otherwise. For instance the man born blind whom our blessed Lord cured.[14] Think what it means to be born blind. He could do nothing for himself, except what he had learned with great labour and trouble. It must have seemed the worst possible thing to him. Think of him as a child, a boy with all his strength for, as far as we know, he was otherwise perfectly healthy, his pent-up energy, and he couldn't walk, ride or swim without someone coming to help and guide him, and tell him which way to go. If you described the beauty of a flower, or the bloom of a fruit, to him, it meant nothing; he was born blind. Horrible, hideous—and yet, what does our Lord say? The apostles, seeing him, said, 'Lord, who has sinned, this man or his parents that he should be born blind?' Of course they put it down to sin (the Pharisees had a doctrine that a man could sin even in his mother's womb), and our Lord said, 'Neither hath this man sinned, nor his parents, but that the works of God should be made manifest in him.' It was just the fact of his being born blind that made the glory of God so manifest. 'It has never been heard of since the world began that a man born blind hath received his sight.' Others, yes, but never one born blind. So just what seemed so cruel to him turned out to be this wonderful miracle, making manifest the glory of God.

So we see that all circumstances, however adverse they seem to be to us, are always favourable to God's plan, always, always, as to the blind man, the best thing for us.

His hands are strong and powerful hands and we can confidently rest there. Can we not sometimes see in the hands of a clever artist, or surgeon, the strength and deftness expressive of the mind that directs their action? But with God, they are not only the hands of power, and not only the hands of wisdom, but of love, and it is only when we leave all things in his hands that we find complete serenity; and then a great peace shall come into our souls.

Every night at Compline we say these beautiful words, 'In manus tuas, Domine, commendo spiritum meum.'[15] That is what we should say at the close of every action of every day, of all our life. It is a perfect prayer of confidence, of trust in the Father, whose tender providence broods over all his creatures. 'Into thy hands.' Where better than in the hands of our Father? And so let us into his hands commend our spirits, and all that our spirits hold most dear. 'In manus tuas, Domine, commendo spiritum meum.'

1. Luke 2:49.
2. John 6:38.
3. John 19:30.
4. Luke 1:38 ('Be it done to me . . . ').
5. Matthew 10:29.
6. Work on the building of the church had started in 1906 and was still going on. The church was consecrated in 1932.
7. 'To work is to pray' (a conventional adage).
8. John 17:3.

9. Luke 9:62.
10. Matthew 6:25, 28.
11. Isaiah 21:11.
12. Matthew 27:46.
13. Luke 25:46, quoting Psalm 30:6 (Vulgate).
14. John 9.
15. 'Into your hands, Lord, I commend my spirit' (from the responsory used at Compline).

97. *Harold J. Laski to BJ. From the London School of Economics and Political Science. 25 October 1923. Autograph.*

I have undertaken to edit a History of European Social Thought for Messrs Benn Bros. and I am anxious, if it is at all possible, to induce you to write a volume for the series. They are to consist of books about 90,000 words in length to sell at half-a-guinea. . . .

I hope you will write a volume on Social Thought in the Middle Ages, along the lines of your admirable essay on medieval socialism.[1] I know no one living who can do this so well, and I should be much honoured by your co-operation. I thought of 12-18 months as a period in which the book might be written.[2] . . .

1. *Medieval Socialism*, London 1913.
2. BJ did contribute a volume to Laski's series: *Social Theories of the Middle Ages*, London 1926.

98. *W. J. Cusack[1] to BJ. From Kempton Manor, Bedford. 19 November 1923. Autograph.*

I rather dread to take up your time knowing the many claims that must be made upon you, but I should like to refer to you a difficulty. Three years ago, Canon Freeland our Vicar General and Diocesan Theologian[2] gave me a copy of the 'Meditations for Layfolk'.[3] I have read one every day since with great comfort, and I hope with profit—certainly with gratitude to the Author. But there is one meditation—The Catholicity of the Church p. 160—that startled me the first time I read it, and it continues to startle me.

After reading it the first time I read it aloud to Mrs Cusack, her sister, and a friend that lives with us. It produced the same impression on them that it had done on me. I then asked Mgr Freeland to read it, and his impressions were the same. Briefly, the impression is this:-

After demonstrating in Parts I and II the Catholicity of the Church you come to Part III.[4]

The Church is Catholic—To that Church I myself belong. Catholic then must be the whole temper of my mind. There must be in me none of that narrowness that would limit the Spirit of God to one single fashion, nor would grudge my neighbour his own way of achieving the purpose of his existence. The liberty I claim for myself, I should gladly concede to others: for, after all, the Church is large enough to include all. If every nation under heaven can find protection under its shadow who am I to dictate to my brother how he should serve God? <Why should I presume to tell an Anglican or a Methodist or a Presbyterian or a Calvinist that he must do as I do, and adhere to the Catholic faith? God does not bind Himself to give grace only in one way.> The self centred spirit of man is too easily persuaded that it alone has found the perfect way, not realizing that what is the way of one, need not be the way of another. Let me then be wide minded enough not to question or be scandalized in my brother. The silly parochialism that would reduce all to one dead level has no part or lot in the Kingdom of God. <We are all aiming at Heaven—what does it matter what boat we sail in so long as we get into harbour?>

I admit that this is not what is meant—I admit that it is not said—and I also admit that it is unfair to garble and interline the text as I have done. But I also think that this impression does irresistibly come to the untrained reader. If the same thoughts and words had occurred in a meditation on some other subject, such as the 'variety of devotions in the Church' or something of that character no dissenting thoughts would have arisen, but it seems as if after making the point of the Catholicity of the Church, the obligation to belong to it is gratuitously surrendered and the world is invited to serve God and work out its own salvation under the conditions in which each individual is born.

Annotated on the back in BJ's hand: 'There is the obvious limit of the Catholic Faith---Within the Church there is also the dogmatic teaching which none may with safety deny---But apart from these fixed truths there are paths and bypaths which each can follow for himself---I must not grudge others.'[5]

1. We have been unable to discover anything about the Cusack family.
2. John Freeland (1861-1940), priest at Bedford, where the Cusacks lived, from 1906-1924. Canon theologian since 1910 and vicar general since 1922.
3. Bede Jarrett, *Meditations for Layfolk*, London 1915 and often reprinted.
4. The next paragraph is a quotation from *Meditations* p. 161, with interpolations by Cusack. The interpolations are identified here by being enclosed within angular brackets (< .... >).
5. BJ's note of his reply consists simply of a passage from the text (also on p. 161), which Cusack had omitted.

99. Provincial's Diary. 27 December 1923.

Went to Laxton Hall for day, met F. Jerome[1] at Wakerley Station and walked and saw over it.

1. Jerome Rigby, appointed headmaster of the school by the 1920 Provincial Chapter; he was destined to preside over the school's move to Laxton in 1924 and to become the first headmaster and superior there.

100. *BJ to John Leather OP.*[1] *From St Dominic's, London. 6 January 1924. Autograph.*

(1) Every best wish for the New Year to you all.
(2) F. Humbert[2] who's settling Byker's business writes to me that the Fathers there cannot get off till Jan 15, when therefore you may expect F. Bugeja.
(3) F. Knapp writes to me (a) that he is very ill, (b) that he asked you to let him off sermons till Lent when he's to be very busy, (c) that you have refused him and put him down to preach every Sunday (including Dec 30) in January—except for St Sebastian's Day.[3] I know you well enough to know that you must have some reason for this seeming harshness and write to ask it if I may. He had previously asked me not to send him out till Lent and I agreed.[4]
(4) Fr O'Leary of Woolwich (F.T.L.'s[5] nephew, you'll remember him) to whom Frs Knapp and Bugeja go for Lent or 3 weeks of it, has asked me whether they could take a 5/- intention Mass each day—I presume only one of them—and I have answered that you will be grateful. Is this correct? . . .

1. Prior of St Sebastian's, Pendleton.
2. Humbert Everest. He was making final arrangements for the Dominicans to hand the parish of Byker, Newcastle, over to the diocese. Bugeja was one of the priests assigned there; when the brethren left Byker, he was due to be assigned to Pendleton.
3. St Sebastian's day (30 January) fell on a Wednesday in 1924, but it was customary to celebrate it on the preceding Sunday, since it was the patronal feast of the parish. This practice was established soon after the priory was opened in 1901. Certainly in 1902 Humbert Everest was invited to preach on St Sebastian on 26 January, as we learn from the Hawkesyard chronicle.
4. Knapp was one of the priests officially deputed by the province to 'mission' work; that is to say, he was available to be sent by the provincial to undertake any kind of preaching work, such as parish missions, anywhere in the country. It was normal for invitations to give missions and special sermons and retreats to be sent to the provincial, who appointed someone to take them up.
5. Thomas Laws. His nephew was Augustine O'Leary, parish priest of Woolwich.

101. *BJ to John Leather OP. From St Dominic's, London. 11 January 1924. Autograph.*

(1) Thanks for approving of my 5/- intention offer from Woolwich.[1]
(2) From all accounts, F. Henry[2] has the makings of a very good preacher. F. Dunstan[3] and F. Humbert[4] both speak of his fire and enthusiasm and his fluency. I really think that he will do well. From *March 23 to April 13*, he'll make his debut in a mission with F. Knapp

at Woolwich. I shall employ him as much as I can: but you spoke of invitations you had received for a preacher so that I shall be glad of anything you can give him. He's very easy to live with and most obliging. F. Paul[5] sang his praises as well as F. Dunstan. But if you do give him any sermons just let me know and I will insert them in my book and so prevent any overlapping. As long as he is free from any engagement of my making for him, you are at perfect liberty to give him any work you like.

(3) Thanks for inviting me for March 2nd.[6] I will certainly come if I can but I am not sure whether I can fit it in or not. You will probably have all sorts of other people there and I shan't be missed! However if I can I will.

(4) As regards F. Knapp,[7] I wrote to you of course because he had appealed to me; whenever this happens, I cannot help myself from applying to the local superior to ask the reason of the action that has occasioned the appeal. Your answer really is that you consider 'his request extravagant' because you do not think he is as ill as he makes himself out to be. That is always a difficulty. Both S. Augustine and the Constitutions say that the sick man must be believed, unless one has very serious reasons for thinking otherwise:[8] the Constitutions particularly urge that one should err rather by kindness than by severity in dealing with sick people.[9] As one who is very seldom sick, I have always felt that I was in a difficult position. It is so easy for the sick man to get upset, contrasting his sickness with the health of the person who refuses his request, and to work himself into a state of distress. There are Priors whose names you will easily guess who have occasioned considerable unhappiness amongst their subjects by this attitude and I only make bold to mention this to you because I do think that one cannot be too careful. I am writing to F. Knapp to say that I have heard from you and that I think you have taken all reasonable precautions and have done very much for him. Nevertheless this is one of the type of things I find so hard to settle[10] in my own mind with justice and kindness.

Forgive my seeming interference: but it is part of this unpleasant provincialate.

1. See above, no. 100.
2. Henry Bugeja, a Maltese priest who had been in England since 1921.
3. Dunstan Sargent, who had lived with Bugeja at Byker.
4. Humbert Everest.
5. Paul Weeks, who had lived with Bugeja at Byker.
6. The silver jubilee of the Dominicans' arrival in Pendleton and the silver jubilee of John Leather's ordination. BJ was to preach special sermons in the priory church, and a memorial window was to be unveiled.
7. See above, no. 100.
8. *Rule of St Augustine* 5.6, edited in G. Lawless, *Augustine of Hippo and his Monastic Rule*, Oxford 1987, p. 96. There is nothing about this in the Constitutions.

9. This is rather an exaggeration of what is said either in the 1872 Constitutions (Const. 166-168) or in the 1923 draft (Const. 333-337), the main difference between the two texts being that the 1923 draft no longer requires that a prior who is inattentive to the sick must be removed from office. However, a section in Humbert of Romans' commentary on the Rule, ed. J. J. Berthier, vol. I pp. 104-106, is headed 'kindness towards the sick is more important than severity'.
10. BJ actually wrote 'so hard so settle'.

102. *Provincial's Diary. 16 January 1924.*

Went with F. McNabb to Laxton.

103. *G. G. Coulton to BJ. From Cambridge. 5 February 1924. Autograph.*

I have just found time to read your review, and sit down at once to thank you very sincerely for it. I sent the book[1] at your request, not for commercial reasons but because I felt sure, whether you reviewed it yourself or deputed it, that I should not be sniped from behind a hedge, and that I should learn something from a competent critic who dissented from my own point of view. I have now learned much more than this; you have given me a lesson in charity, for you have gone further out of your way to praise me—exceptis excipiendis—than my personal friends. . . .

1. G. G. Coulton, *Five Centuries of Religion*, vol. I, Cambridge 1923. Reviewed by BJ in *Blackfriars* 4 (1923-24) pp. 1365-78.

104. *Memorandum submitted by BJ to the Provincial Council for its meeting on 8 February 1924. Autograph.*

I wish to submit to the Provincial Council and to ask their permission to buy Laxton Hall in the county and diocese of Northamptonshire and to transfer there the school from Hawkesyard, to remain dominantly a school for boys who intend to become Dominicans but to include other boys as well.

Laxton Hall is a large stone building, about 80 years old, in very good condition, with water supply, electric light, central heating, telephone, drains of modern equipment, all either recently installed or recently overhauled. The building includes over 30 bedrooms, several spacious reception rooms, a library which is 55 feet long, stone built stables, greenhouses, and 50 acres of land,—the cost being £4000. It is stated that the reason of this low price is that it is not good hunting country, that the size of the place is difficult because of the servant-shortage, and that it is rather remote. It is just under 3 miles from the nearest station, and though a very good centre for trains from all parts is a distance varying from 4 miles to 8 miles and fourteen from the nearest stations whence fast trains can be caught.

Further it should be stated that more land could be bought at £20 an acre and that there is building stone only a few feet under the soil.

Laxton in in the Peterborough, Stamford, Kettering district and within 6 miles both of Uppingham and Oundle schools.

Reasons for transferring

(1) Birmingham diocese objects to our receivings boys not going on for the order;[1] yet these boys to some extent make the school pay and have sometimes become Dominicans in the end.

(2) Difficulty of the House of Studies and the school being in the same establishment and (nominally) under one head is experienced indeed only now and then, and is a difficulty that is superable. Nevertheless the school has to be fitted into the Study House as far as hours of divine office are concerned. We should replace this by 2 separate Priories, each with its own purpose only to consider, as London Priory or Newcastle or Leicester can arrange their hours etc to suit their particular work, i.e. the parish.

(3) Laxton would become a Priory, with divine office (eventually) and sung Compline by the boys every night. At present there are five fathers at work in the School, almost a Community:- Frs Peter, Jerome, Kevin, Clement, Stanislaus.[2]

(4) This would prevent overmuch familiarity with the novices and the Province generally, and yet not leave the boys wholly ignorant (as it is stated they were at Hinckley) of the life as we live it in England.

(5) It would set free the Park at Hawkesyard and the playing field for novices who need it badly and have no other really level ground.

(6) It would set the school on a permanent, efficient basis, and give it a chance to be self-supporting. The Bishop[3] writes unofficially a letter full of welcome. He would be very glad of us in the diocese. We would be restarting Catholicism in that district which only lapsed 70 years ago.[4]

How is the Money to be raised?

(1) It is proposed to borrow £6000 to cover cost, moving, expenses of adaptation etc.

(2) To borrow this on a short loan for one year at 5½ per cent (this works out at about 4½% net, deducting 4/6 in the £1 for income tax) and then after some experience has been gained in the new surroundings to raise the loan of £6000 at 7½% which will mean

repayment of capital as well as interest, and extinction of debt in 20 years. (Mr Bellord[5] tells me he can arrange these loans for us).

(3) To effect this, the school would have to lose the services of its present lay master . . . and would retain the salary paid him, namely £240 per annum. Moreover the school has repaid more than £250 each year of its loan to the Priory borrowed by authorisation of Prov. Council in 1921.[6]. It would seem therefore that the School could carry this new burden without taking more money from the Province than it does at present.

(4) The building would be able to take between 70 and 100 boys, and the increase in numbers would mean a growing increase of profits. The rates and taxes on it at present are however under £200 a year (at Hawkesyard the school pays £136, its share of the rates and taxes of the whole establishment). So that while the larger accommodation and the freedom from the restraints imposed by the Birmingham diocese would enable us to take more boys the expenses would not be considerably above the present expenses except (a) heating, (b) lighting, due to the very much larger building to be heated and lit.

It will be seen however that this financial prophecy is largely guesswork, because we have no figures to go on as to cost and upkeep of Laxton. The figures of the owner, Col. Wyndham,[7] who only left it last November, even if available, would not be much guide.

Consequently it must be admitted that our hopefulness in the scheme depends on an act of faith in the capacity of F. Jerome to pull off this financial scheme. Frs Hugh, Vincent, and Humbert[8] have seen the house, as well as F. Jerome and myself, and I think we are all agreed that it is a bargain at the price and that we are not likely to get so good a place so cheaply again. We intend to incur no unnecessary expense, to make no great stir at the beginning, to proceed warily and gradually to open out the school.

But if we look ahead, I think we shall realise that this venture is really necessary to the establishment of the Province. It is a venture. There can be no doubt of that. But with the school, even in its present restricted way, already holding 42 boys and practically full, we have every prospect of securing a large increase of numbers. It in only a prospect truly, but a not improbable one.

Nor should anyone think, after the allocution of the Master General (*Nov. Dec. 1923 p. 260 Analecta*)[9] at the solemn Profession of the Head of the Lacordaire Teaching Congregation (now a Congragation of the First Order),[10] that a school such as we[11] propose is against the spirit of the order. The Master General uses two phrases about the teaching of boys: (a) 'qui n'est pas nouveau' in the order and (b) 'une des formes les plus fécondes et les plus nécessaires de l'apostolat.'

That it is traditional and that it is a fruitful and necessary apostolate in the eyes of the Master General is enough for us.[12]

1. Cf. above, no. 74.
2. Peter Reader, Jerome Rigby, Kevin Clark, Clement Feeley, Stanislaus Lamb.
3. Dudley Charles Cary-Elwes.
4. There had been a priest living at King's Cliffe, which is not far from Laxton, until 1855, but since then there had been no resident Catholic priest in the vicinity.
5. The province's lawyer.
6. The Council was consulted by post about this loan at the end of May 1921.
7. Lt. Col. Edward Scawen Wyndham (1883-1967), who had bought Laxton Park some years earlier. He was the son of the 2nd Baron Leconfield, and in 1963 he succeeded his brother to become himself the 5th Baron.
8. Hugh Pope, Vincent McNabb, Humbert Everest.
9. *Analecta S.O.P.* 16 (1923-24) pp. 260-261.
10. Lacordaire had founded his teaching congregation in France in 1852, consisting of men who made profession as Dominican tertiaries. On 8 December 1923 the head of this congregation made solemn profession as a Dominican friar, and the congregation was absorbed into the Order.
11. BJ actually wrote 'such we'.
12. BJ was perhaps indulging to some extent in wishful thinking; anyway, he received a letter from the Irish provincial, Finbar Ryan, expressing incredulity about the attitude of the Master General, who had not shown himself particularly enthusiastic about the school run by the Irish province at Newbridge.

105. *Provincial Council Book. In BJ's hand. 8 February 1924.*

LAXTON HALL. Present Frs Vincent McNabb, Everest, Bracey, Thomson, Jarrett. Long discussion from 9.30 to 12.59 ending in 2 proposals:
(1) It is desirable that the school be moved to a diocese where we shall be authorised to receive boys other than those going on for the Order (5 white votes).
(2) It is prove possible to raise a loan of £7000 at 5½% on which only interest shall be payable for not more than 3 (three) years, and subsequently interest and capital in instalments at 7½ per cent, it is agreed to purchase Laxton Hall for sum of £4000 and to raise a loan of £7000 to include expenses for transfer and alterations (5 white votes).

106. *Provincial's Diary. 9 February 1924.*

Bishop of Galloway[1] wrote asking us to take over Annan Mission and dependencies at £4000 debt, with a population of 700 over an area of 6 miles by 40 miles, possessing only one school at which average attendance is 14 children. Wrote back expressing doubts.

1. James McCarthy.

107. *Provincial's Diary. 19 February 1924.*

Interviewed Bishop of Galloway (on his way to Palestine on pilgrimage) at Archbishop's House, Westminster. I told him that we had 2 things to be sure about: (i) that whatever place we take must have at least remotely the prospect of becoming a Priory, (ii) that we were not financially in a condition to support any place we took over from any central fund of Province and that we were therefore compelled to take only such a place as was self-supporting. He answered that to safeguard (i) we should take Gretna, large Govt buildings for sale, 8 miles from Carlisle, of which becoming a residential suburb, but must take over whole debt of £4000 for without Gretna, Annan could not support debt.

108. *Provincial's Diary. 22 February 1924.*

Wrote to V.G. of Galloway[1] refusing Annan at present.

1. Daniel O'Brien, Vicar General since 1906.

109. *Provincial's Diary. 28 February 1924.*

Heard from Master General that he and his Council approve of transferring school from Hawkesyard to Laxton Hall, Northants. Bishop and Chapter of Northampton have already approved and welcomed us. Bank will lend money at 4% for 2 years and after that draw up scheme for repayment of interest and capital. The School is to be dominantly for boys going on for the Order, but open to everyone we care to take. What will it lead to? We shall be the largest establishment in the diocese. Will it mean that one day Norwich will be offered us?

110. *Provincial's Diary. 18 March 1924.*

Signed contract for Laxton with F. Vincent[1] as witness.

1. Vincent McNabb.

111. *Provincial's Diary. 25 March 1924.*

Met Jerome[1] and Sir Albert Ball[2] at Leicester, and we were motored to Laxton where staked out the 50 acres. We agreed that we would take over pay of gardener and electrician, from now, but should continue to pay through Sir Albert till we take possession on June 24. Meanwhile he's to take from garden whatever he wishes.

1. Jerome Rigby.
2. Who had bought Laxton Hall from Col. Wyndham.

112. *BJ to Aidan Elrington OP. From Grayshott. 11 April 1924. Autograph.*

Very strongly approve of your plan.[1] If I can get to Oxford from Hove on Thursday[2] and back shall come but doubt it. Have sermons.[3] Please see that done.

1. Elrington had written to BJ on 9 April with a suggestion about the placing of the windows on the top floor of Blackfriars, which he thought would gain some extra living space in the rooms. On the same day he explained to the architect, 'A student has only *one* room for everything, and it is imperative to get him as much space as possible.' However on 12 April he wrote to BJ again to say that the builder had discovered what appeared to be an insuperable difficulty in the proposed arrangement.
2. There was to be a meeting with the architect on Thursday 16 April.
3. Sermons to preach, that is.

113. *Provincial's Diary. 27 April 1924.*

MASS SAID FOR FIRST TIME AT LAXTON BY FRS JEROME AND KEVIN.[1]

1. Jerome Rigby, Kevin Clark.

114. *BJ to Mrs Tytus.*[1] *Place and date uncertain, but c. May 1924. Autograph.*

. . . that you have done for me this 4 years in which I have held office. They began on June 29 1920;[2] since then Oxford has had its foundation stone and far more than that, dreams solidifying, walls rising, a city of God built in a little place but with a great radiance, we can surely hope, of light and heat. Can I ever forget how much of that is owing to you? You who found as well as founded the place? Nor has your care of it or interest in it ever faltered, and, whenever my courage oozed, have always given me back again my courage. Don't think that I forget or alter. You remember Cosimo de'Medici, when he was told that it was no use building so finely in Florence since the fickle populace would drive him into exile and forget him, answering so well: *I may be driven out and forgotten but my buildings shall remain.*³ True of you surely.

1. On 20 July 1934 Bernard Delany went to visit Mrs Tytus, who was by now seriously ill, and, as he reported to John Baptist Reeves, 'I managed to get from her maid this bundle of letters. There are loads of others, but stored with other belongings of hers.' The province never did manage to retrieve the other letters. The one edited here is only a fragment, whose first sheet is missing. The date is therefore conjectural.
2. The date on which BJ was re-elected provincial.
3. Cf. BJ, *S. Antonino and Mediaeval Economics* pp. 33-34: 'Cynically enough, he admitted his use of the arts to be but an instrument of government: "I know the humours of this city, fifty years will not pass before we are driven out; but the buildings will remain."'

115. *Provincial's Diary. 20 June 1924.*

Paid cheque for £4275 to Bellord to purchase Laxton Hall.

116. *Provincial's Diary. 4 July 1924.*

Signed the purchase deed of Laxton Hall.

117. *Provincial's Diary. 14 July 1924.*

Present at 'break up' of School at Hawkesyard, concert in School, farces, speeches. Felt like a murderer slaughtering a school.

118. *Provincial's Diary. 18 July 1924.*

Assigned F. Reeves to Hawkesyard¹ . . .
   Frs Jerome, Kevin, Clement, Walter, Stanislaus, Adrian, Bernard² to Laxton.

1. Having failed to get his B. Litt. in Oxford in 1924, John Baptist Reeves was sent back to Hawkesyard to resume working on his lectorate. This too was abandoned after a year.
2. Jerome Rigby (superior and headmaster), Kevin Clark, Clement Feeley, Walter Gumbley, Stanislaus Lamb, Adrian English, Bernard Delany. The first five were already teachers at the school at Hawkesyard. English had been doing a B.Sc. at London University, in view of his teaching science at the school. Delany had just finished a B.Litt. in Oxford.

119. *Provincial's Diary. 19 July 1924.*

Exodus to Laxton of Frs Jerome, Kevin, Stanislaus.

120. *Provincial's Diary. 22 July 1924.*

Arrived myself at Laxton.

121. *Provincial's Diary. 24 July 1924.*

Read in F. Jerome as Vicar, and assignations of F. Kevin and F. Stanislaus at Laxton.

122. *Provincial's Diary. 25 July 1924.*

Deeds of Laxton arrived at Laxton.

123. *Provincial's Diary. 4 September 1924.*

Heard from F. Cuthbert Bretherton's brother that F. C. B. is on way home invalided from B. W. I.[1] and due to arrive Sept 6. First I've heard of it! Also F. Moss wrote to me and asked to come home because ill.[2] I answered he was to await election of Provincial 'who no doubt would follow Doctor's orders'.[3] I get a letter from him today (dated Aug 9th) that he's grateful for my letter and is coming home at once 'obeying doctor's orders'. These people are too much for me. I can deal with people who play the game. I can't deal with folk like this: 'The sons of Sarvia are too strong for me.'[4] It's bad for the Province to have me in command. It needs not a Provincial but a Policeman.

1. Bretherton was assigned to Grenada.
2. Moss had been in South Africa since 1921. He had asked BJ to be sent there, although BJ warned him that it would not suit him. 'I asked for South Africa in sheer despair, because I could not face an English winter, and I thought it was hot out here' (Moss to BJ, 9 August 1924). He wrote several times to BJ during 1924, expressing his worries over his health. On 9 August he wrote thanking him for his letter of 16 July telling him, 'Just do what the doctors say'. He had gone at once to the doctor, as soon as the letter arrived on 8 August, and the doctor had told him, 'Get off at once'. He enclosed the doctor's certificate with his letter. He had evidently not understood BJ to be telling him to wait until the Provincial Chapter.
3. The Provincial Chapter was due to begin on 17 November.
4. 2 Samuel 3:39.

124. *Provincial's Diary. 8 December 1924.*

By Sept. 30: 1924 the state of Province debts was as follows:[1]

Loans. Carisbrooke	£5000:0:0
Hinckley	£400:0:0
Pend. Sinking Fund[2]	£64:17:2
Buckler	£23:1:11
Deposits which need investing	£12:12:1
Deposits which may be called in	£548:12:7½
Creditors in small sums	£116:5:0
Capital money that should have been invested and has been used for income	£3338:1:1

1. BJ had been spending the weekend at Carisbrooke, where the provincial bursar was assigned, and had been looking over the accounts. For most of the items llisted, see above, no. 65.
2. The original 'Sinking Fund' was one set up by the British Government in 1717, a capital investment whose interest was meant to 'sink' (pay off) the National Debt. By analogy, the English Dominicans set up sinking funds from time to time, by which a house of the province could make a capital investment in the province, from which it would receive interest, to pay off its own debts. A sinking fund for Pendleton was set up in May 1912. If the province failed to invest funds like this which were deposited with it, they were to that extent treated as provincial debts; this applies to most of the remaining items listed here by BJ.

125. *BJ to Mrs Campbell. No address. 30 December 1924. Transcript.*

It is a good thing to know one gets into the prayers of other people and helps one to know that one is further dispensed from praying for oneself, a dull process that one's glad to be rid of. But to be remembered by others saves time and restores one's self-respect— and to be remembered so often and so regularly allows one to fold one's arms and laze one's way to heaven. So thank you indeed.

I'm glad the book of Letters is out,[1] as a kind of herald to the Royal Book itself,[2] and I do hope it will sell well. Let's hope it's well advertised, for Letters usually sell well. They're human and helpful and stored so often with neat phrases that sum up so much in such small compass. I'll do my best to talk about 'em to God and man: 'We must do the 100th part ourselves'.

The Rosary I can get interested in always by making it intercessory, taking a general intention for each decade connected with the mystery and saying each Hail Mary for one person connected with that intention: Annunciation for all who get bad nerves today, parents, children, priests etc., or Visitation for 10 people whom I know to be travelling, or Nativity for 10 children I know etc. But I suppose each finds his own fashion. . . .

All good things for 1925 to both.

1. W. E. Campbell, ed., *The Last Letters of Bl. Thomas More*, London 1924.
2. Presumably a reference to the projected complete edition of More's English works, of which the first (and only) two volumes appeared in 1931, London and New York. The first volume contained 'The History of Richard III' inter alia.

126. *BJ to Aidan Elrington OP. From Pendleton.[1] 22 January 1925. Autograph.*

I haven't an idea of what the roof looks like nor how the tank placed there will appear: but I leave that to you and to Bell's[2] counsel or rather Williams's.[3] If he approves so do I. The geyser and bath room as a whole may as well be finished off now or at least when the place is ready for it. The sooner the house is evacuated the better for all concerned. I shall hope on my return in Easter week to see the house all swept and garnished, and the Chapel and Tower on a fair way to external completion. With Webb's[4] plans and Williams' leadership we should do well.

As for what's to happen when I am abroad, F. Humbert[5] will be in my place and you will deal with him as you have dealt with me. He'll have all power to decide.

I shall hope to call in for a night during the Reeves Pope week in February;[6] but you will be hard up for rooms. As it will mean a late retirement after the lectures I can't propose to stay either with the Baroness or anyone up there,[7] I shall probably crave hospitality from F. McCann[8] who's always inviting me to stay with 'em.

However---

1. BJ was visitating the community at Pendleton; on 22 January he attended the funeral of Bishop Casartelli.
2. F. Bell of the Andover Building Works, the main contractor for the building of Blackfriars, Oxford.
3. J. L. Williams, Chartered Quantity Surveyor, Birmingham. Williams was in charge when the architect was in Ibiza each winter.
4. The architect, E. Doran Webb.
5. Humbert Everest. BJ was going to Rome to preach the Lent at S. Susanna; he was away from 23 February until 17 April.
6. John Baptist Reeves and Hugh Pope were due to give a series of 8 conferences in the Town Hall, Oxford, beginning on 17 February.
7. Baroness Frances de Paravicini, who now lived at Priory Cottage, next door to the Dominican nuns in Headington. Mrs Davies also lived in one of the cottages there.
8. The Master of St Benet's Hall.

127. *BJ to Aidan Elrington OP. From St Dominic's, London. 10 February 1925. Autograph.*

(1) By your discretion and Williams', please settle which geyser and bath.
(2) Hand basin to be included in fixture of bathroom.
(3) Can not hand basin and bath in bathroom *now* be used?
(4) How is geyser pipe to allow escape of gas-fumes to be settled as to appearance outside?
(5) Already told Miss Davenport that clock will be refixed in new tower. She wrote before.[1]
(6) Please sign and forward to J. B.[2] to sign and post so as to have dividends paid direct to bank.

Dreadful pile of letters!

1. 62 St Giles was the property of the Davenport family until the Dominicans bought it. The Miss Davenport referred to by BJ must be one of the nieces of Miss Susanna Davenport who had lived there until her death in 1917.

2. John Baptist Reeves. It is not known what the documents were that BJ is referring to. They may have had something to do with some investments that BJ had bought from the community in Leicester to add to Oxford's endowment (letter to Elrington, 17 June 1924), about which he wrote to Elrington again on 30 January 1925 to tell him that the dividends were paid in February and March and then again in September and October.

128. *BJ to Edmund Bellord. From Rome. 5 March 1925. Autograph.*

Your letter has just reached me and I feel that I must just say how much I feel for you all in this distress.[1] She had made so gallant a fight for these many months that somehow one began almost to be secure about her or at least no longer to believe in dates and threatenings of dates; least of all did I think that the operation would do more than allay her distress. It has indeed done that for her; it has given her peace, eternal peace.

For you I am sure it will mean even more than you can guess for she has been the centre of your life, even beyond your knowing. All your thoughts have come back to her. Almost her sickness has increased this. But you must be grateful to God that He spared you to be of such help to her, for had she gone like that after you had been taken so many of her happy hours and days would have been denied her. It was good that you were able to hold out in courage, in cheerfulness and hope to the last. It was good that you were able to see that she had all that human skill could provide not only to cure her but to spare her pain. Nothing possible was denied her, even this last operation on which she had set her heart. I saw that you were uncertain; it was her desire that made you surrender against the instinct of your affection that made you feel how unfit she was to face a shock of that sort.

Had I known earlier in the week I would have come over for the funeral. I have not time now to cross over and get back by Sunday; but you may be sure that she will not be forgotten in my Mass. She shall have my Jubilee Plenary Indulgence[2] for such as it may be worth.

One likes to[3] think of Charlie's[4] smile and the double happiness and the Divine Friend over all.

I am sure the memory of her holiness and her courage will be a constant inspiration to her children, and that the living remembrance of it they will not willingly let die.

May God be with you all to comfort you and give you strength to face what yet remains!

1. Bellord had written to BJ to say that his wife had just died.
2. During the Holy Year of 1925, proclaimed by Pius XI, visitors to Rome could obtain a plenary indulgence, on the usual conditions (*Acta Apostolicae Sedis* 16 (1924) pp. 209-215).
3. BJ actually wrote 'of' instead of 'to'.
4. Charles Bellord, Edmund's son, who had died in 1918.

129. *BJ to George Bellord. From Rome. 10 March 1925. Autograph.*

I hardly like to write and yet I feel I must send you a line of sympathy with you in the shock of your mother's going. No one could really wish her pilgrimage prolonged on such terms of pain as she then had when I was leaving and I do not suppose that these lessened any more between that and the operation. So that I can't help thinking that there was almost a feeling of relief on your part when the end came. It was pitiful to have to see so much pain.

From your earliest days as I knew you, you had always an enormous worship for your Mother, and I think she deserved thoroughly every act of reverence and love you ever showed. It must be some comfort however to remember this. Once I suggested in Bruges your not spending so much money on a present for your mother: 'Nothing can be too good for her' was your answer. Your memory will therefore hold the picture of her in her wonderful beauty and her keen mind and her high and noble ideas and no less in her intrepid courage and her long duel with pain. Her great love for you will help you to keep worthy of her and of all 'the more excellent things' for which she stood.

130. *BJ to Mrs Campbell. No address. [May 1925].*[1] *Transcript.*

But surely send one[2] even to the novices, at Hawkesyard Priory, Rugeley, Staffs (*via* the Novice Master)[3] who number some 25 or 26 souls.[4] I'm sure they'd be delighted.

It must have been good to have met G.K.C.[5] and no doubt was a preparation for this luckless day you have just had, a cocktail to help you through the succession of disappointments. The Lord has a quaint sense of humour and believes thoroughly in cocktails, usually before the meal of sorrow, though sometimes it comes as a cognaced coffee after the event. Whichever comes first you know will be surely followed by tother, and so get prepared.

The new Church must be fine and full of amplitude and great effects, especially when empty and void of folk.[6]

1. The date is inferred from the contents of the letter.
2. A prayer card for the novena to the Holy Spirit, which Mrs Campbell organised among her friends from the vigil of Pentecost to Trinity Sunday (cf. below, no. 178), a week later than the official, indulgenced novena. This means that her novena in 1925 would have run from 30 May to 8 June.
3. Paulinus Sweeney was (in modern terms) student master at this time.
4. In the summer of 1925 there were exactly 26 students at Hawkesyard.
5. G. K. Chesterton.

6. The impressive new nave at Downside was completed in 1925, and was used during the Holy Week ceremonies (*Downside Review* 43 (1925) p. 164); there is an enthusiastic comment on it, with a photograph, ibid. pp. 143-145. BJ was present for its official opening on 25 July, ibid. p. 172.

131. *BJ to Bernard Delany OP. No address. 23 July 1925. Autograph.*

F. Jerome[1] will have told you of your departure.[2] He tells me that he has budgeted on your supply and retreat monies so I must leave you attached to Laxton till the end of them on Sept 23. But could you take over the Review[3] before that? I don't know when your holidays are to be, only your Portobello Retreat[4] and the Edinburgh supply and Ushaw.

The copies printed have fallen from 1550, the maximum, to 950: the problem is to fetch up the sale again.

Blackwell has immense belief in your sense of editorship, your scent as to what will sell and what won't, above all in your discovery of controversy.[5] When he took over the Review, he heard of it on all hands as fresh, daring, and sane. He thinks at the moment that it is little more than respectable. Will you please see that it is no longer respectable?

I think that the thing to do is

(α) to have people whom you can depend on and whose views you approve to be your spokesmen on the chief headings,

(β) to build circulation not on 'names' so much as on subjects, helped out when available by 'names',

(γ) to foresee the coming points that will be locally discussed and to provide the Catholic dining population with arguments they can employ after the soup to worsen[6] their adversaries, Protestants, Pagans and the Deadly Sins.

I propose to settle £50 a year on you. You'll see Blackwell's proposal.[7] But it will be long e'er you can touch his figure. I've told him we will risk it till Dec 1926 and then see what has happened.

For yourself I presume the Editorship could be eked out by 'occasional' sermons and by a leisurely D.Litt. and by the Nuns,[8] the Baroness,[9] and Undergraduates.

Please don't curse me. I have so many curses thrown at me of late that I shall burst into tears if you throw me another.

1. Jerome Rigby, superior of Laxton, where Delany was assigned (cf. above, no. 118).
2. His re-assignment to Oxford.
3. *Blackfriars*. Delany had been its first editor, when the journal was launched in 1920. But in 1924 he had been assigned to Laxton, and the Provincial Chapter (17-25 November 1924) appointed Edwin Essex to be editor of *Blackfriars*. This had not been a success, so BJ had asked Delany to take over again.

4. The Dominican convent of Portobello Road was founded from Châtillon in 1896, at the invitation of Cardinal Vaughan. In 1909 it became the Mother House of a new diocesan Congregation, whose constitutions were approved in 1913.
5. Basil Blackwell had offered to take over the publishing of *Blackfriars* early in 1922, and his offer was accepted by BJ and Delany on 3 February. He had let it be known that he saw no future for the journal under Essex's editorship.
6. Thus BJ; presumably he meant 'worst'.
7. In a letter of 17 July Blackwell underlines the financial uncertainty of the journal, and comments, 'The policy of safety, no doubt, is to cease publication at the end of this volume'. But Delany's resumption of the editorship, in his view, gives grounds for hoping that the position is not irretrievably lost. The minimum sale, to make ends meet, would be 1250 copies, but he suggests aiming at 2000 copies, which would allow a proper payment to contributors.
8. The Dominican nuns in Headington. Delany became their confessor in the autumn.
9. Baroness Frances de Paravicini, A Dominican tertiary who lived near the nuns in Headington.

132. *BJ to George Bowring. From St Dominic's, London. 18 September 1925. Transcript.*

. . . Of course my dear brother[1] I quite understand. It is one of the evils attendant on my position that I can really have no 'friends', for a ruler must have none. It's sweet of you to say what you do about our old friendship for I never forget that correspondence and all our hopes. It's comforting to know that I help you more than I'm aware of, and just as well for I'm not aware that I help you at all.

However at Mass I link up with my friends again and can find you there.

1. Bowring was now a student at Hawkesyard, just starting his first year of theology.

133. *BJ to Hubert van Zeller. From Grenada. 1 January 1926. Autograph.*

One advantage of having a monk[1] as my correspondent is that I can palm off odd bits of paper on him without his thinking that their colour[2] is necessarily symbolic. Lay people and modern lay people especially are symbolists; medieval people and the whole breed of monks are not. You see they, we, have the thing and hence symbols are wholly unnecessary.

Well, skipping the rest of the argument which you can work out when you're next doing up the brass (again no symbolic metal for you), I now come to thank you for your letter and wishes and to reconvey to you mine. Yes Christmas isn't nice at first. It is rather a weeping feast in the earlier days of religious life, because it is so pre-eminently a family feast and in one's earlier days pre-eminently one has not left one's family properly nor yet properly fixed on to the house. Between the two, being in one and having the tail-end of one's heart gazing at the other, one gets rather strained in the diverse pulling. However once one's landed one's soul in the vocation as home, final and irrevocable, well one's landed and that's all there is to it.

> There fared a mother driven forth
>   Out of an Inn to roam;
> In the place where she was homeless
>   All men are at home.
> The crazy stable close at hand
> With shaking timber, and shifting sand
> Grew a stronger thing to abide and stand
>   Than the square stones of Rome.
>
> A Child in a foul stable
> Where the beasts feed and foam;
> Only where He was homeless
>   Are you and I at home:
> We have hands that fashion and heads that know
> But our hearts we lost—how long ago!—
> In a place no chart or ship can show
>   Under the sky's dome.[3]

So there you are and cease thy wailing and remember your sorrow no more; but rather thank the Lord you're no lay brother but one who will one day find ever a home between your fingers at the Dawn. Gallus cantat, spes redit.[4] With the dawn, hope.

1. Van Zeller had become a monk of Downside in 1924.
2. The letter is written on blue paper.
3. The first and third stanzas of G. K. Chesterton, 'The House of Christmas', included in his 1915 Collected Poems; cf. *Collected Poems*, London 1933, p. 140.
4. An allusion to the hymn *Aeterne rerum conditor*, 'Gallo canente spes redit' ('when the cock crows, hope returns').

134. *BJ to Aidan Elrington OP. From Convent of the Sacred Heart, New York. 25 March 1926. Autograph.*

Thanks for your letter. I answer it between 'interviews' at this Convent where I'm retreating 300 college girls and their mothers. Miseremini mei, miseremini mei.[1]

As far as I remember the first draft of the kitchen wing supposed that the 13 feet were a right of way; that we discovered from the deeds was not so; for Wyatt[2] gave us only the land marked on the plan and no right of way beyond.

On the final plan, I think the entrance to coal cellar was especially made so that the coal could be carried up and dumped without trespass, either from the side passage (as agreed with the University) or from[3] the back. I don't remember now which. Certainly we mustn't trespass; we can build up to the boundary at the corner, but isn't it possible to shoot the coals in from the prolonged passage? From the side, and not from the back?[4]

I'm afraid I cannot do much to help you as I don't remember now what we settled. I know we had to alter the first plans because E.D.W.[5] misunderstood the 13 or 14 feet to be a common right of way.

All I can suggest is
(1) Entrance to cellar from side, not back.
(2) Cellar-lights must be on our ground.
(3) Wyatt etc was to be brought out by Ashmolean.[6] I presume nothing done by them yet.

Here I'm pretty rushed and as yet no money for Oxford, woe is me!

1. 'Have mercy on me' (Job 19:21).
2. George Wyatt and Son, builders and ironmongers, occupied 67 St Giles, Oxford.
3. BJ actually wrote 'with'.
4. The coal cellar at the back of Blackfriars was in the outcome so placed that the coal could be delivered by being brought along a passage way, belonging to the University and running alongside Blackfriars. The passage way was extended to run round the back of Blackfriars kitchen and into the garden.
5. The architect, E. Doran Webb.
6. The Ashmolean museum, on the further side of Wyatt and Son.

135. *BJ to Hubert van Zeller. From St Dominic's, London. 9 May 1926. Autograph.*

I've just got back and am just going off again i.e. to Madrid (old Madrid), to elect a new Master General.[1] But I must say thank you for the pleasant letter. I shouldn't write at all if I were going to give the retreat and should have preferred to keep back for public discussion the remarks I'd wish to make. Since your Abbot won't tell you the name of the giver of it, I can't either; only I'll say this that he was the hero of the port-wine and banana episode. Wild horses won't tear the name from me'.[2]

Also before I forget a pal of yours called on me yesterday, 'for pleasure', he said, one E.H., late a novice of Downside.[3] He had hoped for a job in a publishing firm, he said, but none came. At the moment he's a special constable guarding a tram that is too frightened to emerge. When the strike's over he returns to Bristol.

Also I enjoyed U.S.A. and B.W.I. and S. Africa, ditto the 21,000 miles of sea I journeyed through, ditto the 5000 miles of land. So my spedometer measures, no, not the spedometer the other thing, I forget its name.

Also I have not written a book on the spiritual life. I think those are the leading questions which you put by way of conversation. Don't say that I haven't answered them and with the soul of wit. Only the soul of wit is possible to me; its body I leave to young monks. Where the corpse is, there are the young monks gathered together—to say office for the dead, of course.

So glad that you did come up to London and got back intact. I'm always afraid what will happen to you, when you emerge. Shall it be Maskelyne and Devant,[4] or the Hippodrome?[5] or even, nay stay wild thought, Eustace Miles?[6] Lord, not a bit of it, Jelly[7] goes to the Doctor and all's right with the world.

Then he asks me what I think of mortification. What do I think of it? As little as possible. I realise perfectly that it is part of the Christian tradition. If I wrote it ἄσκησις, you'd think I knew a lot about it, if you had forgotten your Greek and didn't remember how it should be written. But however it is spelt, the wretched thing like the poor has always been with us. Unlike the poor it has usually lived in the best houses and clung to the most comely of aspect. I knew a boy 14 years ago, whether in the body or out of the body etc.[8] Now he used to practise it. The knowledge of that made me love him; it also made me desperately afraid for him. Mortification is a queer thing. It's restraint, and painful, and a hurting of the human love of comfort. Yet on its physical side it has a curious affinity to sensuality. There's a terrible amount of pleasure to be got out of pain. I think the flesh tortured is almost capable of being nearest in occasion of sin.

That's to be reckoned up when one is doing the mathematics of penitential exercises.

Penance is necessary; its physical form may easily be dangerous; in some way it is yet necessary in its physical form.

Now take monastic observance![9] We should all keep our ideals of what religious life could be. We should also remember that they are ideals and never fully realisable. There never has been a perfect community; but the best is always to be aiming at more than we've got.

This seems true, that the young are attracted, not by religious life made easy for them but by religious life that appeals to their unselfishness. The more comfortable religious life is anywhere the less it will have a chance of attracting the very souls who have an innate tendency to it. The peaks pull the mind upwards and draw all things to themselves.

Hence long and pray always for fuller and more complete observance. Remember that the value of the observance is dependent on the motives, that these motives give equal value to all that is done under obedience, that a subject does more wisely by thinking, praying, and carrying out all he is allowed to do, than by endless discussion and what's called 'using influence' with people. These discussions disturb the serenity and make for discontent. Also one is a subject and doesn't know all the difficulties in the way of what one thinks feasible. But above all never lower your ideals, keep to them, and pray: *in silentio et in spe erit fortitudo vestra*.[10] There that's a Friar Preacher for you!

I remember how hot and cross you were at the walk with A.K.[11] and yet how at once when he bade you you attitudinised on a block of stone for his (not your) amusement. I've always said you had the capacity for greatness. And ahem! behold it has come true. . . .

1. BJ had sailed for South Africa on 27 September 1925, returning on 14 December. On 16 December he set off for the West Indies, from where he went on to the United States. The exact date of his return seems not to have been recorded. On 10 May he left England again to go to the General Chapter at Ocaña in Spain, spending a night in Paris on the way.
2. The retreat-giver was probably Fabian Dix; he was at any rate at Downside 6-12 September, which is the right time for the retreat.
3. A fellow novice of van Zeller's, who had left Downside. The General Strike had recently started, at midnight on 3 May 1926.
4. A famous team of magicians and illusionists, who had taken over the St George's Hall in the West End of London and turned it into Maskelyne's Theatre, the first theatre to be devoted specifically to this kind of entertainment. Until the retirement, early in the first World War, of David Denant, their shows were billed as 'Maskelyne and Devant's Mysteries'. Several generations of Maskelynes kept the business going. The founder of this remarkable dynasty was John Nevil Maskelyne (1839-1917), who had at one stage devoted himself seriously to unmasking the fraudulent tricks of the Spiritualists. Cf. Jasper Maskelyne, *White Magic: The Story of Maskelynes*, London 1936.
5. A revue theatre in the West End.
6. A restaurant in the West End.
7. Van Zeller's nickname.
8. 2 Cor. 12:2.
9. Van Zeller's personal search for fuller and more complete observance was part of a wider movement at Downside for a more 'monastic' way of life. In the last twenty years of the 19th century Cuthbert Butler's name was associated with a 'Downside Movement', which sought to develop autonomous community life in the historic Benedictine houses in England, which had previously been organised on the basis of provinces and priories. This movement received a fillip in 1899 with the erection of the abbeys of Downside, Ampleforth and Douai and the promulgation of new Constitutions. In the following decades Downside became associated with the withdrawal of monks from parishes and a concentration of efforts on the school. By 1926 Dom David Knowles (1896-1974) had emerged as the leader of a party within the Downside community who wanted an almost Cistercian austerity. For the early parts of the movement, see D. A. Bellenger, 'The Downside "Stirs": Personalities, Principles, Documentation', *E.B.C. History Symposium* 6 (1986) pp. 11-66, and 'Vingt ans après: Downside from Ford to Knowles', ibid. 7 (1987) pp. 2-37. For David Knowles, see Adrian Morey, *David Knowles*, London 1979. The supporters of Knowles were known as 'usques', because they wanted to be completely, *usquequaque*, monastic. Van Zeller, austere in appearance and shaven-headed, was always an 'usque'. BJ, in a letter to Cuthbert Butler dated 29 July 1922 (Downside Archives 1404) revealed his sympathy for Butler's ideals at the time of his resignation as abbot: 'It had seemed so clearly that you were in the right and that you had behind you all the progressive forces of the Congregation, the youth of it, the future of it, that one had taken for granted that the victory was already yours—or rather not the victory but the acceptance of the ideals which you maintained. Anyhow, I am sure that your view will come more and more into the front and that monasticism as you have taught and explained it is the only monasticism that can survive.'

'The future,' he concludes, 'and the youth of all the Orders here in England are on your side; even your resignation cannot affect that now.'
10. Isaiah 30:15 ('In silence and in hope will your strength be').
11. Not identified.

136. *Notes of a sermon preached by BJ at Carisbrooke. 25 July 1926.*

God made us from nothing. He makes each soul by a separate act, whereas the rest of creation, though made and preserved by him, acts through secondary causes. He made us directly, and continues the creative act by preserving, fashioning, moulding us.

Like the sculptor, God sees in the soul not only what it is, but what he can make of it if we let him have his way, and offer no obstacle to the hand that chisels, moulds or hews us. Like the celebrated statue of David that was produced from a block of marble spared for any but the supreme artist's hand, and owing the very beauty and genius of the poise to the original shape of the block[1]— so God can make of us masterpieces of his hand and skill, if only we let him. It is not external events which make the differences in our soul, but the way the soul reacts to circumstances, the use it makes of all the materials placed within its reach.

Paul the Persecutor became Paul the Apostle. Magdalen the Sinner became Magdalen the Saint. Augustine the earthly lover changed into God's lover. 'All things make for good to those who love God.'[2] Let us leave ourselves in the hands of God. He knows, and he can do.

1. Michelangelo's 'David' is carved from a single block of marble, but, according to Vasari, it had already been hacked about by an earlier artist to such an extent that it was now considered worthless; Michelangelo was to some extent constrained by the carving of his predecessor, as well as by the nature of the block. Cf. Giorgio Vasari, *Lives of the Painters*, trans. George Bull, vol. I, Harmondsworth 1987, pp. 337-339.
2. Romans 8:28.

137. *BJ to Gwendolen Plunket Greene. No address. 28 July 1926. Transcript.*

Thank you for your letter.

Of course I shall only be too pleased to be of any use to you at all in helping you towards the Faith as far as I can.

At present I am out of London and shall be in London during August only to give retreats to Nuns there; also in early and late September I shall be out of London but probably all the middle part of the month I shall be there.

I am sorry that you should have had to have a serious operation, but I suppose that the enforced quietness now can have its place in some scheme of God to give you a chance to think things out, or rather, since you have evidently thought already a good deal, to pray things out. It is only wise to remember how much goodness of life must help us to see our way, for the love of God after all is our best method of knowing Him and understanding His ways.

138. *BJ to Gwendolen Plunket Greene. From St Dominic's, London. 31 July 1926. Transcript.*

I got back last night to find your letter. Thank you for taking me into your confidences.

I am sure that you are now to be[1] rewarded for your faithfulness to God's showing of the way. No doubt, as you say, your uncle[2] had a horror of the Catholic who was lukewarm and he evidently deferred the fulfilment of your desire till he could be sure there was nothing but the severe force of the will to hold you to the Faith.

The danger of Catholicism is its power to help. It is a Faith that even to those who do not believe seems to carry with it comfort and reality. Yet it is not wise to come to the Catholic Church because you need comfort. It is never wise to join any cause or any ideal for what one can make out of it or get out of it. We should come in for what we can give.

I suppose he was afraid lest you should have been motived by some such thought as that.

I think that the best thing of all is your devotion to Our Lord. It is to give ourselves to Him that we must come. It must be under the inspiration of His unselfishness, of His service of God in man and of man in God, that we seek to join ourselves to Him: there were those who followed *because* they had been fed in the wilderness.[3] This wasn't enough. 'Signs and wonders' are not good enough proofs; the only great proof is that people have followed Him down narrow lanes and over uneven paths and wearing thorns and carrying their cross. It is along that line then that you must pray, that He would help you to give yourself to Him, patiently, indeed serenely. You won't then bother about arguing or the need of it. You will just follow where He leads you, sure that all will be well: 'Be not solicitous.'[4] For the past, remember His injunction to let the dead bury their dead;[5] for the future, remember that the morrow, so He said, would take care of itself.[6] All that's to be done is to hold oneself in the Everlasting Arms[7] or rather be held by them. The rest is peace, that comes of having nothing left.

Do let me know when you are back in London.

1. The typescript has 'that you are now be rewarded', which can be corrected in several ways: apart from the correction proposed in the text, it would be possible to restore 'that you are now being rewarded' or 'that you will now be rewarded'.

2. Baron Friedrich von Hügel.
3. John 6:26.
4. Matthew 6:25.
5. Luke 9:60.
6. Matthew 6:34.
7. Deuteronomy 33:27.

139. *BJ to Gwendolen Plunket Greene. From St Dominic's, London. 4 August 1926. Transcript.*

I shall be free tomorrow at 23 Kensington Square¹ giving a retreat to nuns there and could find an hour suitable no doubt for you if you could let me know days and times that are easiest. I'll be there 10 days . . .²

Of course pain and sorrow and distress, in so far as they are outside and come to us, have their part in the Divine Economy; but our soul's effort is only to remain tranquil under them and serene. It is seldom circumstances that sadden men, it's always some failure of one's own soul: we can never lose what we have once had unless we choose to lose it. Remember too: 'In silence and in hope shall your strength be.'³

1. The convent of the Assumption nuns. BJ actually wrote '27 Kensington Square'.
2. In some notes made after his death, Mrs Greene described her first meeting with BJ: 'I saw him first many years ago when I went to hear him preach at the Carmelite Church on St Teresa, and his livingness remained so clearly to me. (He talked of how St Teresa was always scandalizing people.) When I felt that at last I must become a Catholic, I wrote to him, but he was away. I wrote again the next year, and found him, and went to see him at the Convent at Kensington Square—it was August. I had just had a major operation and he was more than considerable and kind in his plans for me. When he came into the room, I was *almost* disappointed, he looked far less impressive than I expected and not at all ecclesiastical. I had prepared to be very charmed—instead of which he was entirely natural and simple and sat down in his white habit facing the light, and played all the time with his rosary. I sat in a dark corner clutching my umbrella all the time. After I had explained or tried to, he talked a little about my Uncle and how he alarmed him, and then said he supposed I felt I *was* a Catholic. I said yes, and then he went on to say I must not be disappointed if hidden rocks suddenly appeared and made the way difficult, even for some time. He talked of this and his experiences with people, and then when I left he quoted those words with which I end my *Pax* article—"to whom shall I go" ' (John 6:68). (Mrs Greene published an appreciation of BJ in *Pax* August 1934 pp. 103-107.)
3. Isaiah 30:15.

140. *BJ to Gwendolen Plunket Greene. From St Dominic's, London. 15 August 1926. Transcript.*

Well we can wait and see what happens. F. McNabb¹ (as I too) has sent people to Mother Alphonsine² at Kensington Square to be instructed. However there's no hurry about it. Wait till the 21st and

105

see what happens.³ I won't say anything to him and we can leave it to guidance then.

I believe so strongly in troubles settling themselves:

> Leave 'em alone
> And they'll come home
> Bringing their tails behind 'em.⁴

Don't worry about it or the articles of the Faith. They will be better seen as part of a living whole. Isolated bones are singularly unconvincing.

1. BJ had arranged for Mrs Greene to visit McNabb to see about being instructed in the faith before her reception into the Catholic church.
2. Mother Alphonsine Gavin, one of the Sisters of the Assumption in Kensington.
3. Evidently this was the date fixed for Mrs Greene's first interview with McNabb.
4. From the nursery rhyme, 'Little Bo-Peep' (Opie no. 66).

141. *BJ to Gwendolen Plunket Greene. From the Hospital of SS. John and Elizabeth, London. 23 August 1926. Transcript.*

Have just been over to the Priory and arranged matters. All's well. You can go to No. 23¹, ask for M. Alphonsine and all will be then 'according to plan'. Let things settle themselves. They will.

1. The Sisters of the Assumption, Kensington Square.

142. *BJ to Gwendolen Plunket Greene. From the Hospital of SS. John and Elizabeth, London. 26 August 1926. Transcript.*

Just a note to say that what you describe is just the normal act of the will stripped of the accidental accomplishments which may be helpful but which don't add to the moral worth of the action. This bare, naked holding is the effort of the will. Your emotions are on the other side, the pages of Madam Mystic, the operation is agin you, and the excited state of your own nerves, everything is on the other side: against these are simply will and the grace of God.

So don't worry or prepare answers for her or any of them. Let yourself be quiet in the hands of God: *Beneath us the everlasting arms.*¹ Rest there and all will be well with you.

1. Deuteronomy 33:27.

143. *BJ to Gwendolen Plunket Greene. From St Dominic's, London. 6 September 1926. Transcript.*

I have just got back from abroad,¹ had to be out all day on Sunday, I have had to deal with piles of letters that lay on my table for this past 8 days, now I have reached to your three. I am sure that you have only quickly to go through the Catechism to find most of your questions answering themselves. The only thing to do is to leave what puzzles you till some other point of the same problem turns up elsewhere. It will certainly. Then you see how the Catholic answer fits a little better. You see the Thing is for ever lasting. To swallow and digest it all will take eternity. So don't be in a hurry to understand. Love, yes, ever so much in a hurry to do that. But without worrying: 'Sit still, my daughter'. That's what God's saying to you: 'Sit stone still' as Richard Rolle says.²

1. BJ had just returned from a holiday in France.
2. BJ is almost certainly thinking of *Ancrene Riwle* M 414 (not by Rolle): 'Sit with Mary stone still at God's feet.' He had quoted this text in one of his contributions to the CTS volume, *The English Dominican Province 1221-1921*, p. 138.

144. *BJ to Aidan Elrington OP. No address. 6 September 1926. Autograph.*

. . . Please also pray and ask prayers for a special intention, which concerns the expurgation of the History Text Books in use in all the schools of England. There's a big movement of Edward Eyre¹ to get the publishers to accept *proved* corrections dealing with Catholic things and the publishers and authors have accepted a good deal. It's now a question of a final push.

Probably Sept 17 will find me with you.

1. Edward Eyre was an Irishman, who had gone to the United States in his youth, but then settled in London. He was a member of the Catholic Education Council 1909–1931. He died, aged 86, in 1937. His obituary in *The Tablet* 169 (1937) p. 787 notes that 'from an early date he took a particular interest in securing a revision of the historical teaching given under official auspices by the London County Council . . . His forceful intervention . . . secured the withdrawal of many unjustified anti-Catholic assertions and observations in text-books and other widely circulated histories.' At the time of BJ's letter, he had recently made a substantial donation to the chapel of Blackfriars, Oxford. On 24 August 1926 he wrote to BJ, with reference to his campaign for a fairer teaching of history, 'Some measure of success has been achieved and I feel if we persist the success must be complete.'

145. *BJ to Esme Howard.¹ No address. 8 September 1926. Transcript.*

Really you shouldn't have written though it was a real pleasure to see your writing and to have those words.

You really must have had the grinding stones well over you and under you all these[2] weary months and years that your long-drawn agony has lasted. But it certainly has not been wasted since it has brought you into that bleak and barren place where at last all is seen 'to be nought compared to the excellent knowledge' of Our Lord.[3] It's easy enough to preach it but no one can really know it to be true who hasn't had to buy his wisdom at that long price.

In a way you have had it for years. I think of you always asking to find your way there early enough. You hadn't quite the hearty amusements of the other boys, you had chosen rather for your interests the beauty of the arts and of language, the finer emotions of the soul. Well, these when followed in schooldays make their worshippers rather aloof from the crowd. They have not only to see alone but they tend to be avoided by the rest.

Was Oxford so very much easier? I often wondered when I saw you. You seemed not unhappy; but you looked as though at times you felt your isolation.

Nothing isolates like sickness, so that I think, my dear, that you must have been pushed further and further into the lone places. Of course your loved ones have been with you and crept into your heart but your isolation no one can take from you. You would pain them too much if you told them all you had gone through, and so the secrets of the King have to be kept secrets, much as in one way you would be relieved by telling someone of them, yet in another way you would never dare tell them all. How could they bear it? How could you bear it really to tell them, for to tell these things is to live them through again. You could not do that.

So it has been a real progress in loneliness, despite all the affection shown, even because of it. It was so delicious you could not bear to hurt it. And that's the worst terror of life: witness the Garden of Olives and the cry of Eloi.

But you have come to that blessed meeting-place where the isolation diminishes again. Alone? No, I am not alone, for the Father is with me.[4] 'When my Father and Mother deserted me (how could they help it when you slipped out from them) Thou hast taken me up.'[5] 'Though I go down into the valley of the shadow I shall have no fear because Thou art with me.'[6] Thus a sufferer comes at last to the bleak heights, bed of pain and weariness of soul, and finds that the barrenness of the hills has this advantage, it hides not to the eyes of faith none of the contours of God. It seemed to be growing darker, really you were walking towards the light.

He will help you, dear Esme. At my Mass I think of you and Him; find your friendship in Him, the disciple not above the Master, blessed when he's as the Master. As the Master? Alone, naked, crown of thorns, cross. Yes, you answer, blessed to be as the Master, bearing crown of thorns and alone, for I am sure you have real peace in your dreadful sleeplessness and your pain. God bless you always.

1. Esme Howard, the eldest son of the 1st Baron Howard of Penrith (1863-1939), born in 1903, was dying. He was educated at Downside school (1917-21) and New College, Oxford (1921-25). He died on 27 November 1926. 'Shortly after taking his Finals he contracted the painful and baffling malady which ultimately was the cause of his death. Although the last two years of his life were full of pain, he did a considerable amount of serious writing . . . His death . . cut short the promise of a career more than usually brilliant' (*Downside Review* 45 (1927) pp. 64-65). His father printed BJ's letter in his autobiography, *Theatre of Life,* vol. II, London 1936, pp. 527-528.
2. The typescript has 'those', but in BJ's hand 'these' and 'those' are easily confused.
3. Philippians 3:8.
4. John 8:16.
5. Psalm 26:10 (Vulgate).
6. Psalm 22:4 (Vulgate).

146. *BJ to Miss Savielle. From St Dominic's, London. 11 September 1926. Autograph.*

I am sorry if I seemed hard. I had no idea that what I said was unduly severe. It wasn't meant to be.

If you think it will end this 'fuss' as you call it, I should be willing to hear your confession at any time you find F.B.[1] can't manage it or hasn't answered. I don't pretend to be of any use as a Director. I've never done that sort of job and couldn't if I wanted to do so. I haven't the Napleonic mind. But if it would be of any service to you, tell me and I can fix a time that will be not inconvenient for both of us.

It's unpleasant to find people growing embittered. God's world was meant to be a serene place. What a mess we all do make of it, to be sure!

1. Bernard Delany.

147. *BJ to Gwendolen Plunket Greene. From St Dominic's, London. 14 September 1926. Transcript.*

No those are not sins. Remember always that nothing is sinful unless it is deliberately consented to, so that you have no reason for confessing these mere temptations. You will recall no doubt that S. Paul had something of the same to face.[1] It's rather humiliating. P'raps that's why it's let happen. No one knows quite what God's about. The only thing to be thankful for is that it is God who is about, and that what He lets happen must be very good for us.

You have only to 'seek, suffer and trust' as Mother Julian of Norwich says.[2] But what more could be done? or wanted?

1. 2 Cor. 12:7.
2. Julian of Norwich, *Revelation of Divine Love*, Long Text chapter 10.

148. *BJ to Gwendolen Plunket Greene. From St Dominic's, London. 15 September 1926. Transcript.*

You said you'd talk it over with Mother Alphonsine. However you seem now to opt for this place,[1] so please be outside the Sacristy door, or rather, please be in the Church, at the top, on the left-hand side at 11 a.m.—or 11.15 if you like. You needn't bring anyone else. Will Lady Mary[2] be god-mother by proxy?

The only preparation is to be quiet; not excited. Look like the Shepherds did at their sheep till the noises made them look up. When the light faded, they went back to their sheep. Peter went back to his net. It's because we haven't nets or sheep, that we don't keep ordinary in the presence of God. We should.

So Mass when you can and Communion once a week, and see what the result will be. Bed early on Monday night please and Communion early on Tuesday and then bed again. . . .

1. BJ was going to receive her into the Catholic church at St Dominic's, London, on Monday 20 September. The witness was supplied by him—a convert he had received into the church nearly eight years earlier. This is why he tells her not to bring anyone with her.
2. Lady Mary von Hügel, widow of Baron Friedrich, Mrs Greene's aunt.

149. *BJ to Gwendolen Plunket Greene. From St Dominic's, London. 22 September 1926. Transcript.*

Please don't think of making offerings for your reception. I'm grateful for it, and the money shall go to someone in distress. But you must take care at the start of this new life to not to try to do too much; do regularly what you can do, and therefore aim chiefly at what you can do regularly—not the exceptional sanctifies us but the normal done as well as we can do it.

So try to live your old life in a new way, i.e. in a more vividly conscious way; don't throw over what you've done but continue it under a fuller inspiration. S. Matthew of today's feast gave up his job when he became a Christian because it wasn't a decent job for a Christian; but Peter kept to his fishing and Paul to his sail-making, because there wasn't harm in theirs.

150. *BJ to Mrs Tayleur. On the train. 24 September.*[1] *Autograph.*

Just a scribble to thank you for all your kindness to me and mine. I very much enjoyed my 2 days, would have more enjoyed them had you been in less discomfort and distress.[2] It is hard I am sure when nothing else but religion is left to you to have to surrender so much of that, or rather of the exercise of it. But then it is not your fault, but God's, that is no fault at all. Consequently you can be sure you don't lose, even when you seem to be losing. You see religion will only be perfectly carried out in Heaven. So here everything is only a means to an end. When the means are taken away, or one set of means, we are no worse off than before, since there must always be some means to hand of reaching God. Your obvious means is patience, waiting. Did you notice that the last man who swam the channel did most of it *on his back*?[3] This is another Channel, with shores of eternity on either side, 'from Him we come and to Him we go', and it too can be done on one's back! May He give you the staying power, a prudent judgment to catch the ebb-tide, and a quiet sea! . . .

1. The year is conjectured to be 1926. In 1925 and 1926 BJ's letters to Mrs Tayleur several times make mention of her being laid up. There is a letter to Bernard Delany written 'on the train' on 24 September 1926. BJ paid his first visit to Mrs Tayleur in 1922 (cf. above, no. 80), and in 1925 refers to the fact that he has only been there once. In 1925 itself he was giving a retreat at Chiswick 21-26 September, and in 1927 he was again at Chiswick 19-24 September.
2. Mrs Tayleur was for a time severely crippled as the result of a hunting accident.
3. This most promising clue to the date of the letter has proved disappointing, as we have been unable to learn of anyone swimming the channel on his back. If 1926 is the correct date, the last person to swim the channel was Norman Derham, who did it on 17 September.

151. *BJ to Gwendolen Plunket Greene. From St Dominic's, London. 18 October 1926. Transcript.*

Thank you for your letters. I am glad that all went well with confession and I hope confirmation. It means that you are gradually getting into the heart of things. But there's a homeliness about eternal things that makes it a matter not of time but of spirit to find oneself easily amongst them. If one's eager, one's instantly at home.

Thank you for the letter which I return as I never keep anything. It does touch the real point of things, doesn't it? The temporal and the eternal, and both at once.

Of course death isn't frightening in itself; but as I said it's the uncertainties of it that stagger one at times. It certainly is the Will of God, 'Follow thou me', and that's the finer side; but the other haunts none the less:

>   Whether 'tis ampler day
>   Divinelier lit
>   Or the dark night without.

152. BJ to Richard Hart-Davis. From St Dominic's, London. 10 January 1927. Autograph.

. . . As you know, Mrs Hart-Davis[1] first came to me during a retreat at Grayshott[2] where I saw a good deal of her and where she told me a great deal about herself; then she came up to see me here at S. Dominic's. I must own that I discouraged her as I could see—it wasn't so very long before her illness came down on her in its full fury—that with her it might so easily become an obsession and develop into a great fear. Her nature was so intense and concentrated that one dreaded her interest in the things of the Faith, at the beginning of her Catholic life. One preferred she should go quietly at first and then later on develop her spiritual life with growing interest.

But I think she was one of those who are not so much interested in life, human and divine, as consumed by it, to whom religion is not so much a light as a flame. She was burnt up by that fire within.

Alas that I didn't know her well enough to gauge that courage of which Wilfrid Meynell[3] speaks; she certainly had all the glow that illumines courage and that docility of mind that seems so often and so surprisingly to march side by side with it. It was only in little ways that I was able to see the force, directness, and kindness of her character, and her sympathy with all spiritual efforts and distress. . . .

Does she suffer now? Who can tell? We believe that the Presence of God is so holy that only the perfect can enter into it unchanged; but that for all the rest there is purgation, a cleansing and yet not reluctantly or grimly accepted, but eagerly and joyously, since they see clearly then with no unhindered sight that God is the Purpose of their being and that to reach Him there is no road save through this place of preparation. There then (time can't measure it, nor can anyone guess through what means) the souls wait the moment of deliverance into the fulness of Light and Life and Love.

We believe too that prayers can help them, and that we by bearing patiently our troubles, losses, bereavements can offer for them these sorrows and that God may well let us suffer in this way for their saving as they have no doubt on earth at times suffered for ours.

We have no fear for them since they stand in the Hands of God. He loves as we can never love them; moreover He knows them as we have never known them, He knows how much and how little of will in them went into the things that were done amiss. We can't measure guilt; we can't guess the excuse; He knows all, who is love.

We can hope surely that He who let fall on her the darkness of that awful cloud will not be unmindful of her sufferings under it who Himself faced the darkness and the desolation, and whose cry of forsakenness still echoes from the Cross. It's He who will judge her, He that more than any other, from Gethsemani to His ending, faced the unnamed fears.

You can feel sure too that she knows now you three who were dearest to her and that she, if she be already past her purgatory, sees you in her vision of God. She sees you in His care of you; she knows you all in Him.

You seem to have lost her, yet you haven't, for no one loses friends here unless they choose to lose them; death is no division; much more life divides. So that after what came on her by way of distress of mind for her it is a blessed relief.

And for you too there must be a sense of peace after the anguish of those days; to see those whom we love suffer, to be utterly unable to help them in their suffering, to have to stand and watch, is the real agony of love. Now there should be peace for her and for you all, a peace that isn't mute silence but the silence in which souls meet and understand.

May God comfort you! And may that courage of hers help you to be inflamed by it also and walk what yet remains of the lonely way with the same unquenchable spirit that she showed.

1. She had died on 3 January 1927.
2. In October 1923, shortly after her reception into the Catholic church.
3. The writer, Wilfrid Meynell (1852-1948), was an old friend of Mrs Hart-Davis.

153. *BJ to Miss Savielle. No address. 13 March 1927. Autograph.*

I have only a retreat at Chiswick (Tower House) in September. Is that the summer time? It's late in September, 18th, and one can't tell whether it will be cold then or warm; but that's all.

Thank you for your good wishes. I understand that you see much of Mrs Greene. Don't forget that she's delicate and that what shakes her most is distress of soul; so don't have any storms with her? You can be so nice when you think of it; Lord, but how you can storm when you forget!

154. *BJ to Aidan Elrington OP. From St Dominic's, London. 30 April 1927. Autograph.*

Thank you for the specifications which I shall keep by me and not send on at once to Williams:—
(i) Because as the place won't be occupied for 15 months now, it wouldn't do the things good to let 'em remain there unused and untended. Hence I think we can let them be for the moment.
(ii) Because I really haven't any money either for the moment. The £3000 I shall have left when I've paid these bills of Bell and Osborne[1] belong to the Chapel, and I shall have to start a begging appeal—which naturally I hate. I mustn't commit myself to any more for the moment. I'm sorry.

Williams returns me the map which is 'about right' he says, but he suggests another foot of land so as to leave room for a ladder to be put up to clean windows etc.

He adds that he doesn't think the old wall is ours and that there's nothing in the original deed to warrant our thinking it ours!

1. Bell and Co. (the Andover Building Works) were the builders of Blackfriars, Oxford, but the stone work was being done by G. C. Osborne and Son of Newbury.

155. *BJ to Mrs Bullough. From St Dominic's, London. 10 May 1927. Autograph.*

It seems so small a thing to say *Thank you* for so generous a gift, but what else is there to say? I am most grateful. In this begging business, it is always the people who have the less ample means for giving who give most, and in consequence the begging business distresses the one who has to beg because he knows so well that he will receive his best gifts from those less able to spare it. The only comfort is that God will requite their generosity who alone is able to meet it.

May He then bless you and yours, alive and dead!

I receive this gift of yours on S. Antonino's day, another of those Italian Dominicans who seem with their feasts to set some sort of net round your Mother's anniversaries so that this kind gift in her memory arrives under a Florentine's kindly patronage.[1] Every month there will be a Mass in her memory, along with that of other benefactors, living and dead: I am sure that whenever it is that you are to meet her again this will be remembered by her and be between you a pledge of deeper love.

Do you remember that passage in Michelangelo's treatise on art for Vittoria Colonna in which he discusses the merits of Flemish and Italian art?[2] (Why did no one quote it at the time of the Flemish exhibition?)[3] If you remember the phrases in which he puts his thoughts, you will recall that he considers the Flemish as always likely to be the more popular of the two because it deals with the simpler and more obvious things and expresses simpler and more obvious ideas, whereas the Italian will always be rather the art that needs an artist perfectly to understand it. With the exception of half a dozen Italians who have acquired popularity, Raphael, del Sarto, fra Angelico,[4] I presume that this is very largely true.

Don't you think that the faith of the leaders of Italian thought and feeling has been too of that less popular type? We of this side are simpler and more obvious in our acceptance of the Divine Truths. But is not the Catholic faith for some of those large-souled and munificent Italians (like your Mother) understood rather in some inner feeling than in the simple utterances of the Creed? They reached so much of the real princely virtues of the Catholic following of Christ that one feels sure that they reached somewhere into the inner heart of things divine. If the old principle of that supper room of Simon the Leper be a principle of all time, then she will not forgo her reward who so largely illustrated the full phrase: Many sins are forgiven her because she hath loved much.[5] Those who seek in love, however unworthily, not themselves but service, however mistaken, will not be utterly cast out by Him who sought the larger way of love's expression, beyond which even love could no further go.

She who in her large-hearted fashion sought in human love the fulfilment of the generosity of her instincts will not be judged as those who merely have sought themselves and the satisfaction of their self-seeking passions. For her, love was that into which the soul enters rather for what it can give than for what it can get. For the others, it is rather for what they get than for what they give.

May the generosity that prompted your gift—the first answer to my appeal—avail her, if she still needs the help of it, to enter into that Fountain of Love Unlimited of which S. Catherine speaks, that 'Sea Pacific',[6] alone able to reward her who gave herself and held nothing back!

1. Mrs Bullough's mother, the famous Italian actress, Eleonora Duse, died on Easter Monday, 21 April 1924. In the Dominican calendar in use at the time there was quite a cluster of Italian Dominican saints celebrated around this date: Agnes of Montepulciano (20 April), Peter of Verona (29 April), Catherine of Siena (30 April), Pius V (5 May), Antoninus (10 May).
2. There is no treatise on art by Michelangelo; BJ must have been thinking of the conversations in which Michelangelo and Vittoria Colonna were involved, which were written up by Francisco de Holanda (c. 1518-1584) and published in his *Diálogos em Roma*, of which an English translation was published in 1903 and again in 1911. For the relevant text, see R. J. Clements, ed., *Michelangelo, A Self-Portrait*, New York and London 1968, text no. 86.
3. In January and February 1927 there had been an exhibition of Belgian art at Burlington House, London.
4. Three famous Italian painters: Raffaele Santi (1483-1520), Andrea Angeli del Sarto (1486-1531) and Fra Angelico (Bl. John of Fiesole OP) (c. 1400-1455).
5. Luke 7:47.

6 St Catherine often refers to God as 'mare pacifico' (e.g. *Il Dialogo*, chapter 165, ed. G. Cavallini, Rome 1968, p. 493). She does not seem to have used the exact phrase, 'Fountain of Love Unlimited', but for the image of the fountain, cf. ibid. chapter 64, p. 139.

156. *BJ to Frank Sheed. From St Catherine's Convent, Newcastle. 28 May 1927. Transcript.*

Your letter has just reached me here where I am giving a retreat. It very much flatters my pride that you should have asked me;[1] but the reaction went immediately to the idea that I'm not widely read enough for such an undertaking. There for the moment the idea sticks. But I suppose my real trouble is time and opportunity.

Hence I depend largely for my answer on (a) the number of words the book should roughly contain in your estimate of its size and (b) the date when you are to have it. No doubt your answer to (b) will be *as soon as possible*; so my question would more truly be, *how long can you do without it?*

Your offer is exceedingly generous. Thank you indeed.

1. Sheed had asked BJ to write a history of Europe. It was published by Sheed and Ward in 1929 under the title, *A History of Europe*.

157. *BJ to Mrs Campbell. No address. 31 May 1927. Transcript.*

Thank you for reminding me of the novena.[1] I shall indeed be glad to join in, leaving the Holy Ghost to do what he likes about the money. He knows what's really wanted and can fork out the wherewithal if he wants to and will do so. So that's that. However I'll give you your bird bath if the Holy Ghost gives the £10,000; so there!

Yes, I do agree with you over Teresa Higginson.[2] She is one of those holy people who violate all the laws of decent holiness and yet get into heaven. I feel, despite F. Martindale, that S. Aloysius was a bit like that himself[3] though not to the extent that she had it. Of course you needn't believe a word of all those miraculous communions; the real point is, I suppose, her wanting to receive so often each day, even whether she did or didn't. Of course again if she did get it out of our Lord that's one up to her for her desires were therefore approved.

But it needn't be true at all, and then you're left with your own opinion—with which I agree. There's nothing untheological in her desire (the priest duplicates[4] and at Xmas and All Souls says 3 Masses); but I don't think the experience of priests is that this increases devotion.

When all's said and done, one comes back to B. Thomas More as a better type of holiness because it's the infectious holiness of a great soul. I prefer the way of S. Thomas and the miraculously caught herrings: 'The ordinary providence of God is good enough for me.'[5]

1. Cf. above, letter 130 note 2. The novena this year was due to run from 4-12 June.
2. Teresa Higginson (1844-1905) was a gifted school teacher, who became an ecstatic and enjoyed revelations and conversations with Christ and was believed to live on Holy Communion alone. The absorbing interest of her life was devotion to the Sacred Head of Christ as the seat of his divine Wisdom. Some people thought her a fraud, but Edward Powell, her parish priest, who was her director 1879-83, consulted Bertrand Wilberforce OP, who sent him a long letter on 9 November 1882, in which, while disclaiming any competence in mysticism, he demonstrates the theological propriety of the devotion to the Sacred Head (the letter is printed in Lady Cecil Kerr, *Teresa Helena Higginson*, London 1927, pp. 345-354). From 1883 onwards her director was Fr (later Canon) Alfred Snow, and he was convinced she was genuine. A selection of her letters was published by a monk of Ramsgate, London 1937.
3. C. C. Martindale, *The Vocation of Aloysius Gonzaga*, London 1927.
4. When necessary priests had (and have) permission to say Mass more than once in a single day.
5. This refers to the well-attested episode, shortly before the death of St Thomas Aquinas, when he expressed a desire for fresh herring, which would not normally have been available. Miraculously a vendor arrived, thinking he had sardines for sale; he was discovered to have a whole crate of herrings. According to some sources, Thomas refused to benefit from this miracle, preferring to entrust himself to God's providence. Cf. the account given in Tocco and the reports in the Naples Canonization Process (*Fontes Vitae S. Thomae Aquinatis*, ed. D. Prümmer and M. H. Laurent, Toulouse and St Maximin 1912-1937, pp. 129-130, 279, 334). An account has been preserved by one of BJ's retreatants of how he told the story during a retreat for ladies at St Leonards: 'Thomas Aquinas was sick and could not eat anything. Doctor asked if there was anything he thought he could fancy. He then asked for a herring (an impossibility in Italy). His friends could only get sardines but on looking among them a herring was found. The doctor said it was a miracle, but St Thomas said, "Take it away. God's *ordinary* goodness is good enough for me."'

158. BJ to Mrs Mortimer. No address. 19 June 1927. Transcript.

I am glad that the Abbess[1] sent you that notice before you left. She wrote to me to ask me what I thought. Naturally I did not say very much for I did not know very much. I left completely on one side (a) whether you had a vocation and (b) whether you could do it with justice to your family, because I supposed your confessor's judgement was the only one of any good for (a), and the fact of his having told you to go to Arundel was evidence enough. The other point I also omitted partly because I wasn't asked and partly because I wasn't sure. I only stated that when D.[2] did come home on leave he would in any event stay chiefly with your sister and not with you.

You know how I always feel a little uncertain of D. and your duty to him.

However you must go as you are led. The ways of God are not ways that move over the laid roads but they cross fields, hedges, and high hills. You must strive patiently to find out your path, and tread boldly and serenely such of it as you see, and remember that the way is as divine as the goal. 'I am the Way' said God.[3]

1. Of the Poor Clares, Arundel. Mrs Mortimer wanted to join them, but in the outcome Bishop Amigo would not let her go there.
2. Mrs Mortimer's son.
3. John 14:6.

159. *Sermon preached by BJ at the blessing of the communion rails in the Catholic church, Crayford, the memorial to Mrs Hart-Davis. 21 July 1927. Printed text.*

We are here this evening to dedicate, in remembrance of Sybil Mary Magdalen Hart-Davis, this memorial which has been erected to her memory by her husband and her children.

It is not a long life that is commemorated by it, for the span of her years was little more than forty. Yet it is not the stretch of years that can ever measure that fluid string which we call life. Life is to be judged rather by its intensity than by any other quality it may have. Is not that precisely the very meaning of life, its intangible, elusive essence, its mystery that defies alike our definitions and our analysis?

So judged and so measured, the life we are here to commemorate was life indeed, for it was lived intensely at every point of it. So much was intensity the obvious and central characteristic of her, that whoever met her must have been impressed by that in her first of all. I think that one immediate effect of that intensity of hers, in so far as it concerned us who knew her, was that almost immediately after our first meeting with her we felt that we had known her a long time. At once she seemed to give herself. In our meetings with others it takes much longer to obtain the same knowledge of them or the same insight as almost at once we had of her.

Not as though she opened her heart to all, but the flame of her personality burnt so keenly that in all she did and said her own soul was most clearly seen. There was in her, in this intensity of hers, above all, an absorbing interest in beauty. She loved it wherever she found it; and she found it everywhere. In the obvious places where all others found it, naturally she found it too, 'dawn and sunset on moors and windy hills', 'the springing grass and the soft warm April rain', 'the arched white sails of ships', and 'the old chaunt of the sea'. But she saw it where others so easily miss it or even do not remember to look for it, in the souls of men and women and children, of every sort and kind.

She was not one of those who see its exquisite form only in the world of nature and art, for she had that keener eye that sees it in the troubled beauties of the human soul—for all souls must be beautiful since God loves all souls and He loves only what is lovable for He is Love. Those too who see Him in all can see Him only where He sees Himself, in all the world. Every soul she met must have held her by its beauties, for to every soul she met she showed herself to be in sympathetic understanding. As men are moved by a fragment of beauty and are transfigured and spellbound by it, and show that they are moved, by its spell that holds them still, so by her enthusiasms she showed herself caught by the beauty of the souls she met. We only trouble to talk enthusiastically to others when we think they show an interest in what has stirred ourselves. We can only meet all the world on friendly terms when we happen to feel friendly to all the world. So 'God first loved us'.[1]

This sympathy of hers with beauty everywhere made her turn widely to all those who had sought beauty everywhere and found it and had brought back with them from their far journeys precious fragments of the larger thing they had seen. So colour and form and fragrance all touched her and no less the dreams of the poets and the drama of the stage and the harmonies of music; and she loved all those that would freely share with her something of the treasures she had unearthed.

In the experience of all this beauty and in listening to the experience of others, she could not escape hearing those that brought her tidings of the Infinite Beauty which is God. Wide and eager-hearted, fearless, unhampered by barriers, unprejudiced, free, she turned at once and easily to the Catholic faith when she learnt of its power to help in the pursuit of that uncreated beauty whence had come all the beauty that she knew. Of what befell her soul in that new faith of hers, it is not given to us to speak, for with all her enthusiasm and eagerness to share her joys with others she knew well how to keep within herself the secrets of the King.

But of this we are sure. She that loved beauty found it—not as a secret but as a gospel, not as a thing hidden but as a friend revealed.

It is therefore wholly fitting that what those who most loved her and whom most she loved have set up to her memory should be these communion rails. For us who share in her faith, at these rails will come that Infinite Beauty who once came veiled in the winsomeness of childhood, youth, and manhood, and now comes doubly veiled. He will come to those who love Him, at His invitation and out of their need; and (because love humbles souls, so that only in love do they realise their unworthiness of that which they love and still more their unworthiness of being loved in return) here at these rails men and women and children will kneel to receive love's sacrament and in their hearts will be the cry *Domine non sum dignus*[2]—appropriate memory of her whose exquisite humility was not the least of the endearing qualities that linked other souls to hers.

Nor can we Catholics think only of her as one who loved God. As well as remembering her as an inspiration, we shall pray for her to be at rest. The very nature of her soul brought with it dangers; that keenness and that love of beauty, that pursuit of it by every means in the unstable vesture of the flesh, these mean that the soul that has them may the more easily stumble, its very eagerness for adventure becomes an added danger. 'More haste, less speed' is as true of souls as of fingers. Those best know this who, alert and swift in desire, find patience the hardest virtue to achieve. Thus of her very fine and splendid eagerness must have come unconsidered mistakes which she would have wished had not been done. In that true vision of herself which the first vision of her Redeemer brought her, she would have asked our prayers. We must see to it that she asks us not in vain.

The eve of the Feast of S. Mary Magdalene to whom she had so touching a devotion gives an appropriate time to this appropriate thing. Was it not over the Magdalen that our Lord spoke His Word which has since then touched to hope and life many eager yet half-timid souls, 'Much is forgiven her because she has loved much'?[3] Love that had been the Magdalen's undoing was, said our Saviour, what alone could make her whole.

May this memorial of the short Catholic life of Sybil Mary Magdalen Hart-Davis awaken us to her sensitiveness to beauty, to her eagerness in pursuit of it, to her fearlessness in the continuance of that pursuing, and to her gladness in its finding at the close!

And may that Beauty, ever ancient, ever new,[4] which she sought and now has found, give to her such pardon as she needs and at its end Himself at last for ever and thus finish her anxious quest by Himself, her Peace.

We, sons of S. Dominic, to whose order she turned for fellowship and in whose habit, as she desired, she lies buried,[5] shall remember her as men remember a flame or a fragrance or a haunting song, the echo of the word that God spoke when the world was as yet in its dawn, in that stillness of beauty when the stars swung into the world with song and praised Him as they passed.

May she rest in peace!

1. 1 John 4:19.
2. 'Lord, I am not worthy'—said before receiving communion in the rite of the Mass.
3. Luke 7:47.
4. Augustine, *Confessions* X 27:38.
5. She was a Dominican tertiary.

160. *BJ to Rupert Hart-Davis. From Edinburgh. 24 July 1927. Autograph.*

I was exceedingly touched by your letter which I got yesterday morning as I was leaving London to come up here to Scotland. I cannot tell you how much I appreciated all you said.

To have pleased those who best knew her and loved her was all that I could possibly have wished to do; and it was with much hesitation that I endeavoured to speak about her in your presence knowing how little adequate my small experience could be to describe her to you and yours.

It was only her intensity and her directness that made me think something of her real self was visible to one who knew her as little as I did.

I don't wonder that you so loved her, for I think she herself was devoted to you both, more than is common even with mothers. It was you as you were and as you were to be that filled all her mind.

I am sure you realise that her hopes won't be less, nor her care; and that 'death do us part' is only half a truth.

Indeed it will be a pleasure to me to keep this friendship which seems to have been woven out of the tragic ending of your mother. I shall feel that she has had some share in it and still has.

161. *BJ to Frank Sheed. From Downside. 7 September 1927. Transcript.*

You'll think me very rude, but I had a whole series of retreats and then had a week's holiday with no letters following me, and came back late last Friday[1] to find a pile of letters. I've demolished about 70 of them and am now pretty free.

Yes the immense French volumes came. They are too large for transportation; but I can refer to them when I perch at home in between my trips. But 200,000 words by June! It's rather beyond me for sometimes for days I can only manage my proper job and haven't the chance to write anything but letters. However I can but try. My ideas are clarifying and I think I can manage something helpful. But in the time? That's what's uncertain.

1. This letter was written on Wednesday.

162. *BJ to Sr M. Gabriel Fayer OP. From St Dominic's, London. 24 September 1927. Transcript.*

Thank you indeed for your wishes, your prayers, and your wonderful faithfulness in remembering my feast of Vows; it was indeed a Mother of Mercy who looked after me that day.[1] . . . .

May God bless you, especially through your S. Gabriel, next Sunday,² for S. Gabriel began the Rosary and is the cantor who 'gave out' the first versicle of that office of Our Lady's.³

1. BJ made his profession on 24 September 1899, the feast of Our Lady of Ransom. Three years later, on the same day, he made his solemn profession. At this period religious, including Dominicans, took simple (but perpetual) vows after their noviciate, and then solemn vows three years later (cf. 1872 Dominican Constitutions, Const. 274). It was not until the 1917 Code of Canon Law that temporary simple profession was introduced.
2. Sunday, 2 October, was the feast of the Guardian Angels.
3. The Little Office of Our Lady begins with the 'Hail Mary'.

163. *BJ to Bernard Delany OP. From St Dominic's, London. 3 October.*[1] *Autograph.*

... Please don't ask me to find another editor. It is difficult to squeeze things in as it is; and neither of the 2 you mention is available at the moment. Perhaps later on I may be able to do something, but it's difficult at present.

After all editors should ripen by practice and not grow stale. Look at F. Keating SJ![2] And Garvin![3] Wilder and more enthusiastic. Do please. . . .

Yes the windows are little openable in the choir.[4] With the 3 inches of ventilation in roof it's thought that the windows would be too much. I wonder.

Please tell F. Aidan[5] I hope to get off offices and masses of new feast[6] to him this week for you all + nuns.

1. The year is probably 1927. On 3 October 1927 the Provincial Council voted in favour of Delany being confirmed as prior of Hawkesyard.
2. Editor of *The Month* since 1912.
3. Editor of *The Observer* since 1908.
4. At Blackfriars, Oxford.
5. Aidan Elrington.
6. Presumably Christ the King, first introduced in October 1925.

164. *BJ to Miss Reichenbach.*[1] *From Carisbrooke. 8 October 1927. Transcript.*

I am sorry to hear of your loss; and yet not really sorry for after all it is not his gain only but yours as well.

It's true that your friend is gone, but not true that you have lost him for you are less likely now to be misunderstood, less likely to be misinterpreted, more likely to be appreciated and unselfishly loved.

He sees now the life on earth through the unclouded vision, if he sees at all; we don't know the conditions of Purgatorial life, but we do know that when he reaches Paradise he 'will know even as he is known';[2] and knowing God who is the Providence of the world he will see the work of that Providence in the souls dear to him, and now that he is to see clearly he will love where most on earth his love is merited. Have no fear!

1. We have not discovered who Miss Reichenbach was.
2. 1 Cor. 13:12.

165. *BJ to Aidan Elrington OP. From St Dominic's, London. 12 October 1927. Autograph.*

Very many thanks.
(1) Enclosed £10 is for 40 masses a.i.d.¹
(2) Don't like to think of staircase just yet as it will only land me in more debt. Perhaps later on; I know that one should do it now with workmen about but I dare not go into anything beyond what is strictly necessary. Bank charges 5½% on loan!—the villains.
PS I have assigned F.L.W.² to Oxford; have been through his clothes and shall tell the P. of H.³ what he needs.

1. For the donor's intention.
2. Luke Walker, who was just finishing as prior of Hawkesyard.
3. Procurator (bursar) of Hawkesyard.

166. *BJ to George Bowring. From St Dominic's, London. 30 October 1927. Transcript.*

Please don't think that anything you are likely to do will ever cause me the least pain or trouble.¹ In this particular point you raise I have nothing to say at all:
(i) Because you tell me your conscience is sure,
(ii) Because I should hate to have anyone remain in the Province who didn't want to be in it. Only willing members (however loyal they may be, those who are otherwise) are worth the common fellowship of the Province's life.

Naturally I had always hoped that those who loved the observances would remain to help to make weight against the clamorous demands of souls, to secure a balance, and help towards creating year by year more close attention to the monastic side of our life. But I frankly own that this requires a very great deal of hardship for those who throw in their lot with us; it means that they are to work (and live without seeing it) for the achievement of a monastic observance to be enjoyed by others, and hardly by themselves. Precisely because this will mean a very great deal of personal suffering (you are not alone in your desires; I speak of what I know), I gladly spare it to you who feel that you are called to other ways.

Pray for us sometimes who shall be labouring to build slowly out of tumult a fine austerity to the plan of S. Dominic.

1. This letter, with nos. 198 and 220, is an echo of a protracted crisis through which Bowring was passing, which, as he later wrote to Bernard Delany (26 December 1934), BJ handled with remarkable 'sweetness and patience'. He had joined the Dominicans rather than going to Downside because he thought that Dominicans were a kind of 'active Benedictines', among whom he would find 'monastic life plus preaching, teaching, the confessional, the missions', but he was specially devoted to the monastic aspect of the traditional Dominican synthesis as expounded by Mannes Jacquin OP in *Le Frère Prêcheur, Autrefois et Aujourd'hui* (Kain and Paris 1911), of which an English translation by Hugh Pope had been published, London 1915. He was encouraged by his novice master, Eustace O'Gorman, and (more temperately) by BJ in his enthusiasm for monastic observance. When he joined the Order he had not really taken in the extent to which English Dominicans were committed to parish life (personal letters to S.T., 11 March and 3 April 1989). Hugh Pope had encouraged him to hope that he would become a lector at Hawkesyard, and this was one reason why he made his solemn vows in 1925. But in fact he was never admitted as a candidate for the lectorate. Earlier in 1927 it had been decided that he should go to Louvain for his final two years of study after his ordination, but nothing had come of this either. So he was now thinking of transferring to the Canadian province, where he believed he would find a fuller monastic life and be less threatened by the risk of having to do parish work. As he later wrote to Delany, 'you will marvel at my not seeing for so long that unhesitating obedience to the will of my *external* superior must prevail over the judgment of a confessor and several advisers . . . and also over my own settled judgment . . . of my capacities and incapacities.'

167. *BJ to George Bowring. No address. 2 November 1927. Transcript.*

What have I said?[1] I never meant to hurt you or to suggest our friendship would be affected. Why should it, my dear? I merely wrote quiet facts which really seemed necessary to say; I didn't mean to make things harder for you. Don't let anything affect that.

However you won't think of doing anything till your study years are over; so let us talk when I come Nov. 21st.[2] Please let us pray over the will of God. Neither you nor I want anything but that. Either way is a hard way; hardness is of no consequence really, for love robs it of its power to pain.

1. Bowring had been upset by BJ's remark about not being worth the common fellowship of the province's life; see above, no. 166.
2. BJ visitated Hawkesyard 21-24 November.

168. *BJ to George Bellord. From East Grinstead. 17 December 1927. Autograph.*

Just a line to say my sorrow with you and yours![1] Yet I think he lived as long as he wished to live, namely to see you a partner and Bob well set on his life and Betty with the most delicate years over.[2]

Also my dear may I say that I think you have behaved all these years with exquisite sweetness to your father and have walked through your difficulties so as to have not only touched but assured him?

At times he was troubled; at the end he was perfectly content. He realised you'd done rightly.

May you be blest for your generous loyalty always to your mother's memory in him.

1. His father, Edmund Bellord, died on 17 December 1927.
2. Robert Bellord was then 19, and Elizabeth was his younger sister (now Lady Weld).

169. *BJ to Hubert van Zeller. From St Dominic's, London. 24 December 1927. Autograph.*

With your wonderful acumen, like the bloke in the Gospel who said he wouldn't and did,¹ you have timed your letter so perfectly that I got it on Christmas Eve; indeed I have just got it and my watch points exactly to 10.30 p.m.—so you have done the right thing, trying not to.

Behold a parable of the Odol Jelly!² Not a bit of a prophet who lets himself be had by another fellow also claiming to be a prophet (a nasty jar for F. Richard³ to find himself so described); but just the fellow who manages to do the right thing pretending not to, frivoling and ending in a monastery, trying to be romantic and being severely classical, determined to go by the way of self-direction and finding himself diverted into ways chosen by others.

Now listen to me, old fellow my lad; your job is to listen to other people's advice and never pay any further attention to it. Go your own way, exactly as you think God is calling you, only believe that prudence is a virtue and that prudence has got to be practised⁴ in order that the virtue should take proper effect. Don't suppose that prudence is one virtue to be practised at times—say after a good Benedictine breakfast—but it has a share in every virtue and must be present in every good act.

That's the jumping off ground, so you must begin on that.

Now further add this that impulses are not neccessarily inspirations. There's the very deuce of a difficulty in being able to say when they are inspirations and when they aren't: but be obedient to the divine will where it's clear—Catholic Church, obedience καὶ τὰ λοιπά⁵—and you'll be as sane as an human ever can be when you come to its obscurer manifestations.

Hence I'd say that you can stick to your jolly old *no compromise* by all means; only do be prudent in its expression. You'll certainly be happier and freer if you can find your way to it; but side by side be obedient in the least thing to authority. That will keep you sane.

You see, my dear, I do believe that you're one of that die-hard sort by nature and grace, and I'd say don't lay it aside for the sake of anyone, prophet or Lion[6] or blooming provincial: but remember that life is not exact and can't be, because it's life, and that in consequence prudence is always to be present (can you puzzle out the connection between prudence and the non-exact? What is prudence? its work?). Prudence doesn't mean that Good (in my intonation, if you please. Thank you!) is to be modified, but that the good suitable for the moment is to be chosen and not the good unsuitable. That too means *no compromise*.

To sum up—which means to try to get some coherence—I'd say that

A. No compromise is your nature—stick to it.
B. This implies always obedience
    (a) in letter
    (b) in spirit.
C. What's left over from obedience and lies under your free choice should be rigorously followed, whatever others may do or say, so long as you remember to consider the various points and choose (behold prudence), and not merely consider one point and choose.
D. Education in religious life is a rich habit that is trained to look at a thing from many points of view and to hold sanely to the judgement humbly, honestly, and frankly passed when that consideration has been duly and properly weighed.

Of course really there's no solution, except to love God and let Him rule you. No panics, no fears; obedience, loyalty to inspirations, consciousness of the impossibility of arriving at infallible decisions, and the figure of the Crucified as the central object of life are the means whereby you are to become yourself. Above all He will do it in you if you let Him. As Belloc says

> He was so small
> You could not see
> His large intent
> Of courtesy.[7]

He's courteous, He's our lover, our friend, walk with Him and He'll hold on to you;[8] He wants you and won't desert you. He's love.

Christmas and all that!

PS Thanks for booklet; I'm afraid I don't believe much in these spiritual Bradshaws,[9] but I love consulting them. I never get the right answer.

1. Matthew 21:29.
2. 'Jelly' was van Zeller's nickname; why 'Odol', we have not been able to discover. The background to much of this letter seems to be the novice master's belated intervention to overcome van Zeller's ascetic scruples about eating 'a good Benedictine breakfast' (cf. below, nos. 183 and 208). BJ is suggesting that the case is not parellel to that of the man of God in 3 Kings 13, who was told by the Lord not to eat or drink, but was beguiled into disobedience

by another man claiming to be equally a prophet. The unfortunate man of God was killed by a lion.
3. Richard Davey, novice master at Downside.
4. BJ actually wrote 'to practised'.
5. Greek for 'et cetera'.
6. Cf. above, note 2.
7. Hilaire Belloc, 'Courtesy'; see his *Verses*, London 1911, p. 21.
8. BJ actually wrote 'hold on you'.
9. Bradshaws were nation-wide train timetables.

170. *BJ to Rupert Hart-Davis. From St Dominic's, London. 13 January 1928. Autograph.*

Really that wasn't fair to give me a book in return.[1] It took away my complacent feeling of having done something for you and made me small again. That's a tactless way of beginning a letter of thanks, for despite that opening this is a letter of thanks for that book. It is a book which requires reading carefully and I haven't yet got the hang of it, nor seen quite what's the plan. But there are scattered phrases which are marvellous, whatever the poems may else have of obscurity.

'The lovely human counterpoint of pain',[2] 'the intolerable patience of the designing years',[3] etc. Curiously, the poems on the *Respectable woman* seemed to me to have most rhythm and even a sweetness of sound which some of the others lacked; but then I have only got as far as that and must read the others; again I shall have to take[4] them all over. It's so good of you and a much more valuable gift than you know.

You see, a priest wants to try to help people to achieve the knowledge and love of God of which they are capable, and yet he can't help people unless he knows them, but can help, more or less fully, in proportion to his knowledge of them. It's hardest of all for him to know the younger people who have moved from where he stands and he needs to know, not the individual merely but the spirit of the whole generation. Where else more shortly, finely and frankly shall he find this than in the poets? Rupert Brooke could have been but a few years my junior.[5] Already I can see that he's dead; his romanticism, his sureness, his definite knowledge have all lapsed, rubbed by the war from their clear lines to more smudged and vaguer clouds—not lines at all.

I am hoping through *Requiem* to know this new and attractive generation a little better. Perhaps through it, I may one day become a better friend, knowing better and seeing more truly and in the way of a more understanding service, and 'make smooth the path that runs

                from the sea to the sea.'[6]

My pen is dreadful today!

1. BJ gave Hart-Davis a copy of Eric Gill, *Art and Love*, Bristol 1927. In return Hart-Davis gave BJ the recently published volume of poems by Humbert Wolfe (1886-1940), *Requiem*, London 1927. The poems in this volume are gathered under a succession of headings, such as 'The Respectable Woman', which BJ mentions in the letter.
2. 'The Nun', p. 42.
3. 'The Anarchist', p. 49.
4. BJ actually wrote 'I shall to take'.
5. Rupert Brooke (1887-1915), one of the outstanding poets of the first World War.
6. *Requiem*, 'The Builder-II', p. 81.

171. BJ to Miss Savielle. From St Dominic's, London. 23 January 1928. Autograph.

I am sorry that you should have had a return of your old enemy;[1] I am afraid that there must be no remedy from without and that the only safe-guard even can come from within. It is you and no other who can cure yourself, or rather *let God cure you*. The loneliness of Christ has won for all of us the grace to face our loneliness, seeing in it the exlusion of all else but God. Take, if you can get it, the *Hound of Heaven*[2] and read it slowly, tasting one by one the things that failed him and seeing how their removal was only to bring his soul face to face with God. *Then* at last when he had found God all the rest came back to him. That's the line of thought.

1. Depression (cf. below, no. 177).
2. By Francis Thompson. This was a poem which fascinated BJ, who often used it as the basis for talks.

172. BJ to Aiden Elrington OP. From St Dominic's, London. 27 January 1928. Autograph.

Beginning to despair of funds. Can you send me Italian booklet which gives account of the Lucca choir books?[1] It was with the books. I can then see whether I can find a market for 'em. The book was by predecessor of Walz, Taurisano or some such name.[2] At least I think so.

1. Three antiphonars, one gradual and one psalter, with miniatures by Sr Eufrasia Burlamacchi OP, completed in about 1505 in the Dominican monastery of St Dominic, Lucca. In 1929 BJ presented them to the Dominican sisters of San Rafael, California. On 23 October 1929 he wrote to Mother Raymond O'Connor, the prioress general, 'I am glad you enjoyed the books . . . I gave them because I knew they would be appreciated and inspire you and yours. I paid a good deal for them years ago to save them from going out of Dominican nuns, the Lucca nuns having lodged them with a Roman bookseller to sell for them as they were so poor. The nuns got a good price. I tried to resell them to some Dominican nuns in U.S.A. at the same price and failed, some not answering and others not being able to afford them. Then I thought of the poor books themselves and the need they must have for reverential treatment. Also I thought that you had been generous to me. Finally I knew that they would become with you not merely heirlooms but an inspiration for chaunt, illumination, and culture. The great thing

is to employ one's talents to the full. I judged the talents of these volumes would be best and most fully employed at San Rafael's. I was so touched you see by your Dominicanism, its fire and its fidelity, that I longed to do what I could to increase it even more' (from the archives of San Rafael). In 1951-52 the books were on display, and, in a booklet produced for the occasion, the story of their arrival is related: 'In 1929 [this should be 1928] the Very Reverend Bede Jarrett, Provincial of the Dominicans in England, . . . conducted a retreat for the Sisters of the Dominican Order in San Rafael. The Sisters were impressed by Father Jarrett, but, although edified by the retreat, were concerned because he was extremely reserved, hardly speaking to anyone. The Reverend Mother M. Raymond OP, then Mother General of the Dominican Sisters, felt that, perhaps, Father Jarrett had not enjoyed his stay at the College. However, after he returned to England, he wrote Mother Raymond a cordial letter, praising the community of Sisters. In this same letter, he mentioned, quite casually, that, in appreciation of the hospitality extended to him by the Sisters, he was sending a gift of some books to the College. These books were assumed, by Mother Raymond, to be a few volumes for the library . . . The gift arrived on September 2, 1929. They are not ordinary library books at all . . .'.

The art of painting miniatures was favoured in the monasteries of the Dominican reform. Giovanni Dominici OP, himself a gifted miniaturist, taught the art to some of the nuns in Pisa and when, in 1502, the new reformed monastery of St Dominic, Lucca, was established, sisters from Pisa were sent there to help with the new foundation. In 1927 the community of St Dominic, Lucca, moved to S. Maria in Sasso.

2. I. Taurisano, *I Domenicani in Lucca*, Lucca 1914. The artists among the nuns are treated of in pp. 147-183; for Sr Eufrasia see pp. 160-161.

173. BJ to Miss Savielle. From St Dominic's, London. 15 March 1928. Autograph.

. . . As for the idea of mortification, you know F. Baker's distinction between that and penance.[1] He considers that some people (but not all) are called to penance, in the sense of self-inflicted penance; but that all are called to mortifications i.e. receiving patiently those sent them by God. I suppose one starts with the purpose of penance, namely self-control, and works to that by the means most suitable to each. Violent people need the curb of self-inflicted penances; other folk are better without. But patience is good for all of us and needed by all of us, so that there we can hold on at any rate: so put down your food as before but put up with your table companions instead. . . .

1. Cf. Augustine Baker, *Holy Wisdom*, section I chapter 5.

174. BJ to Mrs Tytus. No Address. 1 April 1928. Autograph.

'Ragged looking figures', 'tidies it up', 'looks much nicer'? Dearie me! What's to be said? Sister Ben,[1] what can I say? The grace and gracefulness, the airy toss of the shower of gold, the charming way it's done, stop my heart. What's to be said, Sister Ben? What *is* to be said?

I can only say that it is you exactly as you have always been to me, overwhelmingly kind with jests to cover the kindness, with terrifying sympathy, with a princely width of munificence that shuts one up, voice and pen and heart even: such a flood, to anyone greeted by it, makes one gasp and be silent except for a splutter of noise. That splutter went into a telegram. Twenty thousand thanks, and an earlier fifteen thousands thanks! Thirty five thousand thanks! What can I do but offer my Mass for you whenever I have a free day. But I've done that already since the gift first began its shower: how can I add to that? I can only go on doing that whenever the chance comes.

I believe that I have been left money for the endowment of the place, a £1000 by an aunt of F. Norbert[2] who died the other day, distressed at his death and what befell before it: and another £500 by an old family servant of some cousins of mine, a fine old Bretonne, dying at 82, after being in the family since she was 16. She told me she was leaving me that: so I daresay it will come along. But in neither case have I official information of these bequests: both died in March. This is only to let you see that the continuance of the work in being assured: Blessed those who give having seen the venture come into existence: more blessed you who gave when no stick or stone was visible,[3] believing in the vision when my own brethren did not believe in it, as a practical thing.

I can remember one of the members of my Council looking round at the place in the early days when the foundations were being put in and when the Council was there on the spot[4] looking at the plans and saying: 'Well, we shan't live to see anything built worth calling a building.' I remember how I winced inside. He's alive still to see what your hopefulness inspired and gave.

You see my dear Sister Ben I do realise that you are really thus the founder of the whole in that you gave first and consistently and generously—when you had all sorts of other dreams and ideals as well. It is to you only that I have shown my moments of panic and cowardice: to whom else could I have shown them, than to you, best and most unselfish and most virile of friends? Never anything but a bold front to the rest of the world, to my home and my brethren and the others I know. You have seen me at my worst and have been kinder than those who saw what seemed to them courage and faith: 'they saw the tower; I saw the sun.' So you see, my dear, it's you who have put heart into me and into the building, who have upheld it, inspired the hope that went on with things, and held it together till now.

May God bless you in His Garden of the Resurrection[5] who have in your love for Him been fine enough and delicate enough to help us to fulfil His purposes despite our fears! There are some of us, priests, who under God owe you all. Oh how empty all this sounds! But it's true, true. God bless you.

1. 'Sister Benvenuta' was Mrs Tytus' religious name as a Dominican tertiary.
2. Norbert Wylie, who had died recently, having left the order and the church in the previous year.
3. Cf. John 20:29.
4. See above, no. 55.
5. 1 April 1928 was Palm Sunday.

175. *BJ to Mrs Tytus. From Woodchester. 5 May 1928. Autograph.*

Another birthday![1] Troublesome? Why no! You remember the old saying that the further off from England the nearer 'tis to France, so that however far you drift out from land you're getting nearer to land none the less. So we comfort ourselves from what we're leaving for all the more we are getting to. Here in the new year is always a new hope, a heart reborn.

You so happily hearted with courage won't need these sayings. May God be with you! You shall have my Mass on the 10th.

We've had our Provincial Chapter. It has just finished and I go back to London on Monday. I had an invitation to give retreats in California and as soon as I was elected Provincial sent it on to F. J. B. Reeves as I could no longer take it, I feared. He at once sent it to the Diffinitory (the 4 elected in the Provincial Chapter who boss everything) who ordered me to take it. Nice of him, wasn't it? So off I go in early June to be back at the end of July. It's the O.P. Nuns at San Rafael who've asked and they've sent me £200 to cover expenses! A blessing on their heads! America again!

This Diffinitory settled to open Oxford Whit Sunday 1929, centenary of Catholic Emancipation and our celebration of it. You'll come? The same have ordered every Priory to say a Mass pro Domina Carlotta Tytus eximia benefactrice nostri conventus Oxoniensis![2] I was pleased when they suggested that, themselves.

1. 10 May was the anniversary of Mrs Tytus' reception into the Catholic church.
2. Acta of the Provincial Chapter of 1928, p. 13.

176. *BJ to Mother Dominic Geoghegan. From Woodchester. 5 May 1928. Transcript.*

Thank you indeed. I know that you'll pray for me lest I make even worse messes, without and within.[1]

1. The Provincial Chapter finished at Woodchester on 5 May, and BJ had been re-elected provincial. The priest who transcribed this card noted down the circumstances: 'A post card

from Fr Bede to Mother Dominic, written in reply to a letter from her to console him when he had been re-elected Provincial. He had been down to see her shortly before the Chapter and had told her how much he dreaded being re-elected.'

177. BJ to Miss Savielle. No address. 14 May 1928. Autograph.

. . . Of course the cure from within for depression is not a merely human one but the effect of grace: it can come from closing one's thoughts and imagination to the present day things and troubles, and by remembering with eyes shut that God is in the centre of your being, it means leaning back on God.

Once we see in the quiet darkness of closed eyes that God is within us and that He gives us power from within, that He is infinite joy, that He is the only joy there is to be hereafter, that we hold Him now and that He holds us, then the cause of the depression should be scotched by substituting for it the serene dependence upon God; the rock foundation, which winds and rain and the sea cannot throw down.[1]

1. Cf. Matthew 7:25.

178. BJ to Mrs Campbell. No address. 24 May 1928. Transcript.

Thank you for reminding me. I shall gladly share in the *Novena* from Saturday till Trinity Sunday.[1] The Holy Ghost is so good a friend that we know well He has His charge of the world.

And now He's needed badly while all the world gropes for the light. The destruction of the old ways seem accomplished, while the new ways are not yet clearly marked either by custom or light. Even lawyers whom I have seen lately are worried over the dissolution of principles in law, case after case on appeal is decided by 2 to 3 or 1 or 2 i.e. where there is no clear ruling and where principles have failed. So a number of them, Catholics, have formed themselves into a *Sir Thomas More Society* which has for its object to study law and cognate subjects on the principles of Catholic philosophy.[2] That's good, isn't it? or else we shall become like your little Hedgehog or Ernest Oldmeadow (perhaps he walks the earth at night like that), bristles and spikes.[3] Sir Thomas will give us the due perspective and the spirit of wit, wisdom, and constancy.

1. 26 May—3 June.
2. The Thomas More Society was founded in 1928 by Richard O'Sullivan QC (1888-1963), a leading Catholic barrister, who went on to become Master Treasurer of the Middle Temple and Recorder of Derby. It continues in 1989 as the Thomas More Society of Lincolns Inn. Among its early speakers was John Baptist Reeves OP in February 1928. BJ spoke to the Society on 16 January 1931 on 'The outlook in England'. The Society gave the impulse to the

first Thomas More Exhibition in Chelsea, 1929. Richard O'Sullivan played a leading role in the Friends of Blackfriars and in the Bede Jarrett Memorial Fund, both designed to raise financial support for Blackfriars, Oxford; he was also one of the moving spirits in the Aquinas Society. According to Douglas Woodruff, he was 'a man of wide Catholic sympathies', but 'felt a special attraction to the Dominicans' (contribution to B. A. Wortley, ed., *The Spirit of the Common Law*, Tenbury Wells 1965, p. 16).

3. Oldmeadow was the notoriously prickly editor of *The Tablet*.

179. *BJ to Miss Calthrop. From St Dominic's, London. 5 August 1928. Autograph.*

It is most kind of you to have thought of this and to have organised it:[1] for I am sure it is your doing, the concept of it and the work. You could not have shown your understanding and your sympathy in any better way, and I am indeed grateful to you for it.

Still I do ask you not to proceed with the matter. My reasons are various, but the chief reason is that the mere 25 years of my priesthood is something which I cannot well help. It's perhaps not to my credit that I have lived for 25 years as a priest: certainly it is not my 'doing' but a gift to me. So much does this really mean to me that I have always refused to serve on committees for other people's jubilees. I think the idea wrong. Now having refused others, can I very well let this go forward? Greed urges me, and even more your kindness in thinking of it. But please thank all of those whose names are there, for me, and believe that most of my thanks go to you.

Gratefully for more than gold.

1. Plans were being made for a presentation to BJ to celebrate his silver jubilee as a priest; since he objected to this, a group was started, called 'The Friends of Blackfriars', to build up an endowment for the new priory at Oxford. Later it was decided to keep the Friends in being, as a relatively predictable source of donations to the house. On 3 December 1935, in the course of Vincent McNabb's golden jubilee celebrations in London, Bernard Delany recalled BJ's refusal to celebrate his own silver jubilee and said that BJ had commented 'that it was not very much to a priest's credit to keep a jubilee; if he had done his job properly he would have died long ago' (*The Universe* 6 Dec. 1935).

180. *BJ to George Bellord. From St Dominic's, London. 6 August 1928. Autograph.*

Your news is just perfect.[1] I am so very glad about it and I know that in that other place where the souls of the just see what befalls those whom they love on earth, there will be joy indeed in those two who most cared for you when they were on earth.

Of course if I can, I'd be so very glad to marry you to her, it would be the fulfilment of a dream: so let me have (if you can) a few days of choice when you are finally settling and I'll do everything

I can to be there. I am sure that this will be the real life for you and that you will be with her more thoroughly yourself.

Just off for a series of retreats but shall hope one day to be able to meal with you.

1. His engagement to Marjorie Strangways.

181. *BJ to Mrs Tytus. From St Dominic's, London. 10 August [1928]. Autograph.*

I begin this early . . . to make sure of reaching you in time for August 15,[1] so as to assure you of my Mass for you and him that day. You won't need to be told, I hope, that I shall be saying Mass for you and him then: but I like to tell you none the less. Indeed even more so this time from what you tell me of him on 'the Singing Sands' and you with him and your delight in the house and your disdain of the hotels. You contrast that disdain with today. It's that that makes me want to say that you and he shall be remembered that day, for I can guess at the sorrows that so small a sentence hides and reveals. The whole sense of *home* has gone for you in that human cosy sense: life is a mere *hotel-life*, beggared of him. I suppose it would be so even were you actually settled anywhere definitely, it would be a house but not a home. In one of those American poems in the Anthology I found at San Rafael was a line which redeemed a poem from foolishness. I hope I didn't quote it to you before:

'for life is only a small house and love is an open door'.

The picture is fine, I think, the wee house that all our life ever really reaches to, and then the one big thing in it—love, and love a way out from life. Love is your way out of the 'small house', for love is an open door. In spite therefore of your hotel-existence and all its wanderings, you have never missed that open door, for it has been the unfailing and unquenchable spirit of love in you that has saved you from the else-inevitable bitterness and from the failure of courage that one sees elsewhere, the sunny hearted joyousness that one associates with your presence.

His going has somehow given a golden heart to you which is unchangeable in you all these years.

His death on the feast of the Mother's love, and its complete fulfilment in her, has made it so that you are now never to be separated and even one day to be more closely joined.

I don't think that he will need prayers but one knows so little of God's justice and the mechanism of that other life, that I shall say Mass none the less for you both, for peace for both of you.

Pray for me.

1. The feast of the Assumption, and the anniversary of her husband's death.

182. *BJ to Mrs Tytus. No address. 17 August 1928. Autograph.*

But you have been so swift and so generous! I do thank you! I do thank him. May he and you be blessed for your great kindnesses! May the peace of the Lord and the glory of the Lord be on you both for evermore! The Lord is wonderfully good to me. He sent you and you have been indeed a godsend.

I loved too your quotations, so rich in the simplicity of the ideas. 'Life joyous', why surely! It is love alone that can make it so; Him whom we are set to love is joy incarnate. 'The empty heart cannot be robbed.' That's fine too. The Lady Poverty who tempts no thieves and fears none. It's the Epistle of St Paul, 'having nothing and possessing all things',[1] the fine poverty of the lover of God, who owns nothing and holds All.

> Say not the struggle naught availeth
> The labour and the wounds are vain
> The enemy faints not, nor faileth
> And as things have been they remain.
> For while the tired waves vainly breaking
> Seem here no painful inch to gain,
> Far back through creeks and inlets making
> Comes silent flooding in the main.

P.S. EUROPE[2] being revised!

1. 2 Cor. 6:10.
2. BJ's *History of Europe*. It was finally published in 1929.

183. *BJ to Hubert van Zeller. No address. 29 September 1928. Autograph.*

Thanks for your letter. I am glad that you have been 'through it' and come out into the other side. It is a good sign too that now you don't want people to notice your observance but your good spirits; another leg up will have happened (does a 'leg up' happen or occur or take place?) when you really don't care what folk say of you and indeed prefer to have a goodness that no man sees, knows, or guesses. But really you must aim at sanctity and not merely at being 'a thundering good chap and no more'. You see holiness is the will of God for us: so that we have always to be aiming at it and can't ever be content with less—or rather, we have to alter our whole view of holiness and no longer look on it as something we do but something done to us: 'we are patient of divinity' says Denis.[1] Which means that God works in us. Richard Rolle's phrase you'll remember: 'There's no *doer* but he.'[2] Isn't that the true mysticism? I don't become a saint but I let God make a saint of me. I deliberatlely seek His will where and when I see it, and I know that He will make a saint of me for 'the will of God is my sanctification'.[3] But it is not I, but He, that works.

So that, to use your own way of putting it, one shouldn't expatiate on what folk think of us, but only at the odd comments the Three-in-One might make in their eternal conversation: 'Hubert, all right you know, but rather foolish, the way he won't let Us deal with him. Frightfully pig-headed and all that. Doesn't give a fellow the chance to make him really what he could be, but is bothering about what he's got to do. As though he were anything! Scruples and all that bunkum! Terrified of a hearty breakfast! Frightened of brawn! As though that mattered, when it's under obedience. Rather silly of the Novice master to have let him starve himself to start with. He'll jolly well have to feed to get sane again. But if he'd only realise that he's got to be passive in Our hands, he'd have a happier time than he has, and fruitfuller too. Between You and Me, he's got the makings of a rather charming saintlet. But he won't let himself be led. He will want to put everything right. Yet his character is attractive—a mixture of My humour and My love of high things. He's got the go and the grit and the guts: but he lacks sense!'

That's more or less what I overheard of the *arcana Dei* the last time but one I had an ecstasy; I give it you for what it's worth. Anyhow let the 'dear physician' on his feast-day[4] heal you of your worries with the cool strength of his touch. May he show you, as in his Gospel he loves to do, the innermost recesses of the Prayer of Christ! May he show you how to lie limp in the everlasting arms, *removens prohibens*,[5] getting rid of self more and more, and leaving all to the Wisdom, Love, and Power of God.

1. Pseudo-Dionysius, *Divine Names* 2:9 (PG 2:648B).
2. In fact, Julian of Norwich, Long Text chapter 11.
3. 1 Thess. 4:3.
4. St Luke (cf. Col. 4:14); his feast day was on 18 October.
5. A kind of incidental cause, recognised by scholastic thought, on the basis of Aristotle, *Physics* VIII 255b24: A can be said to move (or effect) B, if it removes something which is preventing a movement or effect which would otherwise be occurring in B. One of St Thomas' examples is that of a column supporting a heavy weight: if the column is broken, the weight will fall, so whatever is responsible for the breaking of the column is indirectly responsible for the weight falling (*In Libros Physicorum* VIII lect. 8:7; Leonine edition vol. II p. 392). In the jargon, this kind of incidental cause is designated 'removens prohibens' (e.g. *Summa Theologiae* I q.19 a.12).

184. *BJ to Mrs Tytus. No address. 20 December 1928. Autograph.*

I am not very sure whether all this fuss over early posting for Xmas is to be taken seriously but in case it is let me thus 5 days before the time send you every blessed wish for Xmas and the New Year. You shall be remembered most in my Midnight Mass which shall be wholly yours, so that He that came may thank you as best He only can for all that you have done for Him to me and those many others whom for His blessed sake you have helped.

He came in that silence that you love, in the dark, that He might accomplish His miracle of love, a miracle of healing and of life-giving, to those that laboured so with death in every form. He came giving; and those whom most He praised and defended were those who gave of their best to Him or in the treasury to the poor. These have never lacked His defence nor ever will. He's on their side always because by giving they have put themselves on His. May He therefore give you always the assurance of His protecting hand! 'Prove me now herewith, saith the Lord of Hosts, if I will not open you the windows of Heaven, and pour you out a blessing, that there shall not be room to receive it.'[1] May he open then His windows and to you who live where His casement is above you (for He dwells in the hills and where the air is more rarefied so that those with clean eyes may see Him) may there come the freshest and most choice of His blessings, the fulness of life and its appreciations, the sense of the full beauty of His world, the love of those you love, and 'a shining peace under the stars.'

I am not quite sure whether your grandchildren are to be with you for Xmas or whether they come to you after that. But your heart will necessarily be with them and you will be now the central home of their lives. It is wonderful thus towards the ending to have inherited at last the love so long deferred, and to you who have been so long an exile that it should be granted to have become yourself a home. Xmas will make you think of all this, and of God over you, and the dead held in with you, and the living turning towards you. It is the feast of gathered memories, and of the keen thoughts of the living. . . .

Have you read *Marius the Epicurean*[2] lately? I am re-reading it and can't think how blithely I can have read it years ago. It is interesting but rather stiff reading now to me. Was I sharper or less observant then? It seems now to require a great deal more thought and leisure for thought than I can possibly have given to it then—and yet I 'loved' it in those days and have ever since recommended it to all sorts of young men whom now I see wouldn't have understood very much of it at all. Do you ever find shocks like that? and wonder what sort of ideas you had when you were young? Or have you always remained the same, gay and sensitive to beauty, with your mature judgement of things and people, and your downright insistence upon the fine niceties of honour? I see all that in the determined pen and its sabre strokes and the undeviating and measured solemnity of the letters. I have at times guessed you have always been the same for you show now both maturity and the gifts of the girl. But this is getting embarrassing. I must stop.

1. Malachi 3:10.
2. By Walter Pater, first published London 1885.

185. *BJ to Hubert van Zeller. From St Dominic's, London. 22 December 1928. Autograph.*

A long Christmas letter? But why? You have all the great O's,[1] you say, bumping all about you, and you'll have the Midnight Mass καὶ τὰ λοιπά. Isn't that enough in all conscience? What can you want more? or at least what more to be said? All that could be said, is said there: for the rest all that remains is silence in which to look at it all again and again till it sinks deeply into the soul. Don't you feel that to say anything on this big feast-day is sheer impertinence?

I hope so, because being a Dominican I love being impertinent, and so how I shall talk after that charming little introduction which breathes the spirit of S. Bernard, Serenus Cressy, and Dom Christopher Batley[2]—whom I have seen at the New Caldey, looking magnificent, without an inch of superfluous flesh or an ounce, with his low-cut habit or rather smock, his chain of silver showing round his neck, his determined mouth while as cellarer he directs the rebuilding of the house and sets Theodore Baily[3] to nail lathes on to the ceiling and marshals the 10 laybrothers to hoist steel girders and chivvies the Subprior-and-Novice-Master[4] out of the way into the fields to say his prayers and keep quiet and not interfere, a veritable S. Bernard indeed, new born, comely, attractive, with eyes like a sailor's, farseeing and impersonal, and the vigour of human energy and a blazing soul in corpore sano. Lord, what a sentence! I feel quite exhausted. But I haven't yet got to Christmas and its lessons.

Speaking of Christopher Batley reminds me of Geoffrey[5] who also is rather a stained glass figure, if he'd only wear long pointed shoes and turn his toes out; well, I supped with him and his-and-your aunt[6] in their half-castle, half-surgery, (high walls, a drawbridge, and a light over the door). Geoffrey's room is rather characteristic, bare, coloured, and with shelves draped. We sat, talked, ate, and talked, chiefly of some Dutch monk I missed (for whom Dutch cheese had been ordered by your tactful elderly relative) and of you, and (whenever Geoffrey went out of the room) about his hard lot, and especially about you. Poor beggar! I can see him in sheer despair becoming a monk too, shocked into its comforts by the disagreeableness of ordinary life (ahem!), except that he's got an aunt about the premises which makes, or who makes, a difference. They followed me to Brook Green where I discoursed on prayer. Needless to say, I have never heard of them again. . . .

Well, I suppose now I can safely come down to Christmas as you can't expect more than a few lines more from me after those 2 pages. A telephone call from Leonard Parker's papa to supply for them and stop over from today till after Christmas has had to be refused reluctantly, because I'd thrill in my lower nature at the prospect of food, fires, and fun; instead I say midnight mass in a nursing home to cheer up some patients and nurses, and dine at night—as always since 1911—with the Bellord family in the charming new flat owned by Geo and Mrs Geo[7] at the end of Kensington High Street! It's all new and upholstered after Mrs Geo's designs, frightfully modern, with yellow cupboards and unlikely looking red splodges and most exacting curves and curlicules, where the chief centre of attraction is the bath and the next the cupboard which turns on its own electric light directly you open the door; at least so it's said. Of course no one can tell whether it goes out when the door is shut for there isn't room for anyone inside to watch and see. It looks as though it were always alight, because when you do open the door, at once---but I really can't go on with the cupboard for it only held her dresses or pocket handkerchiefs, I couldn't tell which and didn't like to ask in the event of her not being able to be sure herself.

Phew! That's three pages! Can I hang on for a fourth? I'll have a good try.

Now Christmas is the feast of the Child. He comes as a Child because that is the sign of His discipleship, the friendliness, the snuggling confidence, the joyous forgetfulness of yesterday and tomorrow, the fine disregard of conventions or 'laws that lackeys make' and the whole concentration on the personal side of life, its not mattering in itself and its intense mattering in relation to everyone else. Things being valuable because of the people who gave them, and places because they are full of memories, and dreams because they are already old, and clothes because they are familiar, and a garden because it is never the same. All that personal philosophy of life, together with an immeasurable power of fancy, is the gift of Childhood and it is the gift of Christ to His followers.

Do you know He only once called them *children*? He named them apostles, He called them friends, He described one as Satan, another as a devil, He called them servants and followers:[8] but only at the end, in John XXI, did he call them children.[9] Through what a discipline had they passed before He gave them that name, through what failures, trials, humiliations, shocks to faith and hope, through what bleak wastes of desolation and lack of prayer, through what weariness had they to go before they became children. It's a thing one has to become. Easily one could see in Bethlehem a high city reached after Calvary by us; we pass the passion to reach childhood. It's not a condition but a goal. There, 'we pass the land of Intarry!'[10]

May Christmas lead you to those blessed and bare heights!

1. A series of Magnificat antiphons, all beginning with 'O', used at Vespers for nine days before Christmas.
2. A monk who had received the habit at Downside, but then transferred to Caldey, and so was one of the community who established the new monastery at Prinknash. Caldey was originally an Anglican monastery, founded in 1906. In 1913 the monks became Catholics, and in 1928 they moved to Prinknash Park in Gloucestershire (here called 'the New Caldey' by BJ).
3. A priest monk, who had been a novice at Downside and then moved to Caldey, moving to Prinknash with the rest of the monks in 1928.
4. Benedict Steuart, who had made his monastic profession for Fort Augustus, but then transferred to Caldey, where he became subprior in 1927. He became prior of Prinknash in 1929.
5. Van Zeller's brother, who later entered the monastery at Downside and was clothed as Dom Simon in 1929.
6. It is not clear which of van Zeller's four aunts this refers to.
7. George Bellord and his wife.
8. Cf. Luke 6:13, John 15:14, Matthew 16:23. John 6:71, John 13:16, Matthew 19:28.
9. John 21:5.
10. We have not been able to identify the source of this quotation, assuming that it is one.

186. *BJ to Mrs Tytus. From St Dominic's, London. 23 December 1928. Autograph*

But dear dear Sister Ben, you really are terrifying in your generosity, and I don't know what to say in thanks except thanks indeed. You have been my good fairy for so many years, waving wands and producing out of nothing the stable achievement of my dreams. What am I to do, who guess but dimly all that this means by way of cost and price and denial to one like you? May the blessed God comfort you and inspire you and give you His best and choicest gifts in every imaginable way and even unimaginable.

I shall write again later when I have recovered my balance but this is a *cri de coeur* of ever so many thanks for your everlasting kindness to me and mine. At the dawn Mass then we shall meet in Him who alone can thank you for me.

187. *BJ to Hubert van Zeller. From Fort Augustus Abbey. 28 March 1929. Autograph.*

As I was saying the other day when you interrupted me by not answering, I think that your vanity gets in your way; a birthday[1] is a good time for considering that point and for making an effort at humility. To be practical on one's birthday is inappropriate, so let's be idealists for the moment and recognise the fact that humility consists in building on God because we recognise that no other foundation is well and truly laid. But building on God gives one unlimited confidence or (as we'd have said 'when we were very young'[2]) unlimited cheek. This in turn means that we aim at any heights and plug away till we die, trusting not to our bodies (plumpifying daily here, there growing thinner) but to His wings. Hence dare anything even to hope one day to see established a more austere way of life (even though God waits till He makes you an instrument of it, not faute de mieux but faute de pieux, for the weak and contemptible has He always chosen) in religious houses everywhere. As a boy from Downside said to me the other day to explain why he wished to join[3] a particular order that he wanted sacrifice, 'sacrifice is attractive at my age.' Is it only at his age or at all ages, dear Jelly lover of disciplines, that sacrifice appeals?

PS I did mean to wish you all blessed birthdayness and the offer of my Mass for more cheek for you.

1. Van Zeller's birthday was 3 April.
2. No doubt an allusion to A. A. Milne's famous book of poems, first published in 1924.
3. BJ actually wrote 'to joy'.

188. *BJ to Mrs Tytus. From East Grinstead. 3 April 1929. Autograph.*

Just a line of such grateful thanks for your letter and its completing gift. You have been a blessed friend in every way possible and even what seemed impossible!

Say a prayer for my mother who is not expected to last through the day.[1] She's not in pain but very drowsy and eager to die.

I watched the nurse holding her hand and surreptitiously feeling her pulse. She also watched the nurse out of one corner of her eye. Said she, 'Is my pulse weaker?' 'No,' said the nurse triumphantly, 'it is quite good.' 'Botheration!' answered my mother. Complete discomfiture of the nurse!

1. Mrs Jarrett lasted a little longer and died on 20 January 1930, aged eighty.

189. *BJ to Frank Sheed. From East Grinstead. 5 April 1929. Transcript.*

I return to London tomorrow where I shall no doubt find that Life of S. Catherine of Siena and shall do what I can for it.[1]

As regards my book,[2] I had a covering letter from Dr McQuaid[3] and also a short criticism from a priest of his congregation who made some corrections in detail but thought I wan't *Catholic enough* or strong enough in my assertion of the goodness of the popes. I know that criticism of that sort is to be expected. But if I don't happen to think them admirable, I can't well say that I do. But I am a little agitated over the reading of the proof-sheets: I shall be away on a Dominican pilgrimage July 31-Aug 14, and am wondering (a) how long the MS is likely to remain in Ireland; it has been there since Sept, (b) when I shall get it back in order to re-read it and correct it in the light of the Irish comments, (c) how long the proofs will take arriving; I shall need to have at the end of the book the lists (with dates of reigns) of Popes, Emperors of East, Emperors of the West, Kings of France, England (not the heptarchy),[4] the Kings of the various Spains and Scandinavias, the same of Russia, Poland, the Italies. Most of these you will find at the end of Hassall's book.[5] Also genealogical tree of the Carolings.

As regards a book for your club,[6] would a book of Meditations do? Somewhat after the type of the Meds. for Layfolk only rather for young men? I could let you have that within the period you have named. But I don't know quite what sort of people subscribe or what they can swallow in the way of pieties. . . .

1. Almost certainly the manuscript of Alice Curtayne, *Saint Catherine of Siena*, which Sheed and Ward published later in 1929.
2. *History of Europe*.
3. John Charles McQuaid (1895-1973), a Holy Ghost father, at this time teaching at Blackrock College, of which he was president 1931-39. He was later a redoubtable Archbishop of Dublin (1940-72).
4. The seven Anglo-Saxon kingdoms which coexisted in England from the 6th to the 8th centuries.
5. A. Hassall, *European History, Chronologically Arranged*, London 1920.
6. The 'Book a Month' club. BJ sent in a text he already had, which was published in 1930 as *The Space of Life Between*. Shortly after it was published he wrote to a friend of his who was at that time working at Sheed and Ward, 'I was rather astonished to hear from you when I was away that the *Space of Life Between* was too small for the ordinary book you have; however since you said so I presumed the book was smaller than I thought. But my astonishment faded when I found on Saturday night that in the hurried business of sending it off to you the last third had got left behind and was reposing peaceful and undisturbed on my shelves. Hence I had another third planned for the book and written 4 years ago! Nobody will be any the worse, that's the sad part about it' (12 August 1930).

190. *BJ to Frank Sheed. From St Dominic's, London. 13 April 1929. Transcript.*

Your letter and the MS to hand. I go away for a week but hope to be able to look at it on my return. Have had meetings all this week; haven't been able to get out at all these last 2 days, business meetings of province and letters (35 yesterday and not all finished that should be written). I only say this to prepare you for some delay in going through the volume. I don't see how I can get it done this month. I'll try but really just now it's going to be rather difficult. It isn't the work but the time: I have to give the Province precedence over everything else. It's my duty. This other's a mere recreation!

Shall work in the statement you suggest about bad Popes and infallibility somewhere.[1]

The Irish comments[2] not yet to hand, so that's as well.

Shall write the description for you. Also a brief preface. . . .

1. The published text of BJ's *History of Europe* does not seem to contain any such statement.
2. See above, no. 189.

191. *BJ to John Baptist Reeves OP. From Hampstead Cenacle. 28 April 1929. Autograph.*

I hope you're better for your holiday. I meant to have a talk with you on Saturday morning but I had misunderstood my retreat time and had to come over for Mass instead of starting, as I thought, on Saturday afternoon.[1]

You must have been ill and overwrought during Lent because you evidently scared the Oratorians, F. D. Sheil[2] especially, by what you said in your week there—about the Bl Sacrament and our Lady and marriage. I can't get hold of what it is that scared them for they have made no complaints to me: but they have scared Canon Roskell[3] and he wants me to send another retreatant to the teachers in your place. I know that you won't have done more than F. V. McN.[4] does, namely putting things in so arresting a way as to startle them for I am sure you wouldn't teach what wasn't the truth. But evidently the teachers have heard of all this and they and D. S. and the Bishop[5] have all made Canon R. think that you will hear of this when you go there and that it will make you self-conscious and uncomfortable and that for your own sake you'd better not go at present.

You know, my dear Father, that I have no fear of you or for you, and that I would trust you to the world's end. But I don't want you bothered. Which would you prefer? To face it? or would you rather I fetched in another. Canon R. is evidently thinking more of you than of the crowd. So tell me and I will back you up whichever you think best.

Aelred could take it or Edwin,[6] I think: so there's no trouble from my end.

If you think it wiser for you not to go, I would like you instead at that time to take the Redcar retreat to the Nuns[7] (I have you down for Torquay at that very date; but I think it must have been revoked). You see I don't believe that you taught what should not be.

Perhaps too you'll have heard that Leicester nearly elected you Prior;[8] in the last scrutiny (3rd) Fabian[9] had 4 votes and you 3! I'm not sorry that you didn't get in there, for it will be worrying, the getting of money for the building of the Church: but somewhere else you'll be elected. Your brethren believe in you. What does the rest matter? As Kipling says, 'the sweetest praise is the praise of an equal'; the most blessed confidence is the confidence of a brother who knows the worst and believes the best.

1. BJ was giving a week-end retreat at the Hampstead Cenacle. 28 April was the Sunday.
2. Denis Sheil (1865-1962). Superior of the Birmingham Oratory (1923-32). He was the last survivor of the community that had lived with Newman. He had been present at Hawkesyard for the dedication of the church on 12 June 1899.
3. John Roskell (1880-1948), administrator of St Chad's Cathedral, Birmingham (1919-1948).
4. Vincent McNabb.
5. Archbishop McIntyre resigned in 1928, and Archbishop Thomas Leighton Williams (1877-1946) was not consecrated until 23 June 1929. During the interregnum the diocese was administered by the auxiliary bishop, John P. Barrett.
6. Aelred Whitacre, Edwin Essex.
7. The Dominican convent of Redcar was founded by the Leicester Congregation of Dominican Sisters in 1896; with the rest of the Congregation, it became part of the new, amalgamated Congregation of St Catherine of Siena in 1929, and was closed in 1930.
8. Leicester had first elected Robert Bracey, but he refused, as he had the right to do, being already prior of Woodchester. BJ is referring to their second election, which had been discussed at a Provincial Council meeting on 26 April.
9. Fabian Dix.

192. *BJ to Bernard Delany OP. From St Dominic's, London. 5 May 1929. Autograph.*

I have just returned from Hawick and Newcastle to find your 2 letters.
(1) Thank you indeed for your generous accepting of this burden;[1] but the fact that all the world assured you that it would come suggests, doesn't it, that all the world felt you were the only possible person. It was either you or F. Robert: of these F. Robert was the lesser.[2] So remember that there's always a blessing that attends the beginnings of things, the sources of rivers, the establishment of a new religious order, the opening of a new house. That blessing will be proportionate to its need. Moreover the more we realise our own insufficiency, the

more we are thrown back upon God, a goodly thing: 'Gladly therefore will I glory in my infirmity that (I may remember the more)³ the power of Christ may dwell in me.'⁴

(2) Yes I have thought of the office, sung and Mass too at Oxford and Hawkesyard: we shall have to call on the generosity of all at the first and we shan't be disappointed. Hawkesyard will be little short of its old complement next year and Oxford will yearly grow.

(3) Shall tell Felix⁵ that Whit Saturday won't do. We must let the ordination stand over.

Ascension day will find me at Stamford Hill triduoing to the Nuns! How I shall envy that last re-union of the youth of the Province at Hawkesyard.⁶ But 'silly point' is my more accustomed rôle these last 13 years.

1. Delany, who was prior of Hawkesyard, had been appointed the first prior of Oxford.
2. Robert Bracey, just finishing his third term as prior of Woodchester. BJ wrote 'leoser', and then corrected it to 'lesser', but perhaps he originally meant 'loser'.
3. BJ first wrote 'that I may remember the more will be given', then put 'I may remember the more will' in brackets and crossed out 'will be given'.
4. 2 Cor. 12:9.
5. Bishop Felix Couturier OP, who was to consecrate the church on 20 May, Whit Monday.
6. On the feast of the Ascension (9 May) the last 'festum collegii' was held at Hawkesyard, celebrated, inter alia, with a cricket match between the Dominicans and the boys of Laxton. Laxton were all out for 40, Hawkesyard all out for 24!

193. *BJ to Mrs Tytus. From St Dominic's, London. 5 May 1929. Autograph.*

I wonder where you are; but dear Brown and Shipley¹ will know so I commit this to their hands in the hope it will reach you to wish you all sorts of gorgeous things for May 10th.² May this new year be a full one of the joyous ways of God! May he help you by showing Himself through to you and making all fuller than ever of His presence and peace! And may that successive act of generosity, on Monday 20th to be consecrated to God,³ bring you even here some of that thrill which it has brought to so many of us.

1. Mrs Tytus' bank.
2. 10 May was the anniversary of Mrs Tytus' reception into the Catholic church.
3. The church at Blackfriars, Oxford, was to be consecrated on 20 May. Mrs Tytus was one of BJ's most generous and persistent benefactors.

194. *BJ to Gwendolen Plunket Greene. From St Dominic's, London. 7 May 1929. Transcript.*

Thank you for your letter. I am glad that anyway Nature is kind to you, even if the debts multiply and the folk jabber after Church and the wretchedness of drink¹ is still apparent. But of course the great thing to remember is that God is in charge of the world and not we; so that all we have to do is the best we can and not to grow wretched because we see those we love wandering foolishly. The Lord is their Shepherd and that is our unquenchable hope. As long as one can hold on to that, for so long does that sickness of the heart mean no real fear but merely the troubled body that will disobey the soul.

I think indeed that the book is a most excellent idea. But I would have preferred one of your own, to another of the Baron's.[2] He has helped you enormously but he has helped you precisely to be yourself; I am sure that the best testimony to him is to show what originality his ideas can provoke. To be merely quoting him is to suggest that he overwhelmed you: the last thing he did and the last thing he would have wished to do. His whole method was precisely to teach you to be yourself. So I'd say *Be Yourself*. Don't let them force you in their dreadful way of 'book-making': but give us instead yourself.

1. Her daughter, Olivia, had a serious drink problem.
2. In 1928 she had published *Letters from Baron Friedrich von Hügel to a Niece*, containing her uncle's letters and reports of his conversations with her. Apparently the publishers, J. M. Dent, were asking for more von Hügel material from her.

195. *BJ to Mrs Tytus. From Blackfriars, Oxford. 19 May 1929.*[1] *Autograph.*

My heart is too full these days to say more than, were you here, I should become emotional, most bad for me. It's as well there are seas and hills between.

May the Spirit of God with His tact and rich store of gifts help you to fulfil your needs.

1. On 17 May the new community of students and lectors from Hawkesyard had arrived to take up residence in Oxford, and on 20 May the church was to be consecrated, followed, on 21 May, by the formal opening of the priory.

196. *BJ to Bernard Delany OP.*[1] *From St Catherine's Convent, Edinburgh. 23 May 1929. Autograph.*

This is only to ask you to thank your community for me for their splendid carrying through of everything those crowded and hectic days. It was wonderful to have been able to organise everything so quickly and smoothly in a new and accustomed[2] house with so much not there to which the student Fathers and Brothers were used. Not only was the singing and liturgy admirably carried out, so judges whose verdict is weightier than mine reported, but the staff work of it all, the instant response to any demand for generosity, and the fine and genial spirit of team-work was striking and affecting.

I am most grateful to them all.

Not least, F. Prior, am I grateful to you for your generous receptance of an uncertain burden, uncertain as to its future financially and every other way. God, who blesses in proportion to generosity, must bless your undertaking richly and beyond our measure.

1. Prior of Oxford.
2. BJ presumably meant to write 'unaccustomed'.

197. *BJ to Gwendolen Plunket Greene. From Stanbrook Abbey. No date.*[1] *Transcript.*

Thank you for your letter which has come here to me. It is certainly a marvellous gift of God to her and to you:[2] to you because it justifies your way of treating her soul, despite all the advice we showered on you, to her because it was an act of Blessed Mercy to have discovered to her the hidden capacities of her soul. Down in the depths of her was that hidden power of love and knowledge, that unselfishness, that exquisite gratitude, that life: it needed some awakening, a moving of the waters, for her soul to emerge healed and cleansed. Then she suddenly saw the whole meaning of it, your unselfishness, and how it too had a deeper meaning, the unselfishness of Christ. A perfect awakening, painful, grim, sad-eyed, but in peace; like in the garden of the Resurrection when Magdalen arrived a little cold, with the deathly paleness of the place when the sun had not yet risen to glow and warm and flood with its heat and glory.

She'll find in Plato that hard and just light (it's always cruel and just) out of which comes the more domestic and family warmth and delight of Christ. Plato is like the light in the room, Christ like the hearth. After Plato, Augustine's Confessions, and then home to Christ, Beauty, Goodness, Truth.

1. BJ was at Stanbrook 25 June–3 July 1929, so the letter must have been written during this period.
2. Her daughter, Olivia, had just become a Catholic.

198. *BJ to George Bowring.*[1] *From St Dominic's, London. 30 July 1929. Transcript.*

(1) If F. Prior[2] approves of your consulting a specialist in London, so do I.
(2) Parishes are abnormal to Dominican life?[3] Of course—so is the consulting of a specialist in London, so are weekend supplies, so is a holiday in Scotland with your father and sister. You won't find these in the Constitutions, nor probably in the lives of the saints. But the Constitutions lie under the power of 3 successive chapters: what these

approve become constitutions as much as anything else.⁴ You will have noticed the introduction of legislation on the subject in the Chapters of 1924 and 1927.⁵ These rule us and not the ideas of any individual or individuals. We are Dominicans and our life is only possible as long as we obey our laws.

1. Bowring had just finished his studies at Hawkesyard (the final examinations being on 16-17 July). At the beginning of September he received an assignation to the parish at Woodchester.
2. Rupert Hoper-Dixon.
3. In the first draft of the revised Constitutions, circulated in 1923, the proposed Const. 1007 reads: 'In the most ancient discipline of our Order there was a strict prohibition on accepting churches with a cure of souls attached; but, with the consent of the Holy See, this ban has been modified in several places for various reasons.' There then followed regulations governing the acceptance and running of Dominican parishes. In the comments from the provinces, circulated in 1924, the Lombard province urges that this text should be changed to read that there 'is' (not 'was') a strict prohibition: 'This ban is most emphatically to be retained for the future.' In the outcome, none of this proposed Constitution was finally accepted, so that the 1925 text made no reference to any ban on the acceptance of parishes (Const. 1045-1055). It is clear, though, that the issue remained contentious in the Order and in the English province. The 1932 Chapter put into the Constitutions (Const. 782-I) a text saying that the Order's regular life 'is not easily combined with parochial life'. The list of Dominican parishes given in *Analecta S.O.P.* 18 (1927-28) pp. 575-580 shows how widespread in fact was the practice of Dominicans taking responsibility for parishes.
4. All changes or innovations in the Dominican Constitutions must be approved by three successive General Chapters; after that, they are fully incorporated into the text.
5. The publication of the new Code of Canon Law in 1917 was followed by a drastic revision of the Dominican Constitutions, called for by the General Chapter of 1920 (Acta paras. 75-77). A draft was circulated in 1923. Legislation on parishes was included in the text passed by the 1924 and 1926 Chapters (Const. 1045-1055). The Chapter that should have been held in 1927 was brought forward a year because of the death of Master General Theissling in 1926.

199. *BJ to a Naval Officer interested in joining the Order. From St Dominic's, London. 2 August 1929. Autograph.*

... Now for your questions:—
1. I should say that the vocation of a Dominican would show itself in a desire to become an apostle and in the absence of anything that would effectually prevent its fulfilment. Hence a natural capacity for public speaking is not, I think, necessary. How few of us have that? At least it is most difficult to tell, for the normal man has such few opportunities for knowing whether he has or not.
2. Moreover, as you yourself imply, the pen is a means as well as the spoken voice: just as Fra Angelico used his paint brush, and S. Thomas Aquinas his philosophy, and Lacordaire his voice. These all are effective and perhaps the voice less effective than the other two. It's so soon only a memory.
3. As for Latin, we require a knowledge of the groundwork of the language: grammar and syntax. Hence declensions and verbs etc. The rest will be a matter of practice. As long as you get those simpler things into your memory (it will require dull slogging to get them

there), the rest will come of itself. One's first year, the novitiate, is not concerned with philosophy or theology, but only with the upbuilding of one's spiritual life and so you will have some spare time each day to yourself, which you can devote to Latin. When you find it at every turn, and say office in it, you will soon find that fluency will come of itself. Stick then to the grammar and syntax, and you can be sure the rest will arrive in due time: *solvitur ambulando*.

I am so glad that you like the contemplative, monastic side of our life besides the more apostolic side. S. Dominic certainly meant us to develop both, indeed to use the silent and liturgical hours to give us the proper spirit for the apostolate, zealous because of our love of God, loving God because we have tried to discover Him and gaze on Him if haply we can find Him,[1] and recruiting zeal and love from the hours alike of silent meditation and of vocal praise. The apostle thus formed will not only want to share with others something of what he has found and known but also will himself be of the temper and spirit best fitted to impart the knowledge he has gained. He will be serene, dignified, patient: just as the sea gives men a freshness, a patience and a tolerance such as other labours in life do not often give, so does the habit of gazing on God (that 'sea pacific' as S. Catherine of Siena calls him[2]) give men a freshness, a patience, and a tolerance even beyond the sailors, fed by the level and unending ocean of the Divine Being.

Practise now while you can that art of looking for God which is the art of the saints; we only find Him when He shows Himself. That's His doing, ours is the search.

1. Acts 17:27.
2. E.g. *Il Dialogo*, chapter 165, ed. Cavallini p. 493.

200. *BJ to Mrs Tytus. From St Dominic's, Stone.*[1] *14 August 1929. Autograph.*

It was nice seeing you that day, nearly a week ago; it would have been nicer if I could have seen you tomorrow[2] to wish you all the blessed things possibly needed for the feast and its anniversary of sorrow and yet release. You may be sure that the Mass shall be yours, and that it shall be his also. May he give you some token of his happiness, some grace of especial comfort, some sudden sense that all is well with you and with him! On their day of release the dead seem sometimes allowed to make their presence evident in times of prayer, especially at the Mass.

Not that you need these things, for you have long since taken to yourself the ideas of faith i.e. of a life in darkness, wherein one does not see but none the less believes. That quietness of the soul that goes with a profound confidence in the mercies of God and His divine provision for every soul, separate or with the dead. Yet we are blessed by God sometimes in a way that, though it doesn't lessen faith, does add an assurance of well-being, 'all shall be well, all shall be well.'[3]

I am wondering whether you are still in London or whether you have gone Oxford way yet. I shall hope to see you there later on, after I have been for 10 days at home. I go there on Monday, with a sermon, or sermons rather, at Ledbury in between that and this, where I finish on Saturday. The Nuns here are all strung up and excited: the 5 Congregations meet on August 26 and elect a Mother General on August 27 and then become amalgamated.[4] The sooner I leave England after that the better for my general health! Actually we leave on September 9 for Rome,[5] I shall travel in second class comfort, for now this year there's a second class sleeper to Rome, 2 nights in the train,—quite good and not too luxurious yet luxurious enough.

F. Aelred[6] is at Hull till tomorrow and on the 22nd he goes to Llandudno: perhaps you'll catch him in between. He evidently loved his walking tour and it did him good.

1. BJ had been at Stone since 8 August, giving the nuns their retreat.
2. The anniversary of Mr Tytus' death.
3. Julian of Norwich, Long Text chapter 27.
4. BJ had hoped to go on a Dominican pilgrimage to places in the south of France associated with St Dominic (cf. above, no. 189), but Rome had insisted that he remain in England to deal with all the business connected with the planned amalgamation of five English Congregations of Dominican Sisters. The Congregations involved included two of pontifical right (Stone, founded in 1844, and Stroud, founded in 1857), and three of diocesan right (Leicester, founded in 1875, Harrow, founded in 1878, and Portobello Road, London, founded in 1897).
The idea of amalgamation had been around for some time. In Ireland, a proposal to amalgamate five separate communities had been made by Louis Nolan OP as early as 1919, eventually coming to fruition in February 1928 with the creation of the new Cabra Congregation. In May 1921 BJ informed Joseph Clayton that it was the policy of Rome to get small religious congregations to amalgamate with larger ones, and that he himself had been involved in persuading one stray Dominican convent to join forces with a community that had 3 convents (the identity of this convent eludes us). Later in the year the Bishop of Nottingham asked BJ's advice about the Leicester Dominican sisters, and BJ promised to give all the help he could in bringing about their amalgamation with some larger group of Dominicans. In 1926-27 he had worked for and achieved the amalgamation of West Grinstead with the Bushey sisters. He also knew that at least two bishops with Dominican sisters in their dioceses were urging the cause of amalgamation in Rome.
What finally started things moving in England was a letter BJ got from Stroud in 1928, to which he replied on Christmas Day, 'Thank you for your letter which has inspired me to resolve to do what I can in 1929 to bring about your dream . . . The time for waiting is over: we must act.' And act he did. On 31 December he wrote to the Mother General of Stone to ask for a meeting on 8 January to discuss 'the project of some sort of amalgamation between the Congregations of Dominican Sisters which say the Divine Office.' Of the five Congregations eventually amalgamated only Harrow was at this stage not saying the Divine Office. At the meeting in Stone on 8 January a scheme was elaborated, on the basis of the Stroud proposals, as developed by BJ, for a common formation programme and a common Mother General, but with the existing Mothers General retaining most of their present authority for the time being,

and a guarantee that no already professed sister would be moved out of her Congregation without her own consent. On 22 January BJ won the agreement of Leicester to this scheme, and on 14 February that of Portobello Road. He then went on to inform the sisters of Harrow what was afoot, and they decided to come in on it too, even though it meant adopting the Divine Office. By now, thanks to Leicester, there was a further condition attached to the scheme, namely, that all existing works would be kept up at their current strength.

Having ascertained that there was a basic willingness on the part of the five Congregations to move towards amalgamation, on the terms outlined, BJ asked Louis Nolan OP, of the Sacred Congregation for Religious, whether Rome would receive favourably an application for amalgamation along these lines. Nolan replied positively, so another round of meetings was initiated. All 5 Mothers General and an assistant from each Congregation met at Stone on 8-10 April and drew up a formal Scheme of Amalgamation, which they all signed and submitted to the bishops in whose dioceses the various convents were situated. At the end of the month and in early May all the convents then voted on the Scheme, BJ himself in many cases visiting the convents to preside over this vote. An overwhelming majority of the sisters voted in favour of it.

Matters now passed into the hands of Louis Nolan. At a meeting of the Mothers General at Stroud in May he insisted that no petition would be accepted in Rome with strings attached, so the Scheme must be rewritten without the two conditions that BJ had written into it. He would not even allow the matter to be proposed afresh to the sisters to see whether they would accept an unconditional amalgamation. His line was that they had voted for amalgamation, and their vow of obedience bound them to accept whatever was lawfully commanded by their superiors. It was for Rome to establish whatever conditions it deemed necessary. He assured the nuns that he was not calling for any substantial change in the plans, only indicating the way it was necessary to proceed if Roman approval was to be secured. Rome would not allow for amalgamation with a built-in delay. It must be all or nothing. It would then be up to the new Mother General of the whole new Congregation to respect the sensibilities of individual sisters.

The emended petition was duly sent round and signed and in July it was submitted to Rome, and it was quickly approved by the Sacred Congregation and by the Pope. A meeting was fixed for late August, at which the Mother General and the Council of the new Congregation were to be elected. The election took place on 28 August, and Mother M. Teresa Lamburn, the Mother General of Stroud (from whom the initial impetus had come at the end of 1928), was elected Mother General of the new Congregation.

BJ was obviously excited about the way in which the scheme gathered momentum. In several letters written during the year he alluded to it in very positive terms. In a letter written to Jerome Rigby on 13 April he bids him urge the brethren to do anything they can to promote it. 'It will mean 21 convents and 450 nuns. Amalgamated, they'd be of vast help to us.' But he feared, not unreasonably, that some of the sisters would feel let down by him, when they discovered how much of the scheme he had negotiated with them had been dropped, on Nolan's insistence, from the final proposal for amalgamation, which had as a result proceeded much further much more quickly than they had anticipated. Nevertheless the new Congregation seems to have gone into operation with remarkably little difficulty and with much good will on all sides.

5. For the General Chapter, due to start on 21 September. Because it was an elective Chapter (a new Master General had to be elected, since Master General Paredes had been forced to resign), the province had to send three representatives: apart from the provincial, there was a diffinitor (Hugh Pope) and the diffinitor's socius (Luke Walker). Cf. below, nos. 201-204.

201. BJ to Mrs Bullough. From The Angelicum, Rome. 19 September 1929. Autograph.

I hope you won't think me interfering but I found among the Dominicans here assembled for the General Chapter a certain Father Alberto Duse, Diffinitor of the Province of Lombardy, and the Parroco now for 20 years in Ancona.¹ So I ventured to ask him his parentage and he gave me the enclosed genealogical tree. He was thrilled to hear that he had relations in England and especially when I told him how devoutly Dominican you and Mr Bullough were, and of the desires of Hugh.²

Hence he gave me also his address; which I take to be a sort of hint for you! . . .

We go to the election³ on Saturday. I was at one time rather nervous of myself as there seem no outstanding figures and anyone might be elected. But I hope now that the Provincial of France⁴ will be the victim and not I.

1. Alberto Duse OP, born in 1870, entered the Lombardy Province in 1885. He died in Venice in 1947. He and Mrs Bullough (née Duse) shared a common great-great-grandfather.
2. The Bulloughs' son, who joined the English Dominican province in 1931 and took the name Sebastian.
3. Election of a new Master General.
4. Martin Gillet.

202. *Provincial's Diary. Note by BJ written on the official list of members of the General Chapter, pasted into the Diary. It records the voting in the election of the Master General.*¹

FIRST SCRUTINY		SECOND SCRUTINY	
Gillet	32	Gillet	46
Jarrett	24	Jarrett	31
Cordovani	11	Szabó	6
Szabó	10	Cordovani	4
Sales	5	Casas	1
Fanfani	1	Caterini	1
Casas	1		
Caterini	1		
Getino	1		
Lottini	1		
Bonhomme	1		
Meagher	1	89 Electors.	

1. The spelling of the names has been corrected, where necessary. Brief notes on the people listed will be found in the biographical notes at the back of the book.

203. *BJ to Austin Barker OP. From The Angelicum, Rome. 21 September 1929. Autograph.*

Just to announce to you solemnly that you are Lector Primarius at Hawkesyard.¹ I am sorry that I can't do anything more impressive than merely write this letter, but it appears that there's no document issued because actually I appoint but the M.G.² confirms; so he's confirmed your appointment. Hence you are hereby L.P. May you not be overwhelmed by the little bits of jobs it will add to the already crowded hours of friend Aristotle.³

We had our election here this morning and Père Gillet romped in at the second scrutiny with 46 votes out of 88, I followed soberly behind with 31, the rest were few indeed.⁴ Naturally I was much relieved. I never did believe that I should end up in Rome as M.G. I thought better of the Holy Ghost than that. But people tried to tell me that I was in the running and even F.H.P.⁵ believed. I told him that I felt sure he was wrong. I know these folk better than he does. Also I know myself better and I couldn't believe the Holy Ghost who also knew me would so far 'violate the conveniences'.⁶ Gillet will be a good man but he isn't the man they think him to be!

I shall hope to leave before the week is out; such a lot of intrigue and dirty work has been about that the Pope is much against us.⁷ That I think Gillet will correct as he's *notus Pontifici*.⁸

1. 'Lector primarius' is the title given to the person running a Dominican study house that is not, in itself, a formal studium. In 1929 the officials of the English studium were moved to Oxford, so that Hawkesyard thereafter was no longer a studium in its own right. Its academic life would be governed by a lector primarius, under the authority of the Regent at Oxford.
2. Master General.
3. Cf. above, no. 89.
4. For the details, and the correct figure of 89 electors, cf. above, no.202.
5. Hugh Pope, diffinitor of the English province.
6. Mock-scholastic for 'do something inappropriate'.
7. Relations between Pius XI and the Dominicans had become embroiled during 1928 in the pope's intransigent campaign against the French movement, Action Française. Master General Paredes had been more or less forced by the pope to resign, and the 1929 General Chapter was forbidden by the Holy See to have any discussion at all of his resignation or to do anything about the revised Constitutions, which should have received their final confirmation at this Chapter; to play it safe, the people running the Chapter decided that it should avoid all legislative activity (Processus Verbalis of the Chapter, AGOP III 1929). This is why, with the permission of the Holy See, it was left to the 1932 Chapter to confirm the Constitutions, and why no decisions, except the election of the new Master General, were taken by the 1929 Chapter.
8. 'Known to the pope'.

204. *BJ to Mrs Tytus. From the Angelicum, Rome. 26 September 1929. Autograph.*

I am just in the throes of ending up the Chapter, with all the wee and wearisome details that accompany such an act, but I think that to be sure of reaching you on the right day I must send you my wishes today for October 1.¹

I hope that England has been kind to you with her weather and that in consequence you will be able to begin your new year without any return of the old ills. May God bless you a thousand and a thousand times for all that you have been to me and all that you have done for me! I shall be back in England on the night of the 30th and able therefore to say Mass for you on October 1st and so give you what I have to give.

The elections were a little troublesome at first as there were some here who wished to put me in but the Holy Ghost made His own arrangements otherwise and my devotion to Him has all the more increased. Not that I should dread the difficulties of the job; but only that I agree with the Holy Ghost in thinking that Père Gillet is the better man for them. He's known to the Pope and that in effect means a good deal.

Indeed at our audience yesterday the Pope spoke of the election of Père Gillet as being 'one of the most consoling facts' of his year of Jubilee:[2] in the present rather unhappy state of things in Rome in regard to the Order, too long to describe here by letter, it is a very great thing to have had the Pope speak thus kindly and encouragingly. Of late he's been rather out of patience with us, *e ha ragione* as they say here. It has been our own fault.

We have had hot weather till lately when it has been delicious, the cool of autumn without yet its tang, just that ever so short period in England, longer here, between the turns of the season, the fragrance of the summer just slowly dissolving, the sun waning in its power, men beginning to strip less for their work, the glorious colours of the flowers a little faded; and yet no taste as yet of that almost salted bitterness of the Fall.

1. Presumably Mrs Tytus' birthday.
2. Pius XI had been ordained priest fifty years earlier, in 1879.

205. *BJ to Robert Bracey OP. From R.M.S. Kenilworth Castle. 12 February 1930. Autograph.*

May I ask your counsel on the proposal of the Bishop of Cape Town[1] that we should take over Stellenbosch parish, 30 miles by road from Cape Town:
(1) The parishes we have in the Transvaal are all over 4000 ft up, and most of them are over 5000 ft. A lower altitude is needed for recuperation from time to time.
(2) Stellenbosch is down on the level of Cape Town; it is the centre of the Dutch culture; it is a purely university town. The university is the centre of the Dutch Reformed Church, of its seminary etc, and the D.R.C. is the great external enemy of the Catholic Church in S. Africa. We should be in the thick of the fight.

(3) We shall need one day to have a Noviciate house in S. Africa. Stellenbosch would be a very good place for it,² rich pastoral and fruit district, healthy, full of sunshine, finest farms in S. Africa, ½ hour by car from sea. Good railway connections with Cape Town and main lines.

(4) The Bishop will transfer the land etc to us; there's a little chapel and a wretched hovel where the priest lives. I should try to get a benefactor to give us a house and land.

(5) There are only 100 Catholics of European descent, 20 coloured, and 3½ miles off a coloured mission run by Dominican lay tertiaries.

(6) There are 20 white children of school age. A number of the Catholics are quite well off.

(7) The collection at present is very small (25/- a week) partly because the Chapel is so wretched that no outsiders are tempted to come in. Living is very cheap.

(8) The P.P. is a Dominican tertiary³ and is anxious for us to have it. He's a magnificent priest, living in great poverty and saving all his monies to buy more and more land. He's done all the pioneer work and has made the Catholic name respected and beloved.

The Fathers in S. Africa all desire it.

All congratulations on the welcome of your Community this record-breaking time.⁴

1. Bernard O'Riley.
2. A noviciate was eventually opened there in 1947.
3. The parish priest was Edward O'Reilly, about whom we have not been able to discover anything beyond what BJ says here.
4. So far the letter has obviously been a circular addressed to Bracey as a member of the Provincial Council. It is typical of BJ to add a personal note at the end: Bracey had just been re-elected prior of Woodchester for his fourth term.

206. *BJ to Hubert van Zeller. From Grenada. 3 June 1930. Autograph.*

Ah me! July 13¹ will find me tossing on the ocean homeward bound. I shall be out of Port-of-Spain on July 9th and should step lightly ashore on July 22 or 23rd. So you see I just can't! Isn't it unpleasant? I can only hope that His Amplitude of Clifton² postpones and so gives me my chance. But you will know that I shall be remembering you that day out on the waste of waters and invoking God's blessing on you and God's furtherance of all your dreams and plans, most especially those plans of yours for Benedictine holiness, downright, thorough, and serene, within the harbourage of your own heart—that you may first be a Benedictine and then inspire Benedictinism, and that this may be true because of the Mass. It has always been the centre of the liturgy, it should always mean the centre too of life. May He who has led you to this and helped you past all your troubles to it, school-troubles and Greek merchants[3] and stomachs and what-nots, give you now through Himself the real purpose of your life: Qui manet in Me et ego in eo, hic fert fructum multum, quia sine Me nihil potestis facere—nihil POTESTIS[4]—either He or nothing possible to us. That you will spend your life discovering and end by knowing yourself to be just nothing at all without Him.

PS Please me, amongst your earliest blest! Don't forget.

1. The date fixed for van Zeller's ordination to the priesthood at Downside.
2. George Ambrose Burton, bishop of Clifton.
3. For a time, before entering the monastery, van Zeller had worked for a Greek firm of cotton merchants in Liverpool.
4. John 15:15 ('he who remains in me and I in him brings forth much fruit, because without me you can do nothing').

207. *BJ to Mrs Campbell. From Grenada. 18 June 1930. Transcript.*

Thank you for your letter forwarded out to me here. I have been on the wander since September last but am well, thank the Lord!
. . .
Try to remember the silence of Christ during the Passion, its dignity, its unselfishness, its God-lookingness, and find in it the strength to the same uncomplaining way as heretofore.

208. *BJ to Hubert van Zeller. From St Dominic's, London. 18 August 1930. Autograph.*

I really can't go on writing to a venerable priest as JELLY:[1] really I can't. I must invent however something less formal than Dom Hubert. Still there's time for all that yet, isn't there? When you're an Abbot I shall have to try again.

It was with distress that I heard from No. 64[2] that I had missed seeing you do the baptism and with more distress that I heard from No. 64 that you weren't looking well. What's going to happen to you? Bath?[3] or what? or where?

Schoolmastering?[4] But your nerves will be in disarray and your innards will be all dithering and your religious scruples will descend on you with devastating force. Really do let me know what's befallen you or about to befall. Not of course that I can do anything. I have already once interfered over your breakfast and got there too late: also it's a settled habit of my spiritual life, partly due to high spirituality and partly to low laziness, never to ask anyone, divine or human, for anything. So I shall not be able to do anything to help you; but with that restless Dominican mind of mine, loving curious information and especially a detailed knowledge of the conditions of those I'm fond of (love is the word now one only applies to naughtiness and complexes and things like grape-nuts or Bradman's batting[5] or curious information for that matter), I'd like really to know how or where or what you're at.

Always yours in things divine and human and especially now in ara Crucis.[6]

PS I LOVE (really) the Mass-card, a composite picture of all 4.[7]

1. Van Zeller's nickname. This letter begins, 'Dear Dom Hubert'.
2. The home of the Geoghegan family. Cf. above, no. 72.
3. The Benedictine mission and residence at Bath was established in the late 17th century and was regarded as one of the Order's most important centres. The Victorian Gothic church of St John, with its tall spire, was joined in 1929 by the equally handsome 'basilican' church of St Alphege, designed by Sir Giles Gilbert Scott (1880-1960). These churches and the parish were handed over to the diocese of Clifton in 1932, as part of the policy of concentrating the Downside community at Downside, so van Zeller was not to be sent on the Bath mission, though in September 1932 he was enrolled at a technical college in Bath to study art and design; however he left after one term (*One Foot in the Cradle* pp. 157-158).
4. Van Zeller taught in the school from 1929-1930 and thereafter until 1946 he spent much of his time as a monk schoolmaster, but the role never suited him and his latter years were spent in chaplaincy and retreat work and also in sculpting and writing books on a wide variety of subjects.
5. Donald George Bradman (born 1908), the Australian cricketer, later knighted. He was the greatest of all Australian cricketers and probably the finest batsman in the history of cricket. In 1930 he was on his first tour of England. The Test series was won decisively by Australia, thanks largely to his batting, which aroused much public interest. A leading article in *The Times* on 12 July observed, 'He does not merely break records; he smashes them.' On 12 July he completed an innings of 334 runs at Leeds, then a record for all Test matches. When BJ wrote this letter, Bradman was in London, playing in the fifth and final Test of the rubber at The Oval. Monday 18 August was the second day of the match, but he did not come in to bat until tea-time; he had however already accumulated a total of 2430 runs at an average of 93.46 in all the matches of the tour. The authoritative account of the tour is P. G. H. Fender, *The Tests of 1930, The 17th Australian Team in England*, London 1930. Also in the Australian team was the graceful batsman, Stan McCabe (1910-1968), cousin to Herbert McCabe OP (born 1926, joined the English Dominicans 1949, teaching in the studium at Oxford since 1967). We are grateful to Fr Paul Parvis OP for the information contained in the note.
6. 'The altar of the Cross'.
7. Apart from van Zeller, the ordinands were Ralph Russell (1903-1970), Andrew Snelgrove (1901-1948) and Oswald Sumner (1906-1964).

209. *BJ to Sr M. Teresa Fay OP.*[1] *From St Dominic's, London. 5 September 1930. Autograph.*

Thank you for sending me a copy of the book[2] but I already have one: I only said that I had not seen your copies with the missing papers. I suppose F. Nolan is still in Ireland and so you won't hear from him for some time yet.

1. The 'very strict rule of wearing woollen underclothing' is a modern accretion. In primitive days the rule forbade linen. Later on wool was positively ordered. At present most of European Nuns can't afford (neither can the priests) to buy wool as the price is prohibitive for them. Consequently, we deliberately reverted to the freedom of the original wording.[3]

2. Again the old law was *officium nocturnum*. The precision of midnight or 3 a.m. is a merely modern interpretation.[4] Where S. Dominic gave latitude, why not we?

3. Hence I suppose all those regulations that now drop, about the black scapular[5] etc., are due to the fact that in many places they are not and cannot be observed. It is better to have a rule that is observed *ut in pluribus* than one that very few are able to keep. Indeed a *regula* is composed for the majority deliberately: else it would not be a *regula* or measure.

4. Undoubtedly there is a drop in the general severity of observance; but remember that the gap between religious life and secular life is probably greater than it has ever been. Austerity is always relative. I fancy that in proportion the austerity you ask is as great as (if not greater than) has ever been asked from girls who desire religious life.

5. Again, have the Nuns ever been asked to discuss these Dominican Constitutions? Is that, though desirable, traditional or canonical?

This book need not be a big blow unless you let it be. It is at your choice to deal with as you think best. You can take the law and obey it and go farther; or you can limit yourselves to the law. I don't think you will do the latter. Unless you do you should suffer no hurt. A religious community lives by its spirit and its interpretation of the law: for the law is not the limit of the horizon but only the lower line of the earth above which the horizon begins.

Don't be anxious. The Spirit you have established will live. Your descendants will be as great as yourselves. Be true Dominicans, live and trust the future generations. Light your flame and leave it not to your care but his who chose you.[6] He looked down the generations and left no complete rule,[7] but trusted to the spirit he had made, to live and enliven what he had begun. He trusted to that more than to the words he fashioned with the others at the General Chapter.

That is Dominican democracy, to work and trust the rest of the world OP.[8]

1. Prioress of the Dominican nuns at Headington, Oxford.
2. *Constitutions of the Nuns of the Sacred Order of Preachers*, Rome 1930. The nuns' Constitutions, like those of the friars, had been drastically revised; the new text was approved by Pius XI on 15 November 1929 and promulgated by Master General Gillet on 7 March 1930. The official English version was published in the same year.
3. Unlike the Constitutions of the friars, those of the nuns had remained unchanged for centuries; in 1868 Jandel re-approved the text exactly as it had been printed in 1566. However,

the nuns were also bound by the ordinations of General Chapters in so far as they were applicable (1872 Constitutions of the friars, Const. 719). The oldest Constitutions of the friars prescribed that the brethren must not wear linen next to the skin (I 19, in Thomas, op. cit. p. 329), and by 1566 the same phrase had been inserted into the nuns' Constitutions (chapter 10). The specific requirement of woollen underwear derives form Jandel's great 'reforming' Chapter of 1871 (Acta p. 44) and was inserted into the 1872 edition of the friars' Constitutions (Const. 187). In response to the 1923 draft of the revised Constitutions, the Californian province proposed that the text should be changed so as to call for 'woollen or cheap clothes' next to the skin (Const. 316), and this was accepted in 1924 and 1926 and, in different words, it became part of the Constitutions of the friars in 1932 (Const. 604). The 1930 Constitutions of the nuns (Const. 61) said nothing at all about the material of their underwear.

4. It was the 1871 Chapter which introduced the idea of Matins 'at midnight or at 3 a.m.' (Acta pp. 40-41). The ancient practice of celebrating Matins at or about midnight had been widely dropped and Jandel wanted it revived; the option of saying it at 3 a.m. was intended as a concession to human weakness. Provinces where night office had been abandoned entirely were required to appoint at least one priory where it would be restored. The 1872 Constitutions reproduced exactly the prescriptions of the 1871 Chapter. The draft prepared for the General Chapter of 1901 (Const. 272) retained the requirement that at least one priory per province must have night office, but said nothing about 3 a.m. The 1923 draft (Const. 232) simply said that provinces that observed night office should go on doing so, but this was considered too lax. The province of Baetica called for compulsory night office at midnight or 3 a.m., except in the case of a dispensation from the Master General. The text which finally emerged called for a revival, where possible, of night office at or about midnight, at least on Sundays and major feasts (Const. 571-II). The 1930 Constitutions of the nuns (Const. 241) tell them to 'rise at night for Matins on Sundays and feast days from the feast of All Saints until the feast of Our Lord's Resurrection' and in Advent and Lent; 'if the custom of the monastery should be stricter, let it be faithfully preserved.'

5. The black scapular, worn by laybrothers and laysisters, had never been mentioned in any legislative text of the Order in connection with the nuns.

6. I.e. St Dominic.

7. From the outset, the Dominican friars had the Rule of St Augustine, which was obviously unchanging, and Constitutions, which could in principle be changed and which have in fact been changed by a continual process of revision, for which successive General Chapters are responsible. The nuns had no universally accepted Constitutions until 1259, and thereafter their Constitutions have been revised much less frequently than those of the brethren, though their law did evolve, all the same, because of the General Chapters of the brethren (cf. above, note 3). It is striking that the Order never produced and apparently never sought to produce anything like a complete customary, so that its laws did not and were not intended to enshrine the whole reality of Dominican life.

8. In spite of BJ's re-assurances, the nuns were evidently not happy with their new Constitutions. On 9 September 1930 Sr M. Suso wrote to BJ: 'I have spent about three hours with our holy Father and his first daughters. It is refreshing to get back to the primitive days of the order, isn't it? More especially just now when I am feeling rather depressed by the new Constitutions. A careful study of the English translation reveals many things which had escaped us in the cursory reading of the Latin text. There is a distinct drop in the level of observance, the translation is less than mediocre, there is no Dominican stamp about the book, in fact the general impression is that the order has let us down badly . . . There is something to be said in favour of the new Constitutions, but very little.' (In an undated letter to Miss Calthrop, BJ confided, 'Of course you show your Dominicanism by the way of freedom and truth. I think sometimes that Mother Suso has little ideas of her own that are not quite OP.')

The nuns of Carisbrooke too were unhappy about the new book, though for rather different reasons. On 21 October 1930 BJ wrote to the prioress saying that, in response to their request, he has obtained permission to dispense them from certain innovative practices, such as spiritual reading in common, having a reading during meditation, and starting with the seniors at the Chapter of Faults.

Even so, on 25 February 1931, he forwarded to Fr Garde, for the Master General, a petition from the nuns of Headington, with the warning that a similar one was to follow from Carisbrooke. The Headington petition (dated 24 February 1931) is effectively a complete rejection of the new Constitutions, except in so far as some changes had to be made because of the new code of Canon Law. The nuns had pleaded with the previous Master General that nothing should be changed or suppressed in 'our holy observances', and they now re-affirm their desire to keep in their entirety the Constitutions approved by Jandel in 1868. They complain that the old text has been completely 'changed or ignored' in the new book. 'The very spirit of our Order has suffered gravely from these innovations and changes'. Carisbrooke voted to associate itself with the plea to be allowed, essentially, to keep the old Constitutions, as had the first Dominican monastery of them all, Prouille. In his covering letter, BJ comments that both the English monasteries are 'rather worried over their new Constitutions. I do entirely sympathise with what they dislike in them. (i) They have very little that is distinctively Dominican in them. (ii) Without austerities the Enclosed Orders have no reason for existence . . . The new Constitutions put into the hands of a modern girl would not be inspiring as they don't demand more sacrifice than would the Constitutions of the Sisters and the sisters teach and labour for souls actively.' The Headington petition is in the Headington Council Book, but no copy of it seems to have been kept in the archives of the Order in Rome. BJ's letter was kept, though (AGOP XIII 65105).

210. *BJ to Hubert van Zeller. From St Dominic's, Newcastle. 20 November 1930. Autograph.*

Dear Ghostly brother!

I can't really say 'son'; it sounds too desperately responsible. And after all I am not going to be treated any more favourably in Heaven because I'm fond of you as I shall die first. Of course you'll get there before I do as I'll be loitering about till I'm smoked like a kipper. But by then you won't be able to do too much for me. The worst will be over by the time you follow me.

However the chief point is that you have written to me and I am that pleased as the people, I mean PEOPLE, say. Your Aunt had written, full of ghastliness, of your state of health, and Switzerland, and an hour on your bed before and after meals, and to be well shaken before taken and all that sort of thing. Of course I was delighted that at last, even at sanguinary last, you were being looked after, so that what filled her with gloom gladdened me. I was more reconciled to S. Benedict or rather to his offspring. He was celebrated, wasn't he, for his prudent kindness and commonsense, both admirable and humiliatory virtues. I could tell you of a monastery where those admirable things suffer from a loss of exercise in regard to a friend of mine. But wild Fords won't tear the name of it from me. (No reference to your recently dead abbot,[1] the inspirer of the abbey of your love).

It was nice to find that Bavaria appealed to you[2] or rather the Bavarians. All I remember of Munich is the Cathedral, the Pinacotek (spelling most uncertain), the beer halls, and a house in the main square or platz (?) on the walls of which the figure of Charlemagne is painted, looking a little like Father Christmas, as I dare say he did, after he had massacred the Saxons. Anyone would have felt genial after that. But there are no Dominicans in Bavaria, barred by the Concordat with the late Govt. They may perhaps be coming back again.

I was interested in your contrast between the respective Benedictinism as it appeared to you, of Germany, Bavaria, and (by retrospect) England. The great point of English Benedictinism is that it has suffered the shock of martyrdom and stood firm. Other forms are nearer the external ideal but have not had either the problems (as you have noted) or the experiment as by fire of martyrdom. The others are like admirably drilled troops; these march as raggedly as the French infantry but have withstood the Verdun of Tyburn.[3] Hence the effectiveness of one has been proved by the fiercest flames. Has the other been fire-tried? I shouldn't wish to belittle the Germans, nor should I wish to take from the Anglo Benedictines their steadfast crown.

Then secondly the secular clergy here seem a slack lot: they probably don't make a half hour's meditation each day, they smoke and read the newspapers, they hardly read a book before Sheed and Ward deceived them into buying pious books by the fraudulent device of an alarmist jacket. The French clergy are most correct and most priestly and live by the rules laid down in all the books on the priesthood (which they have written themselves from their inner consciousness). But the people in England follow their priests. In France they don't. From this learn a parable!!

However the great thing is that you are happy. I have seen that you weren't at Downside. There has been a caged spirit behind those brown eyes. But then I think you were right not to be happy in the sense of contentment, though I believe you were happy in the sense of being serene. After all happiness is the special gift of ETERNITY in any full sense. Moreover ideals are gnawing fevers. They make the eyes sparkle and the lips eloquent but the tummy suffers bad pains. Also the head and the sleep suffer. You live on the clouds and suffer from a very real catarrh!

Now you're away from it, have stepped out of it, and will return when you do return with a better proportioned view of the HOME ABBEY. Ideals are fever making. No one in a fever sees truly. You feel a responsibility at Downside for the incompleteness of the idealism. You feel no responsibility where you are. That will bind up your wounds, beloved; rest and forget and come back clearer-eyed.

Leonard[4] did write after all and explained how he'd written on his honeymoon to me from Paris with a lot of other letters and how he only recently found that these had not been posted by the page boy etc etc and that he'd told you the same story and you'd listened in grave patience and then told him it was jolly hard lines as it was the sort of story no one would ever believe! George and Mrs George[5] seem to flourish . . .

1. Edmund Ford, the first Abbot of Downside (1900-1906), died on 30 October 1930.
2. Van Zeller had left for Germany earlier this autumn, to go and study in Munich, stopping en route at Bruges, Maria Laach and Beuron. Fearing a breakdown in his health—he had had pneumonia in 1915 and his health was never robust— he returned to Downside on 22 December of the same year (cf. *One Foot in the Cradle* pp. 152-156).
3. In 1916 the French had held out against the Germans at Verdun for six months. Tyburn was a place of execution in London, associated in Catholic minds with all the Catholic martyrs who perished there at the time of the Protestant reformation.
4. Leonard Parker.
5. The George Bellords.

211. *BJ to Sr Elizabeth Stourton. From St Dominic's, London. 9 March 1931. Transcript.*

Thank you for your letter. I have noted the state of the case and shall do what I can. Lent is a difficult time to see people other than those one has to see and committee meetings abound and one wastes precious time listening to all sorts of futile chatter that gets nowhere. But I'll call when I can.

The only chance I suppose is to insist that the Encyclical[1] is right, while admitting that it is hard. The Pope has given a loud call and that's all that can be bothered about. The other folk please or try to; he doesn't. The only reason why the Church of Rome has its power is because Popes do that sort of thing etc. I suppose that's all one can keep on saying till at last it gets somewhere home. So cheerio! Hoping this finds you as it leaves me in the pink!

1. *Casti connubii*, 31 December 1930 (*Acta Apostolicae Sedis* 22 (1930) pp. 539-592). In this encyclical Pius XI expressed firmly the opposition of the Catholic church to all artificial methods of birth control.

212. *BJ to John Baptist Reeves OP. From St Dominic's, London. 7 April 1931. Autograph.*

Herewith the *celebret*[1] for 3 months which is all I have power to grant. You must be back by that date, or I must apply to Rome for leave for you to be longer, *extra provinciam*.[2] But I think that should be long enough. Many prophets and kings, which means provincials and priors, have desired to have the things that you have and have not had them![3]

However when you come back, I shall expect to see you more regular in attendance at duties. You will be the better for more regularity, both physically and spiritually. I made various efforts to see you, for the purpose of a long talk, but my times and yours did not agree. However I know that this thought was also in your mind and that for the accomplishment of it you are asking for this longer leave. I know I can trust you to use the leave for work and for contemplation of that which in God will most move you to fit in with community law.

So please in your daily Mass make that the centre and hold yourself to the Strong Son of God to gather His strength in your need.

Also send me a card as to how I can discover F. John's FRA ANGELICO.[4] I must finish it myself as I can't keep him waiting any longer. So please a card to say how I'm to find it.

1. The official document, carried by priests when they travel, asking the incumbent of any church they visit to allow them to celebrate Mass.
2. It is not clear what canonical or constitutional requirement BJ has in mind. According to the canon law of the time (Can. 606 §2) appeal had to be made to the Holy See for any religious to live outside his order for more than six months. According to the 1926 Dominican Constitutions (Const. 949) a provincial could give his subjects leave of absence for up to six months; for a longer period, recourse must be had to the Master General and the Holy See.
3. Matthew 13:17.
4. Evidently the manuscript of John Leather's book, *The Rosary: Its Power and Use, illustrated by the work of Fra Angelico,* had been passed on to Reeves to examine. Reeves had been appointed one of the provincial censors of books by the 1928 Provincial Chapter. BJ apparently took it for granted that Reeves had left it behind in London. The book was published in 1932.

213. *BJ to John Baptist Reeves OP. From St Mary's Church, Derby. 17 April 1931. Autograph.*

Thank you for your letter which much relieved my mind as you evidently had arrived in safety and were resting in peace. But it was heroic of you to take WHY ROME and FRA ANGELICO with you.[1] In my admiration for your enormous sense of duty I never guessed that it would go to such lengths as that! I pride myself on doing (however badly) what I should do: but never have I holidayed like that.

As for the rest I can only say that I will hold you in memory all these days at Mass. I am sure that everyone, man, woman or child, must face what you are facing some time or other in life: else faith is meaningless to them in its heights and depths. Till that fierce fire has tried them, their faith is merely external. Only such fire can make faith run molten and be fused with one's soul. I've known boys in agony over it and come through. I've known, as you must too, some boys even who have failed in it and faith has gone under.

But I'd never wish anyone I was fond of to escape that trial. The value of it is immense. I suppose for some it must be incredibly harder than others: you have both activity of mind and activity of imagination, so you have those two forces to meet. Moreover you have a sensitive body which adds a third contension. So you will have a good triple dose. But they won't hurt you. God never lets anyone be tempted beyond his power,[2] —right up to the edge of his power, yes; beyond it, no. So that you can face whatever has to be faced. That's the fine thing about the Christian view of life that it is manly; it denies no difficulties. It asserts that man will have his troubles within and without, that God dosen't remove troubles even when prayed to, but that God makes us able to cope with our troubles, which is the more excellent way.

However you'll know all this better than I do: you'll know too that the direct answer of walking out of one's entanglements is never an answer. You'll always be entangled, because you are you. If chucking all were really possible it would be a solution: but it isn't possible. You can only exchange not chuck. However Mass is the best answer because it is the supreme sacrifice of the supreme Lover who came as Love does, not like peace but a sword.[3]

PS Excuse this. No paper left and no time to change and buy![4]

1. For *Fra Angelico*, see above, no. 212. We have not been able to discover who wrote *Why Rome*.
2. 1 Cor. 10:13.
3. Matthew 10:34.
4. The letter is written on the back of posters advertising BJ's mission at St Mary's, Derby, 12-19 April 1931.

214. *BJ to John Baptist Reeves OP. From St Dominic's, London. 28 April 1931. Autograph.*

I don't want to write at length, nor do I want an answer. In fact I do ask you not to write, as you will need to rest from all that need not be attended to at once. You have your work and there is the peace of the place in which to think out your thoughts. These shall suffice.

I had no idea you were going to deal so generously with your time in the Leather MS:[1] but I am most grateful for what you have done and can now look forward to the publication of the book without qualms. It will be difficult to call it F. John's book: it will be as difficult to call it yours. We must see later what's to be done about that.

However thank you indeed for the princely spirit in which you have done the work. May God and fra Angelico reward you! And our lady too!

As for the other problem you pose, I am too little versed in philosophy to deal with it as it should be dealt with. But I imagine (a) that nature is God, (b) that God is not nature but a good deal more, (c) that the pagans weren't mere nature either, and (d) that even before the Incarnation He enlightened every man that came into the world.² In fact, natural man is a figment: the problems raised by this and by your poets shall be only solved in the beatific vision where the unveiled Beauty shall be shown us, deeper than faith or reason, nature or supernatura, and where all these torrents and all our hunger shall meet.

1. See above, no. 212.
2. John 1:9.

215. *BJ to Sr M. Agatha Kane OP. From St Dominic's, London. 28 April 1931. Transcript.*

In this moment of your most bitter loss,¹ it is fine that you should so quickly have had the faith and generosity to see that loss from the point of view of your father and mother rather than from your own. For them both it is sheer gain: it is the completion of love human in love divine. It will have given your father time to think of death, to have been in anguish at your mother's loss, to have offered that anguish to God in a spirit of whole-hearted acceptance, and to have been cleansed thereby—to have had all those tendrils of human desire and earthward clinging severed and to have been detached from what might have clogged his soul. He will have gone gladly and without reserve.

May God give you the grace to see His blessed Will in all things and to find Him in death and life, for of Him and by Him and IN HIM are all things!²

1. Sr Agatha's mother had died only a few weeks ago; her father came to visit her at Carisbrooke and now he too had died, at Carisbrooke.
2. Romans 11:36.

216. *BJ to a young woman intending marriage. From St Dominic's, London. 26 May 1931. Transcript.*

Thank you for your letter and for sharing your story with me. I think there comes a time in everyone's life when he or she has to choose between what is personal and what is the opinion of others, what suits and what pleases the circle in which he lives. You have already had once before this choice to make and you chose what was personal and what suited, which happened to be the Faith.¹ But in some people's lives that choice comes twice over; you have the same sort of choice to make again, not in what concerns faith but love.

Again I'd say that to choose what's personal and suitable is as right in love as it is in religion. It's your life that matters and not theirs at all. You have to decide, not they.

With all my heart I wish you joy of what's coming to you. You've had a lonely life, you've had under God to fight your own battles: now He's giving you a helper. Thank Him and be glad!

1. She had been received into the Catholic church by BJ in 1913.

217. *Provincial's Diary. 27 May 1931.*

In answer to telephone call visited Archbishop McDonald of Edinburgh in Euston Hotel. He told me that now all the Canons were agreed and that we would be asked to open a house in Edinburgh in order that we might (a) give weekly lectures in apologetics to the teachers-to-be who frequented the University and (b) be Chaplains to the University students. The restriction however of not having a public chapel he reiterated: but that the Master General is willing to accept thanks to Major Hay. Later on perhaps there may be opportunity to develop a scholastic philosophy chair at the University and a chair of theology[1]—It's the feast of S. BEDE! And within the octave of Whitsunday.

1. In 1930 Archbishop McDonald had started the ball rolling for the Dominicans to come to Edinburgh. He was particularly keen to get them into the University, but on 9 December 1930 he wrote to BJ that there had been a setback, and that it would not, for the moment, be possible to 'bring in a religious', even if the University did agree to the establishment of a Catholic chair of philosophy. 'I believe,' he went on, 'that your activities will find an outlet in another branch of work at this University.' On 16 March 1931 he wrote to say that there was a good chance of the Dominicans being invited to run the chaplaincy for the Catholic students, with a chapel reserved for the use of students. 'I believe it would ultimately lead to recognition of the Fathers as public lecturers at the University.' On 23 April he insisted that 'the question of a chapel open to draw the general public would I think raise insuperable opposition.' Meanwhile Major Hay, without knowing anything of what was going on, had been talking to the Master General in Rome, getting him excited about the possibility of work in Scotland. On 29 April Fr Garde wrote from Rome: 'I have reason to hope that the Master General will grant permission for the opening of the new house . . . Recent conversations with Major Hay (author of "The Chain of Error") have aroused the interest of the Master General in the possibilities of Dominican work in Scotland' (AGOP XIII 61505). BJ wrote to Major Hay, who replied on 24 May, 'Your letter is a pleasant surprise. I had no idea, when I talked with your Master General at Rome, that there was the slightest chance of the Dominicans coming North.' The archbishop himself had broached the matter with the Master General, after Major Hay's visit. On 11 March BJ wrote to Fr Garde about him, asking him to be nice to him: 'He's been such a perfect friend to us, and it is through him that the house has come our way at all' (AGOP XIII 61505). On 15 July the archbishop wrote with a formal invitation to the Dominicans to come to Edinburgh, and the Provincial Council voted to accept the invitation at their meeting a few days later, the only dissenting voice being that of Vincent McNabb, who objected to the ban on them opening a public chapel.

218. *BJ to Blanche Leigh. From St Dominic's, London. 28 May 1931. Autograph.*

I am sorry that my letter should have arrived so late on Wednesday morning. I went out to post the letter before midnight (it was '40 Hours' and I was to watch at 12 so that I wasn't up on purpose for that) so as to ensure it getting to you as soon as I could. . . .

But you mustn't think that I am overworking deliberately, or even that I am overworking. I do just and only what I have to do. The Lord must look after that. I don't seek work. However anyhow I keep alive and about.

Moreover and finally neither you nor Beatrice[1] are in a position to scold people for 'overworking'.

So there!

1. Beatrice Leigh (1866–1949), Blanche's sister.

219. *BJ to Sr M. Dominic Heveningham OP. From St Dominic's, London.[1] 24 June 1931. Transcript.*

All is well!

Pray for us all that we may have quickness[2] to rest quietly on God even though we be disturbed by what happens to us at first. We need depth of character which can only be achieved by resting character on the Eternal. Oh the *depth* of the riches of the wisdom of God![3]

1. There seems to be something wrong here. According to the Provincial's Diary, BJ was visitating Hawkesyard 23–27 June. So either the date is wrong (either the date on the letter or the dates in the Diary), or BJ was using London writing paper but in fact writing from Hawkesyard. Or the transcriber of the letter has made a mistake.
2. The typescript has 'quietness' corrected to 'quickness'; it is possible that 'quietness' is correct.
3. Romans 11:33.

220. *BJ to George Bowring.[1] From Upholland. 31 July 1931. Transcript.*

. . . As to the whole parish problem I think that my views will be very different from yours. But I don't want to labour them. I would only say that since we managed to get parochial life and its regulations into the Constitutions in 1926,[2] we can hardly be said to have deceived people. I have mentioned it to every postulant who has applied to join the Order for the last 16 years.

Moreover I think our ideas of religious life with its regular hours etc is a luxury the middle ages did not contemplate in a friar. They wandered preaching over the country. S. Dominic had far less monastic life than I. That is why provinces like Poland have had parishes since 13th cent.,[3] the Minerva, where the Master Generals lived once they began to settle anywhere (a novel and modern idea!)[4] has had a parish attached to it for centuries.[5] I am confident that the medieval friar had far less monastic life than anyone is ever likely to have in Pendleton.

However that is only a vague statement to show you why I think parishes also have their place in our life. They are of course not the only type of work. The university life is our real life in the sense of what is properly and exclusively ours in theory. But I don't think I am unselfish in being provincial. I can't help it. I have no right to refuse according to the Constitutions.[6] I don't believe a religious should resign except for the gravest reasons. Hence I have felt I had no choice after being confirmed except to obey. I only want the Lord's will.

1. Bowring had been assigned to Pendleton on 29 November 1930.
2. Cf. above, no. 198.
3. It is not clear what BJ's authority for this is; it is perhaps something he had picked up at the General Chapter of 1929, at which he was a member of the commission on parishes.
4. The first Master of the Order to settle at the Minerva, Rome, was Raymund of Capua (Master of the Order 1380-99). The General Curia was moved away from the Minerva in 1885, and was established at Santa Sabina, where it now is, by Gillet in 1936.
5. It has had a parish since 1276. Cf. P. T. Masetti, *Notizie storiche del Tempio di S.M. sopra Minerva*, Rome 1855, pp. 6-7; T. Ripoll, *Bullarium Ordinis Praedicatorum* vol. I, Rome 1729, p. 550.
6. According to the 1926 Constitutions (Const. 557-559) someone elected provincial can refuse, but his refusal has no effect unless it is accepted by the Master General.

221. *BJ to Mrs Tytus. From The Cenacle, Grayshott. 18 October 1931. Autograph.*

. . . Here we have a full house, 40 females! Not room for them all in the convent, some are boarded out in the local pubs! However so far they are an unbothering lot and behave themselves nicely. One or two folk I know well, one or two are people I've heard of and am glad to have met, one or two are people I've heard of and wanted to escape: but the worst one who threatened to come has meanwhile been certified as a mental case and sent off to an asylum, a different asylum to this!

Yesterday I got a letter from the Archbishop of Edinburgh[1] telling me of a house for us in Edinburgh in the very best centre imaginable for our work, in an old-fashioned centre in the University part of the town, called George Square. Also this house has a garden and also 'the largest drawing room in Edinburgh'—sounds well as a lecture room or chapel. But how history repeats itself! We can't buy that house without also buying the house next door. Do you remember how that happened at Oxford when you spied out the land? And what a benefit it has been that we did buy all of it! And how splendid for us that we had someone to give us the whole site at Oxford, right out as you did, so munificently. I am afraid that these things don't happen twice in a lifetime so that I daren't even hope that someone will turn up and offer to do the same here. However when you think of it throw up an orison to St Margaret the Queen of Scotland that we may be able to have what we should have. I had almost despaired of the house when this letter of the Archbishop came. My courage and hope were on the verge of being extinguished. Then this bucked them all up again. What a fool one is not to have confidence in God! I don't know the amount wanted for the houses but I am afraid it will be a stiff price. However the Lord's been good. Blessed be His name.

1. Andrew Joseph McDonald. The search for a suitable house in Edinburgh had been proving very difficult. Edwin Essex had been sent to prospect, and on 22 August he wrote to BJ, 'It seems impossible to find anything really near the University.' A few days later he wrote again to say that the archbishop had suggested that George Square or its near vicinity would be 'the only place for us' and proposed asking the Sisters of Charity in 26 George Square to vacate their convent for the Dominicans, a course of action which does not seem to have appealed to Essex. On 27 August he wrote to say that he thought he had found a good place, but on 30 August he wrote to say that it was too small. Then on 14 October the archbishop wrote to BJ to mention that 24 George Square would be for sale not later than November, and that the occupant of 25 George Square was also going to sell his house as soon as he could find another. McDonald recommends buying both houses. 'One of these could be let and the rent would pay the interest on any money that had to be borrowed for the purpose.'

222. *Edwin Essex OP to BJ. From Edinburgh. 27 October 1931. Autograph.*

On Saturday evening, the Archbishop arrived in great excitement with further news of George Square . . .
a. The Scott-Moncrieff house[1] is to be sold. Price asked £2300. It is large (with the largest drawing room in Edinburgh) and a lot of garden space.
b. The snag. The Scott-Moncrieffs have offered the house
   1. To the University as a residence for the Principal (who doesn't want to live there, nor yet his wife).
   2. Failing the University, to the Royal Infirmary as a hostel for nurses.
   If neither of the above want to buy the house, it will come into the open market.
. . .
d. He has arranged for me to meet Prof. Whittaker[2] today, Tuesday, who will probably be able to give me news of the University's decision . . . The common opinion is that the University have no money to spend at present, but that they'd buy to keep us out. Also, that the

Royal I. have recently bought a lot of property and won't want any more. So there's a chance.

1. 24 George Square. The Scott-Moncrieff family had been in possession of it since David Scott-Moncrieff moved in in 1868. In 1918 his eldest daughter inherited it, and she lived there with her sister. When she was dying, apparently the last word she uttered was 'Dominicans', and it was with the good will of the surviving sister that the Dominicans acquired the property, though neither of them was Catholic.
2. Edmund Taylor Whittaker (1873–1956), Professor of Mathematics at the University of Edinburgh (1912–46), lived at 48 George Square. He was knighted in 1945.

223. *BJ to Edwin Essex OP. From St Dominic's, London. 28 October 1931. Autograph.*

Thank you for your letter with its exciting news.
(1) All we can do is wait and see what the Lord wants for us.
(2) As soon as it is known whether the sale has been effected or not, we shall be able to sing our *Te Deum* or our *Fiat voluntas tua*.[1] In either event, *semper et ubique gratias agens*.[2]
(3) Whatever price is asked we must offer for the Scott-Moncrieff house at once. Your letter seems to imply that the University know we are after it—which would be a nuisance.[3] However we are here in the Lord's hands.

The only point really is that we must offer whatever is asked; it is well worth £2300 to us. We could then buy Wightman's house[4] and let it, and eventually mop up the Convent too.[5] But we now wait on the Lord.

Please consider yourself authorised to offer on my behalf whatever is asked. I must placate the P.C. afterwards[6] like Dizzy and the Suez Canal.[7]

1. 'Thy will be done'.
2. 'Always and everywhere giving thanks', an allusion to the formula found in the Prefaces in the Missal.
3. In a letter of 17 October Archbishop McDonald had warned BJ, 'With regard to any application you might wish to make to acquire any of the buildings mentioned in my last letter, it is very important that this should be done in a manner not likely to arouse antagonism and opposition from the bigotry of interested parties.' Such bigotry had already scuppered the scheme for a chair of Catholic philosophy in the University. On 12 November 1931 BJ explained why the purchase had to be made so quickly and secretly: 'We have had to keep it dark as the University and Hospital were both offered the house and refused it; had it been known we were after it, it would have been bought over our heads out of spite, says the Archbishop. But fortunately no one knew that we were house-hunting. So all was well. That's why I had so terribly to keep things dark' (letter to Kenneth Wykeham-George).
4. 25 George Square, which housed a medical practice recently acquired by Dr Arthur Robertson Wightman. In the outcome Wightman retained possession until 1943, when the house was purchased by Dr Alexander Guthrie Badenoch, who was clothed as a tertiary by Bernard Delany in 1950. His house became quite a Catholic centre. In the late '50s he emigrated to Nova Scotia and died in 1964. The province acquired the house in 1969.

5. 26 George Square, belonging to the Sisters of Charity. The province never did acquire this property. In fact, it expanded its holdings in the opposite direction, acquiring No. 23 in 1936, No. 23A in 1938, and No. 23B in 1960.

6. According to the 1926 Constitutions (Const. 605) the approval of the Provincial Council was required before the provincial could authorise expenditure beyond a limit set by the Provincial Chapter. In 1928 the Chapter had set this limit at £100!

7. In 1875, braving the opposition of his cabinet, Disraeli bought the Khedive Ismail's shares (amounting to about seven-sixteenths of the total) in the Suez Canal for £4 million.

224. BJ to Gwendolen Plunket Greene. From Woodchester. 3 November 1931. Transcript.

Such a letter as this must indeed give you comfort despite the poison fever and the externalisation of life that even this very letter itself implies. Only you did write your books for this very purpose.[1] You must not complain now when your books succeed. You are no failure. You would not have failed were this the only letter you ever had. You have helped him. What more do you ever want? Just be glad in the Lord and ask Him that as you are being used as an instrument in His service He would in turn supply someone, yourself or another, to bring His inspiration to David[2] too.

But no cottage for you yet: instead a spiritual light house. It's most kind of God to use anyone. Don't do anything else but thank Him even for the love in Him that allows the deadness and the pain.

1. She had published *Mount Zion* (London 1929) and *Two Witnesses* (London 1930).
2. Her son (1904–1941).

225. BJ to Hugh Pope OP, Robert Bracey OP & Hyacinth Koos OP.[1] From Holy Cross, Leicester. 12 November 1931. Autograph.

(1) We have now secured a house in the very part of Edinburgh that the Archbishop wanted, No. 24 George Square[2] backing on to the walk that goes from the Meadows past the infirmary to the University.
(2) It consists of 9 bedrooms (including 2 servants rooms), 2 bathrooms, the largest drawing room in Edinburgh, and the garden of two houses.
(3) The house next door (in which the second garden once belonged) will come into the market very soon and we have secured the first refusal of it. Beyond it are two houses formed into a convent of the Sisters of Charity: the Archbishop tells me (but not them yet) that he is going to eject them from their schools and that their convent will ultimately be vacant. To this we should be heirs. We shall thus have provided 4 houses we hope to become the house of studies of the Scottish Province!

(4) The cost of the first house and most expensive is £2400. I have no immediate expectancy of money but I presume that as God has given us a house when it was least expected and where it was wanted He will also give us the money to pay for it.
(5) I think that it would be good (despite the Prince Consort connection) to dedicate the Priory to S. Albert the Great, if he be canonised and doctorated in December.[3] His scientific excellence gives him an aptness as a patron in that city.
(6) We enter into possession Nov 28 the anticipated vigil of S. Andrew![4]

This information can now be made public within the province, I suppose.

1. Three members of the Provincial Council.
2. Cf. above, nos. 221-223. The agent handling the purchase of the house wrote to BJ on 11 November to say that the purchase was definitely concluded.
3. Albert the Great was canonized and declared a Doctor of the Church on 16 December 1931.
4. The vigil of St Andrew should fall on 29 November, but this year that was a Sunday, so the vigil was moved back to the preceding Saturday.

226. *BJ to Edwin Essex OP.*[1] From Newcastle. 23 November 1931. Autograph.

Quite a good house, capable of being a good centre:-
(1) I shall have arranged with a man to distemper the whole house and to mend one chimney—all that needs to be done, thank the Lord.
(2) I shall have arranged with Margaret George[2] for furniture of house and chapel.
(3) I have written to F. Shaw of Tomintoul for a house-keeper (Scottish, necessary here to deal with the local folk) recommended by him to Canon Gray.[3]
(4) I have bought a library from Glasgow for you *via* Henry Bugeja.

So all you can bring in addition will be useful: also and also any cash.
(5) I have opened an account (at present a £1400 overdraft, which I've promised to repay by end of January—Lord be merciful to Thy servants) with a bank and you and I are to sign. I gave your name as Vincent Edwin Essex (so Charles George urged). Will you please sign on this with me and return to the manager, Commercial Bank of Scotland, George Street, Edinburgh?

All for the present but MONEY is greatest need now.

1. It had been decided that Essex was to be the first superior of Edinburgh, though it was not until 1 January 1932 that he officially took up the position.

2. Margaret George worked extremely hard to make the house habitable for the brethren before their arrival. She was the daughter of Charles George, the lawyer who acted on behalf of BJ in the purchase of the house.
3. George P. Shaw was a priest of the diocese of Aberdeen, currently parish priest of Tomintoul. The housekeeper was taken over from Canon John Gray, and a 'little maid' was also employed, who came from Tomintoul (letter of BJ to Miss Coats, 11 January 1932).

227. *Provincial's Diary. 11 December 1931.*

Edinburgh for day, called on Franciscans, Mr George, saw over the house with Margaret George, called on Sisters of Charity at No. 26, on Mr Gumley the agent[1] and on the Commercial Bank of Scotland manager.

1. Louis (later Sir Louis) Gumley, the estate agent who had handled the purchase of 24 George Square.

228. *BJ to Austin Barker OP. From St Dominic's, London. 19 December 1931. Autograph.*

Thank you for your letter, the points of which I have read and mused over: the main doctrine I agree with. I am not so sure that I would agree with some of the asides. Indeed some I would love to tilt over, for instance that the masters of philosophers and theologians should dwell remote from men. True perhaps in the natural order, though not even there true altogether, witness Socrates, Aristotle, Plato etc, not true in the supernatural order, witness the Dominican tradition, the older Universities which were more alive, tumultuous, roaring than ours are and yet were the homes of the Ord. Praed. Surely the cloistral life of the heart is the Dominican's desert: within himself is stillness and the philosopher's mood? However I can't think you really would maintain what your words seem to maintain, namely that to be physically 'off the stage' is a need for the Dominican professor of his brethren.

Even so that is not the main point of what you write. But I do agree with you that the staff both at Hawkesyard and Oxford should be as near permanence as possible, even though Humbert de Romans would only give a professor 5 years' teaching[1] in his very traditional though busy and active world. Nor can I think of any professor I have removed from the staff for any other reason than that I thought he was not a good professor. There is only one sad instance, Luke,[2] where my hand was forced. The Regent[3] told me that I either must remove Luke or accept notice of his (F.H.P.'s) resignation to the Master General. As only one year more remained of his regency and as the office was in the gift of the General, I could only expose the whole situation to F. Garde and explain that I thought the only procedure was for the Master General to allow me to rusticate F. Luke for a twelve month. Perhaps after that he'd be able to come triumphantly back. F. Garde agreed both to the immediate rustication and to the hope of an ultimate return in triumph. I've told F. Luke exactly why I did what I did, and what my hopes are and that Rome seems to be ready to bring these hopes to fruition in 1932.[4]

Were you to be removed then because I thought you a bad professor? Indeed no: but because I was (and am still) distressed over your mood. In a little and remote community like the professorial group at Hawkesyard any one may easily cloud the proper and desired happiness of the whole. I was deeply conscious that of late you had been clouding the happiness of that group. I had talked to you of what was distressing them: you replied that circumstances had happened to make you look at life differently and that you were lonely intellectually and that the older world had gone.

In my distress I could only foolishly repeat in my heart while you were talking, 'The man's sick, he's sick, don't believe him to be bitter, he's sick, ill, that's all.' At the time I was planning Edinburgh in detail, writing to the Archbishop, to Canon Gray, to the Provincial Council. Imagine how my heart smiled, when utterly unconscious of my preoccupation you suddenly began to say how very well you always felt in Edinburgh, what a marvellous change it always made in you, how the air stirred, refreshed you etc. 'Ho! Ho!' thought I to myself 'Is this a hint from the Holy Ghost?' I knew you were blissfully ignorant of what I was at the time occupied with, but I knew that the Holy Ghost was not ignorant and I have always cocked an ear for hints from the Holy Ghost. Perhaps more often than not, I have got the hints wrong, but I have always waited for them to settle my perplexities. One is so sure that there is a divine solution always if one can only find it: 'There's a remedy for everything but death.'

In such a mood as I was then in, dreaming of Edinburgh, finding you (of all people) a cause of unhappiness to your fellows, diagnosing the roots of this to be sickness, imagine what this unexpected and lyrical praise of Edinburgh as a stirrer of your pulse, imagination, life, happiness, seemed to me! Do you wonder that I nearly stopped you with my sudden impulse? However the Holy Ghost seemed to remind me of your exam:[5] 'The beggar will never be ready for his exam if you shift him' I echoed to myself. It had taken me ages to work you up to it: I had had to let Paulinus[6] go because I couldn't move him. Luke was my *only Bachelor*[7] after 15 years! So I muzzled my mouth and laid aside my idea. As I wrote to you the other day, it was the idea of the exam that saved you from being shifted, saved us as well as you.

So there you have the story as I see it of what nearly befell. I have through all these years, war years, post-war years (when I could not satisfy the houses or the missions with the type of men I sent them) husbanded the professorial staff, sending students abroad[8] I could ill spare, refused all requests from the houses to send them the professors. Dear Austin, I've really tried to build a staff that will fashion a future province that will be nearer than the present to S. Dominic's heart's desire.[9]

Now in the autumn I shall end my work anyhow.[10] Others will do better than I have done for the studies, but remember that I had my difficulties as well as my dreams. When I came as Provincial there was no new lector, there had been no new lectors,[11] Luke was home from Palestine,[12] no one was engaged in complementary studies, the war was on, the Regent had not resigned, was not removed, remained still Regent though he was overseas in France.[13] Things had to be begun all over again. It was slow, painful, I made many mistakes, the professors were sometimes to my judgement incompetent, I had to suffer them, there were none others.[14] Gradually things fitted in, I could remove encumbrances, I shifted people I thought ill-adapted to their work. All this was personal, lonely, and difficult to me who had never taught, who did not know the personnel of the house of studies, who had to listen, guess, and act. But I was blessed to have generous and docile people like you and F. Hugh, to have people like you both and Luke who were full of ideas. Such plans as I made were the result of other people's enthusiasms. Now the future of this will be fulfilled as God meant.

Pray for me and forgive me in the name of our common dreams.

1. There is nothing in Humbert's writings or in the Acts of the General Chapters held during his time as Master of the Order to justify this assertion. BJ was probably thinking of something he had published ten years earlier in *The English Dominicans*, London 1921, p. 59: 'The term of teaching varied; but four or five years was considered quite long enough. The chapter of 1334 judged that after that period a lecturer had a tendency to become stale.' The Chapter of 1334 said no such thing; the reference should be to page 334 of the edition of the Chapters in MOPH IV (i.e. the Chapter of 1350), though the Chapter only ruled that no one could be principal lector in the same convent for more than four years, unless he was a Master in Theology, without any explanatory comment such as BJ implies.
2. Luke Walker.
3. Hugh Pope.
4. There had been considerable friction between Walker and Pope. Walker was removed from Hawkesyard in 1927 and sent to Oxford, where he resumed his teaching in 1929, only to be sent away again to Stroud in 1931. At the Provincial Chapter of 1932 his attitude to Pope was alleged as a reason against petitioning for him to be given the STM, though the majority of the diffinitors supported him and he was in fact given the STM. In 1932 Pope was graciously but firmly given his retirement as Regent and Walker was appointed in his place.
5. Barker was due to take (and did take) the exam for STM in 1932.
6. Paulinus Sweeney gave up teaching in the studium in 1927.

7. Luke Walker took the exam for STM in 1930, so was now a Bachelor.
8. The practice of sending students abroad for part of their studies was well established in the province. The English Dominicans had had a college in Louvain until it was lost when the republican French forces invaded in 1794. It was later discovered that the title deeds to the house were missing, so it could not be sold, but the province received compensation in the form of two burses created in the university of Louvain for English students in 1837, and in 1839 it was clarified that preference was to be given to English Dominican students. From 1857 onwards the province nearly always had at least one student at Louvain, and sometimes three or four. The financial value of these burses however dwindled to almost nothing, and complicated negotiations between the British and Belgian governments were involved in their allocation every time one fell vacant, but in spite of all this BJ evidently thought it was worth while to go on making use of them. Because of the war, it was not possible to send anyone to Louvain from 1914 onwards, but in 1917 BJ wrote to the Foreign Office to inquire about the burses and in 1919 he was told that applications could once again be received, so BJ resumed the practice of sending two students to Louvain to do part of their theology there. By 1926 the value of this custom was being questioned in the province, but BJ argued in favour of maintaining it, on the grounds that 'it was good to have as many Dominican educational centres as possible left open to us' and that 'Louvain may perhaps become a place where some special studies may be developed later' (Studium archives). By 1932 the feeling of the lectors was that the province should stop sending students to Louvain, though BJ wanted to continue. With the end of BJ's provincialate the province did in fact stop sending students to Louvain, and negotiations already opened for filling the two available places were abruptly broken off. In 1932-34 there were repeated inquiries from the Foreign Office as to why the burses were not being used, and in 1934 it was arranged that the two burses should be merged into a single one, which could be used even by someone studying in England. In 1935 it was further clarified that the burse could be claimed by someone studying at Blackfriars, Oxford, though still no candidate was proposed (to the evident puzzlement of the Foreign Office). It was not until 1938 that the burse was actually awarded in its new form.

Master General Gillet put pressure on all the provinces to send students to the Angelicum in Rome, which the English province duly did. But in 1933 the lectors made it clear that they were reluctant to go on complying, on the grounds that there were too few students in the province.

The occupants of the Louvain burses were normally not doing extra studies that they could not in principle have done in the provincial studium. But BJ was also keen to send people to university elsewhere, whether abroad or in England, for further studies. Thus Reginald Ginns was sent to Jerusalem in 1920, Wilfrid Ardagh to Fribourg and Adrian English to London University in 1921, Rupert Hoper-Dixon to Rome and Hilary Carpenter to Oxford University in 1923, Ambrose Farrell to Rome in 1927, and Richard Kehoe to Jerusalem, Quentin Johnston to Friboug and Thomas Gilby to Louvain to do a doctorate in 1929.

There were, of course, more mundane reasons for sending people abroad, which perhaps appealed more to some of the lectors. In 1928 they decided that Quentin Johnston should do his lectorate in Rome to 'relieve the pressure on the house'.

9. On 11 July 1932 the lectors in Oxford agreed unanimously to send BJ a letter 'to express to him the very deep feelings of gratitude the teaching staff feels for his generous support of everything that has favoured the welfare of the studies'.
10. The Provincial Chapter was due to begin on 5 September 1932.
11. When BJ became provincial, the teaching staff at Hawkesyard consisted of Austin Barker (who had acquired his lectorate in Jerusalem in 1910 and had been teaching at Hawkesyard since 1911), Paulinus Sweeney (who had been brought into the studium in 1914, but had acquired his lectorate in Louvain in 1909), Vincent McNabb (who had returned to Hawkesyard as prior in 1914, but had acquired his lectorate in Louvain in 1894 and had been teaching at Hawkesyard on and off since 1897), Chrysostom Egan (who had started teaching in 1915, having obtained his lectorate at Hawkesyard in 1912), and Walter Gumbley (who had no lectorate and belonged properly to the school, not the studium, though he had been teaching church history in the studium since 1914). The last people to have obtained the lectorate in the province were Jerome Rigby (1910), who never taught in the studium, and Chrysostom Egan (1912). The next was Reginald Ginns in 1920.
12. Luke Walker had been studying in Jerusalem, but had to leave when war broke out. He arrived back in England early in February 1915.

13. Cf. above, no. 31.

14. BJ's efforts to secure a properly trained staff for the studium can be seen from the minutes of lectors meetings he attended, with considerable regularity, throughout his time as provincial, and also from the references in the Provincial's Diary to his trying to secure lectors from other provinces. His difficulties can be illustrated vividly by the problem of getting Canon Law taught. In 1912 Ethelbert Rigby came from Rome with his doctorate in Canon Law, and he taught the subject at Hawkesyard until 1915, when he enlisted as an army chaplain; he returned disturbed from the war, and never resumed his teaching, and shortly afterwards left the Order. In 1915-16 no one taught Canon Law. Paulinus Sweeney taught it 1916-18, Vincent McNabb 1918-20. After a gap of another year, Walter Gumbley started teaching it, by special permission from the provincial (he was not even officially a lector). As a student of his from this period recalls, 'He evidently did not know Canon Law. The students soon found out that he could not be more than one classs ahead of us, and often he was openly corrected by one of the students, an Irishman [Michael Delahunty], who had followed one year of Canon Law in his own province' (letter to ST from Peter Duncker OP, 7 May 1989). In 1922 Master General Theissling visitated the province and Duncker, a compatriot of his, was urged by the students to point out to him the insufficiency of their Canon Law teacher—which he was evidently already aware of, and he burst out laughing when Duncker passed on the students' message. He had him taken off Canon Law at once, so in October 1922 the lectors petitioned both BJ and the Master General for a proper canon lawyer, but without success. In 1923 Wilfrid Ardagh took the subject on, though it was no more his field than it had been that of any of his predecessors since Rigby. He taught it until 1927, when at last the province obtained the services of a professional, Juan Ylla Barry from the Rosary Province.

In 1920 it was decided that Stanislaus Lamb should specialise in Canon Law after doing his lectorate, but, when he completed his lectorate in Louvain in 1922, he was promptly turned into a schoolmaster instead. In 1923 two more students in succession were earmarked for Canon Law, but both had to be brought back from Louvain because the lectors there were not satisfied with their work, and both in due course left the Order. So in 1924 the lectors noted sadly that, once again, they had no professor of Canon Law in the making. In 1925 Ambrose Farrell was picked to specialise in the subject, but it was not until 1927 that he was ready even to begin specialised studies. In 1929 he came home laureated and took over from Ylla Barry. Also in 1929 Alexander L'Estrange and Kenneth Wykeham-George were earmarked for Canon Law, and the latter did in due course get a licentiate in the subject in 1932 (by which time it was clear that L'Estrange was not going to specialise).

229. *BJ to Mrs Campbell. From St Dominic's, London. 21 December 1931. Transcript.*

Indeed that is the most difficult of all jobs that you have on hand and you will need every ounce of wisdom you have and a good deal more if you are to meet it as it needs to be met. So you must go very quietly along depending on your daily Mass for enlightenment, resting very quietly on the Mass and its meaning, watching it through to the end in such a fashion as shall make it live.

Not least think of the Mother who was 'standing by',[1] the most difficult of all jobs: to be able to do something is much easier, to be unable really to *do* anything and yet to have to watch needs more than human tact. Let her help you on to the way in which you should walk.

I can only hope that your courage will outlast the strain and that you will find your peace in it all. Christmas is the pageant of Peace in a cave, in the cold all alone: *de te fabula narratur*.²

Every blessed wish be yours!

1. John 19:25.
2. 'It is a story told about you.'

230. *Provincial's Diary. 24 December 1931.*

Mrs Tytus gave me £1000 for Edinburgh.

231. *Provincial's Diary. 29 December 1931.*

Said first mass 8.20 at 24 George Square¹ coram F. Giles.² Present Margaret George and Michael³ who served the mass. Gave letters of fraternity to Margaret George who has done everything for the house, its furnishing etc. Blest the house. Archbishop McDonald called and Mr Pat McGlynn⁴ and these two and F. Giles and I discussed the Chaplaincy from 4.30 to 6.10.

1. BJ actually wrote '26 George Square'.
2. Giles Black, who was to be the first Catholic chaplain at the University of Edinburgh.
3. Michael George, son of Charles George.
4. Dr Patrick McGlynn, a Catholic lecturer in Classics at the University of Glasgow.

232. *BJ to a lady just married.*¹ *From St Dominic's, London. 11 January 1932. Transcript.*

I feel a villain; I had intended to wire you on Dec. 30 to the Church at Wincanton with all my best wishes for the 31st, and had noted this down in my diary to be done. Actually I was travelling down from Edinburgh and forgot all about it till the morning of the 31st when I knew I was too late. So I did say Mass for you but had to leave it at that.

I trust that you will both be blest in the New Year and with your new life and have not least the blessing that helps you to have from human love a better understanding of God's love, its generosity, its absorbing nature, its flame.

1. See above, no. 216.

233. *BJ to Sr M. Anthony Morrison OP. From Hinckley. 6 February 1932. Autograph.*

Thank you for your accounts which as usual are admirably done and clear;[1] you seem to manage to run your whole community very cheaply. I think we might obtain a special bull from the Pope to allow you to come to London as secretary to F. Humbert[2] and build you a little cell in the garden, an anchorhold. He could dictate through a window to you and you could save him such a lot of work. That would complete his cure!

He is more cheerful than when he first came and is I think indeed better in health though I think too that he eats less. His breakfast is only toast, and his supper but the fish we have and sometimes a little jam with his bread and butter. But he has little else. A good dinner at midday. He has company however and that perhaps is the best advantage of London to him, the company of his brethren.

Your account of the death of Sister Angela[3] is most touching; it must indeed have been a very great grace to her at the end, no doubt as you say because of her admirable charity all her life. She had—as so many do have—all the great virtues and few of the little ones! In religious life we are inclined to judge fervent religious to be those who do the little obvious things of the life we lead and not to realise that the great commandments are still the great commandments in the cloister as well as outside. Hence we sometimes underestimate our fellows because of their failures in the things that are most visible.

The disarmament of nations must as you say be according to the needs of each nation and no absolute disarmament is possible this side of paradise. I always 'kick off' with the words of Pope Ben XV 'a simultaneous and reciprocal diminution of armaments',[4] that puts the matter simply and well. I am most grateful for your prayers for the meeting: it went well.

1. Sr Anthony was the bursar at Carisbrooke.
2. Humbert Everest, provincial bursar and archivist.
3. Sr Angela Butt OP was a laysister of Carisbrooke, who died 29 January 1932.
4. BJ is probably referring to the letter Pope Benedict XV sent to the leaders of the warring nations on 1 August 1917, in which he called for a negotiated and balanced reduction of armaments on all sides (*Acta Apostoliae Sedis* 9 (1917) p. 418).

234. *Provincial's Diary. 11 July 1932.*

Visited house in Sheffield offered us by Duchess of Norfolk and wrote to her in sense of subjoined report. Forgot to ask name of house. Think it is called Beech Hill.
Good house, worth £70 a year, well built
garden and paddock

hot and cold water throughout, electric light and plugs
4 bed rooms and bath; 2 servants' rooms, 2 attic rooms
dining room and drawing room, lavatory, kitchens, new range etc
outside W.C. as well as one on ground floor
garage with large room over
(1) too far from university to be a good centre
(2) not likelihood to become a good parish
(3) admirable to live in but little else.

235. *BJ to Hubert van Zeller. From Wigton, Cumberland. 19 July 1932. Autograph.*[1]

Dear Claud,[2]

You tell me not to give you advice but to pray for you. Nevertheless I will give you advice. Take down Migne's Patrology vol. 195 (P.L. 195) and read S. Aelred's DE SPIRITUALI AMICITIA. Any of the dialogues will do. All three will do better. The third with its analysis of his two friendships in excelsis will be helpful—or the last chapter of the third book of his SPECULUM CHARITATIS—or indeed any of his works. He'll give you the best point of view from which to look at these things. Or take Powicke's life of him[3] and go away with it into the woods beyond the cricket field and settle down to it with a prayer for guidance. Last Sunday's rather crafty prayer will do![4]

Then as for the point you mention, I would only say this, that I am exceedingly glad. I am glad because I think your temptation has been always towards Puritanism, a narrowness, a certain inhumanity. Your tendency was almost towards the denial of the hallowing of matter. You were in love with our Lord but not properly with the Incarnation. You were really afraid. You thought (here I am imputing all sorts of evil to you without warrant) if you once relaxed, you'd blow up. You bristled with inhibitions. They nearly killed you. They nearly killed your humanity. You were afraid of life because you wanted to be a saint and because you knew you were an artist.

The artist in you saw beauty everywhere; the would-be saint in you said, 'My, but that's frightfully dangerous'; the novice in you said 'Keep your eyes tight shut'; the Claud in you nearly blew up. If P. hadn't come into your life, you might have blown up. I believe P. will save your life. I shall say a Mass in thanksgiving for what P. has been, and done, to you. You have needed P. a long time. Aunts are no outlet. Nor are stout and elderly provincials. You have needed this.

Don't you see that you have got a talent of friendship and that it is very dangerous and that nevertheless it is worse than dangerous to wrap it in a napkin and that it has got to be used. Don't imagine P. will be the last one you'll fall in love with. You were meant to love P. and to be of service to P. You will find that God will use you for others too. . . .

However that is rather beside the main points; there are two. Yourself to wit and God.

For yourself it is the best thing that could have happened to you, both the pleasure and the pain of it. They will both liberate you, give you a new freedom, help you to find yourself. You have been much too stiff.

For God, it is most admirable. You had no vocation to Parkminster.[5] You never did have. You'd have been 'potty' in Parkminster, I mean noticeably 'potty'; for after all---

Now a cloister is not a defence but a battle field. Your noviciate was not to protect you but to train you. You are not to be saved from meeting evil but from being overcome by evil: 'He did not say, Thou shalt not be tempested, but thou shalt not be overcome' (Mother Julian, God bless her).[6]

Now evil is overcome by good, by God, by love of God, by searching for Him everywhere. You must not be afraid of looking for Him in the eyes of a friend. He is there. You can at least be sure of that. To love others is not to lose Him but if possible to find Him in them. He is in them. You don't lose God by loving others; you will find Him if you love them. You will miss finding Him only if you merely love yourself in them. That is the blinding nature of passion; it is self-love masquerading under a very noble disguise.

In this particular case you must indeed be afraid of supplanting God's unique position by substituting one of His workmanship for it; but you will only overcome that danger one way. Other people would find other ways. Your way is a very simple but a hard way. Your only chance is to go on loving P.; if you stop, you'd miss God. If you thought the only thing to do was to retire into your shell you'd never see how lovely God was. You must love P. and look for God in P.

I agree that to say that your desire to bring God to P. is sufficient justification for your friendship is all bunkum. It is terribly like pretending. I hate those dodges and subterfuges. You love P. because you do, neither more nor less, because P.'s lovable. You won't find any other sincere reason however hard you try. Don't allow anyone to hoodwink you into supposing purposes which are dragged in after the event and are humbug—anyhow that's what I think. Perhaps that's worth little as an argument. Anyhow I hate that tosh!

Keep reminding yourself that God is in P. and that God is in you: that you're both monstrances of God. Enjoy your friendship, pay the price of the following pain for it, remember it in your mass and let Him be a third in it. The opening of the Spiritual Friendship: 'Here we are, thou and I, and I hope that between us Christ is a third.'[7] Oh dear friendship, what a gift of God it is. Speak no ill of it. Rather praise its Maker and Model, the Blessed Three-in-One. Beloved Claud, walk joyously now and gratefully. God is good.

1. Because of the very personal nature of this letter, it has been necessary to rewrite a few parts of it slightly. Otherwise much more of the letter would have had to be omitted entirely. In no point has the substance of the letter been affected.
2. Van Zeller's baptismal name.
3. F. M. Powicke, 'Ailred of Rievaulx and his biographer Walter Daniel', *Bulletin of the John Rylands Library* 6 (1921–22), reprinted in 1922 on its own. A revised edition, including the whole text of Daniel's life of Aelred, was published in the Nelson Medieval Classics in 1950.
4. Collect for the 9th Sunday after Pentecost: 'Let the ears of Thy mercy, O Lord, be open to the prayers of Thy suppliants, and that Thou mayest grant them what they desire, make them to ask the things that are pleasing to Thee . . .'.
5. Van Zeller had for a long time dreamed of joining the Carthusians at Parkminster and he later tried his vocation there.
6. Julian of Norwich, Long Text chapter 68.
7. PL 195:661A.

236. *BJ to Miss Calthrop. From St Dominic's, London. 10 September 1932. Autograph.*

Thank you indeed for your letter and its too generous enclosure. I am afraid that it is far too much for you to give at this time of the year anyhow: but I shall indeed gratefully use it on a holiday which I am hoping to take at the end of the month in a remote Italian hill village, far away from everything, where I can forget my many mistakes as provincial and the disasters that ensued.[1] But what I shall never forget is your kindness and devotion, and the unselfish and fierce labours of the Oxford dream now at last come true.

May S. Dominic bless you with a due reward!

1. On 6 September the Provincial Chapter had elected Bernard Delany provincial, thus bringing to an end BJ's sixteen years' provincialate.

237. *BJ to Bernard Delany OP. From Prinknash Priory. 19 September 1932. Autograph.*

Thank you for your letter. I presume from it that you have the intention of confirming me in that priorship.[1] As you can guess it is certainly not what I wanted. I had hoped for other things. However since it is your wish that I should ultimately accept it, I can do so knowing that it must be right for me to do so. As for the rest it must be as God wills.

So again with the Editorship.² I shan't bother you with my feelings but only with my acceptance of course of the work laid on me. I shall cowardwise get F. Thomas³ to do as much of it as his long patience and eager good will will stand.

Thank you too for telling me that my holiday can stand—and also for sending me the celebret by the hands of F. B. P.⁴ whom I met in the drive here (someone has broken the *sigillum* of the Diffinitory and told him that I suggested his name!).⁵ I am grateful as these last 4 years I have found almost intolerable at times with all sorts of physical troubles within. Perhaps a holiday will ease them all.

As for the D. Litt., your suggestion does me much honour but I am afraid that my days of scholarship are over⁶ and that I can only be useful in other ways. And the same applies to preaching. Since the Constitutions say that Priors must rarely even for preaching be absent from their priories⁷ I shall refuse all engagements, except local ones. Hence I return this second Irish letter to your Paternity to be dealt with in that sense.

There is however the New York invitation,⁸ for F. Edwin⁹ or for me. There are strong financial reasons for allowing one or other of us to go (I don't know what his views there anent would be) but his need for the fat cheques is certainly greater than mine. Leicester must raise money privately to buy from the province and the bank the *site* of the Church, owing as it does about £2000 on these loans. It has actually bought the land but owes that amount on the land (hence the detained Oxford investments).¹⁰ F. Edwin by going to New York could clear some of this off. The Oxford needs you know. Perhaps you could let me know in mid October which of us you'd like to accept the invitation (or neither!) so that I can acquaint Mgr McMahon.¹¹

A weekly mass is promised (see adverts) for all benefactors of the Noviciate Guild. I said that mass myself each week, each Sunday when I could. I said it yesterday and the other Sundays since Sept 5 but now I shall leave it to you. Also a mass for the Brethren as the Constitutions advise each superior to say.¹² . . .

1. The Provincial Chapter began on 5 September, when BJ formally ceased being provincial. Bernard Delany was elected on 6 September, and his confirmation arrived on 14 September, so that he formally ceased being prior of Oxford. The electors at Oxford unanimously elected BJ to be their new prior, and the Provincial Council approved the election on 17 September, and Delany immediately wrote to BJ. He formally confirmed BJ as prior on 19 September, the day BJ wrote this letter.
2. The Chapter appointed BJ to replace Delany as editor of *Blackfriars*.
3. Thomas Gilby, appointed assistant editor of *Blackfriars*.
4. Bertrand Pike.
5. Since Laurence Shapcote wanted to resign as Vicar Provincial of South Africa, the diffinitory at the Chapter were concerned to find someone to replace him. At their sixth session, on 8 September, they called BJ in to advise them and he suggested Pike, a suggestion accepted unanimously by the diffinitors (Processus Verbalis of the Chapter). He was then duly appointed (Acta p. 9). The proceedings of the diffinitory were meant to be secret.

6. This had been brought home to BJ by the critical, puzzled and rather sad reviews of his book, *Social Theories of the Middle Ages*, published in 1926.
7. 1932 Constitutions, Const. 433-I.
8. To preach during Lent at Our Lady of Lourdes Church, New York.
9. Edwin Essex, prior of Leicester.
10. The bank at Leicester was holding up some investments which had, in principle, been transferred to Oxford, as security for Leicester's loan.
11. The rector of Our Lady of Lourdes Church, New York, BJ had known him since 1918. In the outcome it was BJ who went, and his conferences were published as *Our Lady of Lourdes*, London 1934. He brought home $4000.
12. 1932 Constitutions, Const. 428.

238. *BJ to Mrs Tytus. From Blackfriars, Oxford. 29 October 1932. Autograph.*

I have now been here just over a week[1] and find life full but not unpleasantly full. It is lovely in Oxford despite rain and wind for the leaves have not all deserted their places and give a golden and red and brown diaper pattern to the old grey walls: the comeliness of decay. But I haven't had very much time for that really as I have to find my way about in the house and its needs. We are a community of 32! That means that two cells alone are vacant, so we shall have to consider the problem of building one of these days! But that is really beyond anyone's thoughts in these days, especially since we have to do a little repair work already to the building. The battlemented parapet round the Church and tower seems to have been badly done; the mortar used was bad mortar; instead of sand, stone-dust was employed which has no binding quality so that as it dried it fell out and left gaps through which the rain very cheerfully found channels for its exit and entrance! The expense of re-mortaring it all is not the trouble so much as the horrid thought that our builders should have served us so ill and that we may find defects elsewhere. Moreover with architect dead and the builder's firm dissolved and since bankrupt there is no one against whom we can bring an action and recover damages. What a disheartening world it is after all, when one wants to believe and trust everybody! One doesn't mind troubles, but one does dislike being let down when one has trusted folk. However I suppose I have let down others in my day and must suffer accordingly.

And you and all your aches and pain? How are you bearing up against our fiercely opposing climate?

1. BJ had arrived to take up his priorship in Oxford on 19 October.

239. *BJ to Bernard Delany OP. No address. 7 November 1932. Autograph.*

But you ought not to give us[1] that cheque, your needs are more pressing than ours! Please don't ask the Prov. Proc.[2] for money for us; I have much too much pride to want money from the Province. It was only the Master General's ruling that made me write like that, much against my will.[3] We shall be perfectly all right. I was only afraid that we were obliged to ask for the money.

Most of his Paternity's letter was written under a misapprehension; I don't yet understand its terms.[4]

We shall indeed remember your retreat in our prayers[5] and hope you will find comfort in it and all the other helps to wear with your accustomed quietness this troublesome crown.[6] How good of your mother to do that for us! We shall be grateful for them.[7]

The £100 for Persia[8] is still in the names of McNabb and Jarrett. If you like it can be transferred to your account. On deposit it collects very little interest: but it is protected from incursions. It is no trouble to me but McNabb and Jarrett are both getting on in years and so---

PS (1) Bishop Myers comes on Dec 17th, Ember Saturday.[9] You know you will be welcome then or at any other time. Your Archdeacon performance will be most acceptable, salva reverentia. We have only the little room on the front to offer as your room will have to be offered to the ordaining prelate.

(2) F. H. P.'s [10] sermons on the condition of our buildings here are rather exaggerated, from all one hears! Also he calls the clerk-of-the-works a fraud! which is either Williams or Aidan[11] who are likely to bring libel actions! But really from all accounts that reach us his sermons are frightening people and giving us a 'bad name'. Also (and worst of all) the money given under this emotion appeal doesn't go to us as presumably the givers mean it to go. We aren't claiming the money—we would like the dreadful account a bit nearer the truth. The *we* represents the Senior Common Room!

1. BJ originally wrote 'me', and then corrected it to 'us'—an interesting sign of how he had to learn new instincts, now that he was merely prior of a properly constituted priory, not a provincial building a priory out of his own pocket. While he was provincial he personally handled much larger sums of money than were normally available to the provincial bursar. All the bills for the building of Blackfriars, Oxford, went to him personally.
2. Provincial Bursar (Procurator)—still Humbert Everest.
3. Master General Gillet had decreed that the Oxford priory should be the financial responsibility of the province, not the provincial, so that the provincial bursar would be ultimately the man in charge of its funding (Acta of the 1932 Provincial Chapter p. 50).
4. Gillet had written a letter, to be read to the Provincial Chapter, after his visitation of the province. In it he complains about the grubbiness of Woodchester and the lack of spiritual direction of the novices; about undue eagerness to adapt the studies to English needs, which Gillet found particularly reprehensible in view of the number of converts in the province, with a 'university training so different from our own'; and about the 'cult of liberty', with the crisis of authority that results from it, both on the part of subjects and 'on the part of superiors who

wield it (sc. authority)—or, rather, scarcely dare to wield it' (Acta pp. 32-70). It is not suprising that BJ was rather flummoxed.

Gillet also indicated that he was unhappy with the division of the studies between Hawkesyard and Oxford. He wanted all the studies to return to Hawkesyard. In July 1935 he sent his assistant, Fr Garde, to make a special visitation, chiefly in connection with the reuniting of the studies. After he had gone, the Provincial Council held a special meeting, at which both the Regent (Luke Walker) and the lector primarius of Hawkesyard (Austin Barker) spoke against the continuing division of studies. On the other hand, there was not room for all the students at Hawkesyard and what was to be done with Blackfriars, Oxford, if all the students were taken away? A compromise solution was accepted, that Oxford would be kept going as a place where simplified and curtailed studies would be available for the less talented students, and Hawkesyard would become the province's formal stadium again. In the outcome, however, nothing was done to implement this plan. So Gillet wrote again before the 1936 Provincial Chapter calling even more explicitly than before for the re-uniting of the studies at Hawkesyard. For Oxford he suggested, in the short term, that it should be used for 'people preparing for the ministry together with those who are taking University degrees with a view to teaching at Laxton'. But in the long run he wanted it to become 'a House of Higher Studies—especially historical studies' to benefit, not just the province, but the whole Order. So his plan was, essentially, to reunite Dominican philosophical and theological studies at Hawkesyard, leaving Oxford to be a university house, specialising in history. At the 1936 Chapter the diffinitors discussed Gillet's letter at length, but without coming to any conclusion. McNabb seems to have been alone in calling for immediate acquiescence in the Master General's wishes. The others maintained that there was not room at Hawkesyard for all the students, and that it was important not to scandalise people outside the order who had supported the foundation at Oxford and were looking for great things to come of it. As a compromise, they suggested the opposite of the plan previously proposed by the Provincial Council: Oxford should be reserved for the brighter students, who were aiming at the lectorate, while the simpler, more basic studies would be done at Hawkesyard (Processus Verbalis of the Chapter). They seem to have been quite out of sympathy with any suggestion that Blackfriars should be more closely associated with the university in Oxford. Because of their inability to come to any clear decision, they put nothing at all into the Acta about the whole issue, which shocked Gillet, who refused to confirm the Acta until this defect was remedied. Delany, who had been re-elected provincial, accordingly wrote to all the diffinitors asking their approval for an insertion into the Acta of a 'commission' charging the prior of Hawkesyard (Hugh Pope) to complete the building there as soon as possible so that the Master General's wishes could be complied with. This was agreed to and duly put into the Acta. However no practical results ensued, and in 1937 Delany wrote to Gillet explaining the difficulties involved, and at last Gillet seems to have been persuaded. He replied that what he had been worried about was the isolation of Blackfriars in relation to the university and now 'tout cela est changé', so he no longer wants all the studies reunited (Acta of the 1942 Chapter pp. 10-11). The studies were in fact reunited much later on, at Oxford rather than at Hawkesyard, when the last students left Hawkesyard for Oxford in 1967.

5. Delany was going to make a private retreat at Hawkesyard, 11-20 November.
6. Of being provincial.
7. It is not known what gift of Mrs Delany's BJ is referring to.
8. The province's interest in Persia began in 1919, when one of the novices, Cyprian Rice, told BJ about his desire to develop a new form of apostolate among Muslims, preferably in Persia. BJ responded with enthusiasm. However, the French Dominicans working in Iraq heard about Rice's interest and, in 1927, got the Master General to assign him, immediately after his lectorate, to Mosul, where he stayed for two years. In 1929 BJ managed to dislodge him from there, and the Apostolic Delegate in Persia asked to see him and got him to stay with him in Teheran. The Delegate secured the pope's interest, so early in October 1930 the Provincial Council was asked (and agreed) to 'accede to the desire of the Holy Father' and make a foundation in Persia. As BJ immediately wrote to Rice, 'I shall nominate you superior at Shiraz and add Alexander L'Estrange and Mark Brocklehurst to you to form a community (letter of 7 October 1930). L'Estrange and Brocklehurst were approaching the end of their studies at the time. Before anything could be consolidated there was a change of Apostolic Delegate, and the new man was much less well-disposed than his predecessor, so in July 1932

Rice arrived back in England, very uncertain whether there was any future for the mission in Persia. Rome, however, was still keen, so at the beginning of October 1933 Rice was assigned back there; in deference to the Delegate's known wishes, Henry Dominic Blencowe was sent with him, to be superior of the mission. But the attitude of the Delegate and the suspicions of the French Dominicans made it impossible for the new venture to prosper, and the mission was abandoned in October 1934.
9. To ordain seven of the students deacon. Candidates for ordination were presented by the provincial, if he was present—this was the 'archidiaconal' role BJ was offering Delany.
10. Hugh Pope.
11. Aidan Elrington.

240. *BJ to Miss Calthrop. From Blackfriars, Oxford. 13 November 1932. Autograph.*

I feel that I must put on paper my very great gratitude for your munificent gift to Blackfriars, all the more munificent because of the times through which we pass and because of the uncertain future that seems so full of menace.

But at least your princely gift, princely in its size and more than princely in the largeness of the hole it makes in your savings, helps to make us realise how beholden we are here at Oxford to the generosity of people, Friends or friends, and how much we have depended upon the efforts of everyone else but ourselves.

We are grateful naturally to the Holy Ghost who has kept us not merely in sufficiency but in abundance of the things we need; it is good for us to feel uncertain of where our help shall come from as long as we are certain from the very nature of Himself that the help we do need He will send.

So please believe that you have all our gratitude. I told the Community that night of your benefaction and we prayed for you immediately with the liturgical prayers for Benefactors in the breviary.

God reward you!

241. *BJ to Bertrand Pike OP. From Blackfriars, Oxford. 6 December 1932. Transcript.*

How sad that you should dislike S. Africa; or perhaps you are of those who hate the new? (not nude but new)? Anyhow it will do your general health good. . . .

Now to business.

(1) Yes, partly Stellenbosch[1] was meant to be an entrance into S. African university life. I hoped that Jo/burg would put us in touch with the English speaking element and Stellenbosch with the Dutch. I knew it would take a long time to break into the Dutch camp because it is Dutch, farmer, and Calvinist, each most stubborn; all

3 together the most stubborn combination in the world. But till it is done the conversion of the young leaders of the African world won't ever come off—humanly. I am sure that F. Wilfrid[2] has worked as hard as anyone could have done and harder than most would and that no one could have got into university life if he couldn't—except a Scotchman (the Dutch are partial to Scotch, Calvinists both) might have done. But I never thought anything would really happen—
  (a) For ten years.
  (b) Till there were novices and students, S. A. born, attending the university. As here in Oxford, it can only be attacked from *within*.

(2) My benefactress[3] promised me in 1930 that she'd give me a large benefaction; but since 1930 American wealth has slumped, hers amongst others. She told me in London in May that she would eventually do what she had promised; but I can't tell you when. From this (she gave me the money to buy the place) I had hoped to start a Noviciate and philosophy-course i.e. till solemn profession: and then send them to Rome or England. But naturally this depended on money. I believe there is money in S. A. to be got for S. A. enterprises. But it takes looking for. However I am absent and have nothing to do with things and can't advise you at all.

(3) Everyone at our meeting at Potchefstroom[4] approved of the Stellenbosch scheme (it and Joburg were considered together).
  (a) A house was needed at lower altitude than our houses in the Transvaal and the Natal border etc. was denied us by the Bishops.
  (b) A house needed in the Cape for the sake of the new arrivals there, coming from overseas; can't always sponge on Cathedral etc.
  (c) Our OP work had been pushed aside by our taking on more parishes and we need preaching centres, one in J. and one in the Cape Province, if we were to develop Dominican work.
  (d) Cape Town and Joburg are the two centres of S. African life and will always remain so. Much else is floating and uncertain in S. Africa; but not these two. Stellenbosch is equally a fixed centre. Other places may easily cease to function (Springs, Brakpan etc) but not this.

(4) It seemed to me also that though the Dutch were so hostile S. Dominic would have gone to them, because they were so hostile. He drove always at the centre. It seemed to me to have been the usual Dominican tactics to do that and always at the universities; but that it was a long job and that it would never be achieved except by getting people into the university—as at the beginning in Paris and here in Oxford. Universities are always exclusive. They only respect

their own folk; you have always to attack them or rather to attract them by sending people to them as students and then these students form contacts with the university, first with other students and then with professors. Only in that insidious way is a breach made. It would be by taking boys like D. S. and first sending him to the university and afterwards getting a noviciate and having him in it etc; and if the brethren out there would rally round the scheme they could get the necessary funds to pay for him at the house etc.

At least that was the plan I had.[5]

I feel so hopeless, to pit myself against the local people in this way and to scheme what everyone else says is impossible and to be quite confident myself that it is the way to deal with the country and that the people out there are on the wrong tack altogether. But that was my judgment and is still.

However I have no personal feelings about it; it seemed and seems the right thing. My successor must make up his own mind and act as he sees the right. I shall not grumble or lament: but my faith in the scheme will remain.

Life is easy really if one holds by the Spirit of God as the governor of life and does what one judges right and leaves consequences and the future severely alone to look after themselves. I would not desire to urge you in my direction. I see it clearly myself in the light of 10 years on and more. But no one can believe on the strength of my faith. Second-hand faith is poor stuff.

However F. Wilfrid has been admirable, especially if you consider F. Wilfrid himself whom no one would have guessed to have either the physical stamina or the strength of character needed to deal with that particular difficulty. Yet he has dealt with it perseveringly and joyously. We owe him a great tribute of praise.

If you are for shutting up houses, Klerksdorp should go! It was accepted to suit a scheme of the Delegate which never eventuated. I would drop Klerksdorp and Potchefstroom! EXCEPT FOR THE BISHOP.

Cheer up, young man! You will have amassed much experience, have made many friends, have wallowed in the dry sunshine, have secured a manly complexion and the firm eye of the bloke what looks across the Veldt. Also you will have twice completely cleaned out your inside.

1. Cf. above, no. 205.
2. Wilfrid Ardagh.
3. Another American benefactress, not Mrs Tytus.
4. During BJ's visitation of South Africa towards the end of 1930.
5. The first Dominican actually to attend the University of Stellenbosch as a student went there in 1938.

242. *BJ to Humbert Everest OP. From Blackfriars, Oxford. 10 December 1932. Autograph.*

. . . May I take the opportunity to thank you for the overwhelming praise lavished on me in the Acta? I recognise the gentle Latinity as yours[1] and have been afraid of looking up while it was read in the Refectory. It has shamed me into confusion; but it was charming of you to phrase it so prettily.

1. Everest was one of the diffinitors at the Chapter (and they are the people who actually write the Acta). The praise of BJ is on pp. 15-16 of the Acta. It comes in the petition to the Master General that BJ should be made an STM. Gillet replied that he did not have the necessary qualifications for an STM, so he made him a Preacher General instead (Acta p. 29).

243. *BJ to Bertrand Pike OP. From Blackfriars, Oxford. 14 December 1932. Transcript.*

I was immensely touched by your letter and by the fact that you wrote to me so frankly of yourself and your dislike of so much of the business of a missionary's life and of how little you have to bring to the work of the gifts that seem so necessary to it, love of adventure, daring, courage etc and of how little too the people appeal to you, the coloured people etc, and indeed of how little the Prov. Chapter can have known of you when it selected you for this job.

Well taking the last point first, it is quite possible that the Chapter did know little about you, the real you, within, when it made its choice; but as I know you know, it was I who suggested your name. In confidence the one they proposed to me before they asked me to suggest someone, was a father who, admirable in many ways, would have been wholeheartedly disliked as a superior in S. Africa. One is bound to secrecy else I'd tell you the name.

Why then did I suggest you? I did know something of you, of what you felt and what you feared, for I had read all your letters from the front (and indeed had re-read them lately when I was going through my papers in London before the Chapter) which were full of your sense of fear. Do you remember that dreadful day you had to cross between trenches at Ypres, when your courage failed you and only after 3 or 4 attempts did you force yourself to get by, and how you found the carved edges of your rosary beads had cut into your finger in your unconscious gripping of them to take a new lease of courage from holding them? Yes I remembered that.

But my dear Bertrand courage and fear are not opposed? Those only have courage who do what they should do even though they have fear; to be fearless is not to be courageous but only not to need courage. Those are courageous who fear and yet do what they should.

Actually I don't think that S. Africa needs adventure at all; I think it needs wisdom. It needs common sense, an independent judgment, and someone who is fond of men. S. Africa is above all a man's country (*vir*, not *homo*). The men are neglected and the boys. They need looking after. It is that that would have attracted me, it is that that puts S. Africa near my heart. It seems to me ideal for you because it requires a certain amount of experience of boys and men here,[1] and yet a width of understanding to realise that conditions are very different, and that the men and boys are more independent and more casual than here. They are as affectionate but their affection is more hidden than even an English boy would make it, more masked by indifference in outward show.

I also hate mountains except at a distance; I have lived all my life with only the Downs for my companions. Those I love but not the hills. A love of hills I could not have brought to the work! I am sure that 'safety first' is the very best motto for the government of S. Africa OP together with your very lively sense of human nature, your intuitive appreciation of youth, and your being able to establish lines of communication with boys despite shyness, awkward independence, and gruffness of manner. You are a man. It matters most that you should be that, in a man's country. Four years will settle S. Africa's affairs; it will have established your own health admirably. Also it will have given you a knowledge of people and openings for boys that will be helpful when you return. Honestly you were the one I thought best of all.

1. Before his appointment as Vicar Provincial in S. Africa, Pike had spent six years as headmaster of the school at Laxton.

244. *BJ to Bernard Delany OP. From Blackfriars, Oxford. 7 January 1933. Autograph.*

Thank you for your cheque from the Province; we have too much money now, so please no more at Easter. We shall easily carry on. We pay sparingly and were about 30/- up when your first cheque arrived and had paid everyone to date.[1]
(1) Oldmeadow[2] has little sense of humour if he thinks *Pictantiae* are serious and that Lord Castlerosse was quoted because we approved of his remark and not because the accusation of snobbery sounded inappropriately from him.[3] However the point is that he accused the Editors of writing a 'dishonest paragraph' (this may be actionable at law!!) because the Editors differed from him in his policy towards the Hunger Marches and considered his use of the word 'imposture'

unjustifiable. That some people with revolutionary purposes made use of the marches to turn them into something other than was intended is possible. We dissent violently from his use of that word and we intend to dissent: and if he considers us dishonest because we dissent from his way of dealing with the matter, he is at liberty to continue to think so—only he must not say it or write it. We are sorry to have entangled you in this affair. If you care to refer him to us we shall deal with him affably---

(2) But please don't order me away. It is less trouble being here than being absent; I am not tired. Indeed people who visit me from London tell me[4] how very different I look! Moreover I have a stream of visitors from today almost till I leave,[5] . . . who have all invited themselves.[6] So please--- . . .

PS A most witty and beautiful concert last night, a grand opera! The voices were wonderful. I laughed and wept!

1. Yet on 10 February the Provincial Council had to approve Oxford's request to be allowed to raise a loan of £400 to meet the cost of some repairs to the building.
2. Editor of *The Tablet*. On 2 January he wrote to Delany to complain about a paragraph in the December number of *Blackfriars*, which contrasted his description of the Hunger Marches as an 'imposture' with a much more benign comment in the *Church Times*. He demanded that the editors should publish a retraction in the *Church Times*. Delany wrote back, asking if he was serious. On 5 January he replied that he was. He also remarked that someone had told him he ought to be flattered to be attacked by a journal so disloyal to the faith as to quote Lord Castlerosse as saying that 'We Roman Catholics are the religious snobs of the world'. The quotation was included in the December 'Pictantiae', a feature only recently introduced into *Blackfriars*, culling amusing dicta from the press (including, in November 1932, a rather preposterous bit of scaremongering from *The Tablet* about a well-known girls' school on the South coast being a hotbed of Bolshevism).
3. Valentine Edward Charles Browne, Lord Castlerosse (1891-1943), later the 6th Earl of Kenmare (he succeeded to the title in 1941), was a journalist and the director of *The Evening Standard* and *The Daily Express*.
4. BJ actually wrote 'him'.
5. For America (cf. above, no. 237).
6. Among the names listed is David Bailey, who soon afterwards, as a Dominican, inherited BJ's name and became Bede Bailey OP, the original editor of this volume.

245. *BJ to a 17-year-old niece of his. From New York. 16 March 1933. Autograph.*

Is it too late? Anyhow you will know that I did remember you and that I shall say Mass on your birthday. God bless you and make you nearer to Him in your memory more and more every year.—I hope that this year will be even more bounding and happy for you and that you may more and more enjoy it. I think we should enjoy always God's world. We have only to remember that He made it and loves it and keeps it in being,[1] to have a perpetual inspiration for getting immense pleasure out of it. But we must do it whole-heartedly, see

Him as the world's lover in pain as well as in pleasure, take life completely from His hands.

1. Cf. Julian of Norwich, Long Text chapter 5.

246. *BJ to Hubert van Zeller. From Convent of Mary Reparatrix, New York. 20 March 1933. Autograph.*

The eve of S.Benedict's day and also more or less the proper interval to give my letter a chance to reach you on the *dies natalis*[1] of the Bl. Claud de Gellée[2] both suggest to me that I should write to you. Which I do herewith.

First and foremost I wish all the proper things for your birthday, past, present, and to come. Past, because I hope that your birthday will help you to see in your year past the hand of God, present, that you may accept the truth of that faith in His will which is essential to our serenity, and future, that you may be sure that what has been done for you shall continue to be done for you by Him to whom past, present and future are tenses or moods fitting to humanity's language but not to His. May the new year see you growing in discontent with self and content with God's management of you! It's a double process which is really one at base.

Here I am kept with plenty to do, thank the Lord, and with all the excitements of this present time, the ups and downs, the violent fluctuations, the collapses and recoveries, the adventures and ruins which make life exhausting but fascinating, which try the spirit that longs for even and smooth waters and has still to face, without escape, the storm. It all makes life interesting but deepens the lines and wrinkles on the faces of generations that have to meet it.

However each age is fascinating to those who live it: no doubt Noah and Queen Victoria would here join hands with S. Gregory and S. Aloysius—except that S. Aloysius might refuse to join hands even with the Old Vic.

But as always the crisis of outward life depends upon the crisis of the inward life: and the crisis within is always one of faith, human and divine. It is always a problem of faith, in man or God or both. The marriage troubles of our day are the troubles of those who have lost faith in themselves to hold on to duty and in others to love them in return. All human problems are at basis problems of love: faith rests upon love or grows up with it. They are mutually co-existent. They agree.

You know this as well as anyone; it is always a problem of believing the other fellow implicitly. All our pains are the pains of those who can't get themselves to trust implicitly, who are jealous or suspicious or who can't believe their good fortune can last. Whereas, blow it all, we should be merely and happily made humble and recognise indeed that we are not worthy of the friends God sends us but also recognise that since they are friends they must be accepted as friends.

It is just nasty to think, 'I shall always be loyal and faithful, but how about him?' It is nasty because it pretends to be humility and is nothing but blasted pride. It sounds so pathetic but is really vanity preening herself on her goodness. It sounds like the publican not daring to look up to love's heaven but is really the old Pharisee saying beween sobs 'I am not like the rest of men, I remember but they forget.'[3]

Why should I say all this to you? Why does one say anything to anybody, except in order to ventilate one's own self-examination, on the basis that all the world is as rotten as I. So you get it. I dare say the ladies here will get it in ten minutes when I talk to them of the spiritual life. But you get it because I venture to think of you as a specimen of humanity something like myself, having much the same sort of hungers, desires, hopes, and fears. So I give you the results of my vast self-musings, coming from looking at this bloke that is myself. Now I find that my friendships have cost me far more pain than my hatreds, loving costs more than fighting, but only because I see that I was loving myself all the time, that I was thinking rather well of myself, and that I couldn't hope to credit other people with the same friendship for me that I had for them. It seemed like asking too much. But I see now that love should be like that, love once given should be taken for granted, one shouldn't question just as one shouldn't nag. And so the pains of friendship were the result of my own selfishness. And life would have been happier if it had only been less selfish. It has had so many nice things and especially nice people in it: and all the troubles have been of our fashioning because I didn't believe and so couldn't really have loved.

There now! See what a letter I have written with my own hand.[4]

1. 'Birthday'.
2. Claud was van Zeller's baptismal name, Jelly (here Frenchified as 'de Gellée') his nickname.
3. Cf. Luke 18:11.
4. Gal. 6:11.

247. *BJ to Kenneth Wykeham-George OP. From Our Lady of Lourdes, New York. 1 April 1933. Autograph.*

But let prudence go hang! and let me write and thank you for your letter without thought of subject or superior[1] or letter covers or distinctive writing. There's spring in the air and I feel sentimental and at peace; have just finished a harassed retreat, females without number and without mercy and all wearing black hats—the fashionable colour of hats, if black is a colour, I forget.

But I did give your love to Baltimore[2] and thought of my visit to you though I couldn't remember the number of the house in Charles St. It was 2000 or 3000 odd I believe, but I forget which it was. I remember the stairway and the rooms and your mother and the emergence of you all from school. I stayed this time out at the new seminary in Roland Park, a very fine place. I lectured for an hour to the 350 students on their spiritual life and they asked me to give them another talk on Oxford so I had to give them a second hour immediately. It was late when we all got to bed, only to have thunder and lightning all night!

It must be a relief to have all your examination behind you;[3] I hear from the students that your sermon was very much liked indeed; sermons I think the letter said. Anyway much appreciated. Procede et regna.[4] God bless you in this as in all else beside.

The family troubles have been very difficult to put up with and are none easier to bear because they seem to have been occasioned originally by folly and need never have happened. I don't know that one gets comfort by that. The past is best left alone, I think. One keeps what's going, one leaves the past. That is my philosophy. Let the dead bury their dead,[5] deal with today, let tomorrow take care of itself;[6] the lovely life of a child is the more perfect, live wholly for the moment and distill from it all you can. Religion is to help one to enjoy all life; so too culture is given us to enjoy life in all its richness, to miss nothing. Religion is so fine because it deals with the soul, because it enables man to be independent of circumstances, to triumph over them, at least not to be defeated by them, to hold his own against them, not to let himself be fussed by them, to accept whatever is coming to him, indeed to be hurt (he can't help being sensitive) and wounded by others and yet somehow as well to use that very experience to enable him to appreciate all the more gratitude when he finds it, and loyalties and affection and all the other blessed gifts of God to us through men. We have to make ourselves be honest and sincere and true and yet endlessly happy because we have an inner spring of happiness that works against our surroundings: 'Stone walls do not a prison make.'[7] We can use them as a protection against an invading world. The prisoner and the hermit each have a cell and their difference between irksomeness and happiness is due to their ways of looking at the very same circumstances---and so on till you fall asleep.

1. Wykeham-George was assigned to Oxford, so BJ was his prior. Throughout his long provincialate BJ insisted that, as superior, he 'could have no friends' among the brethren.
2. Where Wykeham-George had lived as a boy.

3. He had just taken his Licenciate in Canon Law at the Angelicum, Rome.
4. Psalm 44:5 ('Go forth and reign').
5. Luke 9:60.
6. Matthew 6:34.
7. Richard Lovelace (1618-1658), 'To Althea, from prison'.

248. *BJ to Mrs Bullough. From Blackfriars, Oxford. 20 November 1933. Autograph.*

But of course; masses shall be said at once for Stefano d'Italia;[1] under that name shall he be prayed for that all may be well with him in his difficulties and temptations. I shall tack him on to the 'Bullough list' who are included in my daily mass. I am sure that you will have given him comfort and inspiration by your talk with him. You have all the gifts for that familiar apostolate which is so needed and so fine.

It is good to know that you have been to Italy and that you have come back refreshed; now-a-days when so much is in perplexity and bewilderment, the Italian situation is most interesting. I wish I knew it better. The interesting part of it is not the dictatorship, which is a phase that must pass, but the corporative State which may well survive as the new form of national life. Salazar, the dictator of Portugal (I believe he is a practising Catholic) has now plumped for it.[2] Spain may now easily follow,[3] as the Right is royalist temperately,[4] but more especially fascist in its ideals. It will be interesting if after a multiple experiment il Duce shall arrive at that, and create a new era of national organisms.

I have written to B.O.W.[5] to offer—if they will buy it for me—to translate selected letters of Savonarola from the princely edition I see now advertised from Italy.[6] I hope that I shall learn that you and your husband have already embarked on such a volume yourselves. But one wants to create in the imagination of our people a new image of him not as the thunderer but as the saint. We think of him brandishing lightning and not enough of him with his flaming heart.

1. 'Stefano of Italy'; we have not identified him more precisely.
2. On the authority of a plebiscite, he introduced a new constitution, setting up a corporative state in Portugal, in March 1933.
3. Election results in Spain on 19 November 1933 showed a pronounced swing to the Right. On the same day, the Spanish Fascist party was founded.
4. BJ perhaps meant to write 'temperamentally'.
5. The publisher, Burns Oates and Washbourne.
6. Ed. R. Ridolfi, Florence 1933.

249. *BJ to Mrs Campbell. From Blackfriars, Oxford. 26 December 1933. Transcript.*

Your life indeed has fallen in hard times these last three years; but the time has not, I am sure, been wasted really, for life is so little to be measured by what we do, and so much how we accept what's done to us, so little by our actions and so much by our reactions: hence, though it may be that there seems little to show for it, you are not one of those who would measure life by what is seen. You have lived well and finely, serene and helpful and seeking to alleviate the distress you have been conscious of, patient, wise, unselfish.

The Worth adventure[1] must indeed have meant a severing of ties; for though the monks have technically gone there for a while, I suppose actually they won't return. For a short time they will be visibly Downside but then later they will draw apart and go on their own ways. That's life: 'We are born in another's pain.'

1. Under Abbot John Chapman the Downside community was finding itself short of space in the monastery. This was on account of an increase in vocations and the closure of Downside parishes as well as a renewed emphasis on life in community. Abbot Chapman purchased a large property called Paddockhurst at Worth, near Crawley in Sussex, in 1933. Worth was a dependent priory of Downside from 1933 to 1957, when it became independent. Since 1965 it has been an abbey. Worth never developed, as some had hoped, as a 'primitive observance' house, and its chief work in its Downside days was as a Preparatory School for Downside.

250. *BJ to Mrs Bullough. From Blackfriars, Oxford. 2 January 1934. Autograph.*

I wish I could come to Cambridge but now I don't go anywhere. Priors are bidden in our Constitutions only to be absent rarely from their houses,[1] so I find that it isn't possible to rule and go about preaching; so preaching and all wandering has ended. Fortunately one hasn't to settle the knotty problem as to what sort of life one would prefer but only to accept the life settled for one: it doesn't save trouble so much as enable one to know what's to be done right. Hence however it is little likely that I shall be at Cambridge at any time or free to go—though I'd dearly love to go. I have so much I'd like to talk to you both about. Political things like a lecture I have to give for the Burge Foundation[2] on the Catholic Church and what she's done and is doing for peace. About that I know little enough. Your good Professor[3] once lent me books to read on this: but it is your talk I'd like, your ideas, your views.

But there are other things as well: deeper and more important and needing chatter to bring them out. However perhaps the Lord will find me a chance to see you; if He does, then I shall be pleased. You were so ill when I did see you last time, and time itself was so short, that I doubt if I even was able to speak to you.

Stefano[4] and your poet[5] must indeed be often in your prayers; I can't believe that your mother won't prevail with him in the end. An eagle whose talons have been caught by the indecencies it preyed on! But an eagle's right place is with eyes on the Sun. Stefano naturally doesn't grow individual yet, but a man in danger who knows he's in danger is seldom kept from the danger's neighbourhood; he can be upheld. Which is nobler perhaps. . . .

I am hoping to persuade S. & W.[6] to let me 'do' some of Savonarola's letters,[7] if I can only get a little time. . . .

1. 1932 Constitutions, Const. 433-I.
2. On 14 December 1933 BJ's old tutor, Ernest Barker, wrote to him: 'I have been connected, since its foundation, with the Burge Trust—a trust in honour of Dr. Burge, once Bishop of Oxford [1862-1925]. The object of the Trust is to promote international friendship on the basis of the common Christianity of Europe and other nations. We have a yearly lecture on some topic connected with our object. My earnest desire is that you should deliver the lecture, and that you should speak of what your great Church has done, and is doing, in the cause of world peace.' BJ accepted the invitation, and the lecture was to be given in Lincoln's Inn on 30 May.
3. Mrs Bullough's husband, who had recently become a Professor at Cambridge.
4. See above, no. 248.
5. Gabriele D'Annunzio, who had famously been the lover of Mrs Bullough's mother, Eleonora Duse.
6. Sheed and Ward.
7. Cf. above, no. 248.

251. *BJ to Mrs Bullough. From Blackfriars, Oxford. 18 January 1934. Original typescript with autograph additions and corrections.*

Thank you for letting me read that letter and for commenting on it too, for else I would never have understood it. The comments are charming![1] As it is, it is a charming account of one indeed of 'good will'. That is redolent on every page. . . . I should feel that the real misunderstanding on his[2] part (if I have properly understood the Italian) is as to the relation between goodness and evil. I think that he takes too absolute a view of goodness in its human form. If I understand him, in that passage in which he describes what you have called 'the festering sore' he seems to imply that unless a man were completely free from sin of this sort or that, he could not be called to holiness or prayer. I should feel inclined to say that he drew too hard a line between good and bad people. Goodness and evil are poles apart; but saints and sinners are not. Is it not a common error to divide the world up like that; as though the saints were not also sinners and some, sinners intermittently? The real point is that the saint knows he's a sinner but is trying to react against his sin. The sinner, truly so, is the one who has lost courage. In Ephesians somewhere S. Paul speaks of those who 'in despair' have surrendered themselves to impurities.[3] That is the true sinfulness, not doing evil but the surrender to evil. That is dreadful for it is the rejection of the power of God to alter man or of the love of God to wish to do so.

He seems to me, if I rightly follow him, to be maintaining that unless one's heart was pure there was little use in praying or in aiming at holiness. The answer to this is of course that no saint ever thought of praying *because* he was on the way to holiness. No saint ever thinks in terms of his personal success. He looks on himself as a failure, considers himself to have done no good in life at all; that indeed was the very phrase of S. Francis when he was dying.[4] I am sure that Stefano does not judge himself to be as evil as S. Francis thought himself to be. It is no answer to say that in fact the saint had his heart set on goodness. He didn't think so. All the saint would have hoped was that he was *trying* to love God. He couldn't be sure. No one can be.

Hence in this case I would suggest that what he needs is instruction in the virtue of hope and fortitude; that fortitude is the virtue by which we continue to fight even when we are always losing—Botticelli's Fortitude,[5] the tired woman sitting down, who is nevertheless perfectly ready to go on if needs be. Fortitude is not the virtue of going on when you are succeeding (that's no virtue but natural and easy) but when you are failing; and the saints did think of themselves as failing and yet held on. The argument is S. Paul's everywhere. We are useless but we go on because our uselessness does not affect the power of God; and since good comes from God and not from man, He can pull off sanctity, where man shows only wrong. Man has therefore to remember that he won't ever be much good but that it does not matter very much as long as he is willing to go on making efforts towards goodness.

Of course I am speaking without much knowledge of the case so that my diagnosis may be all wrong. But I feel that what he most needs is not to make acts of faith but acts of hope, for he is already a man of good will. Once you have that in your penitent, you can be sure that the chief point has been gained; for the rest what is needed is that he should continue to make efforts against his failings, senza poesia or con poesia. I think that he has all the proper dispositions since he has good will and does desire to do the right thing. I am not sure however whether he goes to the sacraments or not. I fancy from what you say that since his conversion he has been regularly. Well, that is right.

As to whether the two should have been left to help each other towards a love of God, I cannot tell which decisions would have been better. I am sure that it would have been harder to do that well but much more wonderful, so that I can understand the Dominican carrying Teresia off away from the occasion of evil.[6] But it would have been far more splendid if it had been possible to leave them to help each other—a prolongation of that saying of the Imitation that he that loveth knoweth the voice of divine love.[7] Or again those sayings of S. Paul that marriage is a sacrament of the love of husband and wife,[8] even (we can suppose) of the love of one for another whether they be husband and wife or merely friends, so long as the love be lawful.

But I should say that his need, to repeat, is to realise that what God asks from man is not success but continual effort. This is the greater heroism.

This all looks tame and jejune; after I have read my letter through, it doesn't seem to say anything very much but I do believe that his need is *hope* rather than faith or love, for these two he seems to have.[9]

1. These four words are written in as an afterthought, above the last words of the previous sentence.
2. Stefano, Mrs Bullough's Italian friend, for whom she had been asking for prayers; cf. above nos. 248, 250.
3. Eph. 4:19.
4. It is not clear what BJ was thinking of; the detailed accounts we possess of St Francis' death do not contain any such comment as BJ implies.
5. 'La Fortezza' in the Uffizi Gallery, Florence.
6. It is not known who Teresia is, or the Dominican who took her out of harm's way, but the nature of this episode can be inferred from the letter.
7. *De Imitatione Christi*, ed. T. Lupo, Vatican City 1982, III 5.23.
8. Cf. Eph. 5:25-32.
9. This last paragraph is added in BJ's handwriting.

252. *BJ to Mrs Bullough. From Blackfriars, Oxford. 23 January 1934. Autograph.*

You have such courage, such humility, and such dainty vigour of language that you ought to convert anyone who naturally has sympathy with the things of Christ. If the Poet[1] is not moved by what you write, I shall feel disappointed in him: he has power, he almost has wings. Moreover I am sure that where 'she'[2] is she has not forgotten and that her native generosity (now a thousand times re-inforced) will be poured out, the more and not the less, because of what she sees above and below her.

That other soul! S. Catherine had her Stefano, who turned Carthusian.[3] What prayer, what gay wit, what affection was needed, before he found his way there! But he found it.

Years! Ah what are they? To us at times they seem so rich, so to be desired: but not time matters but intensity. Offer for him, to be what God wills of him, offer for the Poet and the rest (that they wake and find themselves in a dark wood[4]), no other thing than yourself: Non nisi me Domine![5] But most offer Him your will to accept His own wherever it points, for that is a whole burnt offering, a consumed sacrifice.

God bless you and all your house!

1. D'Annunzio (cf. above, no. 250).
2. Mrs Bullough's mother, Eleonora Duse.
3. Stefano Maconi (c.1350–1424). He was a close friend, from childhood onwards, of Tommaso Caffarini OP (c.1350–1434), who joined the Dominicans c.1364 and came to be a fervent admirer of St Catherine of Siena, whose biographer he later became. Maconi joined the ranks of Catherine's 'family' in 1376 and often accompanied her on her travels and acted as one of her secretaries. On her prompting he became a Carthusian at Pontigliano in 1381, and was superior in a variety of Carthusian monasteries from 1382 until his death. 'That other soul' is Mrs Bullough's friend, Stefano; cf. above, nos. 248, 250 and 251.
4. Dante, *Inferno* I 2.
5. An allusion to the episode in the life of St Thomas Aquinas, when the Lord appeared to him and asked what reward he wanted for writing so well about him. Thomas replied, 'Domine non nisi te' ('Lord, nothing except you') (in Tocco's life of Thomas, chapter 34; ed. D. Prümmer, *Fontes Vitae S. Thomae* II, Saint-Maximin, n.d., p. 108).

253. BJ to Bernard Delany OP. From Blackfriars, Oxford. 9 February 1934. Original typescript.

. . . When I have heard approvingly from Mrs Tytus and Mrs Weguelin, to whom I have written, I shall ask your leave with details (in case you think it should be asked also from Rome) to sell the cloth-of-silver vestments[1] and the old furniture in the common room[2] and the bursar's office.[3] We have had to overdraw our account three hundred and thirty pounds and shall have to pay another hundred pounds out at the middle of February. I don't bother you with our troubles because I guess that you are in no condition to help us as we need to be helped. We ought to do something for ourselves. The council here agrees we must do something. We should try to sell the vestments to a church in New York, the cathedral if possible. Don't rack your brains to help us but when the time comes let us help ourselves.

1. The Jerningham vestments (cf. above, no. 79). Mrs Tytus and Mrs Weguelin were both important benefactors of Oxford (indeed, Mrs Weguelin had presented a set of red vestments for the opening of Blackfriars in 1929); it is not clear quite in what capacity they were being consulted now. In the outcome, the Jerningham vestments remained at Blackfriars.
2. BJ omitted 'room'.
3. BJ campaigned for the use of the word 'bursar' (as being more in line with Oxford practice), rather than the traditional Dominican word 'procurator'.

254. *BJ's last Conference. 17 February 1934.*

BJ was booked to give a week-end retreat to the Little Oratory in Kensington[1] *on 17–18 February. On Oratory writing paper he wrote these brief notes for the first conference, at 5 p.m.*

HOLINESS
WHAT NOT: series of good deeds.
　Mass & justice & charity & patience
　Father & husband, son, brother
RETREAT NOT TO HELP THAT
DEEPER: OUR LORD PROTESTED
WHEN ASKED FOR LAW, NO THINGS
　COMMANDED, LOVE.
VAGUE, UNCERTAIN? Yes more
　difficult to be sure of—
AT BACK MOTIVE – KNOW HIM[2]
AT END OF RETREAT, THAT. Not
　self but God, not exam of con-
　science—
May He help us to know &
love Him—

1. The Little Oratory was a large, lay confraternity attached to the London Oratory. According to their records, 'about 120 brothers and visitors took part' in the retreat.
2. The rest of BJ's notes are in pen, but 'KNOW HIM' is pencilled in.

255. *BJ's last conference. The Little Oratory, Kensington. 17 February 1934.*

Father Antony Holland, the director of the Little Oratory, took notes of BJ's conference, of which a copy has been preserved:

We are here to know God.
Christ was a hater of hypocrisy and cant.
Realise that the essence of goodness is not in 'action' but in 'motive'. Not to ask ourselves 'Am I doing it' etc., but '*Why* am I doing.'
　Motive: Love. Do I love God.
One means of increasing love of God—to get to know God better. What time do you give to that? Do you ever think what sort of a Person he is?
Know, love, serve.
A good deal of it is Prayer—that God will help us when the Retreat is done to know him better.
Goodness in terms of action—What Our Lord found and wanted to break through.

Goodness of itself could become a substitute.
'I'm better than I was because I am *doing* more things than I was. Our Lord came to teach something quite different and the New Testament is continuing to echo that.'
What do we mean by Goodness and Holiness? . . . so keen on *doing* that they completely ignore there is spiritual life.
Do you love God?—the only thing that matters.
The Pharisees' goodness could be measured—decorum, respectability.
The Magdalen was a saint—because she had loved much.[1]
How do I stand in the sight of God?—I don't know.
Man knoweth not whether he be worthy of love or hatred.[2]
Not *what* you do, but *why*. Dominant *motive* in going to Mass and Holy Communion.
What motive in being pure etc.
Holiness never to be measured by action but by motive.
Of two persons the more perfect may love God less.
Of two children the one who gives her Mother the more trouble may *love* its mother more.
Love is a queer thing.
What is a Retreat for?—Forget yourself.
Something much more important—God.
I'm to love God.—How? If you *know* him you *will*.
Christianity is the knowledge and love of God. If I knew God more I'd love him more. What is Heaven. The Vision of God. Why are the Saints loving God? Because they can't help themselves.
We should examine God.

1. Luke 7:47.
2. Ecclesiastes 9:1.

256. *Bernard Delany OP to Mrs Bullough. From St Dominic's, London. 23 February 1934. Autograph.*

How very kind of you. I very much appreciate your sympathy. I saw F. Bede this morning and he seems (to me) visibly weaker. There are other things besides the stroke (which was only slight) and it seems that his kidneys are badly affected and his general condition of exhaustion gives him little power of resistance.

We can only go on with hope and entire trust in the divine will. F. Bede himself seems to think he is dying. We are getting in another doctor this afternoon on the advice of Dr Reid and Dr Walshe.[1] A recovery is not impossible and we can pray.

1. Dr F. M. R. Walshe wrote to the provincial, Bernard Delany, after BJ's death, saying that he had heard that BJ's hospital expenses were being paid for by friends, but that if this was not the case he would not wish to be paid. The provincial should simply tear up the bill.

257. *Bernard Delany OP to David Bailey.*[1] *From St Dominic's, London. 24 February 1934. Autograph.*

I am opening Fr Bede's letters because he is much too ill to receive them and we mustn't let him talk much. He is being magnificent like the wonderful saint he is. We thought he was going to die on Thursday; but today's news is a most distinct improvement. He is managing to retain liquid food and it is most hopeful. I will tell him when I am allowed to see him for a minute tomorrow that you wrote and that you are praying and that will cheer him.

I have put him under obedience to get well and that has made him want to try and live. He seemed to want to die before that.

1. Now Bede Bailey OP, the original editor of this volume.

258. *Sr Mary Evangelist*[1] *to Bernard Delany OP. From the Hospital of St John and St Elizabeth, London. 24 September 1934. Original typescript.*

The Reverend Father Bede Jarrett O.P.

Complete resignation from the first moment of his illness. He accepted each change and each symptom without question and never gave way to depression.

Perfect self-control. He never flinched even in those awful spasms of hiccough which were characteristic of his illness in the first few days.

Simplicity. His wants were always simple. He wanted something to read and asked for a child's picture of the Life of Our Lord—not elaborate, but large and coloured.

During the Novena to Blessed Thomas More he would ask every day at 10 o'clock for the prayer to be said with him. He could only manage two or three words at a time and would repeat them slowly, often stumbling over a simple syllable and correcting himself with pain. After 'Blessed Thomas More, pray for us' he would often say 'And now please if you can spare a moment one "Hail Mary" '.

Generosity. When flowers and fruit came for him he was most anxious to share them.

When the Cardinal[2] came to see him he rang for the Nurses afterwards and said, 'I have told the Cardinal about my Nurses and I want you to go now and ask him for his special blessing.'

Humility. 'I have learned a lot from watching you Sisters. I have never been as thorough in my work as you are in yours.'

His detachment from all earthly things was so very marked. Heaven meant so much to him. He once asked for prayers that he might have Courage, Patience and Contrition. He called these the three outstanding virtues which he needed so much.

1. Sr M. Evangelist Simmons was matron of the hospital where BJ died.
2. Cardinal Bourne; he had first met BJ in 1898, just before BJ joined the Order, and they became good friends. He wrote to Bernard Delany on 18 March 1934: 'You have my deepest sympathty in the death of F. Bede, which is a grievous loss not only to your Order but to the Church in England, for which he seemed destined to do still greater work even than in the past. I met him first when he was eighteen, and followed his life with affectionate interest—and for long years found in him one upon whose friendship and assistance I could always count.'

259. *Bernard Delany OP. Provincial's Diary. 17 March 1934.*

I saw Fr Bede Jarrett this morning and found what seemed to me a vast improvement. There was a kind of glow of health in his face: he was cheerful and bright and we talked for ¾ of an hour and I came away with the happy feeling that now recovery was only a matter of time. At recreation I told the fathers that Fr Bede was very much better and seemed definitely to have turned the corner.

Between 2 and 2.30 F. Vincent McNabb (the subprior) came to my room and said they had phoned from the Hospital to say F. Bede had had an attack. We both hurried off to St John and St Elizabeth's and F. Bede was dead before we got there.

After his meal the sister was arranging the pillows and settling him up for the afternoon when he complained of a sudden onset of pain in the heart and immediately collapsed. The doctor came and administered oxygen and artificial respiration. He was dead. Requiescat in pace.

BIOGRAPHICAL NOTES

AELRED, St (1110-1167). Born at Hexham, he became a Cistercian at Rievaulx in Yorkshire. In 1143 he was appointed the first abbot of the new foundation at Revesby, and in 1147 he became abbot of Ricvaulx. He is particularly famous for his elevated doctrine of friendship, enshrined in such works as the massive *Speculum Caritatis* and the treatise *De Spirituali Amicitia*. Cf. A. Squire, *Aelred of Rievaulx*, London 1969.

ALBERT THE GREAT, St, OP (c. 1193-1280). Leading scholastic philosopher and theologian. He entered the Order in Padua in 1229, but was immediately sent back to his own country, Germany, where he soon became a lector. Later he was sent to study in Paris, where he became a Master of Theology in 1245. In 1248 he was appointed first Regent of the new studium generale in Cologne. In Paris and in Cologne he had Thomas Aquinas among his students. In 1254 he was elected provincial of Germany, a position he retained for three years. In 1260 he was appointed bishop of Regensburg, but he resigned the following year; after doing odd jobs for the pope for some years, he returned to his teaching in Cologne. He was one of the leading pioneers in the serious study of Aristotle, and was a highly inquisitive natural historian, as well as being a biblical commentator and speculative theologian. Canonised and declared a doctor of the church in 1931. Cf S. Tugwell, *Albert and Thomas*, New York 1988.

AMIGO, Peter (1864-1949). Bishop of Southwark 1904-1949; in 1937 he was given the title of Archbishop. Cf. Michael Clifton, *Amigo: Friend of the Poor*, Leominster 1987.

ANCRENE RIWLE. An English 'rule' for nuns, written c. 1220 by a Victorine canon of Wigmore Abbey. Vincent McNabb believed that the author was a Dominican, a claim he presented in a succession of articles: *Modern Language Review* 11 (1916) pp. 1-8; ibid. 15 (1920) pp. 406-409; *Archivum Fratrum Praedicatorum* 4 (1934) pp. 49-74. BJ accepted his conclusions (*The English Dominican Province 1221-1921*, London 1921, p. 119). On the provenance and authorship of the work, see E. J. Dobson, *The Origins of Ancrene Wisse*, Oxford 1976.

ANGELICO, Fra, OP (Bl. John of Fiesole) (died 1455). The most notable Dominican painter. The date of his birth and of his entry into the Order remains controversial but probably he was born c. 1400 and entered the Order in Fiesole between 1420 and 1422. After the work of rebuilding San Marco, Florence, began in 1438, he moved there and contributed his famous frescoes to the new convent and church. Eugenius IV, having seen his work there, invited him to

Rome in 1445, where he did several paintings in St Peter's and the Vatican, living meanwhile at the Minerva. Apart from a stay of some months in Orvieto in 1447, Fra Angelico remained in Rome until 1449, when he returned to Fiesole, where he was prior 1450-52. In 1453 or 1454 he went back to the Minerva. Beatified 1982. Cf. S. Orlandi, *Beato Angelico*, Florence 1964. For a contrary view of his chronology, see T. S. Centi, *Il Beato Giovanni pintore Angelico*, Siena 1984.

ANTONINO PIEROZZI, St, OP (1389-1459). Entered the Order in Florence in 1404 or 1405, drawn by the preaching of Giovanni Dominici; in 1406 he was one of the friars who, under the leadership of Giovanni Dominici, established the new, reformed convent of Fiesole. After being prior of several convents, in 1432 he became Vicar General for the Dominican reform in Tuscany. In 1436 the community of Fiesole took possession of the monastery of S. Marco in Florence, and Cosimo de' Medici provided the funds for a lavish programme of rebuilding. In 1439 Antonino became prior of the joint communities of S. Marco and Fiesole, a position he retained until 1444. In 1466 he was made archbishop of Florence. He was a prolific writer on moral, historical and theological topics. BJ published a book about him, *S. Antonino and Medieval Economics*, London 1914. See R. Morçay, *Saint Antonin*, Paris 1914; S. Orlandi, *S. Antonino*, 2 vols., Florence 1959-60.

ARDAGH, Wilfrid, OP (1896-1980). Born in Birmingham and educated at St Philip's Grammar School there, he entered the Order in 1913. After taking his lectorate at Hawkesyard in 1921, he went to Fribourg, where he obtained a doctorate in theology at the end of 1923. At the beginning of 1924 he was assigned to Hawkesyard to teach, and he moved to Oxford in 1929 when the studium was re-established there. In 1930 he was appointed to the newly founded house at Stellenbosch, South Africa, where BJ hoped to launch an important mission in the heart of Afrikaanerdom. Returning to England in 1936, he was assigned to Newcastle, where he was prior 1941-44. Prior of Leicester 1944-47. After that he was in London 1948-58, giving extra-mural lectures on theology and moral philosophy. Then he was sent to Barbados, where the English Dominicans were taking over what had till then been a Jesuit mission. In 1961 he returned to Stellenbosch to teach in the studium there. He retired to England in 1969. He ended his days at Oxford.

ARUNDELL OF WARDOUR, Lady Anne Lucy (died 1934, aged 92). Daughter of John Errington of High Warden, Northumberland (1807-1878), in 1862 she married the 12th Lord Arundell

(1831-1906). In the absence of children, the Arundell succession passed first to the 12th Lord's brother, Everard Aloysius Gonzaga (1834-1907), who was a priest, then to his Cousin, Edgar Clifford (1859-1921), then to another cousin, Gerald Arthur (1861-1939). Lady Arundell was a Dominican tertiary and frequent benefactor of the English province. In 1913, for instance, she gave £1000 to set up a burse for educating English students (She insisted that they must be genuinely English, not Scottish or Irish). She took a great interest in plans for expanding the work of the province, and volunteered to pay for all the stone needed for the building of Blackfriars, Oxford, and she also asked that the architect should be her own local man, E. Doran Webb. For a time Francis Burdett SJ was chaplain to Wardour Castle. Lady Arundell 'was a dragon built on the lines of Jane Austin's Lady Catherine de Bourgh, but Fr Burdett was no Mr Collins. Once a week he was summoned to dinner at Wardour Castle, where for years the bill of fare had been one sardine followed by rice pudding. According to Fr D'Arcy, Burdett was the only chaplain who dared to confront Lady Arundell on this score: every time the butler hovered near his chair, he asked for another helping until he had a plateful of sardines and for this the old lady came to respect him. When, later on, private benefices and lay interference in church affairs was finally brought to an end, Lady Arundell refused to comply or even surrender the key to the chapel and the bishop was forced to excommunicate her' (C. Scott, *A Historian and his World*, London 1984, p. 70).

ASHWORTH, Mary Veronica, OP (1881-1965). Professed as a nun of Carisbrooke in 1901, she became novice mistress when she was only 26 and held that position for thirteen years. Prioress 1920-26 and 1932-38. Her sister, Mary Imelda (1896-1979) made her profession at Carisbrooke in 1921 and was prioress 1941-47, 1950-56 and 1962-68. Their aunt, Mary Clare Ashworth OP (1842-1905), received the habit at Carisbrooke in 1868, the first nun to be clothed there after the community moved there from Hurst Green in 1866.

BAILY, Theodore (1898-1966). Entered the noviciate at Downside in 1914, then transferred to Caldey in 1920, and went with the other monks to Prinknash in 1928. He was ordained priest in 1927. Later he moved to Farnborough. He was a painter.

BAKER, Augustine (1575-1641). A convert to Catholicism, he became a Benedictine in Padua in 1605, and later worked at Cambrai, Douai and in England. Author of various ascetical writings, later collected by Serenus Cressy and published under the title of *Sancta Sophia* or *Holy Wisdom*, first printed in 1657.

BAKER, Elizabeth Anstice (1849-1914). Daughter of John Baker (1813-1872), who emigrated to Australia in 1839 and was an enthusiastic and independent-minded politician; he was a member of the South Australian Legislative Council 1851-61 and 1863-72. His son, Sir Richard Baker (1841-1911), was the first president of the Australian Federal Senate (1901-1906). Elizabeth was born at Morialta, where her father had built himself a mansion, but later moved to England. Dissatisfied with the Anglicanism, of which her father was an eager promoter, she began a long exploration of various religions, eventually becoming a Catholic in Paris on 15 December 1877. In *A Modern Pilgrim's Progress*, London 1906, she describes the process of her conversion. One important influence was a speech she read by R. Suffield, a Dominican who had become a Unitarian, in which he maintains that the only realistic alternatives are Unitarianism and Ultramontane Catholicism (*A Modern Pilgrim's Progress* p. 52). She was finally convinced that she must become a Catholic by a sermon she heard in Paris by a young Dominican priest, Etienne Le Vigoureux, who received her into the church in the chapel of the Carmelite nuns, Avenue de Messine, Paris; she become one of his closest friends. Her sponsor was Lady Blount, wife of Sir Edward Charles Blount, who was the landlord of BJ's parents. She afterwards become a Dominican tertiary and a benefactress of the English Dominicans. As she says in her book, p.241, 'The spirit of the Dominican Order is a spirit of light and liberty'. In 1883 she instigated and paid for the sending of some of the Dominican sisters from Stone to start a new mission in Australia, returning there herself for some years, though she then returned to England.

BALL, Sir Albert (1862-1946). Mayor of Nottingham in 1909-10 and 1920. He bought Laxton Hall as a speculation.

BARBERI, Bl. Dominic (1792-1849). Entered the Passionists in Italy in 1814. In 1841 he opened the first Passionist house in England, at Aston Hall, Staffordshire. His work in the Midlands around the Potteries brought him into contact with the foundress of the Dominican sisters of Stone, Mother Margaret Hallahan (1802-68). In 1845 he received Newman into the Catholic church. Beatified in 1963.

BARKER, Austin, OP (1885-1947). Born in Birmingham, he was educated at the Dominican school at Hinckley and Hawkesyard (1897-1902), and then joined the Order in 1902. After his ordination, he studied at the École Biblique in Jerusalem 1908-11. The rest of his life was spent at Hawkesyard. After the first World War he played a prominent part in the reformation of philosophical and theological studies in the English province. He was lector primarius at Hawkesyard from 1929, when the studium in Oxford was opened and the Regent was moved there, until 1935, and again from 1938 until his death. He was elected prior of Hawkesyard in 1917, but BJ asked him to resign in 1919 'because seldom at Meditation or Prime'. He had a great influence on the Ditchling community, started by Eric Gill and his friends. In the early years he was a close friend of BJ's, but later he became disillusioned with his policies. In 1932, during the visitation of Master General Gillet, he was examined for the STM, which he was awarded later in the same year. He died suddenly in a public house in Cannock, where he had gone to telephone for a taxi to take him to the Dominican sisters at Brewood.

BARKER, Ernest (1874-1960). Obtained a triple first at Oxford in classics and modern history. Classics fellow at Merton (1898-1905) and lecturer in modern history at Wadham (1899-1909), then fellow of St John's (1909-13), then fellow of New College (1913-20). Principal of King's College, London (1920-28). Professor of Political Science at Cambridge (1928-39). A polymath and 'character'. He was BJ's tutor at Oxford. He was knighted in 1944.

BARKER, Osmund (Francis) (1894-1939). Educated at Hawkesyard School (1907-12), he joined the Dominican Order in 1912. Having completed his studies, he was sent to Grenada in 1920, but was back in England in 1922 and was assigned to Newcastle. In 1925 he was sent to Leicester, then back to Newcastle in 1929. In 1932 he was assigned to Pendleton. In 1933 he left the Order, and was laicised the following year. He died in Newcastle.

BARRETT, John P. (1878-1946). Auxiliary to the archbishop of Birmingham 1927-29; bishop of Plymouth 1929-46.

BARTLETT, Henry, OP (1829-1905). He was received into the Catholic church in 1851 and almost immediately took steps to join the Dominicans. He was sent to study for a time at Hinckley and Leicester, then went to Woodchester in 1854, where he received the habit. Assistant novice master 1858-61 and 1862-63, novice master 1863-79. In 1895 he was assigned to Hawkesyard. After a time in London (1896-98) he was elected prior of Hawkesyard (1898-1901). He was prior there when BJ arrived as a student in 1900. He then returned to London, where he died.

BELLOC, Hilaire (1870-1953). Born in France, he was educated in England at the Oratory School, Birmingham, and at Balliol College, Oxford. After a brief career in politics, he settled down to being a writer and journalist. He was a Catholic apologist of great vehemence, a brilliant poet and a perceptive, if not entirely scholarly, historian and biographer. In the public mind he was closely associated with G. K. Chesterton.

BELLORD, Edmund (1858-1927). Educated by the Benedictines of Ramsgate, he became a partner in the firm of solicitors, Witham, Roskill, Munster and Weld; he was solicitor to the English Dominican province and a constant adviser to BJ. His wife, Agnes, died in 1925. His eldest son, Charles Edmund, born in 1900, was at school at Downside 1910-1916; after a year at Balliol College, Oxford, he volunteered for the RAF in 1918 and, after six months' training, went to France and died three weeks later of wounds. *The Oxford Magazine* 37 (1919) p. 133 describes him as 'very mature in character, yet with plenty of humour and a charm which made him a delightful friend.' A younger son, George (1904-1963), was also educated at Downside and later joined his father's firm; he was solicitor to the English Dominicans from the death of his father until 1958. Another son, Robert (1908-1970), also later joined the firm. Edmund's daughter, Elizabeth, married Joseph (later Sir Joseph) William Weld in 1936.

BENSON, Robert Hugh (1871-1914). Son of Edward White Benson (1829-1896), who was archbishop of Canterbury from 1883. Ordained in the Church of England in 1894, he joined the Community of the Resurrection at Mirfield in 1898. In 1903 he became a Catholic, and was ordained priest in 1904, devoting the rest of his life chiefly to preaching and writing. Author of many lively religious novels. Cf. C. C. Martindale, *The Life of Monsignor Robert Hugh Benson*, London 1916.

BEZZINA, Gabriel, OP (1887-1947). Joined the Maltese province in 1905. After serving as a military chaplain during the first World War, he was sent to the English Dominican mission in South Africa in 1920, but in 1924 he asked to be allowed to return to Malta as soon as he could be replaced, and permission was granted for this. He was replaced in 1925. Thereafter he worked in Australia, California and India.

BLACK, Giles, OP (1887-1954). Educated at Merchiston Castle school and at Oxford, where he graduated in 1908, he was ordained in the episcopalian church in Scotland and appointed to Aviemore. In 1916 he came into the Catholic church, with a number of his parishioners. In the same year he joined the French army, and was decorated with the Croix de Guerre. In 1919 he joined the Dominicans in England and he was ordained in 1925. In 1926 he was assigned to Newcastle. At the end of 1931 he was appointed to the new community in Edinburgh as university chaplain, a position he retained until ill-health obliged him to retire in 1944. 'By sheer goodness and patient charity he did an enormous amount of good there and his name is still remembered throughout Scotland' (Bernard Delany in 1952). In 1944 he was assigned to Hawkesyard, where he soon became novice master for the laybrothers.

BLACKWELL, Basil (1889-1984). Joined the staff of his father's bookshop in Oxford in 1913, and took charge of it, on his father's death, in 1924. He built it up to become one of the largest and most respected bookshops in the world. In 1921 he started his own publishing firm as well. He was knighted in 1956. Cf. A. L. P. Norrington, *Blackwell's 1879-1979*, Oxford 1983.

BLENCOWE, Henry Dominic, OP (1879-1960). Entered the Order in 1905. After ordination in 1911 he was sent to Pendleton, but at the beginning of 1913 he was appointed to Grenada, where he remained until 1928, returning there again 1944-53; in 1958 he offered his services yet again to the West Indies and was appointed superior in Barbados, though at the end of the year he went back to his familiar Grenada. In between his times in the West Indies he worked mostly in various parishes in England: London (1928-33), Leicester (1935-44) and Newcastle (1953-58). In 1933-34 he was superior of the ill-fated English Dominican mission in Persia.

BONHOMME, Romain, OP (1870-1937). Entered the Toulouse province in 1899. Provincial of Toulouse 1928-32.

BOURNE, Francis (1861-1935). Entered the Dominican novitiate at Woodchester in April 1880, but soon decided to become a secular priest instead. He was ordained in 1884. In 1896 he was consecrated coadjutor bishop of Southwark, succeeding to the diocese in the following year. In 1903 he became archbishop of Westminster, and was created a cardinal in 1911. Cf. Ernest Oldmeadow, *Francis Cardinal Bourne*, 2 vols., London 1940-44.

BOWRING, George Charles Aldhelm SSJ (formerly OP) (born 1903). Born in Mauritius, he joined the English Dominicans in 1921. After finishing his studies in 1929, he was sent to Woodchester as assistant parish priest and assistant novice master. In September 1930 he was assigned to the parish in Pendleton. In October 1932 he set off for Grenada, where he worked until 1970, except for a year spent in Alabama (1947-48), where he became convinced that his true mission was to work with American Blacks. At last, in 1970, he was allowed by the provincial to go to the United States to work with the Josephites (an American order founded for work with the Blacks), and since 1975 he has been a Josephite.

BRACEY, Robert, OP (1870-1954). Born in Birmingham, he was received into the Catholic church at Birmingham Oratory in 1887. Joined the Order in 1891. After ordination he was assigned to London in 1896 as a missioner. In 1899 he was sent to Leicester, and in 1901 he was sent back to London as acting parish priest. In 1906 he was elected prior of Woodchester, and in 1908 prior of London. In 1911 he was assigned to Woodchester, but the following year he was appointed vicar provincial of Grenada. In 1916 he was elected prior of London again. Soon after the end of his term of office in 1919 he became superior of Stroud, then, in 1920, prior of Woodchester again, and he held this position for four consecutive terms, until January 1933, when he was sent to Carisbrooke to be chaplain to the Dominican nuns. There he remained until his death.

BRETHERTON, Cuthbert, OP (1889-1966). Joined the Order in 1907. After the completion of his studies he was sent to Leicester and then, after a few years, to Byker. He worked in Grenada 1922-29 and went back there again the following year (having been assigned to Woodchester in between as a missioner). In 1933 he came back to England and was assigned to Pendleton as a missioner. Apart from being superior of Cambridge 1948-51, he spent the rest of his life as a parochial missioner.

BROCKLEHURST, Mark, OP (1906-1967). Born at Hinckley, he went to Hawkesyard School (1919-23) and joined the Order in 1923. In 1931 he won his lectorate at Oxford and was sent to Leicester to await an assignation to Persia that never came. He remained at Leicester until 1940 and was then sent to Hawkesyard to teach ethics, but after less than a year he was called back to Leicester to be prior. After that he was prior of Hawkesyard (1944-47, 1953-56) and Woodchester (1948-51, 1961-65) and taught in the studium at Oxford (1947-48, 1951-53) and in the school at Llanarth (1956-61).

BROOKES, Jerome, OP (1877-1903). Entered the Order in 1896, having already begun a course of priestly studies at Oscott College. After ordination in 1901 he fell ill and was sent to Leicester for a year. In 1902 he went to Jerusalem to study at the École Biblique, but died before he had even been there a year.

BROWNE, Joseph, SJ (1856-1917). Went to Stonyhurst in 1870 and entered the Society in 1874. Taught at Stonyhurst from 1892 and was rector there 1898-1907. After there years in Liverpool, he became provincial 1910-1915.

BUCKLER, Reginald, OP (1840-1927). The youngest of three brothers in the Order, the other two being Albert (1830-1913) and

Edmund (1835-1911). He was received into the Catholic church in 1855 at Woodchester, where Albert was already a Dominican. He himself joined the Order in March 1856, only three months after Edmund. After his ordination he worked at Woodchester until 1867, then assignations followed in rapid succession: Littlehampton and London (1867), Leicester (1868), Clifton (1896), Stone and Leicester (1870), Woodchester again (1871), London again (1872), Newcastle (1878), Woodchester again (1879). Chaplain to the nuns at Carisbrooke 1884-86, then London again. In 1891 he returned to Woodchester, then to London again in 1892. Novice master at Woodchester 1895-98, then London yet again. He was re-assigned to Woodchester in 1902. Student master at Hawkesyard 1905-1908, then back to Woodchester. In 1911 he volunteered to go to Grenada, where he worked for the last sixteen years of his life.

BUGEJA, Henry, OP (1885-1957). Entered the Order in Malta in 1900. He came to England in 1921 and joined the province in 1933. After working briefly in Byker, he was sent to Pendleton in 1924 as a missioner, and there he remained until deafness made it difficult for him to continue his work. In 1937 he was moved to Stone, where he served as chaplain to the Dominican sisters. In 1950 he was made a Preacher General.

BULL, Theodore, OP (1880-1952). Educated at the Dominican school at Hinckley (1892-97), he joined the Order in 1897. After ordination he was sent to Newcastle, but in 1907 he became bursar in Leicester, a role in which he excelled and which he filled in several houses. He was thought by BJ to be the practical man of the province in building matters, so was a member of the group overseeing the construction of Blackfriars, Oxford. After doing two terms as bursar of Leicester (1907-1913), he became sacristan there. In 1916 he was commissioned as an army chaplain. In 1922 he became bursar at Pendleton, a position he retained for three years. In 1926 he was sent to Grenada, where he stayed until 1931, when he returned to England and was promptly made bursar of London, which he remained until 1938, when he became bursar of Newcastle. In 1941 he was re-assigned to London, becoming bursar there again early in the following year. In 1946 he was sent to Leicester, where he remained until his death.

BULLOUGH, Mrs Enrichetta (1882-1961). Daughter of Eleonora Duse. In 1908 she married Edward Bullough (1880-1934), who became a fellow of Gonville and Caius College, Cambridge, in 1912, where he taught modern languages. He was University Lecturer in German 1920-23, University Lecturer in Italian 1926-33, Professor of Italian 1933-34. He was received into the Catholic church by Fr

Martindale SJ in 1923 and soon afterwards he and his wife became Dominican tertiaries. Both their children became Dominicans. After Prof. Bullough's death, their 'Italian villa' in Cambridge was given to the Dominicans and now forms part of Blackfriars, Cambridge. Edward Bullough was for a time chairman of the Friends of Blackfriars, Oxford.

BULLOUGH, Sebastian, OP (1910-1967). Son of Enrichetta Bullough. He went to Hawkesyard School in 1924 and was one of the boys who went with the school to Laxton later in the same year. Leaving Laxton in 1926, he went to Cambridge, where he did a degree in Hebrew and Aramaic. He joined the Order in 1931. After doing philosophy at Hawkesyard, he was sent to the Angelicum, Rome, in 1935 to do his theology, and he obtained the lectorate there. Returning to England in 1939, he was assigned to teach at Laxton, where he remained until 1954, when he was elected prior of Woodchester. In 1957 he went to Oxford, where he taught for two years. Then, after a very brief spell at Llanarth, he went to Cambridge in 1960. There he taught Hebrew in the university. Apart from his published works, he wrote a history of the Dominican school from its beginnings in Bornhem up to Laxton and Llanarth in the 1950s.

BURDETT, Francis (1882-1943). Son of Sir Henry Burdett (1847-1920), he was received into the Catholic church in 1901 at St Dominic's, London, by Gilbert Tigar OP. In 1903 he became a Jesuit, and was a student at the Jesuit Hall in Oxford 1908-11, leaving Oxford in March 1911 to try his vocation as a Carthusian at Parkminster, to the consternation of Ernest Barker, his tutor. He left Parkminster after three months and returned to the Jesuits. He was ordained in 1916 and was parish priest of Tisbury, Wiltshire, 1918-21, which involved also being chaplain to Lady Arundell of Wardour. He was at St Aloysius, Oxford, 1922-24. He left the Society in 1926 and joined the diocese of Clifton, but from 1929 until his death he was on sick leave. He 'combined intellectual brilliance with great personal holiness' (C. Scott, *A Historian and his World*, London 1984, p. 50).

BURLAMACCHI, Eufrasia, OP (c. 1478-1548). The Burlamacchis were a rich, noble family in Lucca, prominent in both politics and trade. Many of the family fell directly or indirectly under the influence of Savonarola, and several of them became Dominicans. Eufrasia became a nun at the Dominican monastery of S. Nicolao, Lucca, but was one of a group of nuns wanting a stricter way of life; in 1502 they founded a new, reformed monastery of S. Domenico. Eufrasia and her older sister Gabriella had been chosen to belong to the founding community of the new monastery, but when the day came for the foundresses to depart, their names were not called. Later in the day, noticing that the door was open, the two sisters fled to their father's house, and the family used their influence to ensure that they were allowed to join S. Domenico after all (cf. D. Di Agresti, *Sviluppi della Riforma Monastica Savonaroliana*, Florence 1980, pp. 217-219). Eufrasia became the most notable of the miniaturists in the community.

BURTON, George Ambrose (1852-1931). Born in Hull. Bishop of Clifton 1902-31. Philip Hughes includes him in his 'trio of really eloquent bishops' from this period. 'He stands in a class apart for the distinction which marked his whole episcopal action . . . A spirit touched with genius, who never realised all his quality promised, so exacting was his taste; a rarely cultivated mind; theologian, scholar, and artist breathed into a sturdy north-country character' (G. A. Beck, ed., *The English Catholics 1850-1950*, London 1950, p. 193). It was he who ordained BJ priest in December 1904.

BUTLER, Cuthbert (1858-1934). Leader of the reform movement in the English Benedictine Congregation, monastic historian and scholar. He became abbot of Downside in 1906 and was Abbot President of the Congregation 1914-21. His monastic ideas were published in *Benedictine Monachism*, London 1919.

BUTT, Angela, OP (1865-1932). A lay sister at Carisbrooke, where she made profession in 1887.

CADOGAN, Lady Adele (died 1960, aged 80). In 1911 she married the 5th Earl Cadogan, George Henry (1840-1915). She was one of the leading ladies of the Catholic church in London, actively involved in many charitable and apostolic works.

CAJETAN, Tommaso de Vio, OP (1469-1534). After lecturing for many years at Padua, Pavia and Rome, and after serving as Procurator General of the Dominican Order (1501-1508), he became Master of the Order (1508-18). Created a cardinal in 1517, he became bishop of Gaeta in 1518. One of the main contributors to the revival of Thomism in the sixteenth century, and an important commentator on St Thomas, he nevertheless retained his intellectual independence, becoming for instance much more sceptical than St Thomas was about the possibility of philosophical proofs for such beliefs as the existence of God and the immortality of the human soul.

CALLUS, Daniel, OP (1888-1965). Born in Malta, he entered the Order there in 1903. After studying in Florence and Rome, he taught in Malta for a while. In 1921 he was assigned to Hawkesyard to teach, but in 1923 he was sent to La Quercia to take charge of the studies there. In the same year he was made an STM. Later he was Regent of Studies at Rabat in Malta. In 1931 Rome asked the English province to take him 'for a while', and he was duly assigned to Hawkesyard again, where he taught elementary Hebrew for a year. He was then moved to Oxford, where he taught Scripture for a year. In 1932 he applied to join the English province, but the Provincial Chapter declined to consider the application, on the grounds that the province did not yet know him well enough. In 1933 he embarked on a doctorate at Oxford university, thus launching himself on what was to be his essential career as a medievalist, to which the rest of his life was devoted with much success and to widespread acclaim. In 1942 he was appointed Regent of Studies at Oxford, and this time he was allowed to become a member of the English province. He died in Malta, where he had gone on a visit to celebrate the diamond jubilee of his profession.

CALTHROP, Muriel M. C. (1871-1945). Associated with the Socialist group of Joseph Clayton, she was received into the Catholic church by BJ in 1910 at St Dominic's, London. In 1913 she became a Dominican tertiary. She was quite a serious historian and in 1914 was asked to become a member of the Board of the Catholic Record Society, through BJ's mediation. She also did some work towards an edition of Humbert of Romans. In 1919 she was accepted as a postulant at Carisbrooke, but left after little more than a month on the doctor's advice. She founded the Friends of Blackfriars and was their first secretary. In 1938 she was given letters of fraternity as an acknowledgement of all she had done for the province. She was something of an eccentric, but BJ had a high regard for her intelligence and confided in her as a friend.

CARPENTER, Hilary, OP (1896-1973). Born in Cheltenham, he was educated at the Dominican school at Hawkesyard (1910-15) and then joined the Order in 1915. Having obtained his lectorate at Hawkesyard in 1923, he was sent to Oxford to study in the university. There he obtained a B. Litt. in 1926. He taught in the studium at Hawkesyard 1926-29 and Oxford 1929-33 and then he returned to Hawkesyard, but on 16 March 1934 he was appointed prior of Oxford, a position he retained until 1940. He was also pro-Regent of Studies 1936-42, and editor of *Blackfriars* 1934-40. In 1940 he became a chaplain in the RAF. In 1945 he was again elected prior of Oxford, and in 1946 he became provincial, in which office he remained for twelve years. In 1960 he was summoned to Rome to be one of the Assistants of the Master General, and there he remained until his death.

CARY-ELWES, Dudley Charles (1868-1932). Bishop of Northampton 1921-32. A friend of BJ.

CASARTELLI, Louis Charles (1852-1925). Bishop of Salford 1903-25. 'A distinguished orientalist . . . singularly free from the conventional narrowness of the Victorian cleric, a man of really cosmopolitan mind, with a breadth and variety of intellectual sympathies that recalled Wiseman' (P. Hughes, in Beck, *The English Catholics* p. 38). He was the only Catholic bishop to welcome the Malines Conversations between Catholics and Anglicans. Born in Manchester, where his father had emigrated from Italy, he studied at Ushaw College, taking an external London MA there in 1873 (he later expressed strong disapproval of such external degrees, which he regarded as a tyrannical oppression of local universities). In 1884 he won a doctorate in Oriental Literature at Louvain. He taught at St Bede's College, Manchester, of which he became Rector in 1891. Professor of Zend and Pahlavi at Louvain 1900-1903. As bishop of Salford, he lectured on Iranian languages at the university of Manchester 1903-20. On 12 December 1904 he formally opened the library at Hawkesyard.

CASAS, Juan, OP (1869-1952). Entered the province of Betica, Spain, in 1895. Provincial 1911-15. He was a member of the General Curia of Masters General Theissling and Paredes. During the Spanish Civil War he survived the massacre of most of his community in Almagro by the Communists.

CATERINI, Filippo, OP (1881-1966). Entered the Roman province in 1896. Elected prior of S. Maria Novella, Florence, in 1910, and of the Minerva, Rome, in 1914. He was Procurator General of the Dominican Order from 1917 until ill-health forced him to retire in 1946.

CATHERINE OF SIENA, St, OP (c. 1347-1380). Doctor of the church. Drawn by a vision of St Dominic, she entered the Dominican Order of Penance c. 1365 and later embarked on an extraordinary career of 'preaching' and letter-writing. Her doctrine is expounded in numerous letters and, more systematically, in her book, *Il Dialogo*. She was influential in persuading Gregory XI to move the papacy back from Avignon to Rome. She had a profound effect on many people, including Raymund of Capua (c. 1330-99), Master of the Dominican Order and a leading figure in the reform of the Order. Cf. K. Foster and M. J. Ronayne, *I, Catherine*, London 1980.

CECIL, Hugh, Baron Quickswood (1869-1956). A member of the Cecil dynasty of Hatfield House. Member of Parliament 1895-1937, representing Oxford University 1910-37. Provost of Eton 1936-44. He was an accomplished classical orator and a devout Anglican, much interested in church affairs. Chesterton said of him, 'He was, and probably still is, the one real Protestant . . . From time to time he startles the world he lives in by a stark and upstanding defence of the common Christian theology and ethics, in which all Protestants once believed . . . It was George Wyndham who once confirmed this notion of mine, by noting what he called the extreme Individualism of Lord Hugh Cecil . . . (He) might be called the one strong pillar still upholding the England in which I was born' (*Autobiography*, London 1936, pp. 263-264).

CHASES, Casimir, OP (1905-1967). Born in Leicester, of Lithuanian parents, he entered the Order in 1923, after being at Hawkesyard School (1917-22). In 1930 he was assigned to Grenada, but early in 1933 Master General Gillet asked for him to be sent to Lithuania as quickly as possible, where there were hopes of reviving the Lithuanian province, which was in fact restored in 1935. In 1939 the outbreak of war necessitated his return to England, where he was assigned to London, where he spent most of the rest of his life. Prior of Woodchester 1945-48. In 1963 he was appointed superior of Hinckley, a position he retained until his death.

CHESTERTON, Gilbert Keith (1874-1936). He began to train as an artist, but then settled for journalism instead. Abandoning the free-thinking agnosticism in which he was reared, he became, first, an Anglican and then, in 1922, a Catholic. He was closely associated with Hilaire Belloc (together they were known as 'Chesterbelloc') and the combination was a force to be feared by those they combatted. He was a master of paradox and a brilliant controversialist, whose comments are often as topical today as when they were first penned. His most famous creation was the priest-detective, Father Brown. On 3 December 1935 he attended Vincent McNabb's Golden Jubilee at St Dominic's, London, and addressed the assembly in the priory common room; he called McNabb 'almost the greatest man of our time' (*The Universe* 6 December 1935).

CLARK, Kevin, OP (1887-1965). Born in Newcastle, he was educated at the Dominican school at Hawkesyard (1901-1906) and then joined the Order in 1906. He studied in Louvain 1912-14. He was then appointed to teach at the Dominican school, first at Hawkesyard, then at Laxton (1914-29). In 1929 he was assigned to Grenada, where he remained until his death. He was a geologist and a friend of the distinguished French prehistorian, Abbé Henri Breuil (1877-1961) and also of Teilhard de Chardin (1881-1955).

CLAYTON, Joseph (1868-1943). Journalist and member of the Fabian Society, to whose meetings he introduced BJ. He was put on to BJ in 1909 by Raphael Moss, and was received into the Catholic church by BJ in 1910. Until the outbreak of the first World War he used to take a weekly walk with BJ, ending with tea at his house, where BJ took him and his wife through points of Catholic doctrine. He was a member of the first editorial board of *Blackfriars*.

COLE, G. D. H. (1889-1959). A prominent Labour Party intellectual and member of the Fabian Society. Chichele Professor of Social and Political Theory at Oxford 1944-57.

COLONNA, Vittoria (1490-1547). Married in 1509 to Ferrante d'Avalos, Marchese of Pescara (died 1525). Religious poet and enthusiast for the reform of the church, a concern which linked her specially with Cardinal Pole.

CONNELLY, Cornelia (1809-1879). Foundress of the Society of the Holy Child Jesus. Born in Philadelphia, in 1831 she married Pierce Connelly, an Episcopalian clergyman, by whom she had several children. In 1835 she and her husband became Catholics, and in 1845 she made a solemn vow of chastity, so that he could become a priest. He was ordained in the same year. She was received as a postulant at the Sacred Heart convent of La Trinità in Rome, but Bishop Wiseman persuaded her to come to England to start a new institute, for the education of children, and in 1846 she and her first companions received the habit of the new society. In 1848 her husband, having left the church, started legal proceedings to get his wife back, which were finally defeated only by an appeal to the Privy Council in 1851. Pierce then published a stream of sensational anti-Catholic pamphlets, which were received enthusiastically by the Protestant public. He made no more attempts to disturb Cornelia personally, though, and, when she died, he sent a sympathetic letter to her community. He returned to the Anglican ministry. Cf. Mother Marie Thérèse SHCJ, *Cornelia Connelly, A study of Fidelity*, London 1963.

CORDOVANI, Mariano, OP (1883-1950). Entered the Roman province in 1900. Taught at the Minerva, the Angelicum and then at the Catholic University of Milan between 1910 and 1927, when he returned to the Angelicum as Regent of Studies (1927-32). At the 1929 General Chapter he was diffinitor of the Roman province, whose provincial he became in 1933. In 1936 he was appointed Master of the Sacred Palace. He was a keen opponent of Fascism from its inception. A friend of Mgr Montini, later Paul VI. Cf. R. Spiazzi, *P. Mariano Cordovani dei Frati Predicatori*, Rome 1954.

CORMIER, Hyacinthe, OP (1832-1916). Ordained priest in 1856, he immediately joined the Dominican Order at Flavigny. Ill health prevented his profession, but Master General Jandel sent him to Italy, where he was professed in 1859. In 1861 he was appointed prior of Corbara, Corsica, where a general noviciate was being established. In 1865 the province of Toulouse was restored and Cormier was its first provincial, a position he retained until 1874. Prior of Marseilles 1874-78, then provincial again 1878-82. After being prior of Toulouse and then of Saint-Maximin, in 1891 he was appointed socius to Master General Frühwirth. In 1896 he became Procurator General, then Master General in 1904. He resigned in 1916 and died very shortly afterwards. He was a musician and a prolific writer. He founded the Angelicum, whose first academic year began in 1909.

COULTON, George Gordon (1858-1947). Historian and controversialist. He was ordained in the Church of England in 1884, but later devoted his life to medieval history, especially church history, and to fierce controversy with Catholics. In 1919 he became a fellow of St John's, Cambridge. In 1921 he successfully blocked a proposal that Cambridge should award honorary degrees to Cardinals Gasquet and Bourne. He was deeply suspicious of Catholic historians, whom he regarded as too fettered by dogmatic constraints to be capable of doing objective history. When he could not get his vituperative attacks on Catholic positions published, he printed and distributed them at his own expense. David Knowles acknowledged him to be 'one of the most learned medievalists of the day' (*The Historian and Character*, Cambridge 1963, p. 258). Cf. A. N. Wilson, *Hilaire Belloc*, London 1984, pp. 348-54. Coulton published an autobiography, *Four Score Years*, Cambridge 1943.

COUTURIER, Felix, OP (1876-1941). Born at La Foré, in France, his English mother brought him to England when he was a young boy, after the death of his French father. He was educated at the Dominican school at Hinckley (1892-95) and joined the Order in 1895. After ordination in 1901 he was assigned to London to teach in the short-lived Grammar School run by the Dominicans there at this time. When the school closed in 1903 he was sent to teach at Hawkesyard School. In 1905 he went to Pendleton as a missioner, and to Woodchester in 1906. In 1910 he was elected prior of Hawkesyard. In 1913 he was sent to Leicester as a missioner, but shortly afterwards in the same year he was assigned to Woodchester. In 1914 he was commissioned as an army chaplain. In 1919 he was appointed Visitor Apostolic to Egypt and consecrated a bishop. In 1921 he was translated to the see of Alexandria, Ontario.

COWGILL, Joseph Robert (1860-1936). Born at Broughton, near Skipton, Yorkshire. He was consecrated as coadjutor to the bishop of Leeds in 1905 and succeeded to the see in 1911, remaining bishop of Leeds until his death.

COX, Charles, OMI (1848-1936). Vicar Apostolic of the Transvaal 1914-25 and titular bishop of Dioclea.

CRESSY, Serenus (c. 1605-1674). Graduated at Oxford in 1623 and in 1627 became fellow of Merton. He took Anglican orders and, with the rise of Oliver Cromwell, felt obliged to leave England. In 1646 he became a Catholic and in 1648 he joined the English Benedictines at Douai. In about 1651 he was sent to be chaplain to the English Benedictine nuns in Paris. In 1652 he was made subprior at Dieulouard, then he was at Douai again 1653-60. During this period he wrote a variety of spiritual, historical and polemical works. In 1660 he came to England and was chaplain to Queen Catherine of Braganza. He spent his last years at West Grinstead. He published the first printed edition of Julian of Norwich, and edited some of Augustine Baker's works under the title *Sancta Sophia*.

CROSSE, Aloysius, OP (1856-1920). Educated at Winchester, he was received into the Catholic church at Farm Street in 1880. Joined the Order in 1882. After two years of study at Woodchester, he was sent to Louvain, whence he returned in 1888 and was appointed immediately to the school at Hinckley. He was a very successful and popular schoolmaster there, and, when the school moved to Hawkesyard in 1898, he became its headmaster. In 1902 he was taken off school work and never settled down again in the Order. One assignation after another failed to satisfy him, and he kept leaving the Order and coming back again until, in 1913, he was authorised by the Sacred Congregation for Religious to live outside the Order, and his repeated pleas to be reinstated in the Order were rejected by the province, though he never formally left the Order and was buried as a Dominican. He became chaplain to the Assumption nuns in Boxmoor and lived in lodgings in Hemel Hempstead.

CUYPERS, Lambert, OP (1877-1920). Born and educated in Belgium, in 1895 he joined the Picpus Fathers. Ordained in 1901, in 1903 he was sent to their newly established house at Eccleshall, Staffordshire. In 1904 he received permission to join the Dominicans at Woodchester. After his profession in 1905 he taught at the Dominican school at Hawkesyard until 1910, when he was assigned to Newcastle, where he stayed until 1913. He was then briefly appointed to be chaplain at Carisbrooke, but was withdrawn for reasons of health. He was then sent to Spetchley, the Worcestershire home of the Berkeley family. In the hope that a warmer climate would do him good, he was assigned to South Africa in 1919, but never actually got there, and to Grenada in 1920, where he died very soon after his arrival.

DANELL, James (1821-1881). Bishop of Southwark 1871-1881.

D'ANNUNZIO, Gabriele (1863-1938). Italian poet and dramatist, a leading light in the Italian culture of his day. Friend and, for some years, lover of Eleonora Duse.

DARLEY, Philip, OP (1882-1951). Born in Birmingham, he was educated at the Dominican school at Hinckley and then Hawkesyard (1895-1900) and then joined the Order in 1900. In 1908 he was assigned to Woodchester, where he was parish priest 1914-21. In 1924 he was assigned to the parish in London. Chaplain to the Dominican sisters at Stroud (1928-31 and 1932-38); for a short time he was bursar at Oxford (1931-32). In 1938 he became chaplain at Templewood, near Stroud, and there he remained until his death.

DAVEY, Richard (1889-1963). Monk of Downside, where he was novice master for most of the period 1922-33. Later he was prior of Worth and of Downside, and titular abbot of Glastonbury.

DAVIES, Mary Magdalen, OP (1892-1982). A convert from Judaism in her late teens, under the influence of Miss Baker, she received the habit at Carisbrooke in 1920. A member of the founding community of Headington in 1922. Her parents were the chief benefactors of the new monastery; they found and bought the house for it and they acquired a house for themselves nearby and continued to help the nuns with all manner of gifts and kindnesses. They were known to the nuns as 'Mammy' and 'Daddy Davies'. On 2 October 1920 BJ wrote to the prioress of Carisbrooke, 'Really you must make her (M. Magdalen's) retreat before clothing a novena to storm her people into the Church. Her father really has been an *Israelita in quo dolus non est.*' On 12 October 1922 Mrs Davies (Mary Esther) (1870-1945) was baptised. On 20 December 1938 she was clothed as a Dominican tertiary by Hilary Carpenter, and was professed in 1943 by Walter Gumbley. Sr M. Magdalen was prioress of Headington 1937-43 and 1946-55. In 1967, when Headington was closed, she moved to the monastery of Estavayer, Switzerland.

DELAHUNTY, Michael, OP (1893-1940). Entered the Irish province in 1910. His studies were extended to incorporate a period at University College, Dublin, and in 1921 he was sent to Hawkesyard for a year. After that he was assigned to Newbridge, where he taught until his death.

DELANY, Bernard, OP (1890-1959). Born in London, he joined the Order in 1907. After the completion of his studies in 1916 he was assigned to Woodchester as a missioner, but in 1917 he signed up as an army chaplain. On his return, he was assigned to London. In 1921 he was one of the first people assigned to the new house in Oxford. He was the first editor of *Blackfriars* (1920-24, 1925-32). In 1924 he obtained a B. Litt. in the university of Oxford. In the same year he was assigned to Laxton, but was called back to Oxford in 1925. In 1927 he was elected prior of Hawkesyard, but he resigned in 1929 to become the first prior of Blackfriars, Oxford. In 1932 he was elected to succeed BJ as provincial (1932-42). In 1942 he became prior of London, and when his term of office was finished was appointed superior in Cambridge, and then, soon afterwards, superior of Edinburgh (1946-51). He was then sent to South Africa, where, in 1954, he became student master at Stellenbosch. In 1958 he returned to England for the Provincial Chapter and was taken ill. He died in London.

DE LISLE, Ambrose Philips (1809-1878). Received into the Catholic church in 1825, he was accepted into the Dominican Third Order in Rome in 1831 by Francesco Ferdinando Jabalot (1780-1834), who was acting Master General and was elected to be Master General in 1832. In 1833 he took possession of one of the family homes, at Grace-Dieu in Leicestershire, and in 1835 he gave some of his land there for the establishment of a Cistercian monastery, opened in 1837 as Mount St Bernard. De Lisle was deeply disappointed that the monks, being good Trappists, were unwilling to undertake apostolic work. In 1837 he laid the foundation stone for the new monastery at Atherstone, to which the Dominican nuns were to move (they moved in in 1839, and left again in 1858), and also the foundation stone of the new church which was to be built for the Dominican mission in Nuneaton. In 1838, on a visit to Paris, he visited Lacordaire's bishop, the archbishop of Paris, Mgr Quelen (died 1839; archbishop of Paris 1821-39); with his support, he launched the Association of Universal Prayer for the Conversion of England. He hoped for a speedy return of England to the Catholic faith, and in particular he believed that the Anglican church could be converted en bloc; to this end, in 1857, he helped to found the Association for the Promotion of the Unity of Christendom, though he obediently withdrew from it, when Manning and others secured its condemnation by the pope in 1864. In 1868 he was High Sheriff of Leicestershire.

DENIS, John Mary Egidius Francis (1834-1900). A Breton priest, he worked in Alderney in the Channel Islands and then, briefly, in Rotherhithe, before moving to West Grinstead, where he was parish priest 1863-1900. He was responsible for inviting the Dominican sisters to establish a convent in West Grinstead.

DENIS, Pseudo-. Sixth-century Greek-speaking theologian, who wrote under the guise of St Paul's convert, Dionysius the Areopagite. His writings were extremely influential in the Middle Ages. There is a translation of them into English in the series, *Classics of Western Spirituality*.

DE PARAVICINI, Frances (died 1930, aged 85). Daughter of W. W. Williams of Oxford, in 1872 she married Baron Francis de Paravicini, who was a don at Balliol College, Oxford (1872-1908), and died in 1920. She was received into the Catholic church in 1878, and subsequently became a Dominican tertiary. She was an historian, and befriended BJ when he was an undergraduate in Oxford, encouraging his interest in the old Dominican sites there. She was a benefactress of the Order and took a particular interest in the foundation of the new Oxford priory. In 1917, at BJ's request, she made a full report on the houses he was thinking of buying in Oxford, and he cited her 'expert testimony' to persuade the Provincial Council. After the establishment of the Dominican nuns in Headington, she moved into one of the cottages near the monastery, but in 1927 she moved to Torquay, where she had previously had a house, to live in the guesthouse attached to the convent of the Dominican sisters at St Marychurch. She gave her furniture to Blackfriars, Oxford. In 1928, finding it too cold in the convent, she moved into an hotel in Torquay. She was taken ill just before Christmas 1929 and died 6 October 1930. She was buried in the Dominican habit by Bernard Delany.

DEVAS, Raymund, OP (1886-1975). Born in Waterford, he was educated in England at Beaumont College (1897-1904) and joined the Order at Woodchester in 1904. In 1912 he was assigned to Woodchester. He was a great admirer of Jandel and sought to realise his vision of Dominican regular observance throughout the province. In 1916 he was commissioned as an army chaplain; he was awarded the MC. After the war he was sent to Hawkesyard and then, in 1920, to Newcastle, but in 1922 he was assigned to Grenada, where he was to spend much of the rest of his life. He acquired a reputation there as an ornithologist, and was awarded the OBE for his work in the Caribbean in 1969. In 1926 he was brought home and assigned to Pendleton, but in 1928 he returned to Grenada as Vicar Provincial. The 1932 Provincial Chapter appointed him novice master at Woodchester, but he caused offence by his sermon to a pilgrimage of the Friends of Blackfriars to the tomb of BJ on 30 September 1934, by reminding his hearers that BJ needed their prayers more than their veneration, and he was shortly afterwards dismissed from his post and sent to London, from where he returned to Grenada in 1936. At the end of his life, in hospital in Barbados, when he was the oldest living member of the province, he still retained a lively interest in the affairs and politics of the province.

DHORME, Edouard Paul (1881-1966). Entered the French province of the Dominicans in 1899 and became a member of the École Biblique in Jerusalem. He was an expert on Assyriology. In 1931 he left the Order and abandoned the faith. He became a professor at the Sorbonne in Paris. Some of his former Dominican colleagues, notably P. Spicq, continued to befriend him, and many Dominicans, including Lagrange, prayed for him with great fidelity, and their loyalty was rewarded when, at the end of his life, he returned wholeheartedly to the faith.

DIX, Fabian, OP (1877-1953). He was a convert and had been a clergyman in the Church of England, like his father. He joined the Order in 1905. After the completion of his studies, he was assigned to Woodchester in 1912, and then to London in 1913. In 1918 he was commissioned as an army chaplain. In 1920 he became subprior, then prior, of London. In 1923 he was assigned to Leicester as a missioner, becoming subprior there in 1926 and prior in 1929. He was superior in Edinburgh 1932-42, then prior of Pendleton 1942-51. From 1951 until his death he was superior of Cambridge.

DOMINIC GUZMAN, St, OP (c. 1174-1221). Founder of the Dominican Order. Born in Castile, he became a canon and later subprior of Osma. In 1206 he was deputed to the papal preaching mission designed to combat heresy in Languedoc, and in 1215 found himself at the head of a new 'institute' of preachers in Toulouse. On the advice of Innocent III this 'institute' was turned into a religious Order, which progressively took shape and acquired recognition as 'The Order of Preachers' between 1216 and 1220. Dominic's life was characterised by extreme generosity towards the needs of others, and a willingness to throw himself tirelessly into the various tasks laid upon him by authority or by circumstances, combined with a certain pragmatism and great firmness of decision.

DOMVILE, Lady Margaret (1840-1929). Daughter of the 3rd Earl of Howth (1803-1874), in 1861 she married Sir Charles Domvile, 2nd Bart. (who died in 1884). She was the author of several books. She was introduced to BJ on one of his visits to West Grinstead, where two of her nieces lived, one of whom later recalled, in a letter to Bernard Delany (23 July 1934), her confidence that they would have 'so much in common, for she was very literary, keen on politics (especially the Irish) and appreciative of his wit and humour'. She wanted him to attend her deathbed and, quite unexpectedly, he arrived shortly before she died; her niece had written to him, asking for prayers, when she was taken ill, and he, finding the letter on his return from Scotland, immediately went down to see her, though he had been there only a week before. 'My dear old aunt—past speech—gave him a lovely smile, squeezed his hand and died almost at once' (testimony of the niece in her letter to Bernard Delany).

DUNCKER, Peter, OP (born 1898). Joined the Dutch province in 1916, and was sent to study at Hawkesyard in 1920. He obtained his lectorate there in 1924 and then went to the École Biblique, Jerusalem, for two years. After a year of teaching in Holland, he completed his biblical studies in Rome and obtained the licentiate in 1928. After teaching for a few years in the provincial study house at Zwolle, he returned to the Angelicum, Rome, where he taught 1934-1984. Since then he has lived in Holland.

DUSE, Eleonora (1858-1924). Born into a family of travelling actors, she was forced onto the stage from an early age. After playing the part of Juliet in 1873 she succumbed to the fascination of acting and soon became the most famous Italian actress of her time, with an international reputation rivalling that of Sarah Bernhardt. Her special talent was to identify herself entirely with the part she was playing, so that it could be said that she did not act on stage, she lived. From her mother she learned early in life to give, and throughout her life she gave herself utterly, whether in her art or in her loves. Her admirers included Queen Victoria and Bernard Shaw, Rilke and Pirandello. In 1881 she married Tebaldo Checchi, by whom she had one daughter, Enrichetta (later Mrs Bullough), but the marriage broke up in 1885. After several more or less unhappy love affairs, her most famous amour was with Gabriele D'Annunzio, with whom she remained on friendly terms even after they had parted. She died in Pittsburgh. Her body was repatriated on the orders of Mussolini and, on the way, it 'lay in state' for three days in the Dominican church of St Vincent Ferrer in New York. In her last years she returned to christian belief, though not to the formal practice of Catholicism. Hers was undoubtedly a deeply religious personality, and her daughter's profound Catholicism owed much to her inspiration. Cf C. Fusero, *Eleonora Duse*, Milan 1971; W. Weaver, *Duse, A Biography*, London 1984.

EGAN, Chrysostom, OP (1887-1951). Educated at Hawkesyard School (1900-1904), he joined the Order in 1904. In 1912 he was sent to Rome to study, and in 1913 Master General Cormier sent him to teach theology in the Benedictine monastery of Ettal, Bavaria. In 1914 he returned to England and was sent to Hawkesyard to teach in the school. In 1917 he was assigned to Newcastle. In 1922 Master General Theissling appointed him to the Leonine Commission in Rome, but in 1927 ill health forced him to return to England. In 1928 he was sent to South Africa, where he remained until 1939, when he came back to England and was assigned to Newcastle. Shortly before he died he became chaplain to the nuns at Carisbrooke.

ELRINGTON, Aidan, OP (1870-1942). Son of Gen. Frederick Elrington (1819-1904), one-time governor of the Tower of London, he was received into the Catholic church in Kansas, USA, in 1893. Entered the Order at Woodchester in 1894. In 1897 he was sent to Louvain to finish his theological studies, and he then remained there until 1906 to acquire a doctorate in science. Taught in the Studium at Hawkesyard 1906-1907, then moved to London. Taught biology at the Angelicum, Rome, 1909-1920, when he was sent home as his lectures were 'not scholastic enough'. The provincial of New York then asked for his services for a few years, and he taught at Providence College, Rhode Island, for a year (1920-21). He was superior of Oxford (1921-29) throughout the building of the priory and the church. He was then assigned to Pendleton, but in 1930 he was asked to help run a home for mentally defective children at Besford Court. Assigned to Woodchester in 1935, two years later he was elected to be one of the founding members of the new community in Cambridge, where he was procurator until his death.

ELTON, Godfrey (1892-1973). Went up to Balliol College, Oxford, in 1911 with a classical scholarship, and obtained first class honours in Classical Moderations in 1913. He then switched to modern history, but was commissioned in 1914 instead of completing his degree. After the war, however, in 1919, he was awarded a fellowship at Queen's College, Oxford, in modern history. He joined the Labour Party and stood for parliament, without success, in 1924 and 1929. In 1934 he was made the 1st Baron Elton of Headington and played an active part in the House of Lords. In 1939 he retired from teaching, while remaining a supernumerary fellow of Queen's.

ENGLISH, Adrian, OP (1891-1938). A native of Newcastle upon Tyne, he entered the Order in 1914. After completing his priestly studies, he was sent to study for a B.Sc. in London, which he obtained in 1924. Taught at the Dominican school at Laxton 1924-28. After that he worked on the parish in London until he was elected prior of

Newcastle in 1935. He resigned in 1938 and was appointed first superior of Blackfriars, Cambridge, but he died soon after.

ESSEX, Edwin, OP (1891-1966). Born in Hull, he was educated at the Dominican school at Hawkesyard (1904-1909) and joined the Order in 1909. After completing his studies, he was sent to Leicester and then, in 1920, he was assigned to Woodchester and, at the end of the same year, to London. In 1924 he was sent to Oxford to be editor of *Blackfriars*, but he was taken off that job in 1925 and assigned to Pendleton. At the end of 1926 he was sent to Leicester, but in the following year he applied for and was given permission to become a naval chaplain. He resigned his commission in 1928 and was appointed to London. In 1931 he was sent to Edinburgh to try and obtain a house where a Dominican community could be established, and at the beginning of 1932 he was appointed the first Dominican superior there. Later in the same year, though, he was elected prior of Leicester. In 1935 he was appointed Vicar Provincial of South Africa, but he came back home the following year, without leave, and went to Oxford and was then assigned to Pendleton. In 1945 he was sent to Woodchester, and in 1950 he became chaplain to the Marist sisters at Nympsfield, near Woodchester, where he remained until shortly before his death. He was a well-known preacher and published several books, including some of his own poetry.

EVEREST, Humbert, OP (1868-1952). Joined the Order in 1887, and studied theology in Louvain 1889-94, where he earned the lectorate. Taught at Hawkesyard 1894-96. After two years in London and two years in Leicester, he returned to Hawkesyard in 1900, where he taught until 1911. He was also student master 1900-1904, lector primarius 1904-1906, prior 1904-1907 and bursar 1907-1911. In 1907 he went to Louvain to take the examination for STM. In 1911 he was elected provincial and, at the end of his term of office in 1916, he was awarded his STM. After three years at Hinckley, he was appointed provincial brusar in 1919, a post he retained until 1942. Until 1931 he lived at Carisbrooke, where he was also chaplain to the nuns; thereafter he lived in London until his death. He was a man of diplomacy and tact. During BJ's time as provincial he often acted as his deputy, when BJ was absent from the country.

FANFANI, Ludovico, OP (1876-1955). Joined the Roman province at the age of 16 and made profession in 1898. Provincial of the Roman province 1924-33 and 1936-40. In 1946 he was made a member of the Master General's curia. He was one of the main founders of the congregation of Dominican sisters, The Missionaries of the Schools. Master General Theissling called him 'a model for the Order' (cited in the obituary in *Analecta S.O.P.* 32 (1955-56) pp. 240-244).

FARRELL, Ambrose, OP (1898-1977). Born in London, he was educated at Hawkesyard School (1913-1916) and then entered the noviciate in 1916. He was then called up for military service and had to leave the Order, but he returned in 1919. After obtaining the lectorate at Hawkesyard in 1927, he went to the Angelicum, Rome, where he got a doctorate in canon law in 1929. After that he taught at Oxford 1930-32, at the Angelicum 1932-34, at Oxford 1934-46, at Fribourg 1948-52, and at Oxford 1952-65. He was superior of Cambridge 1946-48. In 1952 he was created STB, and STM in 1954. Regent of Studies 1954-60. After leaving Oxford, he was for a time chaplain to the Dominican sisters at Harrow. His last assignation was to Cambridge.

FAY, Mary Teresa, OP (1882-1974). Born in Nice, France, she was unable to become a Carmelite there, as she wanted, because of the anti-religious laws; she therefore went to Carisbrooke, where her friend Emily Hurdle-Williams (Sr M. Suso OP) was already a nun, and made profession there in 1905. In 1922 she went, with M. Suso, to the new foundation at Headington. She was prioress there, in succession to M Suso, 1928-31. In 1967 she moved to Siena Convent, Drogheda, Ireland.

FAYER, Mary Gabriel, OP (1873-1940). Made profession as a nun at Carisbrooke in 1893.

FEELEY, Clement, OP (1893-1972). Born in Sligo, where his father was a member of the Royal Irish Constabulary, he joined the English province in 1913. He taught in the Dominican school from 1922-34, then went to Grenada. He returned to England in 1945 and went to Woodchester, from where he was shortly moved to Leicester. Bursar at Oxford 1948-52, then at Pendleton 1952-56, then at Hawkesyard 1956-57, when he became chaplain to the Dominican sisters at Stone. After two years there he went to Woodchester. His last years were spent in the home run by the sisters at Stone.

FITZGERALD, Stephen, OP (1872-1957). Educated at the Dominican school at Hinckley (1891-94), he joined the Order in 1894. After completing his studies, he was sent to Pendleton. In 1904 he was assigned to Newcastle, and to Woodchester in 1914. He shortly afterwards became superior at Stroud. Prior of Leicester 1919-29, he planned the building of the present church there. After that he was in London until 1933, and then spent the rest of his life at Pendleton, where he was subprior 1933-45.

FLETCHER, Ceslaus, OP (1847-1911). He was received into the Catholic church at Woodchester in 1861 and in the following year went to the Dominican school at Hinckley, where he remained until 1866, when he joined the Order. Having done his studies in London, he was ordained in 1872 and returned briefly to Woodchester. In 1873 he was assigned to Newcastle and to Leicester in 1877, becoming superior there in 1878 and the first prior of the newly erected priory there in 1882. In 1885 he went back to London. In 1890 he was reelected prior of Leicester, returning to London again in 1893. Chaplain to the nuns at Carisbrooke 1895-96, when he went back to Leicester. After a breakdown in his health, he was moved to London in 1897 and formally assigned there in 1899. In spite of his bad health, he was bursar there from 1902 until his death.

FLOOD, Vincent, OP (1844-1907). Born in County Longford, Ireland, he entered the Order in Dublin in 1860 and was ordained in 1867. In 1887 he was consecrated coadjutor to Archbishop Gonin of Trinidad, whom he succeeded in 1889. It was he who arranged for the Cathedral parish in Port of Spain to be entrusted to English-speaking Dominicans, and in 1897 it was specifically handed over to the Irish province. In 1901 he asked the English Dominicans, some of whom had been working in Trinidad, to take charge of the island of Grenada, and the refusal of the English to accept this mission, unless it were made independent of the Master General's vicar in Trinidad, led to the creation of two seperate provincial vicariates, one of the Irish province in Trinidad and one of the English province in Grenada.

FOLGHERA, Jean Dominique, OP (1870-1945). Joined the French province in 1889, and came to Hawkesyard as a lector in 1905. When Hawkesyard was made a formal studium in 1906, he was appointed its first pro-Regent of Studies; in 1912 he was awarded the STM and became Regent. When war broke out in 1914 he was in France and was unable to return to England, since no one would issue him with a passport, the French authorities maintaining he was Italian, and the Italians insisting that he was French. In 1920 he was re-assigned to the French province and formally resigned as Regent. Thereafter he worked in Paris, though he was present for the official opening of Blackfriars in 1929. He translated and edited several volumes in the Revue des Jeunes edition of the *Summa Theologiae*.

FORD, Hugh Edmund (1851-1930). Went to school at Downside in 1861, and in 1868 joined the English Benedictine noviciate at Belmont, returning to Downside in 1871. Concern for his health led to his being sent to Australia in 1873, where he remained until 1876, leading a healthy outdoor life and hunting the local fauna. After being ordained in 1877, he was soon appointed Prefect of Studies in the school, under Aidan Gasquet, who became prior in 1878. In this position he did much to modernise the school. In 1885 he was elected prior of Downside, and campaigned actively to restore the monasteries of the Congregation to their proper independence. In 1888 he was not re-elected prior, but in 1889 the President of the Congregation called for just such changes in its régime as had been urged by Ford. In 1890 the Holy See ordered these changes to be made. Meanwhile Ford himself had gone to start a new mission at Beccles, where he remained 1889-94. Then he was elected prior of Downside again. In 1899 Leo XIII appointed a commission to draw up the new Constitutions which had been called for in 1890, but had not been produced. Gasquet was president of this commission and Ford was closely involved in its work. In 1900 the new Constitutions were promulgated, and Downside became an abbey. Naturally Ford was elected the first abbot. He resigned in 1906 for reasons of health, and was appointed superior of Ealing, a position he retained for ten years. His increasing need to seek a warmer climate during the winter led him to ask in 1916 to be relieved of all reponsibilities. As Abbot Cuthbert Butler said in his obituary, 'Abbot Ford more than any man can claim the title "Maker of Modern Downside" ' (*Downside Review* 49 (1931) p. 21).

FRÜHWIRTH, Andreas Franziskus, OP (1845-1933). Born in Austria, he entered the Austro-Hungarian province in 1863. Prior of Graz 1876-1880, provincial 1880-84, prior of Vienna 1889-91. Re-elected provincial in 1891, later in the same year he became Master General (1891-1904). In 1907 he was made papal nuncio to Bavaria and consecrated archbishop. In 1915 he was made a cardinal. Cf. A. Walz, *Andreas Kardinal Frühwirth*, Vienna 1950.

GARDE, Thomas, OP (1887-1960). Entered the Irish province in 1903. After studying in Jerusalem, under Lagrange, he taught at the Angelicum, Rome, 1915-25, and was awarded the STM in 1924. In 1929 he was summoned by Master General Gillet to join the General Curia of the Order. Rector and prior of the Angelicum 1946-49. Provincial of Ireland 1949-56. In 1956 he was again summoned to join the General Curia.

GARVIN, James Louis (1868-1947). Editor of *The Observer* 1908-1942. As a young man he was a verger at St Dominic's, Newcastle. He left the Catholic church. His retired cook told Fr Bede Bailey in Newcastle that he was the most admirable man she had ever met. The Rolls Royce used to take the servants to their doctors' and dentists' appointments.

GASQUET, Francis Aidan (1846-1929). Monk of Downside. A crucial figure in the achievement of the new Constitutions of the English Benedictine Congregation (1899). Member of the Commission on Anglican Orders (1896). He was made a cardinal in 1914. He preached at the laying of the foundation stone of Blackfriars, Oxford, in 1921. Cf. Shane Leslie, *Cardinal Gasquet*, London 1953.

GATTY, Charles Tindal (1851-1928). A convert to Catholicism, for twelve years he was curator of Liverpool Museum. In 1892 he stood for parliament as a Home Rule for Ireland candidate, but without success. In 1903 he moved to Dublin, where he lived for many years before returning to England. He was a great promoter of Irish art.

GAVIN, Mother Alphonsine (1854-1940). Born in Limerick, Ireland, she joined the Sisters of the Assumption in Kensington, London, in 1876, beginning her formal noviciate in France in 1877. She was something of a character, endowed with a great sense of fun, but she lived her religious life with entire simplicity and much devotion. Amid the various responsibilities she was called upon to discharge, her favourite task was instructing converts, for which she acquired a considerable reputation.

GEOGHEGAN, Mary Dominic, SHCJ (1859-1944). Aunt of Terence Geoghegan. Since her mother was ill, she had to run the family home from an early age, but in 1883 she was able to join the Holy Child nuns at Mayfield, and she was soon made assistant novice mistress, a position she held until 1902. In 1916 she returned to Mayfield as guestmistress. She was much appreciated as a friend and counsellor, and she was particularly devoted to befriending and helping priests. She had known BJ since he was a boy.

GEOGHEGAN, Terence (1903-1921). His family lived on Parliament Hill, Hampstead, not far from St Dominic's. He went to school at Downside in 1917. He died after a short bout of pneumonia in 1921. The obituary in *Downside Review* 39 (1921) p. 137 describes him as being 'of singular excellence in every form of athletics; and yet withal a character deeply sensitive to religious influences and capable of carrying supernatural principles into the most unlikely of his occupations.'

GEORGE, Charles (1865-1941). Educated at Fort Augustus and at Edinburgh university. Solicitor of the Supreme Courts of Scotland since 1890. He organised the buying of 24 George Square, Edinburgh, for the Dominicans. His daughter Margaret (who died in 1982, aged

82), made the house habitable for the brethen's arrival. His son Michael, who served at the first Mass there, died in 1981, aged 63.

GETINO, Luis Alonso, OP (1877-1946). Entered the province of Spain in 1892. Taught at Salamanca 1901-1909. Founded *La Ciencia Tomista*, which he edited 1910-13 and 1916-22. Provincial of Spain 1922-26. Enthusiastic Dominican historian. One of his lasting achievements was the revival of interest in Francisco de Vitoria OP (died 1546), often regarded today as the father of international law.

GILBERT DE FRAXINETO, OP (13th century). Leader of the first group of Dominican friars sent to England in 1221. They went straight to Oxford, where they arrived on 15 August 1221 and made their first English foundation. More generally known as Gilbert of Fresney.

GILBY, Thomas, OP (1902-1975). Born in Birmingham, where his father had a wine business. His parents both became Catholics, and he was received into the Catholic church when he was eleven. Joined the Order in 1919. Henry St John, a convert parson, fresh from the trenches of Flanders, was a great influence on him. He took his lectorate in 1927 and received a Ph.D. in Louvain in 1929. He then taught in the studium at Hawkesyard until 1931 and at Oxford 1931-35. Early in 1936 he was assigned to London, where he gave London University Extension Lectures. In 1939 he went to Cambridge, but soon afterwards became a chaplain in the Royal Navy, a role he filled with considerable success. He was offered the post of senior chaplain in the navy, but declined it. He returned to Cambridge after the war and, in spite of continuing restlessness, he lived there for the rest of his days. He was the moving force in the Blackfriars edition of the *Summa Theologiae*, himself translating thirteen volumes.

GILLET, Martin, OP (1875-1951). Entered the French province in 1897. Taught moral theology at Louvain, where BJ was a student of his, then at Le Saulchoir, then at the Institut Catholique in Paris. Elected provincial of Paris in 1927, and Master General in 1929. In 1946, having finished his term as Master General, he was consecrated titular archbishop of Nicea. He founded the Revue des Jeunes edition of the *Summa Theologiae*. In a letter of 4 October 1929 BJ wrote to Alban King, 'F. Gillet was my professor for a year in Louvain, talker, preacher, reads modern psychology, good ideas, a bit drawn to centralising, plenty of energy, master of advertisement, the type that will enjoy being Master General.'

GINNS, Reginald, OP (1893-1987). Born at Hinckley, he was at Hawkesyard School 1907-1912. Joined the Order in 1912. Studied at the École Biblique, Jerusalem, 1921-23. Then he returned to Hawkesyard, where he taught until 1938, being student master 1928-33 and lector primarius 1935-38. In 1932, during Master General Gillet's visitation, he took the examination for STM at Hawkesyard, and was awarded the STM in 1936. Prior of Woodchester 1938-41, after which he served as a chaplain in the RAF. After the war he returned to Woodchester, and then to Hawkesyard, where he resumed teaching and become lector primarius again in 1948, until near the end of 1950. After a few years in London, in 1954 he was appointed novice master at Woodchester, but in 1956 he was relieved of this position, and shortly afterwards he went to Edinburgh. In 1959 he was appointed chaplain to the nuns at Stone, and he remained in Stone until his death.

GIOVANNI DOMINICI, Bl., OP (c.1355-1419). Entered the Order in Florence in 1374. He was an ardent supporter of the Dominican reform, launched by Raymund of Capua. In 1406 he founded the convent of St Dominic, Fiesole, to be a house of strict observance. In 1408 he became archbishop of Ragusa, and, shortly afterwards, a cardinal.

GONIN, Louis, OP (1815-1889). Born at Bourgoing, France, at the age of three he was taken to Mauritius, where he in due course became a lawyer. In 1852 he returned to France and received the Dominican habit from Lacordaire. Ordained in 1855, he was sent to Paris and then to Sorèze. In 1856 the Master General sent him to be novice master at Woodchester, where he became prior the next year, a position he retained until, in 1863, he was appointed archbishop of Port of Spain, Trinidad. He took one English father with him, Thomas Greenough, when he sailed in 1864, and later secured the service of other Dominicans from France, to work with him in Trinidad. Thus he laid the foundations for what became in due course a vicariate of the Master General and, in 1901, a vicariate of the Irish province.

GOODIER, Alban, SJ (1869-1939). Educated at Stonyhurst, he entered the Jesuits in 1887. Before his ordination he taught at Stonyhurst, where he had Cyril (Bede) Jarrett as one of his pupils in 1894. He recalled that 'one afternoon, while the boys were doing some writing exercise, I called Cyril to my desk on the plea of correcting his Latin theme with him; and when I whispered to him, "Cyril, if you can't keep quiet now, what will you do when you grow up?" "What will I do when I grow up, sir? I'm going to be a priest, sir" ' (letter to Bernard Delany, 6 March 1934). In 1915 he was sent to St Francis Xavier College, Bombay, to resolve the crisis caused by the forced withdrawal of the German Jesuits. In 1919 he was made archbishop of Bombay. In 1926 Pius XI asked him to resign, so that the complex politics of the archbishopric, involving both the British and the Portuguese governments, could be sorted out. He retired to England. On 21 May 1929 he preached at the opening of Blackfriars, Oxford. On 4 August 1934 he preached at St Dominic's, London, at the 7th-centenary celebration of the canonization of St Dominic.

GRANT, Thomas (1816-1870). Born in northern France, he studied at the English College, Rome, of which he was subsequently rector. In 1851 he was consecrated the first bishop of Southwark.

GRAY, Canon John (1866-1934). Convert to Catholicism. A friend of Oscar Wilde. He was ordained priest in 1901 and lived thereafter in Edinburgh. He was closely associated with Marc André Sebastian Raffalovich, with whom he made repeated attempts to get the Dominicans to Edinburgh. He left his money to the Dominicans to support their work there. Cf. Brocard Sewell, *In the Dorian Mode: A Life of John Gray*, Padstow 1983.

GREENE, Gwendolen Maud Plunket (1878-1957). Daughter of the composer, Sir Hubert Parry (1848-1918); her mother was the sister of Lady Mary von Hügel. In 1899 she married Harry Plunket Greene (1865-1936), who sang the part of Gerontius in the first performance of *The Dream of Gerontius*. She became a Catholic in 1926 and was received into the church by BJ. She edited Baron Friedrich von Hügel's letters to herself, *Letters to a Niece*, London 1928. Her book, *The Prophet Child*, London 1935, bore the dedication, 'In memory of Fr Bede Jarrett O.P. I believe in the Holy Ghost, the Lord and giver of life.' She and her family had a considerable hand in Evelyn Waugh's becoming a Catholic in 1928. Waugh wrote of them, 'I had in fact fallen in love with an entire family and . . . had focused the sentiment upon the only appropriate member, an eighteen year old daughter', Olivia, who 'suffered from morbid self-consciousness' and was 'a little crazy; truth-loving and in the end holy' (*A Little Learning*, London 1983, pp. 216, 218). Gwen lived with her children and their friends 'on terms of serene equality' (ibid. p. 218). Olivia Plunket Greene (1907-1955) became an alcoholic; she never married and ended her days living a sort of eccentric religious life with her mother.

GREENOUGH, Thomas, OP (1834-1907). Went to the Dominican school at Hinckley (1852-1854) and was then sent to Woodchester, where he received the habit in 1855. After his ordination in 1860 he was sent for reasons of health to Carpentras, returning to England in the spring of 1861, to become chaplain to the Dominican sisters at Clifton. In 1863 he initiated the new Dominican mission at Littlehampton. Then in 1864 he accompanied Archbishop Gonin to Trinidad, where he worked until 1895 when, after a few months in Grenada, he returned to England and was assigned to Newcastle. In 1898 he became superior and parish priest of Hinckley. In 1901 he was appointed the first Vicar Provincial of the new English Dominican mission in Grenada. In 1903 he was replaced as Vicar Provincial, but continued to work in Grenada, as far as his health would permit, until his death.

GROSSETESTE, Robert (died 1253). Bishop of Lincoln 1235-53. Controversy surrounds the dating of his birth and the details of his earlier career. He was born either in the mid 1170s or in the mid 1160s. Studied in Oxford and possibly Paris. According to some scholars, he was the first chancellor of the University of Oxford, though others place his chancellorship later, and in any case it seems that he was obliged only to use the old-fashioned title 'Master of the Schools'. He was the outstanding philosopher and theologian of his time in England. From 1229 or so he was lector in the Franciscan school in Oxford, to which he bequeathed his library. He was also friendly with the Dominicans.

GULSON, Helen (1834-1910). Received into the Catholic church in 1885. She was the niece and heiress of Josiah Spode of Hawkesyard Park. After his death, she handed over the house and property to the English Dominicans in 1894 and built the church and priory there. She herself lived at The Cottage, on the estate, and was a veritable 'mother' to the students there (she styled herself their 'Mother General'). She was also a considerable benefactress to St Dominic's, London, and left the English province her remaining possessions when she died.

GUMBLEY, Walter, OP (1887-1968). Educated at the school run by the Dominican sisters at Stone, then at Hawkesyard School (1901-1906), he entered the Order in 1908. Studied at Louvain 1912-14, without taking any degree. He taught at the school at Hawkesyard, and also taught church history in the Studium 1914-24, then he went with the school to Laxton in 1924. In 1931 he was assigned to Pendleton, where he was prior 1933-36. Then he went to Oxford. In 1938 he was appointed archivist of the province and moved to London. He remained archivist until 1965. He was very much the historian of the province. Prior of Oxford 1942-45, then he returned to London until 1951, when he moved back to Oxford, where he spent the rest of his life.

GUMLEY, Louis Stewart (1872-1941). Senior partner in the firm of Gumley and Davidson, Valuators, Surveyors and Property Agents, who handled the sale of 24 George Square, Edinburgh, to the Dominicans. He was also a fairly prominent local politician, and was Lord Provost of Edinburgh 1935-38. He was knighted in 1937.

HALIFAX, Viscount (Charles Lindley Wood) (1839-1935). A leader in the Catholic revival in the Church of England and a life-long worker for the reunion of the Anglican and Catholic churches. He occasioned the inquiry into Anglican orders in 1894. On 3 August 1901 he visited Hawkesyard and was shown round by the prior, Henry Bartlett. He was the instigator of the Malines Conversations (1921-26), in which at one time he wanted BJ to take part. Cf. J. G. Lockhart, *Charles Lindley, Viscount Halifax*, 2 vols., London 1935-36.

HALPIN, Charles, OP (1871-1952). One of the first boys at the re-opened Dominican school at Hinckley (1885-90), he entered the Order in 1890. After the completion of his studies, he was sent to teach at the school in Hinckley, and went with the school to Hawkesyard in 1898. He was at Pendleton 1899-1902, then returned to the school for another two years. Student master at Hawkesyard 1904-1905, then he resigned and was sent to Pendleton. Novice master at Woodchester 1906-1908, then student master again at Hawkesyard until 1911, when he returned to Woodchester as novice master. He was chaplain to the Dominican sisters at Stroud 1912-13, then went to Pendleton until 1916, when he was appointed to Grenada, where he worked for the rest of his life. He was a pious man, of limited outlook; he was evidently suspicious of the whole idea of sending BJ to Oxford as an undergraduate and fearful of his influence on the other students.

HART-DAVIS, Sybil Mary (1886-1927). Daughter of Alfred Cooper FRCS and Lady Agnes Flower; sister of Duff Cooper, Lord Norwich. Married Richard Hart-Davis (1878-1964) in 1904. Her son, Rupert (born in 1907, knighted in 1967), published a memoir of her, *The Arms of Time*, London 1979. Her marriage was not a success, though she and her husband stayed together. She had a succession of lovers, being 'as generous in love as in everything else' (*The Arms of Time* p. 24). In 1923 she was hurriedly received into the Catholic church in Paris; later on, she received instruction in the faith from Fabian Dix OP at St Dominic's, London. In October 1923 she attended a retreat given by BJ at Grayshott Cenacle and wrote to her son,

'Father Bede Jarrett gave us an address. He is wonderful!' (ibid. p. 120). She became a Dominican tertiary and was buried in the Dominican habit (ibid. p. 145).

HAY, Major Malcolm Vivian, of Seaton (1881-1962). Scottish Catholic historian and man of letters. Author of *A Chain of Error in Scottish History*, London 1927.

HERRIES, Baroness (Gwendolen Mary Fitzalan-Howard) (1877-1945). Daughter of the 11th Baron Herries (1837-1908), she inherited the Scottish barony in her own right. In 1904 she married the 15th Duke of Norfolk (1847-1917); the community at Hawkesyard, including BJ among the students, sent the Duke a letter to express their good wishes, recalling the role of Cardinal Howard in the revival of the English Dominicans (a copy of the letter is preserved in the student Chronicle of Hawkesyard).

HEVENINGHAM, Mary Dominic, OP (1898-1969). Her father was architect to the Duke of Norfolk. She went on a retreat given by BJ at Grayshott Cenacle and was at once attracted to the Dominicans. She made profession as a nun of Carisbrooke in 1927. She was one of a team that made vestments for Westminster Cathedral.

HOLLAND, Antony (1883-1956). Ordained as an Anglican, he served as a military chaplain in the first World War. After the war he became a Catholic, and joined the London Oratory in 1924. He was ordained priest in 1928. Director of the Little Oratory 1929-39. Both as an Anglican and as a Catholic, he had a wide reputation as a preacher. The outbreak of war in 1939 brought on a serious collapse in his health, from which he recovered enough to be able to say Mass, but not enough to be able to return to the strain of life in London.

HOPER-DIXON, Rupert, OP (1894-1935). Born in Norway, he was brought up in Malaya, then went to school at Stonyhurst. Being declared medically unfit for military service in 1914, he entered the Order in 1915. Having obtained the lectorate in 1923, he was sent to the Angelicum, Rome, where he obtained a Ph.D. in 1926. After teaching for a year at Laxton, he was sent to teach philosophy at Hawkesyard, where he was prior 1929-35.

HOWARD, Philip, OP (1629-1694). Brother of Thomas Howard, Duke of Norfolk. Entered the Order in Italy in 1645. To foster the revival of the English province, he founded a priory for it in Bornhem, Belgium, in 1657, and established a house of English Dominican nuns, also in Belgium, in 1660. Vicar general of the province 1661-75. In 1662 he became the principal chaplain to Queen Catherine of

Braganza. In 1675 he was made a cardinal. See Raymund Palmer, *Life of Cardinal Howard*, Lndon 1888.

HUMBERT OF ROMANS, OP (died 1277). Fifth Master of the Dominican Order (1254-63). It was under his governance that the institutions of the Order were clarified and tidied up. He supervised the standardisation of the Dominican rite, the re-editing of the Constitutions, the production of a common book of Constitutions for the Dominican nuns, and the development of the Order's academic structures. He wrote extensively on Dominican life and institutions, some of his writings acquiring almost official standing. For centuries his book on the officials of the Order was published together with the Constitutions. He was a respected and influential churchman and was an important adviser to Gregory X before the second Council of Lyons in 1274.

HUNTER-BLAIR, Sir David Oswald, Bart. (1853-1939). Became a Catholic in 1875 and a monk of Fort Augustus in 1878. A graduate of Magdalen College, Oxford, he was the first Master of the private hall established by Ampleforth in Oxford university (now St Benet's Hall) (1899-1908). Abbot of Fort Augustus 1913-17.

HURDLE-WILLIAMS, Mary Suso, OP (1882-1958). A convert to Catholicism, she entered Carisbrooke in 1903, and was prioress there 1914-20. In 1922 she moved to the new monastery at Headington, to be its first prioress, a position she retained until 1928, when she became novice mistress. She was crippled by disease from 1931 until her death. BJ did not entirely approve of her extreme devotion to what she took to be traditional observances. As he confessed to Miss Calthrop in an undated letter, 'I think sometimes that Mother Suso has little ideas of her own that are not quite OP'.

JACQUIN, Mannes, OP (1872-1956). Entered the French province in 1894. Taught church history and the history of doctrine at Le Saulchoir 1904-14. After the first World War he became professor of ecclesiastical history at Fribourg. He retired in 1937 and went to the Dominican house in Dijon. His major work was his *Histoire de l'Eglise* in three volumes, Paris 1929-48

JANDEL, Vincent Alexandre, OP (1810-1872). In 1841 he joined Lacordaire's little group of recruits, to restore the Dominican Order in France, though it soon became clear that there were grave differences between them on what such a restoration meant. Lacordaire was most interested in the Order's apostolate, and believed that its religious life had to be adapted to facilitate such work in present conditions; Jandel believed that only a return to strict primitive observance, with a minimum of adaptation, would revitalise the Order. In 1850 Jandel was put at the head of the whole Order by Pius IX, and in 1855 he was appointed Master General, a position he retained until his death. Cf. H. M. Cormier, *Vie du R.P. ALexandre-Vincent Jandel*, Paris 1890; Raymund Devas, *The Dominican Revival in the Nineteenth Century*, London 1913; Raymund Devas, ed., *Ex Umbris*, Hawkesyard 1920.

JARRETT, Col. Henry Sullivan (1839-1919). Gazetted Ensign in the Bengal Army in 1856, he was promoted to Major in 1876 and Lieutenant-Colonel in 1882. He served during the Indian Mutiny (1857-59) and on the North West Indian frontier. Member of the Board of Examiners, Fort William, Calcutta, and Assistant Secretary of the Legislative Department of the goverment of India (1870-94). He was a good orientalist and published several translations; he also published a translation of the poems of Heine. In 1874 he married Agnes Delacour Beaufort (1850-1930), who became a Catholic after the birth of her oldest son. They were the parents of BJ.

JOHNSTON, Quentin, OP (1896-1981). Born in India, where his father was a High Court Judge, he was brought up by his grandparents in England. Commissioned in the Royal Artillery, he was in France during the first World War, and was there received into the Catholic church. He entered the Order at Woodchester in 1921. After finishing his studies in the province, he went on to the Angelicum, Rome, to get his lectorate, and then to Fribourg, where he obtained a Ph.D. in 1931. He was then sent to teach mathematics at Laxton, but in 1932 Master General Gillet had him assigned to Hawkesyard to teach philosophy. In 1948 he went to Edinburgh and in 1950 to Cambridge. He was chaplain to the Assumption nuns at Hengrave Hall 1955-69, but then blindness forced him to retire, and he spent the rest of his life in nursing homes.

JOWETT, Benjamin (1817-1893). Regius Professor of Greek at Oxford university 1855-70. Master of Balliol College 1870-93.

JULIAN OF NORWICH (1342-after 1416). English theologian and spiritual writer, in whom interest was revived early in this century. Her *Revelations of Divine Love* became a favourite of BJ's.

KANE, Mary Agatha, OP (1884-1958). Born in Gateshead, she was introduced by Laurence Shapcote to Jane (later Sr Anthony) Morrison, and the two became friends and entered Carisbrooke together in 1908, making their profession there the following year. Sr Agatha had a good singing voice and was chantress from 1913-1954. She was one of the nuns who made vestments for Westminster Cathedral.

At the time of her death she was preparing for her golden jubilee by making little gifts for each of the sisters.

KEATING, Joseph, SJ (1865-1939). Entered the Society in 1883. In 1907 he became assistant editor of *The Month*, of which he was editor from 1912 until his death.

KEHOE, Richard, OP (1905-1981). Educated at Hawkesyard School 1919-21, he entered the Order in 1921. After finishing his studies at Hawkesyard, he was sent to the Angelicum, Rome, where he got his lectorate in 1929, and then to Jerusalem. After a short break in his studies, he returned to Rome, where in 1933 he won the licenciate in Sacred Scripture. He then returned to Hawkesyard to teach, moving to Oxford in 1935, where he taught until 1947. He lectured for two years at the studium of the Chicago province at River Forest (1949-51). In 1952 he returned to Oxford, but ill health prevented him from resuming his teaching and he effectively withdrew from the Order, though he never formally left it, and took up farming.

KENEALY, Anselm, OFMCap (1864-1943). Born in Wales of Irish parents, he joined the Capuchins in 1879. Minister Provincial of the English province 1902-1905. In 1906 he became the rector of the newly established Capuchin school in Cowley, Oxford (taken over by the Salesians in 1920), a position he retained until 1908. In 1910 he was appointed the first archbishop of the newly created archdiocese of Simla, India. Because of ill health he resigned in 1936, and retired to England. See A. Meersman, 'Franciscan Bishops in India and Pakistan', *Archivum Franciscanum Historicum* 72 (1979) pp. 154-155.

KINDERSLEY, Aelred (1860-1934). Monk of Downside. Abbot of Belmont 1920-34. There is a memoir by Dom Roger Hudleston in *Downside Review* 53 (1935) pp. 1-9.

KING, Alban, OP (1874-1962). Educated at the Dominican school at Hinckley (1888-93), he joined the Order in 1893. Studied at Louvain 1899-1901 and obtained the lectorate there. Taught philosophy at Hawkesyard 1901-1905 (having BJ among his students in 1901-1902), and was then assigned to London. In 1906 he went to Woodchester to teach theology, remaining there, even after the studies were all reunited at Hawkesyard in 1907, to work on the parish. In 1912 he was assigned to Pendleton, where he was elected prior the following year, being re-elected in 1916. In 1919 he was sent to Newcastle as a missioner. In 1923 he was appointed Vicar Provincial in Grenada. In 1928 he was assigned to Leicester, becoming prior there in 1935. From 1918 until his death he was assigned to Newcastle.

KNAPP, Albert, OP (1866-1944). Born in London, he was educated in France, where he was received into the Catholic church. Entered the French province in Corsica in 1886 and subsequently worked in the United States and in Canada. In 1910 he came to England and was assigned to Pendleton as a missioner. In 1914 he became an army chaplain. After the war he returned to Pendleton, where he was subprior 1920-23. In 1923 he became a member of the English province. He remained in Pendleton up to 1925, then went to London, where he remained until 1939. In that year he went to France for reasons of health and was caught in the German occupation and was unable to return to England. He was a popular preacher and was made a Preacher General in 1932. He was also an enthusiastic conjuror and became a member of the Magic Circle.

KNOX, Ronald Arbuthnott (1888-1957). Son of the Anglican bishop of Manchester, he was received into the Catholic church in 1917. Catholic chaplain to the university of Oxford 1926-39. A witty, scholarly and versatile writer. Cf. Evelyn Waugh, *Life of Ronald Knox*, London 1959.

KOOS, Hyacinth, OP (1863-1944). Entered the Order in 1889. After completing his studies, he became bursar at Hawkesyard, then, in 1896, bursar at Leicester, where he was assigned as a missioner. In 1898 he was appointed the first superior of the new mission in Pendleton, becoming its first prior in 1901. In 1904 he went to Newcastle, where once again he served as bursar, then in 1906 he was appointed Vicar Provincial of Grenada. He was sent to Woodchester in 1912 to be novice master, but in January 1914 he was elected prior of Newcastle. In 1917 he went to Leicester as a missioner, but in 1918 he was given special work in Trinidad among the East Indian immigrants. In 1925 he was invalided home and went to Woodchester. He worked in Leicester 1929-31, was chaplain at Carisbrooke 1931-33, was prior of Woodchester 1933-38. In 1938 he was appointed prior of Leicester, retaining the position until 1941, then he was novice master and student master at Hawkesyard (where the noviciate had been transferred because of the war).

KÜBBEN, Bernard, OP (1882-1941). Entered the Belgian province in 1902, and studied for the lectorate at Louvain, where he was a contemporary of BJ's. He later worked in Louvain and Brussels.

LACORDAIRE, Henri Dominique, OP (1802-1861). Revived the Dominican Order in France. As a secular priest, he published his *Essay on the Re-establishment in France of the Order of Preachers* (published in English in Dominican Sources, vol. 2) in 1839, and, in the same year, entered the noviciate at La Quercia, Viterbo, in Italy. His first house in France was opened in 1843 and in 1850 the province of France was formally restored. He was a famous preacher, but his liberal and democratic sympathies made him some enemies in the French church. Cf. Lancelot C. Sheppard, *Lacordaire*, London 1964.

LAGRANGE, Marie Joseph, OP (1855-1938). Entered the Toulouse province in 1879. In 1890, with the encouragement of Cormier, his provincial, he founded the École Biblique in Jerusalem. He described it as the 'practical school of biblical studies' (cf. F. M. Braun, *L'Oeuvre du Père Lagrange*, Fribourg 1943, p. 28). He also launched the *Revue Biblique*, whose first number appeared in 1892. In 1912 he was accused of modernism and removed from Jerusalem, but he returned soon after the election of Benedict XV in 1914. In 1921 the French government opened the École Archéologique Française de Jérusalem to collaborate with the École Biblique. Lagrange's literary output was immense, including substantial commentaries on all four gospels and on some of the epistles of St Paul.

LAMB, Stanislaus, OP (1893-1941). His family lived in the parish of St Dominic's, London, and he entered the Order in 1913. In 1920 he was sent to Louvain to obtain the lectorate, and it was planned that he would then go to Rome to study canon law, but in fact he was brought back in 1922 to teach at the school at Hawkesyard, and in 1924 he went with the school to Laxton, remaining there until 1931. After that he taught for a year at Hawkesyard, then became bursar at Woodchester (1932-35), at Hawkesyard (1935-37) and at London (1937-41).

LAMBURN, Mary Teresa, OP (1868-1951). Professed as a Dominican sister at Stroud in 1890, in 1925 she became Mother General of the Stroud Congregation, having previously been at different times novice mistress and prioress of Newcastle and prioress of Brewood. In 1929 she became the first Mother General of the amalgamated Congregation of St Catherine of Siena, Stone. Her last years were spent at Brewood.

LANE-FOX, Mary Agnes Emily (1877-1962). Daughter of the 2nd Viscount Halifax, in 1903 she married the politician, George Richard Lane-Fox (1870-1947), who became 1st Baron Bingley in 1933.

LASKI, Harold Joseph (1893-1950). Political theorist of the Labour Party. Lectured at McGill University 1914-16, Harvard 1916-20, and then at the London School of Economics, where he spent the rest of his life. He was Chairman of the Labour Party in 1945, and in the election campaign that year he was presented by the Conservatives as inciting revolution. Cf. Kingsley Martin, *Harold Laski*, London 1953.

LAWS, Thomas, OP (1839-1923). Born in London. Married in 1864, he went to Hinckley as a postulant after his wife died in 1866, and then to Woodchester, where he received the habit in 1867. After doing his studies in London, he returned to Woodchester in 1872 and was ordained priest. In 1875 he was assigned to Leicester. Prior of Woodchester 1886-89, after which he returned to Leicester, where he became subprior in 1891 and prior in 1893. In 1896 he was sent to London, where he became prior in 1900. In 1902 he resigned to become prior of Newcastle, resigning that priorship in 1904. He then returned to Leicester, to resume his very successful work as a missioner. Re-assigned to London 1907, where he remained until his death.

LEA, John (1871-1958). Won a scholarship to Gonville and Caius College, Cambridge, in 1889 and graduated with 1st class honours in Natural Science in 1892. He was a demonstrator in biology 1892-93. He started to train as a doctor, first in Cambridge, then at the London Hospital, but, when he had nearly completed his training, he was forced to abandon the course by ill health and financial constraints. In 1905 he joined the Indemnity Mutual Assurance Company. In 1907 he took his MA and began to work for the extra-mural department in London University (then known as the Board to Promote the Extension of University Teaching). Appointed full-time secretary to the Registrar in 1907, he was Registrar from 1912 until his retirement in 1936. He did a great deal to promote extra-mural work in London. He was a member of the Secondary Schools Examination Council 1912-30 and of the Adult Education Committee of the Board of Education 1921-25. He published several books on natural history.

LEATHER, John, OP (1872-1938). Educated at the Dominican school at Hinckley (1887-92), he joined the Order in 1892. He was sent to do his theology in Louvain 1894-99, and was then assigned to London, where he was parish priest both during BJ's time on the parish staff and while he was prior there. In 1920 he was assigned to Pendleton, where he was prior 1921-24. In December 1924 he was assigned to Newcastle. Novice master at Woodchester 1934-36, after which he returned to London. He was an ardent advocate of the rosary. In the Provincial's Diary, Bernard Delany wrote of him, 'People are afraid to be considered "pious". Fr John was one of those simple souls—direct and single of vision—who didn't even seem to think what others thought about his piety. He was pious in a very natural and un-selfconscious way.'

LEIGH, Blanche (1864-1946). Granddaughter of William Leigh of Woodchester Park, she was BJ's first cousin. She was also his godmother. She ruled the village of Nympsfield like a Victorian matriarch, deciding everything by herself, such as the form and position of the village war memorial.

LEIGH, William (1802-1873). Received into the Catholic church in 1844. He became the owner of Woodchester Park and, in 1850, invited the Dominicans to take charge of the church and parish he had established there, after the Passionists quitted. In 1859 his son and heir, William (1829-1906), married Mary Victoria Jarrett, sister to BJ's father.

LESCHER, Wilfrid, OP (1847-1916). Born into an old Catholic family in London, he entered the Order in 1864. After his ordination in 1873 he was assigned to Stroud, then, in 1874, to London and not long afterwards to Prudhoe Hall. In 1881 he was sent to Woodchester, and in the following year to Leicester. In 1883 he was allowed to go to Louvain to study for a year, then he was appointed to London. Prior of Woodchester 1889-92, superior of Stroud 1892-95. Assigned to Leicester in 1895, he was appointed superior of Hinckley in 1904. In 1907 he went to Carisbrooke as chaplain to the Dominican nuns. In 1910 he was elected prior of Pendleton, but resigned later in the same year. He had a serious mental breakdown and had to be hospitalised for three years, but afterwards he recovered completely and was able to resume pastoral work. In 1914 he was sent to Hinckley. Although most of his life was spent in pastoral duties, he was a constant student and wrote various works. In 1893 he produced and got printed a pamphlet on *The Scholastic Idea of the Universal*. He pioneered the English translation of the *Summa Theologiae* in 1907, and was officially put in charge of it by the Provincial Interchapter in 1910, though in the outcome most of the work was done by Laurence Shapcote.

L'ESTRANGE, Alexander, OP (1905-1951). Entered the Order in 1923, receiving the habit from BJ at Woodchester. Studied in Louvain 1929-31, winning the lectorate there in 1931. On his return he was assigned to Newcastle, but in 1932 he was sent to Grenada. In 1936 he was sent to teach philosophy at Hawkesyard, but in 1937 he was moved to Oxford, where he taught moral theology. Student master in Oxford 1938-43. In 1946 he went to London and in 1947 he returned to Grenada, where he became Vicar Provincial in 1950.

LE VIGOUREUX, Étienne, OP (1848-1922). After beginning to train for the diocesan priesthood, he entered the French province in January 1870 and was ordained priest on 21 September 1875. In 1876 he was assigned to the recently established community in the Faubourg St Honoré, Paris. Prior of Lille 1883-89 and of Le Havre

1889-92. In 1895 he was elected prior of Jerusalem, where he presided over the building of the convent and church at the École Biblique. In 1901 he was elected prior of Lille again, and, later in the same year, prior of St Jacques, where he remained until the brethren were scattered by the anti-religious legislation of the French goverment in 1903. He was one of the brethren who stayed in France, even though normal religious life was not possible. He was renowned as a preacher.

LORENZO OF RIPAFRATTA, Bl., OP (1373-1456). Received the Dominican habit from Bl. Giovanni Dominici, probably in 1396 or 1397, and made his noviciate at Cortona, where he remained at least until 1401. He subsequently became a lector and worked for many years at Fabriano, where he was also prior for a time. Probably in 1432 he became a member of the community at Pistoia, where he had already lived for a short while around 1425; there he remained until his death, serving in various capacities, such as lector and prior. He was an ardent supporter of the Dominican reform. Cf. S. Orlandi, *Il Beato Lorenzo da Ripafratta*, Florence 1956.

LOTTINI, Giovanni, OP (1860-1951). Entered the Dominican Congregation of San Marco in 1875. He worked in the Holy Office from 1905, and was Commissary General there from 1919 until his death.

LOWE, Anthony, OP (1881-1939). Educated at the Dominican school at Hinckley (1894-96), he entered the Order in 1898. Assigned to Newcastle in 1905, and to Leicester in 1907, in 1909 he was sent to Grenada, where he remained until 1919, except for a brief spell at Pendleton (1913-14). In 1923 he went to South Africa, but ill health brought him back again in 1924 and he was assigned to Leicester, moving to Newcastle in the following year and to Pendleton in 1926. In 1927 he returned to Grenada, but again ill health struck and he was sent to Woodchester in 1930 more or less on sick-leave. In 1933 he returned to work in Leicester, but in 1935 he became a complete invalid and was assigned once more to Woodchester. He died in a nursing home near Staines.

McCANN, Justin (1882-1959). Educated at Ampleforth (1895-1900), he entered the common noviciate of the English Benedictines at Belmont in 1900. Studied in Oxford at Hunter Blair's Hall, where he was a contemporary of BJ's, and obtained a first in Greats in 1907. He then returned to Ampleforth, where he taught in the school. After a brief period as curate in Liverpool (1919-20) he returned to Oxford as Master of St Benet's Hall (1920-47). He spent the rest of his life at Warrington, being made titular abbot of Westminster in 1949. It is said that, on one occasion, BJ found him in a state of considerable gloom, reading *The Imitation of Christ*; BJ seized the book from him and threw it in the fire. There is an obituary of him in *Ampleforth Journal* 64 (1959) pp. 129-133.

McCARTHY, James (1853-1943). Bishop of Galloway 1914-1943.

McCUSKERN, Wulstan, OP (1883-1962). Educated at the Dominican school at Hinckley and Hawkesyard (1896-1901), he joined the Order in 1901. After completing his studies, he was sent to Pendleton and then, in 1911, to London. Novice master at Woodchester 1914-21, then he went to Newcastle, where he was subprior 1922-23. Prior of London 1923-32. In January 1933 he was appointed student master at Oxford, and he was subprior there 1933-36. Prior of Pendleton 1936-39, after which he was assigned to Woodchester and became chaplain to the Dominican sisters at Stinchcombe. Prior of Woodchester 1941-44, then chaplain to the Sisters of Charity in Woodchester Park for a few years. He retired to Woodchester and stayed there until his death. He was made a Preacher General in 1946.

McDONALD, Andrew Joseph (1871-1950). Monk of Fort Augustus, where he was abbot 1919-29. Archbishop of St Andrews and Edinburgh 1929-50. BJ said of him, 'He's been such a prefect friend to us' (Letter of 11 March 1931 to Thomas Garde in Rome, AGOP XIII 65105).

McGLYNN, Patrick (died 1973, aged 81). He took his MA in Glasgow University in 1913, and was appointed a lecturer in Humanity in 1919, against considerable opposition, caused by his being a Catholic, as was the head of the department, Prof.John Swinnerton Phillimore (1873-1926). He taught Latin at Glasgow until his retirement in 1957.

McINTYRE, John (1855-1934). Professor at Oscott College 1880-1912, and canon theologian from 1900. Auxiliary to the archbishop of Birmingham 1912-14 and 1917-21, being Rector of the Beda College, Rome, in between (1914-17). Archbishop of Birmingham 1921-28, when he retired. He was a consultor of the Biblical Commission in Rome. Philip Hughes includes him in his trio of prelates who were preachers 'well beyond the average of good preaching' (Beck, *The English Catholics* p. 193).

MACKEY, Peter Paul, OP (1851-1935). Entered the Order in 1871, and was sent to study theology in Louvain in 1874. Having obtained his lectorate, he returned to England in 1880 and was appointed to teach philosophy and canon law at Woodchester, but in 1881, on the recommendation of his teachers in Louvain, he was sent for to join the Leonine Commission in Rome, where he spent the rest of his life, engaged in the edition of the works of St Thomas. One of his main contributions was the study of St Thomas' autograph of the *Contra Gentiles*. For the last five years of his life he was given the title of President of the Leonine Commission. In 1892 he was awarded the STM. In 1909-10 he also taught archaeology at the Angelicum.

McMAHON, Joseph Henry (1862-1939). Ordained priest in 1886, he was stationed at St Patrick's Cathedral, New York, where he pioneered the development of the Cathedral Free Circulating Library, which became the best Catholic library in the country; it was merged in 1904 with the New York City Public Library. In 1892 he also pioneered the Catholic Summer School of America. In 1901 he founded Our Lady of Lourdes parish in Washington Heights, New York, of which he remained pastor until his death. He invited a succession of English preachers, including several Dominicans, to visit his parish to give series of conferences during Lent; one of these preachers was BJ, who went there several times.

McNABB, Vincent, OP (1868-1943). Born in Northern Ireland, he entered the Order at Woodchester in 1885. He studied for the lectorate in Louvain (1891-94) and then taught at Woodchester (1894-97), Hawkesyard (1897-1900) and Woodchester again (1900-1906), after which he was sent to London. In 1908 he became prior of Leicester, where he remained until 1914, when he became prior of Hawkesyard and resumed his teaching there. Although his term of office as prior finished in 1917, he continued his work as a lector there until 1920, when he returned to London, where he was assigned for the rest of his life. In 1910 he passed the examination for the STM, which he was awarded in 1916. In London he became one of the most famous preachers of his generation. He was the author of a great many books. Cf. Ferdinand Valentine, *Father Vincent McNabb*, London 1955.

MacNAMARA, Richard (1875-1915). Educated at the Dominican school at Hinckley (1890-94), he joined the Dominican Order in 1894 and studied at Woodchester (1895-96) and Hawkesyard (1896-1900). He was then assigned to Newcastle for a few years and then, briefly, to Pendleton. In 1905 he was sent to teach at the school at Hawkesyard. From 1909 onwards he was a missioner, assigned to Hawkesyard, though no longer teaching at the school. In 1910 he fell ill and went to his mother's house in Leicester, where he remained, without leave from his superiors. After consultation with Rome, the provincial three times summoned him to return and, when he refused to comply, suspended him from priestly functions. In December his mother sued him for the costs of his board and lodging, and in his defence he alleged that the province was responsible for his upkeep, a plea which was not accepted by the court, since he was absent without permission from his priory. The provincial then initiated moves to have him expelled from the Order. In 1911 he was told to find some bishop to accept him as a secular priest, having asked to be secularised; but the process of secularisation did not go through. In May 1912 he was given permission to live outside the Order for a year, and this was renewed for another year in February 1913, together with absolution from all censures incurred, on condition that he found a bishop to accept him. He was accepted by the archbishop of Vancouver, but quickly fell into new trouble there, and in July 1913 he was asked to go elsewhere. He seems to have gone first to New Zealand, and then to Australia, where he was found dead in the desert early in 1915. He had apparently been quite destitute and died of thirst.

MANNING, Henry Edward (1808-1892). Educated at Harrow and Balliol College, Oxford. Fellow of Merton College, Oxford, 1832-33. Ordained in the Church of England, in 1833 he became rector of Lavington and married Caroline Sargent, his predecessor's daughter. His wife died 1837. In 1841 he became archdeacon of Chichester. Received into the Catholic church in 1851, he became provost of Westminster in 1857 and archbishop of Westminster in 1865, in which capacity he attended the first Vatican Council (1869-70), where he strongly supported the definition of papal infallibility. Made a cardinal in 1875. He was opposed to Catholics attending British universities. He was famous for his active and effective social concern.

MARTINDALE, Cyril Charles, SJ (1879-1963). Received into the Catholic church in 1897, he joined the Society in the same year. Studied at the Jesuit Hall in Oxford 1901-1905. He was a distinguished author, broadcaster, retreat-giver and teacher. Based in London from 1927 onwards, he travelled widely throughout the world until he retired to the retreat house at Petworth in 1953. Among his many writings are included several popular, though serious, saints' lives.

MEAGHER, Raymund, OP (1872-1954). Entered the New York province in 1888. First prior of St Antoninus, Newark, in 1906, but later in the same year he became prior of St Vincent Ferrer, New York. Prior of Washington 1910-1913. Provincial 1913-30. As provincial, he presided at the Requiem mass for Eleonora Duse on 1 May 1924. After finishing his fourth term as provincial, he was parish priest of Memphis until 1939, and spent the rest of his life in Washington.

MEDICI, Cosimo de' (1389-1464). The first of the Medici 'dynasty' that effectivley governed Florence for centuries. He was an important patron of the arts, and his generosity was responsible for some spectacular architectural achievements in the city. He provided the funds for the restoration of the church and convent of San Marco, famous for its frescoes by Fra Angelico and for the preaching of Savonarola. He also secured possession of a large library for it, which has been described as 'the first public library in Europe' (R. Morçay, *Saint Antonin*, Paris 1914, p.78).

MICHELANGELO BUONARROTI (1475-1564). Major Italian artist and sculptor, also a poet. From c.1537 until her death, he was much influenced by the religious ideas of Vittoria Colonna.

MOORE, Leo, OP (1870-1953). Joined the Order in 1890. He studied in Louvain, where he was awarded the lectorate, returning to the province in 1897, when he was sent to Woodchester. Taught philosophy at Woodchester 1897-1907, having BJ as his student in 1899-1900. After that he became bursar at Newcastle. Novice master at Woodchester 1908-10. Lecturer and student master at Hawkesyard 1910-14. He was appointed Vicar Provincial in Grenada in 1915, but soon returned to England, where he became subprior of Leicester in 1917 and then prior of Pendleton in 1919 and prior of Hawkesyard 1921-24 (during which time he resumed his teaching in the studium). He was then moved to Stroud, where he was superior 1924-29. He spent the rest of his working life in London, and retired in 1940 to Hawkesyard.

MORRIS, Lady Isabel (died 1934). Daughter of Wellmein William Le Gallais (1833-1869), who was born in Jersey but emigrated to Newfoundland, where he was ordained in the Anglican church in 1859. He was an energetic missionary in true Tractarian style and died tragically at sea in 1869. Isabel married Edward Patrick Morris (1859-1935) in 1901, having previously become a Catholic. He was one of the most notable politicians in Newfoundland, of which he was prime minister 1909-1918. He was knighted in 1901 and created the 1st Baron Morris in 1918. Thereafter they lived in Hampstead, London.

MORRISON, Mary Anthony, OP (1887-1952). Born in Newcastle in the Dominican parish, she was only 7 when she first wanted to be a nun. Laurence Shapcote introduced her to Emmie (later Sr Agatha) Kane, and the two of them entered Carisbrooke together in 1908, making profession there the following year. Sr Anthony inherited her father's business sense and she was made assistant bursar in 1913 and thereafter, in one capacity or another, she was responsible for the temporalities of Carisbrooke for most of her life.

MOSS, Raphael, OP (1863-1945). Joined the Order in 1883. He studied at Louvain 1884-90, though his studies were interrupted by ill health. He obtained the lectorate in 1890, and then taught at Woodchester 1890-94. He knew BJ as a very small boy. After spending some years in London, he returned to teaching in 1901, when he was elected prior of Hawkesyard; he was prior and lector primarius there until 1904 (with BJ among his students). After a year at Pendleton, he did another year of teaching at Hawkesyard 1905-1906, then returned to Pendleton. In 1908 he was assigned to Newcastle, and two years later he went to Woodchester again, where he was prior 1911-14. Then he was sent to Leicester. In 1916 he was appointed Vicar Provincial in Grenada, a position he retained until 1921, when he was brought back home after complaints about him in Grenada. He asked to go to South Africa, thinking the climate would suit him, but he was unhappy and unwell there and came back to England in 1924. He returned to Grenada 1925-38. In 1935 he was made an MBE. After two years in Hinckley, in 1941 he was assigned to Woodchester. He died in a nursing home in Bristol. He was a remarkable 'Victorian' preacher and there are many manuscript sermons of his in the provincial archives.

MYERS, Edward (1875-1956). Ordained priest in 1902, he was president of St Edmund's College, Ware, 1918-1932. In 1932 he was consecrated to be auxiliary bishop of Westminster, a position he retained until 1951, when he was made coadjutor archbishop.

NAYLOR, George, OP (1878-1927). Received into the Catholic church by Wilfrid Lescher at Holy Cross, Leicester, he went to the Dominican school at Hinckley and then Hawkesyard 1897-1900 and joined the Order in 1900. After completing his studies he was sent to Leicester, and then worked in Grenada 1909-13. He was then assigned to Pendleton. In 1916 he was commissioned as an army chaplain, after which, in 1919, he went to South Africa. Returning to England in 1922, he was assigned to Stroud, but shortly afterwards became chaplain at Errwood Hall, Derbyshire, where he remained until his death. In 1927 he asked to become a naval chaplain, but nothing came of it.

NEWMAN, John Henry (1801-1890). Having been one of the leaders of the Catholic revival within Anglicanism, in 1845 he was received into the Catholic church by Dominic Barberi. After being ordained priest in Rome, he established the Birmingham Oratory in 1849. His theological beliefs, nurtured more on the patristic tradition than on contemporary scholastic manuals, struck a somewhat controversial note in the church of his time, but he was made a cardinal by Leo XIII in 1879 as a gesture of appreciation, and he is now regarded as one of the most important theologians of his century.

NILAND, Mary Rose, OP (1860-1947). Foundress of the Dominican Congregation of St Catherine of Siena, Newcastle, Natal. Born to Irish parents in South Africa, she was educated by the Irish Dominican sisters in Port Elizabeth. In 1880 she entered the Dominican convent at Kingwilliamstown. In 1890 the convent of Oakford, Natal, founded the previous year, became independent of Kingwilliamstown and Sr Rose joined it, and in 1892 she was sent to open a house in Newcastle, Natal. When the Oakford sisters wished to withdraw, Sr Rose and five others remained and in 1893 she was appointed superior there. Thus began the new Congregation of Newcastle. In the following years houses were founded in Europe as well as in South Africa, and in 1926 Sr Rose acquired the property in Bushey, England, which became the mother house of the Congregation. She remained Superior General until 1947. She died just two months after the General Chapter at which she retired from office.

NOLAN, Louis, OP (1878-1944). Entered the Order in Ireland in 1900, but spent most of his religious life in Rome. Prior of San Clemente, Rome, 1912—18. In 1920 he became a consultant of the Sacred Congregation for Religious, a position he retained for many years and to which he devoted much of his time and energy. As prior of the Angelicum (1928-31) he supervised its move to its present site. He was the Master General's assistant for the English-speaking provinces 1923-29. In 1939 he was appointed provincial of Malta, a position to which he was later re-elected, and he died in office.

O'BRIEN, Daniel (1860-1937). Educated at Maynooth, he was ordained for the diocese of Killaloe in 1888, but then transferred to Galloway, where he was administrator of the cathedral 1893-1936, Vicar General 1906-36, and provost 1927-36. He was made a canon in 1908, and protonotary apostolic in 1923. He retired in 1936.

O'CONNOR, Mary Raymond, OP (1882-1943). A graduate of the Dominican Convent Upper School, San Rafael, California, in 1903 she entered the convent and became a teacher. In 1914 she was elected prioress, and in 1919 she was one of the foundresses of the Dominican College of San Rafael, of which she was president 1920-35. In 1929 she became Prioress General of the Congregation of San Rafael, a position from which she resigned only shortly before her death.

O'GORMAN, Eustace, OP (1884-1935). Educated at Hawkesyard School (1899-1903), he joined the Order in 1903. He was assigned to London in 1911, being appointed socius to BJ (the other representative of the London community) for the Provincial Chapter of 1916, which elected BJ provincial. In 1919-21 he was prior of Hawkesyard, then he was made novice master at Woodchester, though Humbert Everest advised BJ, 'I feel it is a grave step to shut Eustace up in the noviciate', and expressed his regret 'that Eustace cannot be left free for a more public career' (Letter to BJ, 18 May 1921). In the outcome he remained novice master until 1932 and was perhaps the most successful novice master the province has had this century. In 1932 he was sent to Oxford as student master, but in 1933 he became prior of London on 20 January. On 2 April he resigned because of ill health. He was taken to hospital after a serious heart attack at Christmas 1934 and died on 23 June 1935.

OLDMEADOW, Ernest (1867-1949). A convert to Catholicism. Editor of *The Tablet* 1923-36, a position he used as a platform for the rather magisterial style of controversy he enjoyed. In 1933 he published a virulent denunciation of Evelyn Waugh's *Black Mischief*, which was itself attacked in a letter whose signatories include BJ and Fathers D'Arcy, Martindale and Steuart SJ (cf. Martin Stannard, *Evelyn Waugh, The Early Years 1903-1939*, London 1986, pp. 336-338).

O'LEARY, Augustine (1869-1937). Ordained for the diocese of Westminster in 1898, in 1909 he transferred to the diocese of Southwark. Parish priest of Woolwich 1915-34. His mother, Mary Emily, was the sister of Thomas Laws OP.

O'NEILL, Herbert Charles (Hilary) (1879-1953). Joined the Dominican Order in April 1899 and received the name of Hilary. Because of ill health he was ordained a year early, in December 1903, and was sent to Pendleton, where he became a student at Manchester University. In 1906 he left the Order and married. In 1910 he initiated moves to regularise his position, and he was reconciled to the church by BJ. He had a distinguished career as a journalist and was assistant editor of *The Westminster Gazette* and then of *The Observer*. He retained a life long admiration for BJ.

O'RILEY, Bernard Cornelius (1868-1956). Born in Cape Town, he became Vicar Apostolic there in 1925, and was consecrated bishop in 1926. He was Vicar Apostolic for about seven years, after which he retired, though he continued to live in Cape Town.

PAGNINI, Santes, OP (1470-1536). Entered the Order in Fiesole in 1487. After studying in Bologna he returned to Fiesole and devoted himself to biblical and oriental studies, under the influence of Savonarola. From 1502-1519 he was constantly in demand as a superior and was Vicar General of the Congregation of San Marco 1508-10. He was noted for his preaching and for his pastoral concerns, but he was above all a scholar. He wrote several important works of philology, but his main work was a complete new Latin translation of the bible, from the original languages, the first such translation since that of St Jerome. Much of his time, after his last term of office as prior, was devoted to getting this translation published. In 1525 he was allowed to move to France, and in 1527 he settled in Lyons where, in 1528, his bible was published at last. It was the first bible in which the verses of each chapter were numbered in the modern fashion. Cf. I. Taurisano, *I Domenicani in Lucca,* Lucca 1914, pp. 94-111; T. M. Centi, *Archivum Fratrum Praediocatorum* 15 (1945) pp. 5-51. Pagnini was one of the theologians who supported Henry VIII in his attempt to get his marriage with Catherine of Aragon annulled (cf. G. Bedouelle and P. le Gal, edd., *Le 'Divorce' du Roi Henry VIII,* Geneva 1987, pp. 393-394).

PALMER, Raymund, OP (1819-1900). Received into the Catholic church in 1842, he went to Hinckley as a postulant in 1853 and then to Woodchester in 1854, where he received the habit in 1855. After ordination, he was librarian and bursar at Woodchester until 1866, when he was sent to London; in 1867 he joined the newly established priory at Haverstock Hill, London. During 1881-82 he worked on the Leonine Commission in Rome, then he returned to London, where he remained assigned until his death, being provincial archivist until 1898. He was also provincial bursar 1884-94. His main work throughout his Dominican life was the study of the history of the province, on which he published innumerable articles. In recognition of his achievements, he was awarded the STM in 1898.

PAREDES, Bonaventura Garcia, OP (1866-1936). Joined the Rosary province at Ocaña, Spain, in 1883. After his ecclesiastical studies there and at Avila and Salamanca, he went to university in Valencia and in Madrid. Then, in 1898, he was sent to teach at the Dominican university of St Thomas in Manila. In 1901 he was recalled to Spain to be rector of the Dominican college in Avila. In 1910 he was elected prior of Ocaña and then, very shortly afterwards, provincial, a position he retained until 1917. He was then put in charge of a new house being founded by the province in Madrid, of which he became superior. On 22 May 1926 the General Chapter at Ocaña (at which BJ was present) elected him Master General (BJ got two votes in this election). In 1929 he was forced to resign, and he retired to Ocaña.

On the outbreak of the Civil War he fled to Madrid, and there he was murdered by the Communists on 12 August 1936.

PARKER, Leonard (1902-1972). Cousin of George Bellord. Was at school at Downside 1912-20 and then went up to Trinity College, Oxford, where he graduated in 1924 in Law. He was called to the Bar in the Inner Temple. He married in 1928 and then joined Watneys. During the second World War he served in the RAF, and then returned to his firm. He retired in 1962. In 1934 he wrote to John Baptist Reeves, enclosing some of the letters he had received from BJ, which he said 'are all that remains of the most wonderful friendship I could ever experience.' 'Father Bede' he said, 'wrote to me practically every week of my life from 1919 up to within a few weeks of his death.'

PATER, Walter Horatio (1839-1894). Author and critic. Fellow of Brasenose College, Oxford. Of *Marius the Epicurean* Edmund Gosse wrote, 'Modern humanism has produced no more admirable product than this noble dream of a pursuit through life of the spirit of heavenly beauty' (*Dictionary of National Biography* XV p. 459). He died at his house, 64 St Giles, Oxford, on the site of the present priory of Blackfriars.

PEACH, Laurence, OP (1845-1919). Educated at the Dominican school at Hinckley (1859-60), he joined the Order in 1860. He was ordained at Downside in 1869, then returned to Woodchester. In 1870 he was sent to Littlehampton, in 1871 to Hinckley and in 1872 to Stroud and then to Stoke. In 1881 he was assigned to London. In 1884 he went to Newcastle as prior, remaining there after the end of his term of office in 1887. In 1895 he was appointed to Stroud. Prior of London 1902-1908 and of Woodchester 1908-11, when he returned to Stroud. He was provincial bursar almost continuously from 1902 until 1919. He was made a Preacher General in 1912. In 1914 he went to Carisbrooke to be chaplain to the nuns, and there he died.

PICKERING, Silvester, OP (1891-1965). Educated at the Dominican school at Hawkesyard (1908-1909), he joined the Order in 1909. In the course of his third year of studies at Hawkesyard (1912-13) he had a serious mental breakdown and spent the rest of his life in hospital.

PIKE, Bertrand, OP (1884-1954). Joined the Order in 1905. He spent most of his life working, very successfully, in the parish in London (1914-16, 1918-28, 1935-40, 1944-54). In 1916 he was commissioned as an army chaplain, and he was taken prisoner during the war. In 1928 he was appointed headmaster at Laxton, and in

1932, on BJ's recommendation, he was made Vicar Provincial in South Africa. He was parish priest of Woodchester 1940-44. The church in London was unable to accommodate all those who came to his funeral.

PLATER, Charles Dominic, SJ (1875-1921). Entered the Society in 1894. Master of the Jesuit Hall in Oxford (Plater's Hall) 1917-21. He was instrumental in launching the Catholic Social Guild in 1909. Cf. C. C. Martindale, *Charles Dominic Plater SJ,* London 1922.

POPE, Hugh, OP (1869-1946). Son of Thomas Vercoe Pope, a master at the Oratory School in Birmingham, where he himself was educated. He started to train as a doctor, but joined the Order in 1891. After obtaining his lectorate at Louvain (1896-98), he taught scripture at Hawkesyard. He gained the licentiate, then the doctorate in Sacred Scripture in Rome (1908, 1909). Taught scripture at the Angelicum, Rome, 1909-13. He was awarded the STM in 1911. In 1913 he was accused of modernism and removed from his post in Rome; he returned to England. After six years as prior of Woodchester (1914-20), he was appointed Regent of Studies at Hawkesyard in 1920. When theological studies in the province were transferred to Oxford in 1929, he went too, continuing to be Regent. In 1932 Master General Gillet relieved him of his post, commenting in his letter to him, 'If today the province of England is distinguished for its intellectual life, that is due in large part to your example and your unwearying tenacity as a professor and as Regent' (letter of 25 September 1932). Returning to Hawkesyard, he was prior there 1935-41. In 1942 he became superior of Edinburgh. He was one of the founders and perhaps the chief inspiration of the Catholic Evidence Guild. Cf. K. Mulvey, *Hugh Pope,* London 1954.

POWELL, Edward (1837-1901). Born in Liverpool, he was ordained in Rome in 1862, and became secretary to the bishop of Liverpool. Parish priest of St Alexander, Bootle, 1866-85, then of Lydiate 1885-1901.

PROCTER, John, OP (1849-1911). Born at Pendleton, he went to Hinckley School 1863-66, and joined the Order in 1866. His uncle was Augustine Procter OP (1797-1867). After finishing his studies in London, he was ordained in 1872 and sent to Louvain, where he obtained the lectorate in 1874. He then worked in London until 1878, then in Newcastle, where he became superior in 1880. In 1882 he returned to London as a missioner. Elected prior of Leicester in 1885, he resigned in 1887 and returned to London and to his preaching work. Prior of London 1888-94. Provincial 1894-1902. During his second term of office as provincial, the first foreign mission of the province was started in Grenada, West Indies. In 1902 Master General Cormier made him an STM. In 1903 he was sent to California as visitor, and on his return to London he resumed his work as a missioner. In 1907 he became superior of Hinckley and, on Shapcote's resignation as provincial, vicar of the province. In October he was elected prior of Hawkesyard and in November he became provincial again. He died in office as provincial.

RAFFALOVICH, Marc André Sebastian (1864-1934). Convert to Catholicism. A connoisseur in many fields. He provided the initial funds to build a church in honour of St Sebastian at Pendleton, and was a signal benefactor of the province. He was a friend of Canon Gray and the two of them did all they could to secure a Dominican presence in Scotland.

RAMSAY, Henry Leander (1863-1929). An Anglican clergyman, who became a Catholic in 1896. In 1897 he entered the noviciate at Belmont, at that time the common noviciate of the English Benedictine Congregation, as a monk of Downside. Head Master of Downside 1902-18. He retired from the headmastership with what was diagnosed as terminal cancer, and busied himself with editing the works of St Cyprian. But he survived to become abbot in 1922. There is a memoir by Dom Roger Hudleston in *Downside Review* 47 (1929) pp. 99-122.

READER, Peter, OP (1850-1929). Converted to Catholicism as a boy, he took his degree at Merton College, Oxford, and then went to Rome to undertake clerical studies. He joined the Order at Woodchester in 1876. Ordained in 1878, he immediately transferred to the Carthusians at Parkminster, but he soon returned to Woodchester, where he made his solemn profession in 1881. After brief assignments to London and Leicester, he was back at Woodchester in 1884. In 1888 he was sent to London again. In 1893 he was appointed moderator of studies at the Dominican school at Hinckley. He was re-assigned to Leicester in 1896, returning to the school in 1898, going with the school later in the year to Hawkesyard. In 1902 he went to Woodchester and in 1904 to Leicester again. In 1915 he became director of the school at Hawkesyard. In 1924, when the school went to Laxton, he went to Hinckley, being moved to Stroud in 1925 and back to Hinckley in 1926. He was a highly competent and meticulous botanist, and published a detailed catalogue of the plants found on the estate at Hawkesyard in the Transactions of the North Staffordshire Field Club, vols. 57 (1923) pp. 105-117 and 60 (1926) pp. 118-132. His botanical collection was presented to the Bristol Museum.

REEVES, John Baptist, OP (1888-1976). Joined the Order in 1912. He was a well-known preacher and lecturer, with a brilliant mind and a fertile imagination, but, apart from a first in classics at London University before he entered the Order, he was not an academic success. He abandoned his lectorate in 1919, because of ill health, and was assigned to London. In 1921 he was one of the first brethren to move to Oxford and in 1922 he matriculated to work for a B.Litt, but he failed to satisfy the examiners in 1924. He then returned to Hawkesyard to resume working for the lectorate, but once again nothing came of it. After teaching there for a year, he returned to Oxford. In January 1929 he was assigned to London. Then began a period of considerable difficulties in faith, in which he was much supported by BJ. After BJ's death he wrote a biography of him, which the censors rejected when it was completed in 1936. A time spent with his old novice master, Hyacinth Koos, at Woodchester apparently enabled him to come to terms with life. He was superior of Cambridge 1939-45 and then prior of London 1945-47, after which he went to South Africa. In 1952 he went to Edinburgh, where he was superior 1953-59. After two years at Hawkesyard, he became the first superior of the new house in Manchester, founded after the closure of Pendleton; he retained this position until 1967, when he resigned and effectively retired from active life, in protest against 'the changes'. From being something of an enfant terrible in his younger days, he became a pillar of correctness and conservatism in his old age, though he never abandoned his intellectual independence.

RICE, Cyprian, OP (1889-1966). Born at Woodchester, where his father was the Baptist minister. After leaving school, he joined the Levant Consular Service and was sent to Cambridge to study Arabic, Persian and Turkish. While there he became a Catholic. He entered the Order in 1919 and obtained his lectorate in 1927. He was then assigned to Iraq by the Master General, and in 1929 he went to Teheran, where he remained for three years. In 1933 he was sent back to Persia, where the English province was trying to establish a mission, but the project was thwarted by the Persian government and the local ecclesiastical authorities, and he returned to England in 1934 and spent several years doing parish work, in Newcastle up to 1938, and then in London until 1941, when he became parish priest of Stroud. After being superior there for three years he returned to Newcastle. In 1947 he was sent to the Dominican Oriental Institute in Cairo, and in 1950 to the Angelicum, Rome. After only a year there he was brought back to the province, where he taught Greek for a while at Hawkesyard, then worked in Pendleton for a few months, and then went to Leicester. In 1956 he returned to Rome, where he spent the next ten years as a penitentiary at S. Maria Maggiore. He returned to England in bad health in 1966 and died shortly afterwards.

RIGBY, Ethelbert (John) (1882-1965). Joined the Dominican Order at Woodchester in 1902. After finishing his studies at Hawkesyard in 1908, he went to Louvain, where he obtained his lectorate in 1909, and then to Rome, where he obtained a doctorate in canon law in 1912. Taught canon law at Hawkesyard 1912-15, when he became an army chaplain. After the war he returned to Hawkesyard and became bursar, but he never resumed his teaching. In 1922 he left the Order and was laicised.

RIGBY, Jerome OP (1884-1948). Born in St Dominic's parish, London, he was educated at Hawkesyard School (1898-1902) and joined the Order in 1902. He was Ethelbert Rigby's brother. In 1910 he became the first person to be examined for the lectorate at Hawkesyard. All his life as a priest he spent teaching in the Dominican school, first at Hawkesyard, then at Laxton. He was a friend of BJ, of whom he wrote in 1934, 'He will remain the greatest personality we have known and a man of singularly rare virtue and attractiveness.'

ROLLE, Richard (c.1300-1349). An eloquent English spiritual writer, both in Latin and in the vernacular; although his doctrines have aroused controversy from his own time until ours, his influence on late medieval piety was considerable.

RUTHERFORD, Anselm (1886-1952). A convert to Catholicism, he joined Downside in 1909, after studying at Cambridge. He had a distinguished and varied career as prior of Worth, prior of Fort Augustus and, from 1934-39, Head Master of Downside School.

RUTTEN, Ceslaus, OP (1875-1952). Entered the Belgian province in 1890 and acquired his lectorate in 1899 and a doctorate in social sciences at Louvain in 1900. He devoted his whole life, until sickness finally forced him to rest, to teaching and to social action. In 1934 he inaugurated a new Chair at Louvain to expound the church's social teaching. In 1904 he laid the foundation for the Algemeen Christelijk Vakverbund, which attracted a large following of workers. In his obituary (*Analecta S.O.P.* 30 (1951-52) pp. 366-367) he is described as having been 'truly the founder of Christian democracy in Belgium'.

RYAN, Finbar, OP (1882-1975). Joined the Irish province in 1899, and went to study in Rome in 1902. He returned to Ireland in 1906 and was assigned to teach at Newbridge. In 1908 he went to Dublin, where he was prior 1916-19. As well as being much in demand as a preacher, he edited *The Irish Rosary* 1911-20 and launched a new periodical for school children, *The Imeldist,* which was a remarkable success. Elected prior of Cork in 1920, he became provincial in 1921 and remained in office until 1926. He was re-elected provincial 1930-34. In 1937 he was consecrated archbishop, to serve as coadjutor to the archbishop of Port of Spain, Trinidad, to which see he succeeded in 1940. He retired in 1966 and spent his last years in Cork.

ST JOHN, Henry, OP (1891-1973). Son of an Anglican parson, he became a parson himself, but in 1917, after several discussions with Vincent McNabb at Hawkesyard, he was received into the Catholic church by Paulinus Sweeney. He joined the Order in 1919. From 1927-54 he was a schoolmaster, first at Laxton, where he was headmaster from 1932, then at the new preparatory school at Llanarth from 1948. In 1954 he became student master at Hawkesyard. Provincial 1958-62. After spending some time as chaplain at Carisbrooke, he passed his last six years at Cambridge. Throughout his life he had a passionate interest in ecumenism (which he tried, with limited success, to pronounce with the accent on the first syllable). Cf. Henry St John, *Essays in Christian Unity,* London 1966, pp. xi-xix.

SALES, Marco, OP (1877-1936). Entered the province of S. Pietro, Turin, in 1892. Taught at the Angelicum 1909-11 and at Fribourg 1912-25. In 1925 he was appointed Master of the Sacred Palace.

SARGENT, Dunstan, OP (1879-1956). Educated at Ushaw, he was a soldier in the Boer War, then joined the Order in 1906. He worked on the parish in London for a year after his ordination, then, in 1913, was sent to Grenada. Returning to England in 1917, his boat was torpedoed and he was lucky to escape. In 1917 he was commissioned as an army chaplain. In 1922 he was assigned to Leicester, and in 1926 became prior of Newcastle. Parish priest of Stroud 1929-34. He then worked as a missioner, based at Leicester, until in 1938 he was sent to Multan in what is now Pakistan. In 1947 he was assigned to Pendleton, and in 1950 to Newcastle. He died in hospital at Milford-on-Sea. In 1925 he was made a fellow of the Royal Geographical Society.

SAVIELLE, Margaret A. (died 1949, aged 73). A lonely soul, who confided in BJ and treasured the many letters he sent to her. She was a Friend of Blackfriars. She lived for many years at Sion Convent in London.

SAVONAROLA, Girolamo, OP (1452-1498). Entered the Order in 1475 in Bologna. In 1482 he was appointed lector in San Marco,

Florence; in 1487–88 he was Master of Studies in Bologna. In 1490 he was re-appointed lector at San Marco, where he became prior in 1491. Dissatisfied with the reform already achieved in the Order, he secured in 1493 the separation of San Marco from the Congregation of Lombardy, thus launching the new, doubly reformed, Congregation of San Marco, of which he became Vicar General. Other priories, beginning with Fiesole, continued to be added to this Congregation until 1496, in spite of an attempt by Alexander VI to return San Marco to the Congregation of Lombardy in 1495, and another attempt, in 1496, to absorb San Marco into a new and larger Congregation, in which Savonarola's influence would be less. As an educator he stressed the importance of scripture, studied in the original languages. He wanted to create a christian culture, in opposition to the 'pagan' culture of the humanists, though he continued to enjoy a paradoxical friendship with some of the leading humanists in Florence. From about 1490 he adopted an apocalyptic style of preaching, claiming the authority of divine revelations, in the light of which he announced an impending divine judgment on the corruptions of the church and of society. This prophetic stance, and the reforming activity that followed from it, won him the increasing hostility of Alexander VI and eventually he was arrested and condemned for schism and heresy and was hanged and burned on 23 May 1498. Controversy still rages as to whether he was a saint and a prophet or a fanatic and trouble-maker. In 1895 John Procter published an article in *The Catholic Times* (3 May) to show that he was a good Catholic, against Dean Farrar's claim that he was a forerunner of the Protestant reformation, and this article was soon reprinted as a pamphlet. *The Dominican Savonarola and the Reformation,* and in 1896 it was published in Italian translation. Towards the end of his life, BJ was hoping to translate and publish some of Savonarola's letters.

SHAPCOTE, Laurence, OP (1864–1947). Born in the Orange Free State, South Africa, the son of an Anglican parson, he was received into the Catholic church, with his mother, in 1866, after the family's return to England. His father became a Catholic in 1868 and was for many years assistant editor of *The Tablet*. His mother published several volumes of verse. He entered the Order at Saint-Maximin, in the province of Toulouse, in 1880, but almost at once the community had to seek refuge in Salamanca from the persecution of religious by the French government. In 1884 he transfiliated to the English province and was sent to finish his theological studies at Louvain, where he obtained the lectorate in 1888. Taught at Woodchester 1889–90 and 1891–1900, spending a year teaching at Hinckley School in between. He then taught at Hawkesyard and was lector primarius there 1900-1901 (with BJ among his students). In 1901 he was elected prior of Newcastle and in 1902 he became provincial. Re-elected in 1906, in 1907 he went to Rome and resigned, returning later in the year to Hawkesyard, where he taught in the studium 1907-14 and was prior 1913-14. In 1914 he became prior of Leicester, resigning in 1917 to pioneer the English Dominican mission in South Africa, where he remained until 1946. In 1907 he was one of the people involved in plans for an English translation of the *Summa Theologiae* and in 1910 he was officially appointed to be one of the translators. Shortly afterwards he was appointed editor. From 1919 onwards he was the sole translator, and in addition he translated several other works of St Thomas. The English *Summa* was published 1912-36.

SHAW, George P. (1876-1938). Ordained in 1899, after being educated at Blair's College and the Scots College, Valladolid. He died at Blair's College.

SHEED, Frank (1897-1981). Married Maisie Ward in 1926; together they started the publishing house of Sheed and Ward.

SHEPHERD, Robert Aloysius Eric (1892-1955). Matriculated at Easter 1910 as a non-Collegiate student in Oxford, then transferred to Christ Church in 1911, but left in 1913 without taking a degree. He was received into the Catholic church in Oxford in 1911 and took the name Aloysius. Published a book of religious poems, *The Blue Communion,* London 1912, and an edition of the religious poems of Richard Crashaw, London 1914.

SIMMONS, Mary Evangeline (1878-1946). Entered the Convent of Mercy at St John's Wood, London, in 1902. She trained as a nurse at the hospital run by the nuns there, Saints John and Elizabeth, and was matron there 1913-36. After she retired from active nursing, she was put in charge of the Trained Nurses Corporation, administered from the hospital.

SIXTUS OF SIENA, OP (1520-1569). A convert from Judaism, he became a Franciscan and fell under the influence of the controversial, self-taught Dominican theologian, Ambrosius Catharinus (1484-1553), though he later repudiated his views. He travelled widely as a preacher 1540-50, but was then stopped by the Inquisition, after he was accused of heresy. He readily abandoned the errors he was accused of, but then apparently fell into worse heresy and was condemned by the Inquisition. He was taken under the protection of the Dominican Commissary General of the Inquisition, however, Michele Ghislieri (later Pius V), who gave him a much more solid doctrinal education and clothed him personally in the Dominican habit. Thereafter Sixtus was himself employed by the Inquisition. In 1566 he published a large and very erudite introduction to scripture, *Bibliotheca Sancta,* a work which was long held in high esteem and was several times reprinted. See A. Mercati, *Rivista di Storia della Chiesa in Italia* 5 (1951) pp. 374-80; R. Galli, *Archivum Fratrum Praedicatorum* 44 (1974) pp. 93-98.

SMITH, Ambrose, OP (1841-1909). Received into the Catholic church in 1862, he entered the Order in 1865. After obtaining the lectorate in Louvain in 1872 he was appointed to teach at Woodchester, where he remained until 1887, teaching, at various times, philosophy, moral theology and dogmatic theology. At weekends he served several mission stations. From 1881-85 he walked to Cirencester every week. In 1887 he was made superior of the mission at St Patrick's, Leicester, where he stayed until 1894. After two and a half years in London, he became prior of Woodchester in 1897 and resumed his teaching there. It was he who gave BJ the habit in 1898, but he did not teach in 1899-1900, the year in which BJ was a student at Woodchester. In 1902 he was put in charge of the Dominican house and parish in Stroud, and in 1907 became prior of Hawkesyard, where he taught scripture almost up to the time of his death. In 1887 he was awarded the STM. He wrote an unfinished history of Pickering, Yorkshire, his birthplace.

SMITH, James A. (1841-1928). Bishop of Dunkeld 1890-1900; archbishop of St Andrews and Edinburgh 1900-1928.

SMITH, Oswald (1854-1924). Abbot of Ampleforth 1900-1924. He was a popular retreat-giver to nuns, though 'he had no special gift of oratory and was by nature an indifferent speaker', as the obituary in *Downside Review* 43 (1925) p. 55 observed.

SNOW, Alfred (1845-1922). Educated at Downside, he was ordained in 1873 for the diocese of Liverpool. Became a canon of Liverpool in 1901.

SPICQ, Ceslas, OP (born 1901). Joined the French province in 1920. After studying at the École Biblique, Jerusalem, he taught scripture at Le Saulchoir and, more recently, at Fribourg, where he still lives in retirement.

STEUART, Benedict (1880-1963). Professed as a monk of Fort Augustus, he later transferred to Caldey, where he became subprior in 1927. After the move to Prinknash he became prior there 1929-38. Later he moved to Farnborough Abbey.

STEUART, Robert, SJ (1874-1948). Entered the Society in 1893. Served at St Aloysius, Oxford, 1920-26, and thereafter in London. Author, preacher and retreat-giver. Cf. K. Kendall, *Father Steuart*, London 1950.

STOURTON, Elizabeth (1871-1945). A friend of the Blounts, who were the landlords of BJ's parents in East Grinstead, she knew BJ from the time he was a boy. She was the granddaughter of the 19th Baron Stourton (1802-1872), daughter of Albert Joseph Stourton (1835-1902). In 1917 she entered the Convent of Mercy at St John's Wood, London, attached to the hospital of Saints John and Elizabeth, where BJ died. Although she was not a nurse, she was present at his death. She is remembered as having been a tall, dignified lady, with great self-control, though always liable to exclaim 'How perfectly ghastly!' She was superior at St John's Wood 1930-33, after which she went to the nuns' 'rest house' at Hillingdon, where she was superior 1936-39.

SUFFIELD, Robert Rudolph (1821-1891). His father was a lapsed Catholic, but a relative had him baptised nonetheless, but he was later baptised formally as an Anglican. In 1843 he became a Catholic, and was ordained priest in 1850 for the diocese of Hexham. In 1860 he entered the Dominican Order. After his noviciate he served for a time in Woodchester, Littlehampton and Husbands Bosworth. In 1870, having been deeply troubled by the debates over papal authority surrounding the first Vatican Council, he became a Unitarian minister, first at Croydon, then at Reading.

SWABY, Alfred, OP (1869-1925). Joined the Oblates of St Charles, and was ordained in 1894. In 1918 he joined the Dominicans. In January 1920 he was assigned to Leicester, then to London in December of the same year. There he remained assigned until his death.

SWEENEY, Paulinus, OP (1879-1953). Joined the Order in 1902. Obtained the lectorate in Louvain in 1909 and then went to study social sciences at Fribourg. Returning in 1913 he went first to Woodchester, then taught at Hawkesyard 1914-20 and was pro-Regent of Studies 1916-20, and also student master 1914-20. Taught moral and pastoral theology at the Angelicum 1920-21, then returned to teaching and to being student master at Hawkesyard. BJ had scholarly ambitions for him, which were never realised. In 1927 he was moved to London, where he gave extension lectures for the university. In 1938 he was elected prior of Newcastle, and in 1941 he returned to London, with his health already seriously deteriorating.

SWETCHINE, Anne Sophie (1782-1857). A Russian convert to Catholicism. When her husband, General Nicholas Swetchine, fell from favour with the Czar, they moved to Paris in 1816. Her salon there attracted such Catholic intellectuals as Lacordaire.

SZABÓ, Sadoc, OP (1869-1956). Entered the Austro-Hungarian province in 1885. Provincial 1898-1906. In 1909 he was appointed first Regent of Studies at the newly created Angelicum in Rome and, apart from the first World War, he remained there as Regent and lecturer until 1927. At the 1926 General Chapter, at which Paredes was elected Master General, he had been considered a favourite candidate. Lecturer at Fribourg 1927-30. He was diffinitor for his province at the 1929 General Chapter. Provincial again 1930-34. Most of the rest of his life was spent in Hungary. He founded the periodical, *Angelicum*. Cf. *Analecta S.O.P.* 32 (1955-56) pp. 368-72.

TALBOT, Lady Edmund (Mary Caroline) (1859-1938). Eldest daughter of the 7th Earl of Abingdon, in 1879 she married Lord Edmund Talbot (1855-1947), who became 1st Viscount Fitzalan of Derwent in 1921. She was a Justice of the Peace for the county of London, and founder of the Catholic Social Union clubs for girls in London and Sheffield. Her husband was one of those present at the Little Oratory retreat in 1934 at which BJ collapsed after his first conference.

TAURISANO, Innocenzo, OP (1877-1960). Entered the Roman province in 1898. For nine years, from 1914, he was archivist of the Order and editor of *Analecta Sacri Ordinis Praedicatorum*. Throughout his life he wrote a great many books, articles and pamphlets on Dominican history.

TAYLEUR, Lilian (1869-1954). Daughter of James Scott Elliot of Dumfriesshire, Scotland, in 1897 she married Eric Tayleur, who served in the yeomanry in the South African war. She was a woman of great character. In her early married years she and her husband lived in southern Ireland and hunted with various packs of hounds. She was a fearless rider. In 1904 they bought the lease of Kirkconnel Lea in Dumfriesshire. In 1907 she started a Boys Club in Dumfries, mainly for football, and it was a great success, its members coming to be known as 'Tayleurians'. After her husband left her, she became a Catholic, as a result of an Irish Dominican mission in Dumfries. In 1913 she became a tertiary in Ireland. Her great hope was to see the Dominicans re-established in Scotland, and she wanted to give the Order her house to this end. She was generous to the point of being improvident, and reduced herself to poverty through her kindness to the Order; even so, she refused to realise some assets she had set aside to bequeathe to the Dominicans. In 1941 the English provincial council resolved to sell the lease of Kirkconnel Lea, which she had given to the province, and return the money to her.

TAYLOR, George, OP (1904-1975). Born in St Petersburg, he had a good working knowledge of Russian. He joined the Order in 1927 and, soon after his ordination in 1933, was sent to join a group of Dominicans in France, who were preparing to work in Russia with a view to re-establishing the Lithuanian province. In 1936, however, he was sent to Grenada instead. In 1940 he became a military chaplain. After the war he was assigned to Leicester, and in 1948 to Edinburgh, then, after a few months, to South Africa. He returned to London in 1956, then became novice master in 1958, but in 1959 he was assigned to Pendleton. In 1961 he went back to London, where he remained until his death, except for a year at Carisbrooke (1973-74).

THEISSLING, Ludovicus, OP (1856-1925). Entered the Order in Holland in 1873. Provincial of Holland 1896-1908. Master General 1916-25. As provincial, he paid a brief visit to Hawkesyard in 1903, while BJ was a student there. As Master General he visitated the province in 1922. When news came of his death, BJ wrote in the Provincial's Diary, 'A great loss, pious and genial, fatherly, with understanding and a very large heart.'

THOMAS AQUINAS, St, OP (1226-1274). The greatest and most influential medieval theologian. His masterpiece is the unfinished *Summa Theologiae,* a systematic introduction to the whole of theology. Cf. S. Tugwell, *Albert and Thomas,* New York 1988.

THOMPSON, Francis (1859-1907). The outstanding English Catholic poet of his age. Born in Preston, he studied for the priesthood, then medicine, but in 1885 he went to London, where he lived for a time in the utmost destitution, until his poetic gifts were discovered in 1888 by Wilfrid Meynell. His first volume of poems was published in 1893, including 'The Hound of Heaven'. In 1893-97 he stayed at the Franciscan friary of Pantasaph.

THOMSON, Lewis, OP (1845-1927). Went to the Dominican school at Hinckley in 1860 and entered the Order in 1861. He was assigned to London in 1871, but, falling ill, was sent to Stone, where he became parish priest in 1872. When the parish was surrendered to the diocese in 1878, he went to Hinckley, where he was superior until 1887, when he became prior of Leicester. In 1890 he returned briefly to Hinckley, but was then appointed to Newcastle. In 1901 he became superior of Hinckley again, and was prior of Newcastle 1904-1910.

He was then made superior of Stroud, but in 1911 he was elected prior of London. In 1914 he was assigned to Leicester. In 1915 he was appointed to the Provincial Council by the Master General. In 1916 he became parish priest at Byker. In 1918 he returned to Stroud, to be chaplain to the Dominican sisters, becoming superior as well in 1920. In 1924 he retired to London.

TICKELL, Benedict, OP (1844-1905). Educated at the Dominican school at Hinckley (1861-64), he then joined the Order in 1864. In 1867 he went to the newly established study house at St Dominic's, London, returning to Woodchester for his final year of theology 1870-71. In 1873 he was assigned to Leicester in February and then to Newcastle in November. In 1884 he returned to Woodchester as parish priest, and in 1889 went to Hinckley. In 1891 he was moved to London. Prior of Newcastle 1894-97, after which he went back to Leicester, from where he returned to London in 1899 to become rector of the Grammar School there. The winter decided him to take steps to move to a more benign climate, and he asked the Master General to authorise him to go to New Zealand, which he eventually did. He worked there for five years, even though at first he was only given permission for six months, dying there shortly before he was due to return to England.

TIGAR, Gilbert, OP (1861-1942). Entered the Order in 1888, after a spell working in the commercial department of the Board of Trade. After ordination he was sent to Hinckley, and then worked briefly in Newcastle and Leicester, before being assigned to London in 1898. In 1901 he was sent to Grenada. He was in New Zealand 1907-14, then came home and enrolled as an army chaplain in 1914. He was in South Africa 1919-25, then in Newcastle 1925-30 (where he was subprior from 1926). He manned the parish in Nympsfield, near Woodchester, 1930-32, then moved to Leicester, where he was subprior from 1935 until his death. In 1936 he was made a Preacher General.

TRELAWNY, Sir Harry, 7th Baronet (1756-1834). Ordained as an independent minister at twenty, he became an Anglican parson and was appointed to an Exeter prebend in 1789. He was converted to Catholicism in 1806 and, after the death of his wife, ordained in 1830. For many years he had hoped to be ordained as a married man.

TURVILLE, Carrington Francis (1689-1749). After he became a Catholic, he asked the Dominicans to supply a chaplain to his house at Aston Flamville, near Hinckley. The first Dominican priest to be sent in response arrived in 1734, and he established a wide-ranging mission there. After Turville's death, the mission was moved to Hinckley in 1765.

TYTUS, Charlotte Jefferson (died 1936, aged 86). Mrs Tytus was one of BJ's principal benefactors. She was an American widow, who had been received into the Catholic church in England. In 1917 she was clothed as a Dominican tertiary by BJ, taking the name of Benvenuta. She bought the site for the Oxford priory and continued to give large sums of money towards the building of it. She also made a donation to the Dominican house in Edinburgh. At the end of her life, her health deteriorated badly. Her funeral was held at St Dominic's, London.

VAN ZELLER, Hubert (Claud) (1905-1984). Born in Egypt, he went to school at Downside (1914-23). After working for a short time in Liverpool, he joined the monastery in 1924. He was a prolific writer and sculptor, and was also in demand as a retreat-giver. He wrote three loosely autobiographical works: *Family Case Book*, London 1951; *Willingly to School*, London 1952; *One Foot in the Cradle*, London 1965. He was profoundly influenced by BJ, and kept letters which he had received from him over many years. He later gave these letters to the English Dominican archives, saying that they were his greatest treasure.

VAN ZELLER, Simon (Geoffrey) (1910-1988). Hubert van Zeller's brother. He was at school at Downside, and then entered the monastery in 1929. In the 1930s he was an 'usque' disciple of David Knowles. Novice master 1939-42. He was dogged by ill health and his last years were very withdrawn.

VAUGHAN, Herbert Alfred (1832-1903). Educated at Stonyhurst and Downside, he was ordained in 1854. In 1855 he became Vice-President of St Edmund's College, Ware, and in 1857 he joined the Oblates of St Charles. In 1861 he left Ware to travel round, trying to raise money for a new missionary college in England; as a result, St Joseph's, Mill Hill, was founded in 1866, and in due course several religious congregations came into being, including the Mill Hill Missionaries. In 1872 Vaughan became bishop of Salford and in 1892 he was made archbishop of Westminster, being named a cardinal a year later. He was influential in securing the removal of the ban on Catholics attending the universities of Oxford and Cambridge in 1895. Cf. Arthur McCormack, *Cardinal Vaughan*, London 1966.

VINCENT, Louis Hugues, OP (1872-1960). He joined the Lyons province and, while still a novice, was assigned to Jerusalem, where he made his profession in 1891. He spent most of the rest of his life there. He was a disciple of Lagrange and became a leading authority on Palestinian archaeology, and was editor of the *Revue Biblique* 1931-38. Fellow of many learned societies, including the British Academy. After Lagrange's death he wrote a biography of him, which was so thoroughly suppressed by the censors that it has never been seen since: cf. B. Montagnes, 'Deux lettres du P. Hugues Vincent au sujet du P. Lagrange', *Sources* (Fribourg) 14 (1989) pp. 137-141.

VON HÜGEL, Baron Friedrich (1852-1925). Born in Florence, he settled in England in 1867, where he married in 1873. His wide-ranging intellectual interests and his concern for the relationship between religion and history and his belief in 'the mystical element in religion' (a phrase he used as the title of his major work on St Catherine of Genoa, published London 1908) brought him friends among the Catholic modernists, with whose position he sympathised, though he himself never fell foul of the anti-modernist condemnations. He was highly regarded as a spiritual adviser.

WADE, Francis, OP (1848-1923). Entered the Order in 1867. He was sent to study in Louvain in 1874, but ill health brought him home again the following year. He was assigned to Hinckley and worked for about two years at Normanton Hall. In 1877 he was sent to Woodchester, and in 1880 to London. In 1883 he returned to Woodchester to teach, but the following year he was appointed to London again. In 1885 he was sent to teach at Hinckley School, where he remained until 1893, when he went to Parkminster to try his vocation as a Carthusian. The following year he returned to London, and was appointed student master and lector at Hawkesyard in 1896. In 1900 he was assigned to teach at the Grammar School in London, and, when that closed in 1903, he went to Grenada as Vicar Provincial, remaining there for another four years after the end of his term in 1906. In 1910 he returned to Woodchester. In 1917 his health deteriorated seriously and in 1920 he was moved into a nursing home in Bristol.

WALKER, Luke, OP (1887-1936). Educated at Hawkesyard School (1899-1904), he joined the Order in 1904. Studied at Louvain 1909-12 and at the École Biblique 1912-14, where he and his fellow student, Thomas Garde, narrowly escaped with their lives when they were captured by the Turks. Taught at Hawkesyard 1916-27, then went to Oxford, where he taught 1929-31. In 1930 he took the examination for the STM in Rome, and was awarded the title in 1932, in which year he became Regent of Studies. He was a considerable theologian, but wrote nothing except occasional articles in *Blackfriars*. He was an admirer of Friedrich von Hügel and a friend of Canon Gray and Raffalovich.

WALKLEY, Bruno, OP (1886-1945). Born at Amberley, not far from Woodchester, he spent his boyhood in India. Went to Hawkesyard school in 1904 and joined the Order in 1905. He went to Hawkesyard as a student in 1907. After completing his studies in 1913 he was assigned to Newcastle, and in 1919 he went to Pendleton, returning to Newcastle in 1921 to take charge of the parish of Byker and to be superior there. In January 1924 he was assigned to London, moving to Woodchester four months later, where he remained until 1936, when he was sent back to Newcastle. After a period of ill health, he returned to Woodchester in 1939, and was elected prior there in 1944.

WALMESLEY, Herman, SJ (1850-1927). He came of a family having long association with Stonyhurst, where he himself went in 1860. Entered the Society in 1867. Rector of Stonyhurst 1891-98, after which he went to South Africa as rector of St Aidan's College, Grahamstown (1898-1907). Assistant to the General 1908-23, after which he retired to the Gesù, Rome.

WALZ, Angelus, OP (1893-1978). Member of the Austrian province. He entered the Order in 1912 and spent almost all his life teaching history at the Angelicum (1921-69). He made many contributions to Dominican history, including his *Compendium Historiae Ordinis Praedicatorum,* Rome 1930 (2nd ed., Rome 1948).

WARD, Bernard (1857-1920). Son of W. G. Ward. President of St Edmund's, Ware, 1893-1917. Bishop of Brentwood 1917-20. He took the initiative that, with the generosity of the 15th Duke of Norfolk, resulted in the foundation of St Edmund's House (now College), Cambridge. A notable historian.

WARD, Wilfrid Philip (1856-1916). Son of W. G. Ward (1812-1882), the former Oxford don and leader of the Tractarian movement, who had followed Newman into the Catholic church and who adopted a rigorously Ultramontane line (he once said of himself, 'You will find me narrow and strong—very narrow and very strong'; cf. Maisie Ward, *The Wilfrid Wards and the Transition,* vol. I, London 1934, p. 7). Wilfrid's intellectual sympathies were broader than those of his father, but they both enjoyed tough arguments in matters of philosophy and theology. The father was a member of the Metaphysical Society, and the son was one of the founders of its successor in 1896, the Synthetic Society, both devoted to discussions of philosophy and theology. Wilfrid was influential in persuading the English bishops to obtain permission for Catholics to attend British universities in

1895. His friends included statesmen like A. J. Balfour (1848-1930) and George Wyndham, Anglican High Churchmen like Charles Gore (1853-1932) and Lord Halifax, agnostics like T. H. Huxley (1825-1895), Catholic churchmen like Cardinal Vaughan and Catholics of a liberal, if not downright modernist, temper, such as Friedrich von Hügel and George Tyrrell (1861-1909). Cf. Maisie Ward, op. cit., 2 vols., London 1934-37.

WATSON, Maurice, OP (1857-1948). Received into the Catholic church by Bertrand Wilberforce at St Dominic's, London, on Christmas Day 1873, he went to St Edmund's, Ware, to study for the priesthood, moving on later to the English College, Rome, where he was ordained by Cardinal Manning in 1880. In 1885 he joined the Lazarists and was assigned to the Chinese mission, where he worked until 1895. After trying his vocation as a Carthusian at Parkminster, in 1896 he joined the Dominicans. In 1899 he was sent to Hawkesyard as a missioner, and in 1902 he was moved to Leicester. In 1904 he volunteered for the missions again and was sent to the Dominican mission in Amoy, China. In 1905 he became a naval chaplain to the British sailors in China. In 1915 he returned to England and promptly volunteered to be an army chaplain. After the war he was assigned to Hinckley, where he remained until 1930, when he was sent to Hawkesyard. He continued his mission and retreat work until he was over 80. In 1946 he was named a Preacher General.

WEBB, E. Doran (died 1931). Architect and antiquary. He lived at Tisbury and was patronised by Lady Arundell. Among his buildings are the Newman Memorial Church, Birmingham, and Blackfriars, Oxford.

WEEKS, Paul, OP (1874-1932). He started training to be a civil servant, but joined the Dominicans instead in 1896. In 1901 he was appointed to assist at Hawkesyard School, being headmaster there from 1904-14. He then became subprior and bursar of Hawkesyard. Early in 1917 he was commissioned as an army chaplain. After the war he was appointed to Woodchester, and in 1922 he was sent to Byker. When the parish was handed over to the diocese in 1924, he was assigned to Leicester to take charge of a new mission at Aylestone. In 1925 he was assigned to Newcastle and in 1928 to Pendleton and, after a few months, back to Leicester again.

WEGUELIN, Ada (died 1938, aged 70). A life long friend of the second Mother General of the Harrow Congregation of Dominican sisters, she and her first husband, Claude Watney, assisted the community at Harrow (founded in 1878) to raise funds for the building of the chapel. He died in 1919, and his widow made a large donation to the chapel building fund in his memory. In 1925 she married Bernard Weguelin. She was an extremely, not to say rashly, generous benefactress to the sisters, and she also contributed generously to the brethren. When BJ asked to borrow a set of red vestments for the opening of Blackfriars, Oxford, she insisted on giving them to him. In 1923 she was awarded the Gold Cross Pro Ecclesia et Pontifice.

WHITACRE, Aelred, OP (1882-1945). Nephew of Gabriel Whitacre OP, and one of BJ's closest friends. He was educated at the Dominican school at Hawkesyard (1895-99) and joined the Order in 1899. Taught philosophy at Hawkesyard 1907-16. In 1916 he was assigned to London specifically in view of the public lectures the province launched in that year at Caxton Hall. He became a military chaplain in 1918. After the war, in 1919, he was assigned to Rome to work on the Leonine Commission. In 1922 he returned to the province to be a preacher and missioner, based at Woodchester at first, then, for a short time, at Hinckley. In 1932 he became a member of the first Dominican community in Edinburgh. In 1942 he was re-assigned to Woodchester, but was taken ill in 1944 and moved to a nursing home in Guildford. He was a sculptor, musician, philosopher, theologian and practical man; a very remarkable and lovable person.

WHITACRE, Gabriel, OP (1847-1917). Born in Ireland, but the family came to England when he was a boy. He joined the Order in 1865. After completing his studies in London, he was sent to Stone. In 1878 he was assigned to Leicester and, soon afterwards, to London. In 1880 he returned to Leicester, but in 1882 he was appointed novice master at Woodchester. In 1886 he went back to Leicester, and in 1889 to Newcastle. Prior of Woodchester 1894-97 and of London 1897-1900. Novice master again 1900-1906, after which he returned to London. In 1907 he was elected prior of Pendleton, after which, in 1910 he went to Carisbrooke. In 1913 he was sent to Newcastle.

WILBERFORCE, Bertrand, OP (1839-1904). Grandson of William Wilberforce (1759-1833), who campaigned for the abolition of slavery. His father, Henry (1807-1873), was tutored and befriended by Newman at Oxford; in 1834 he married Mary Sargent, sister-in-law of H. E Manning, and Bertrand (Arthur) was born at Lavington in Manning's house. In 1850 the whole family became Catholics. Bertrand (Arthur) was sent to Ushaw College, where he prepared for ordination. Ordained on 1 May 1864, on 7 May he was clothed in the Dominican habit at Woodchester. His parents later moved to Woodchester and his father became a Dominican tertiary. In 1869 he was appointed to Stroud, and in 1872 he was elected prior of London. In 1875 he was sent back to Woodchester, and to Stone in 1877, Newcastle in 1878, London in 1880 and Leicester in 1882. In 1889 he was assigned to London again, and to Hawkesyard in 1896, his last assignation before his death. He was a tireless itinerant preacher, travelling up and down the country throughout most of his Dominican life. He also wrote several books on Dominican saints and personalities. He translated into English some of the works of the Benedictine spiritual writer, Louis de Blois (Blosius) (1506–1566). It was claimed, on the authority of Blanche Leigh, that it was he who baptised BJ at Blackheath on 30 August 1881, but this is shown to be false by the baptismal register there. Cf. H. M. Capes, *Life and Letters of Father Bertrand Wilberforce,* Edinburgh and London 1906.

WILLIAMS, Antoninus, OP (1836–1901). Was educated at Hinckley School (1852–54), and joined the Order in 1855. He was sent to study in Rome in 1857, and then to La Quercia in 1859. He was ordained in Rome in 1860. Returning to the province in the same year, he went first to Woodchester, then, in 1861, to Hinckley and to Stone the following year. In 1864 he was assigned to Newcastle, where he superintended the building of the church. In 1878 he became prior of London, where he once again set himself to work to complete the building of the church. He was still prior of London when he was elected provincial in 1882. In 1885, as provincial, he re-opened the Dominican School at Hinckley. After he finished being provincial, he went to Carisbrooke in 1886. Prior of Woodchester 1892–94. In 1894 he became the first superior of Hawkesyard. In 1898 he was appointed novice master at Woodchester, where he had BJ as one of his novices. In 1900 he was elected prior of Newcastle, but he soon resigned. He died at Woodchester Park. He was a 'big' man in every way. Fifty years after his death he was remembered as a man of great and sweet character.

WOLSELEY, Cuthbert, OP (1850–1920). Fourth son of Sir Charles Wolseley, 8th Bart. (1813–1854). His grandfather, the 7th Bart. (also Sir Charles) (1769–1846), was converted to Catholicism in 1837 by Ambrose Phillips de Lisle; he had gone to Ashby-de-la-Zouche to preside at a No Popery meeting, and de Lisle invited him home afterwards and in due course converted him. His son, the 8th Bart., followed him into the Catholic church. Cuthbert joined the Order in 1869, and studied in Louvain 1874–78. He then went to Woodchester and, almost at once, to Stroud. In 1884 he was assigned to Newcastle, and in 1889 to Leicester. From 1895–1913 he was in the West Indies, working in Trinidad and then in Grenada. He came home in poor health, and in 1914 was allowed to go to Ibiza for the winter. When he returned in 1915 he was sent to London. In 1920 he was given permission to go to Rome, but died in a Paris hospital on the way. His finances tended to be chaotic, and he was helped out of his difficulties by his relatives, including his 'cousin', Lady Arundell.

WYKEHAM-GEORGE, Kenneth, OP (1904-1961). He was baptised by BJ at St Dominic's in 1905. Joined the Order in 1923. After gaining the lectorate in 1931, he went to the Angelicum, Rome, where he obtained the licenciate in canon law in 1932, after which he went back to Oxford to teach canon law until 1934, when Ambrose Farrell (who was a Doctor of Canon Law) returned. In 1933 he was matriculated through St Catherine's Society to study for a B.Litt., which he won in 1937. In 1935 he went to Hawkesyard, where he taught philosophy until 1940, when he became a military chaplain. After the war he returned to Oxford, where he taught dogma for a year, then resumed his role as lecturer in canon law (Ambrose Farrell having become superior of Cambridge). Prior of Oxford 1946-52. In 1953 he moved to London, and in 1954 became superior of Cambridge, and in 1958 prior of Woodchester. He died in office.

WYLIE, Norbert (1879-1928). He became a Catholic in 1897 and joined the Dominican Order in 1898, the same year as BJ. After he completed his studies he was assigned to Leicester, but in 1909 he went to London, where he remained until he was elected prior of Leicester in 1917. In 1919 he was elected prior of London, but resigned in 1920 and went back to Leicester. In 1923 he was assigned to Stroud, but about two years later he went to be chaplain at Spetchley. His health was already giving grave concern (he suffered from Bright's disease). Early in 1927 he was re-assigned to Stroud, but he soon after left the Order and became a Unitarian minister in Reading. When unconscious and dying, he was heard to say, 'Tell Father Bede I shan't be in for supper', and BJ managed to get there before he died, though not before he lost consciousness for the last time. As BJ reported, 'In his conscious moments he gave no sign that we should have liked; but when unconscious kept on repeating *Agnus Dei qui tollis peccata mundi*' (BJ's letters to Jerome Rigby of 22 and 28 January 1928). After his death, he 'appeared' at Holy Cross, Leicester, causing quite a stir in the local newspapers.

WYNDHAM, George (1863-1913). Educated at Eton. Gazetted in the Coldstream Guards in 1883, in 1885 he was ordered to Egypt. In 1887, shortly after his marriage, he was asked to become Private Secretary to A. J. Balfour (1848-1930), the Chief Secretary for Ireland. In 1889 he became Conservative MP for Dover, a position he retained until his death. He himself was Chief Secretary for Ireland

1900-1905. Chesterton, who found him far more congenial than most other politicians, even though he was a Conservative, remarked, 'The wonderful thing about George Wyndham was that he had come through political life without losing his political opinions, or indeed any of his opinions' (*Autobiography*, London 1934, pp. 121-122, 264). Cf. J. W. Mackail and Guy Wyndham, *Life and Letters of George Wyndham*, 2 vols., London 1924.

YLLA BARRY, Juan, OP (1877-1956). Entered the Rosary province in Spain in 1892. After ordination, he taught at the Colegio de San Juan de Letrán and, later, the University of St Thomas, in Manila, acquiring a doctorate in both Civil and Canon Law. In 1921 he became rector of San Juan de Letrán and in 1923 rector of the University of St Thomas, a position he retained until 1926. He taught canon law at Hawkesyard 1927-29, then returned to Manila, where he was rector of San Juan de Letrán again 1930-33, and then rector of the Interdiocesan Seminary in the University of St Thomas until his death.

ZIGLIARA, Tommaso, OP (1833-1893). Born in Corsica, he joined the Roman province in 1851. After this noviciate, he studied philosophy in Rome and theology in Perugia, where he was ordained by Cardinal Pecci (later Leo XIII). After further studies in Rome he was awarded the lectorate. He taught at Viterbo (1861-70) and then in Rome (1870-79), becoming Regent of Studies in 1873. In 1879 Leo XIII made him a cardinal and appointed him director of the commission set up to edit the works of St Thomas (soon to be known as the Leonine Commission). He was the author of a widely-used textbook of Thomistic philosophy, which ran to 17 editions in Latin and was used in the English province when BJ was a student. Cf. *Analecta S.O.P.* 1 (1893-94) pp. 258-263.

INDEX OF PERSONAL NAMES

Aelred, St xxi, xxii, 180, 182, 206
Albert, Prince 69, 70
Albert, St 172, 206
Aloysius, St 116, 193
Amigo, P. 42, 118, 206
Ancrene Riwle 107, 206
Angelico, Fra 67, 115, 148, 163, 164, 206, 251
Antonino, St 67, 114, 207
Ardagh, Wilfrid 62, 176, 177, 188, 189, 207
Arnold, Matthew 70
Arundell, A. L., Lady 24, 25, 33, 54, 207, 215, 272, 275
Ashworth, Veronica 67, 208
Augustine, St 84, 103, 120, 147

Badenoch, A. G. 170
Bailey, David (later Bede) 192, 204
Baily, Theodore 138, 208
Baker, Augustine 129, 208, 222
Baker, Miss E. A. xxxi, 17, 18, 209, 223
Ball, A. 90, 209
Bañez, Domingo 13
Barberi, Bl. Dominic xi, 209, 252
Barker, Austin 5, 7, 8, 11, 13, 14, 16, 17, 18, 19, 20, 22, 23, 24, 26, 71, 72, 152, 173-5, 176, 186, 209
Barker, Ernest 20, 95, 198, 210
Barker, Osmund 55, 210
Barrett, J. P. 143, 144, 210
Bartlett, Henry xix, 210, 238
Batley, Christopher 138
Beaufort, F. xvi
Bell, F. 93, 94, 114
Belloc, Hilaire 35, 126, 127, 210, 219
Bellord, Agnes xxvii, 72, 75, 95, 96, 211
Bellord, Charles 58, 59, 64, 95, 211
Bellord, Edmund 87, 91, 95, 124-5, 211
Bellord, George xxiii, 62, 96, 124, 133, 139-140, 162, 211, 256
Benedict XV 179, 244
Benson, R. H. 12, 13, 211
Bezzina, Gabriel 53, 211
Black, Giles 178, 211
Blackwell, Basil 97, 98, 212
Blencowe, H. D. 187, 212
Blount, E. A. 18
Blount, E. C. 16, 17, 209
Bonhomme, Romain 152, 212

Botticelli, S. 199
Bourne, F. xv, 35, 62, 63, 204, 205, 212, 221
Bowring, George 65, 98, 123, 124, 147, 148, 167, 168, 212
Bracey, Robert 32, 88, 144, 145, 154, 155, 171, 213
Bradbury, J. S. 40
Bradman, D. G. 157
Bretherton, Cuthbert 92, 213
Breuil, H. 219
Brocklehurst, Mark 186, 213
Brooke, Rupert 127, 128
Brookes, Jerome 15, 16, 213
Browne, J. 4, 213
Bruce, C. N. 9
Bruce, R. 70
Buckler, Charles 52, 55
Buckler, Reginald xvii, 55, 213
Bugeja, Henry 83, 84, 172, 214
Bull, Theodore 42, 214
Bullough, Edward 152, 197, 214
Bullough, Enrichetta 114, 151, 196, 197, 198, 200, 203, 214, 227
Bullough, H. (later Sebastian) 152, 215
Burdett, Francis 71, 208, 215
Burlamacchi, Eufrasia 128-9, 215
Burton, G. A. xxiv, 155, 156, 216
Butler, Cuthbert 102, 216, 232
Butt, Angela 179, 216

Cadogan, Lady xxx, 29, 216
Caffarini, Tommaso 201
Cajetan 21, 216
Callus, Daniel 71, 216
Calthrop, Miss M. M. C. xxvii, xxviii, 133, 159, 182, 187, 217, 240
Campbell, Amy 73, 93, 96, 116, 132, 156, 177, 197
Campbell, W. E. 73, 93
Carden, D. 63
Carpenter, Hilary 176, 217, 223
Cary-Elwes, D. C. 86, 88, 89, 218
Casartelli, L. C. 61, 94, 218
Casas, Juan 152, 218
Castlerosse, Lord 191, 192
Caterini, Filippo 152, 218
Catharinus, Ambrosius 263
Catherine of Siena, St 115, 116, 142, 149, 200, 201, 218

277

Cecil, Hugh 35, 218
Chapman, John 197
Chardin, Teilhard de 219
Charles I 39
Chases, Casimir xxix, 219
Chesterton, G. K. 35, 96, 99, 219, 276
Churchill, Winston 47
Cicero xxi, xxii
Clark, Kevin 86, 88, 90, 91, 92, 219
Clayton, J. xxvii, 57, 150, 217, 220
Coats, Miss E. 29, 33, 51, 173
Cogan, Mrs S. 52, 55
Cole, G. D. H. 62, 220
Colonna, Vittoria 114, 115, 220, 251
Connelly, Cornelia 73, 220
Conway, Placid xiii
Cordovani, Mariano 152, 220
Cormier, Hyacinthe 20, 21, 22, 24, 27, 221, 228, 244, 258
Coulton, G. G. 50, 85, 221
Couturier, Felix xxx, 29, 145, 221
Cowgill, J. R. 30, 31, 222
Cox, C. 26, 27, 29, 30, 31, 34, 222
Cressy, Serenus 138, 208, 222
Crosse, Aloysius xxiii, 23, 24, 222
Cusack, W. 81
Cuypers, Lambert 55, 222

Danell, J. 41, 223
D'Annunzio, G. 198, 200, 201, 223, 227
Darley, Philip 5, 8, 9, 223
Davenport, Miss 94
Davey, Richard 125, 127, 223
Davies, Mrs 71, 94, 223
Dawson, Aelred 14
Delahunty, Michael 177, 223
Delany, Bernard vii, xxxi, xxxii, xxxiii, 1, 18, 62, 71, 91, 97, 98, 109, 111, 122, 124, 133, 144, 145, 146, 170, 182, 185, 186, 187, 191, 192, 201, 203, 204, 205, 224, 225, 226-7, 245
Delattre, A. J. 22
Delhaise, H. 52, 55
De Lisle, Ambrose P. 224, 274
Denis, J. F. 41, 224
Denis, Pseudo- 136, 225
De Paravicini, Baroness xxvi, xxx, 94, 97, 98, 225
Devas, Raymund 46, 225
Dhorme, E. P. 19, 20, 226
Disraeli, B. 170, 171
Dix, Fabian 65, 102, 144, 226, 238

Dominic, St xxix, 10, 31, 45, 48, 49, 50, 124, 149, 150, 158, 159, 167, 175, 182, 188, 226
Domvile, Lady Margaret xxviii, 34, 35, 36, 37, 38, 39, 40, 46, 56, 57, 226
Dummermuth, Antoninus xxvi, 13-4, 15, 16
Duncker, Peter 177, 227
Duse, Alberto 151-2
Duse, Eleonora xxiii, 114-5, 198, 200, 201, 214, 223, 227, 250

Edward VII 47, 48, 69
Egan, Chrysostom 26, 176, 227
Eleanor of Aquitaine 40
Elrington, Aidan 53, 71, 74, 90, 93, 94, 95, 99, 107, 114, 122, 123, 128, 185, 186, 187, 228
Elton, G. 62, 228
English, Adrian 62, 91, 176, 228
Essex, Edwin 97, 98, 144, 169, 170, 172, 183, 184, 229
Evans, A. 21, 22
Everest, Humbert xv, xix, xx, xxiv, xxix, 5, 6, 7, 14, 22, 23, 26, 27, 40, 51, 54, 55, 83, 84, 87, 88, 94, 179, 185, 190, 229, 254
Eyre, E. 107

Fanfani, Ludovico 152, 229
Farrell, Ambrose 176, 177, 230, 275
Fay, Teresa 157, 230
Fayer, M. Gabriel 121, 230
Feeley, Clement 86, 88, 91, 230
Fitzgerald, Stephen 77, 230
Fletcher, Ceslaus 20, 21, 23, 231
Fletcher, C. R. L. 9, 10
Flood, Vincent xiv, 231
Folghera, J. D. xv, 23, 26, 175, 231
Ford, Edmund 160, 162, 231
Francis, St 199, 200
Freeland, J. 81, 82
Frins, V. J. 14
Frühwirth, A. F. 1, 221, 232
Fry, C. B. 9

Garde, Thomas 159, 166, 174, 186, 232, 248, 270
Garvin, J. L. 122, 232
Gasquet, F. A. 63, 221, 232, 233
Gatty, C. T. 35, 40, 233
Gavin, Alphonsine 105, 106, 110, 233

Geoghegan, Mother Dominic 56, 131–2, 233
Geoghegan, Terence 38, 42, 43, 44, 56, 58, 59, 60, 64, 65, 233
George, Charles 172, 173, 178, 233
George, Margaret 172, 173, 178, 233
Getino, L. A. 152, 234
Gilbert de Fraxineto 48, 234
Gilby, Thomas 176, 183, 234
Gill, Eric 128, 210
Gillet, M. S. xxvi, 152, 153, 154, 158, 159, 166, 168, 174, 176, 185, 186, 190, 210, 219, 232, 234, 235, 241, 257
Ginns, Reginald 53, 176, 235
Giovanni Dominici, Bl. 66, 129, 207, 235, 247
Gonin, Louis xiv, 231, 235, 237
Goodier, Alban xvii, 235
Grant, T. 41, 236
Gray, Canon J. 55, 172, 173, 236, 258, 271
Greene, David P. 171
Greene, Gwendolen Plunket 103, 104, 105, 106, 107, 109, 110, 111, 113, 145, 147, 171, 236
Greene, Olivia P. 146, 147, 236
Greenough, Thomas xiv, xv, 235, 236
Grimes, J. 12
Grosseteste, R. 49, 50, 237
Gulson, Helen xx, 53, 55, 237
Gumbley, Walter 26, 63, 91, 176, 177, 223, 237
Gumley, L. 173, 238

Haig, D. 36
Halifax, Lord 47, 238, 244, 272
Hallahan, Margaret 209
Halpin, Charles xxiv, 6, 7, 238
Hart-Davis, Richard 112-3, 238
Hart-Davis, Rupert 121, 127, 238
Hart-Davis, Sybil xxiii, 112-3, 118–20, 121, 238
Hay, Major 166, 239
Henry II 40
Henry VIII 255
Herries, Angela, Lady 66
Heveningham, M. Dominic 167, 239
Higginson, Teresa 116, 117
Hill, W. 4
Holland, A. 202, 239
Holland, B. 57

Hoper-Dixon, Rupert 147, 148, 176, 239
Howard, Esme 107-9
Howard, Philip xxvi, 8, 239
Humbert of Romans 50, 85, 173, 175, 217, 240
Hunter-Blair, D. O. 14, 240
Hurdle-Williams, M. Suso 66, 67, 159, 230, 240

Imitation of Christ 200

Jabalot, F. F. 224
Jacquin, Mannes 124, 240
Jandel V. A. xi, 46, 158, 159, 160, 221, 225, 240
Jarrett, Agnes xvi, xvii, 16, 141, 241
Jarrett, C. H. B. 18
Jarrett, H. S. xvi, xvii, xx, 1, 2, 3, 16, 241
Jarrett, Hubert xxv
Jarrett, Mrs Thomas xvi, 1
Jerningham, H. 65, 201
Johnston, Quentin 176, 241
Jowett, B. 38, 39, 241
Julian of Norwich, 109, 110, 136, 150, 181, 182, 193, 222, 241

Kane, Agatha 165, 241, 251
Keating, J. 122, 242
Keats J. 69, 70
Kehoe, Richard 176, 242
Kenealy, A. 25, 242
Kindersley, Aelred 70, 242
King, Alban xix, 31, 234, 242
Kipling, Rudyard 144
Knapp, Albert 83, 84, 243
Knox, R. A. 62, 63, 243
Knowles, David 102, 221
Koos, Hyacinth 171, 243, 259
Kübben, Bernard 17, 243

Lacordaire, H. D. xvii-xviii, 46, 66, 67, 69, 70, 88, 148, 224, 235, 240, 243, 266
Lagrange, M. J. 15, 19, 21, 22, 226, 232, 244, 270
Lamb, Stanislaus 86, 88, 91, 92, 177, 244
Lamburn, Teresa 151, 244
Lane-Fox, Mrs 47, 244
Laski, H. J. 81, 244
Lawrence, F. W. Pethick 19

Laws, Thomas 83, 245, 254
Lea, J. 60, 61, 245
Leather, John 83, 84, 163, 164, 245
Le Gallais, W. W. 251
Leigh, Beatrice 167
Leigh, Blanche xxiv, 1, 167, 245, 274
Leigh, William x-xi, xvi, 55, 245, 246
Leo XIII 22, 253, 276
Lescher, Wilfrid 21, 246
L'Estrange, Alexander 177, 186, 246
Le Vigoureux, Étienne 17, 209, 246
Limbrick, W. 73
Lloyd George, D. 36, 47
Lorenzo of Ripafratta, Bl. 67, 247
Lottini, Giovanni 152, 247
Louis VII 40
Lovelace, R. 195-6
Lowe, Anthony xxv, 55, 247

McCabe, Herbert 14, 157
McCann, Justin 14, 71, 94, 247
McCarthy, J. 68, 70, 88, 89, 248
McDonald, A. J. 166, 168, 169, 170, 171, 174, 178, 248
McGlynn, P. 178, 248
McIntyre, J. 61, 62, 71, 144, 248
Mackenzie, Compton 59
Mackey, Peter Paul xiv, xviii, 11, 12, 248
McMahon, J. H. 183, 249
McNabb, Vincent xix, 12, 21, 22, 26, 29, 30, 40, 41, 42, 47, 61, 63, 71, 85, 87, 88, 89, 105, 106, 133, 143, 144, 166, 176, 177, 185, 186, 205, 206, 219, 249, 261
MacNamara, Richard 20, 21, 23, 24, 249
Maconi, Stefano 200, 201
McQuaid, J. C. 142
Manning, H. E. 33, 224, 250, 273
Mannix, D. 47, 48
Manoel II 30
Martindale, C. C. 116, 117, 215, 250, 254
Maskelyne, J. 102
Meagher, Raymund 152, 250
Medici, Cosimo de' 90, 207, 251
Meynell, Wilfrid 112, 113, 267
Michelangelo 103, 114, 115, 251
Milne, A. A. 141
Montfort, St. Louis G de 33
Moore, Leo xviii, 16, 23, 40, 41, 251
More, St Thomas 117, 132-3, 204

Morris, Lady 72, 251
Morris, P. 31, 32
Morrison, M. Anthony 178, 241, 251
Mortimer, Mrs 67, 68, 117
Moss, Raphael xvi, xix, xx, xxiv, 5, 6, 41, 92, 220, 252
Mussolini, B. 196, 227
Myers, E. 185, 252

Naylor, George 76, 252
Newman, J. H. viii, x, xi, 209, 252, 273
Niland, Rose 29, 42, 253
Nolan, Louis 150, 151, 157, 253
Norfolk, Duchess of 66, 179, 239

O'Brien, D. 89, 253
O'Connor, M. Raymond 128-9, 253
O'Gorman, Eustace 32, 63, 65, 124, 254
Oldmeadow, E. 132, 133, 191, 192, 254
O'Leary, A. 83, 254
Oman, C. 9
O'Neill, Hilary xix, xx, 13, 22, 23, 254
O'Reilly, E. 155
O'Riley, B. 154, 155, 254
Osborne, G. C. 114
O'Sullivan, R. 132, 133

Pagnini, Santes 15, 254
Palmer, F. B. 12
Palmer, Raymund xxvi, 255
Pankhurst, E. 19
Paredes, B. G. 26, 151, 153, 160, 186, 218, 255, 266
Parker, Leonard xxiii, xxviii, 37, 41, 42, 43, 44, 56, 58, 59, 62, 63, 69, 75, 139, 161-2, 256
Parry, Hubert 236
Pater, W. 37, 38, 39, 137, 138, 256
Paul VI 220
Peach, Laurence 6, 7, 52, 55, 256
Petrie, F. 9, 10
Phillimore, J. 248
Pico della Mirandola, G. 39
Pickering, Silvester 52, 55, 256
Pike, Bertrand 63, 183, 187, 190, 256
Pius V 263-4
Pius XI 95, 153, 154, 158, 162, 236
Plater, C. D. 35, 257
Pope, Hugh xiii, xvi, xix, 12, 13, 15, 21, 22, 23, 26, 27, 72, 73, 87, 88, 94, 124, 151, 153, 171, 173, 175, 185, 186, 187, 257
Powell, E. 117, 257

Power, J. 52, 55
Price, Mrs 76
Procter, John xiv, xvii, xviii, xxvii, 1, 2, 3, 15, 20, 21, 22, 23, 257, 262
Prümmer, D. xv

Raffalovich, M. A. S. 32, 55, 236, 258, 271
Ramsay, Leander 70, 258
Raymund of Capua, Bl. 168, 218, 235
Reader, Peter xxiii, 86, 88, 258
Reeves, J. B. 71, 91, 94, 95, 131, 132, 143, 162, 163, 164, 256, 259
Reichenbach, Miss 122
Reynolds, W. 74, 76
Rice, Cyprian xxix, 186, 259
Rigby, Ethelbert xvi, 8, 15, 16, 177, 260
Rigby, Jerome xx, xxv, 4, 5, 6, 8, 10, 12, 13, 15, 16, 17, 18, 19, 63, 82, 83, 86, 87, 88, 90, 91, 92, 97, 151, 176, 260, 275
Rolle, Richard 107, 136, 260
Roskell, J. 143, 144
Russell, Ralph 157
Rutherford, Anselm 74, 76, 260
Rutten, Ceslaus 17, 260
Ryan, Finbar xxxi, 88, 260

St John, Henry 234, 261
St John, Mrs 32, 33
St Lawrence, W. 32, 33
Salazar, A. de O. 196
Sales, Marco 152, 261
Sargent, Dunstan 83, 84, 261
Savielle, Miss 58, 109, 113, 128, 129, 132, 261
Savile, Lady Mary Louisa 45
Savonarola, G. 4, 39, 196, 198, 215, 251, 255, 261
Sayce, A. H. 9, 10
Scott, G. G. 157
Scott-Moncrieff, Miss 169, 170
Shakespeare, W. 69, 70, 72
Shapcote, Laurence xviii, xix, xx, xxix, 11, 12, 20, 21, 23, 26, 27, 29, 31, 183, 241, 246, 251, 258, 262
Shaw, G. P. 172, 173, 263
Sheed, F. 116, 121, 142, 143, 263
Sheil, D. 143, 144
Shelley, P. B. xxi-ii, 70
Shepherd, R. A. E. 62, 63, 263
Simmons, M. Evangeline 204-5, 263
Sixtus of Siena 15, 263

Smith, Ambrose xviii, xix, 3, 4, 264
Smith, J. A. 32, 264
Smith, Oswald 5, 264
Snelgrove, Andrew 157
Snow, A. 117, 264
Spicq, Ceslas 226, 264
Spode, J. 237
Stefano of Italy 196, 198-200
Steuart, Benedict 138, 140, 264
Steuart, R. 71, 140, 254, 265
Stourton, Elizabeth xxxiii, 18, 162, 265
Strachey, L. 69, 70
Studd, H. W. 57
Studd, Mrs 46, 57
Suffield, Rudolph 209, 265
Sumner, Oswald 157
Swaby, Alfred 33, 265
Sweeney, Paulinus 14, 16, 26, 96, 174, 175, 176, 177, 261, 265
Swetchine, Mme 70, 266
Szabó, S. 152, 266

Talbot, Lady Edmund 17, 266
Taurisano, Innocenzo 128, 266
Tayleur, Mrs 28, 68, 111, 266
Taylor, George xxix, 267
Theissling, Ludovicus 25, 27, 29, 30, 31, 87, 89, 148, 177, 218, 228, 229, 267
Thomas Aquinas, St xx, 11, 13, 21, 48, 71, 117, 136, 148, 201, 206, 216, 249, 263, 267, 276
Thompson, Francis 128, 267
Thomson, Lewis 40, 88, 267
Tickell, Benedict xiii, xv, 268
Tigar, Gilbert xv, 53, 215, 268
Trelawny, H. 33, 268
Turville, C. F. x, 55, 268
Tytus, Mrs 90, 91, 129, 131, 134, 135, 137, 140, 141, 145, 146, 149, 153, 168, 178, 184, 201, 269

Van Zeller C. (later Hubert) 62, 63, 64, 65, 74-6, 98, 99, 100-3, 125, 135, 138, 141, 155, 156, 157, 160, 162, 180, 193, 269
Van Zeller, F. 76
Van Zeller, G. (later Simon) 138-40, 269
Vaughan, H. A. 33, 98, 269, 272
Vincent, L. H. 20, 269
Vincent Ferrier, Mother 41
Vitoria, F. 234

Von Hügel, F. 57, 104, 105, 146, 236, 270, 271, 272
Von Hügel, Lady Mary 110, 236

Wade, Francis 53, 270
Walker, Luke xvi, 11, 12, 26, 123, 151, 173, 174, 175, 176, 186, 270
Walkley, Bruno 17, 18, 271
Walmesley, H 2, 271
Walton, P. 8
Walz, Angelus 128, 271
Ward, Bernard 33, 34, 271
Ward, Wilfrid 46, 47, 271
Watson, Maurice xv, xxiii, 272
Watson, W. 11, 12
Waugh, A. 59
Waugh, Evelyn 236, 254
Webb, E. Doran 94, 100, 208, 272
Weedall, H. xi
Weeks, Paul 84, 272
Weguelin, Mrs 201, 272
Whitacre, Aelred xvii, xx, xxi, xxii–iii, xxiv, 3, 23, 144, 150, 273
Whitacre, C. 3
Whitacre, Gabriel xix, 3, 21, 273
Whittaker, E. T. 169, 170
Wightman, R. 170

Wilberforce, Bertrand xxiii, 117, 272, 273
Wilde, Oscar 236
Williams, Antoninus xviii, 3, 274
Williams, J. L. 93, 94, 114, 185
Williams, T. L. 144
Willson, Dominic 14
Wiseman, N. P. S. xi, 220
Wolfe, H. 127-8
Wolseley, Cuthbert 24, 25, 274
Woodruff, D. 133
Wortley, E. 52, 55
Wyatt, G. 99, 100
Wykeham-George, Kenneth 170, 177, 194, 195, 275
Wylie, Norbert xxv, 25, 26, 130, 131, 275
Wyndham, E. 87, 88, 90
Wyndham, F. M. 32, 33
Wyndham, George 35, 40, 219, 272, 275
Wyndham, Guy 35
Wyndham, P. L. 35

Ylla Barry, J. 177, 276

Zigliara, T. M. xviii, 14, 16, 71, 276